LEADERS AND PERIODS OF
AMERICAN FINANCE

ALEXANDER HAMILTON

LEADERS AND PERIODS
OF
AMERICAN FINANCE

BY

THEODORE J. GRAYSON

Essay Index Reprint Series

BOOKS FOR LIBRARIES PRESS
FREEPORT, NEW YORK

First Published 1932
Reprinted 1969

HG181
G7

STANDARD BOOK NUMBER:
8369-1240-3

LIBRARY OF CONGRESS CATALOG CARD NUMBER:
68-29211

PRINTED IN THE UNITED STATES OF AMERICA

TO MY WIFE
GRACE BLAKISTON GRAYSON

*Without whose constant sympathy and
encouragement this book would
not have been written.*

CONTENTS

CONTENTS

LIST OF ILLUSTRATIONS

FOREWORD

THIS book resulted from a conversation I had a number of years ago with the late Charles Custis Harrison, for many years Provost of the University of Pennsylvania, a man of outstanding ability and one who possessed an intimate knowledge of American history. I had been very much interested in the career of Robert Morris, an ancestor of Mrs. Harrison, and on the occasion in question I was discussing his career with Dr. Harrison when he suggested that in his opinion a novel and effective method of teaching the history of American finance would be to develop the subject as far as possible through the lives of the leading financiers of the United States. This idea germinated in my mind and at the earliest opportunity, I began the preparation of this review of the principal periods and some of the most important characters of our financial history.

Naturally in dealing with the careers of the financial leaders selected for the purpose of this volume, emphasis has been placed primarily upon the things they did which were either directly or indirectly connected with the growth and development of finance in the United States. This will account for the fact that sometimes matters which would be dealt with extensively in an ordinary biographical sketch are condensed in this book because they are of minor interest from the standpoint of finance. Biography in these pages is therefore of a somewhat specialized character. It is hoped, however, that it is nevertheless reliable and effective. The best existing authorities have been consulted and every effort has been made to attain factual accuracy. It is further hoped that a happy medium has been struck between the old chronological methods of biographical writing which were often lacking in emphasis and proportion and the new method which even when employed by such masters as Maurois and Ludwig is frequently haphazard, full of unexplained omissions, and emphatic whenever the author's desire impels him to make it so.

There is today entirely too much straining after big effects in biographical writing. After all, history has enough romance when the truth is religiously followed and no biographer who is dealing with the life of an important man needs to resort to artificial means or forget his responsibilities and turn to fiction instead of fact.

It will be easily observed that this is not a chronological history of American finance. There are a number of evident omissions which would not have occurred had it been a history in the ordinary sense. Thus, the period between 1845 and 1860 is not dealt with except incidentally in Chapter XI on Martin Van Buren and the Panic of 1837 and in Chapter XIV dealing with the Tariff as an Issue in the United States. This is because it was thought unnecessary to give space to the financial history of the Mexican War as that was not very important in its financial phase, or to deal intimately with the panic of 1857 in view of the basic similarity of panics and depressions, the panic of 1837 having been already described. It has also been thought unwise to write about any man still alive.

The controlling purpose has been to show how our private finance developed from the firm basis of public finance which first arose in the brain of Alexander Hamilton, and then to describe the gradual evolution of American business enterprise through the century and a half just past.

At the end of the volume, arranged by chapters, the reader will find a reference bibliography containing a list of the principal authorities consulted.

And now for a number of acknowledgments which I am glad to make. My friend and colleague, Dr. Edward S. Mead,

has rendered valuable assistance by reading the book in proof
and making many helpful suggestions. My colleague, Dr. W.
Christie MacLeod, also gave much constructive advice and
furnished most of the material for the chapter on Land Speculation upon which subject he is a recognized authority. Sincere
thanks are also due to my colleague, Herman S. Hettinger,
and to his wife, Sarah Hettinger, for the painstaking care with
which they have read my manuscript, checked it throughout,
and for many suggestions in connection with the book which
have proved to be both sound and helpful. Mrs. Hettinger also
prepared the index.

I am further indebted to the following publishers who so
kindly gave me permission to quote from their publications:
G. P. Putnam's Sons—*"Forty Years of American Finance"* by
Alexander Dana Noyes. Yale University Press—*"Chronicles of
America."* Longmans, Green & Company—*"Financial History
of the United States"* by Davis R. Dewey. Houghton Mifflin
Company—*"The Autobiography of Andrew Carnegie."* Uni-
versity of Chicago Press—*"The Panic of 1837"* by R. M.
McGrane.

Finally I shall send forth this book upon which I have expended considerable time and effort with the hope that in spite
of its imperfections it will stimulate in its readers an interest
in the financial history of their country. The preparation of
this volume has been a labor of love. I have been fascinated by
my subject and I hope I can arouse a similar interest in the
minds of others.

THEODORE J. GRAYSON

Philadelphia, Pennsylvania
March 1, 1932.

LEADERS AND PERIODS OF
AMERICAN FINANCE

CHAPTER I

COLONIAL FINANCE

IT IS often profitable to visualize the past, and so it may help us to come to a correct understanding of the conditions surrounding colonial finance if we picture to ourselves a fair or cattle show in a New England town somewhere about the end of the seventeenth century. At this period there were still many Indians in the eastern country and the population was pioneer in character although already the town dwellers were beginning to form a small but important group.

Let us suppose therefore that we are standing on the small common surrounded by sturdy, low-built houses, the entire scene dominated by the single church which served at once as a place of worship and a community center. We shall be sure to notice the absence of anything like a modern road but will also perceive one broad beaten path running through the town bedded with planks and after a storm little more than a quagmire. This is the main avenue of communication; along it have come the farmers and itinerant vendors of goods who are to take part in the day's proceedings. The town itself may not be stockaded, but if that primitive defense has been reduced, nevertheless the houses themselves if observed closely will be seen to be individually capable of adequate defence against the enemy. Windows are few, and those that do exist are heavily shuttered. Indeed, it is a town in its infancy, and the country itself is equally young with all the vigor and crudity of youth. On the common where we are standing are perhaps a dozen booths where various kinds of food and merchandise are displayed. There is an abundance of rough homespun cloth and a meager quantity of linen and dress stuffs of higher grade. There are live stock, hats, beaver skins, corn, vegetables and for the Indians some gaudy trinkets, bright colored blankets and the inevitable hard liquor with which our ancestors did so much to bring culture to the aborigines. The space between the booths is filled with a constantly shifting crowd composed of the townspeople in their brown and gray homespun clothes severely plain but serviceable enough, and in addition, though in smaller proportions, a far more colorful group of trappers, hunters, and Indian braves more or less gaudily arrayed and infinitely picturesque—the hunters with their coon-skin caps and garments made from the well-tanned hides of game animals, and the Indians tall and sinewy; the squaws wrapped in cloaks manufactured from the skins of wild animals or perhaps swathed in blankets acquired from the settlers, and the braves wearing as little as the season will permit.

The proceedings are much like those of a general fair held in any century during the Christian era. There is much chattering and a wealth of conversation which sometimes results in the consummation of a sale and sometimes not. There is a general background of quiet good nature, and in spite of the diverse types taking part the whole affair seems to progress in a thoroughly amiable way. It is evident that business of some kind is actually being performed. The question of interest to us, however, is how that business is being done. Briefly, what are the people paying for the goods? The answer is not easy. If we step from booth to booth we shall be quickly mystified by what we see. We may observe one of the selectmen decently dressed in sober gray tender a few veritable English shillings made of unquestioned silver to a greatly astonished merchant in exchange for a large bolt of imported English goods which the selectman's wife desires for a Sunday gown. Such a transaction would be so unusual, however, that the merchant would soon be surrounded by an eager crowd all agog to see the English money, which is evidently as much a curiosity as though it had come directly from a museum.

A little further down the line we might see a tall Indian chief tendering a long string of exquisite wampum or delicately woven beads in exchange for a hatchet with a drink of rum as a bonus. We might see a dark-skinned hunter, apparently from the Canadian border, offering some dubious French coins of small value and a beaver skin in exchange for a quantity of powder. But what we should be more likely to observe all about us would be a frank exchange of one commodity for another—the boys of the town offering rabbit skins, coon and wolf pelts in exchange for powder, knives or hats, while the good wives of the town and their husbands would offer various kinds of farm produce for the manufactured articles which they had been unable to make for themselves. The general character of the trade carried on would be of the primitive type known as barter. Goods for goods, commodity for commodity, a species of exchange characteristic of young races and older than history.

We should leave the fair completely convinced that whatever advantages England had sought to give to her American colonies she had certainly not furnished them with an adequate currency, and for lack of a reliable medium of exchange they had been forced to adopt a system of makeshifts, and in the last analysis, to resort to extensive bartering. We should be right in making such an assumption, and the scene we have just imagined may make it of interest to inquire how such a curious situation came about.

From the earliest period, the possessions of Great Britain in America presented innumerable problems which arose largely from the varying characteristics of the colonies. The original thirteen states were made up of many types of men

who had left the mother country at different times and for
various reasons. They settled at widely separated points in the
New World, where they encountered unlike conditions, cli-
matic, political, economic, and social. The result was that, long
before the Revolutionary War, essential differences, mental as
well as physical, developed among the early colonials.

The first settlers of New England were in large part Puri-
tans who had left the mother country to avoid religious persecution. They were hardy, frugal, and self-sacrificing, and they
believed in a just though wrathful God. Contrast these
pioneers with the early settlers of Virginia, most of whom had
fled from Oliver Cromwell and his triumphant followers in
order to find in the New World an opportunity to avoid the
very things which the New Englanders had come here to
foster. Truly, there was little in common between the brave,
roistering, lax, and cheerful followers of the Stuarts, and the
cold, dour, strict, yet industrious children of the Reformation.

To these dissimilar personal characteristics must be added
certain environmental differences which induced a series of
definite economic distinctions, concentrating fisheries and
manufactures in the north and agriculture in the south. With
this picture of colonial conditions it will readily be seen that
fundamental differences in the financial systems of the colonies were inevitable, when the time arrived that they were
able to construct anything which could be called a scheme of
finance.

Great Britain never developed a uniform scheme of government for her American colonies. It is not to be supposed that
her failure to do so was owing to any sinister design, but rather
to the fact that her political leaders were always busily engaged elsewhere. Whenever the interests of the colonies became an issue their ears were assailed by the selfish pleas of
narrow-minded British merchants who greatly feared the competition of the colonies in matters of trade.

The methods by which the colonies were governed were curiously haphazard. They were controlled largely by the Privy Council but partly by the Admiralty and to some extent by the Bishops. The immediate authority for them usually rested on colonial governors appointed by the Crown. These governors, however, had to rely upon the colonial legislatures for their salaries, and hence, for more than a hundred and fifty years, a constant warfare went on between the governors and the elected representatives of the various colonies. The general policy of the colonials was to pay the governors as little as possible and to drive a hard bargain before they gave them that little.

In addition to these governmental agencies, the colonies were subject to the acts of Parliament in the formation and passage of which they had taken no part. From the beginning, this was a source of constant irritation, and eventually was one of the prime causes of the Revolutionary War.

The English Government always maintained a series of restrictive laws which were irritating to the colonials. The Navigation Acts which greatly hampered the growing trade of the colonies and discriminated against them in favor of British traders and ship-owners, are a case in point.

There never was a healthy friendly feeling between the British Government and the American colonials, and although there were doubtless faults on both sides, it was this lack of mutual understanding which not only brought war in the end, but, long before war was ever thought of, deeply affected the financial affairs of the colonies. This is a point in which we are especially interested.

It was due to this lack of mutual understanding that England made no adequate provisions for the financial growth of its colonies in America. Thus, although the British administered American affairs for a period of nearly two hundred years, they established no mint in this country, nor did they make any real effort to supply their colonies with a circulating medium. As a necessary corollary to such neglect, they failed to extend to their subjects overseas any banking facilities whatever. If we look at the situation in the light of present-day conditions, we can hardly conceive how the colonists could have gone on so long without currency, without banks, and without any credit structure worthy of the name.

However, we must not look at the situation in the light of the present day. We must, as a matter of fact, divide the long period of almost two centuries into two parts. If we say that the earliest era of our colonial experience closed about 1700, we will not be far wrong, and we will also be correct, in principle at least, if we assume that, during the last half of the seventeenth century, our ancestors led a life so primitive, so patriarchal, that they did not greatly feel the absence of a currency system, much less the non-existence of banks. On the other hand, from the beginning of the eighteenth century, these needs were increasingly felt, because, at that time, the colonies began to manufacture their own goods, and also to develop a thriving trade with the British West Indies and with the colonies of France and Spain. The export trade of the colonies increased steadily throughout the eighteenth century. It was extremely varied in character. The New England settlements exported lumber in rough and manufactured forms, and also from Rhode Island and neighboring localities a great deal of sugar, rum and molasses was shipped abroad. Furthermore, the New England colonies developed large fisheries which have continued to be an important feature in their commerce up to the present day. The middle colonies early began to export wheat and other cereals, while the southern colonies exported tobacco, and later on large quantities of cotton together with a considerable amount of rice.

These exports, in many instances, were not sent direct to England, although England was the actual trade objective of all the colonies. From the mother country, they wished to import numerous articles which they needed to make their pioneer lives richer and more comfortable. England, however, had little need of most of the goods and raw materials which the colonies were able to supply. These were too crude and simple for her sophisticated tastes. It made little difference to the colonies, however, whether they traded directly with England, so long as they obtained a purchasing power which they could employ in England. They, therefore, by a species of triangulation in trade, sold in one market and bought in another. They developed a brisk commerce with the West Indies and the other French and Spanish colonies, and with the proceeds of that commerce expressed in Pound Exchange they entered the English market and purchased the goods they desired. The restrictions of the Navigation Acts in favor of British ships and British masters doubtless were a factor in establishing such a trading policy. The main reason, however, was that the colonies' best available market in the early days was with other colonies in the south.

Along with the steady increase of the export trade which we have just noted, commerce with the Indians was maintained, and soon grew to large proportions. It was at this time that the foundation was laid for the great traffic in furs which subsequently became the outstanding business enterprise of eighteenth century America.

There were no commercial banks in those times, and the earliest banking transactions developed through the merchants of the new land and were entirely individual. Also, as has been said, there was no uniform circulating medium—indeed, in the beginning there was very little money of any kind. Instead, the early colonists used a system of barter and trade closely resembling that in vogue in Great Britain under the Tudors.

A certain amount of barter will always be going on in the world, but no civilized nation will permit such a situation to continue if it is possible to avoid it. It would have been quite possible to avoid it in the American colonies if the British Government had taken the simplest measures to do so.

The stage of barter, although, so far as the Indians were concerned continued for many years, was early supplanted among the colonials themselves by an era of mixed currency exchange. With the development of agriculture and the genesis of manufactures, the export trade grew up. Under normal conditions, this trade would have meant that a certain amount of British gold and silver would have come to the colonies and circulated among them; but while the colonials were developing a not inconsiderable export trade, they were at the same time improving their own economic conditions. Planters on the Potomac and the James were importing from England the firm red bricks with which they built the fine old mansions of the South. Sober and successful citizens of New York and Philadelphia were importing household goods, clothing, and many luxurious commodities for themselves and their families. Thrifty New England farmers were seeking abroad improved implements of agriculture with which to till the hard-won acres of the North. Thus, despite the growing trade of the colonies, the financial balance set steadily against them. Through the very necessities of pioneer life and development, they were buying more from the continent than they were selling to it.

Whatever gold and silver left the shores of Britain for America was speedily returned whence it came, and the lack of currency had to be supplied, when it was supplied at all, through trade with other lands. For many years the Spanish milled dollar, known as "pieces of eight," was the leading currency unit of the American colonists. Our present monetary system based upon the dollar unit directly resulted from the unofficial adoption of this Spanish coin. However, it had many competitors. Numerous French and Portuguese coins and English shillings mixed with the Spanish dollars in a mass of miscellaneous currency. Moreover, the value of each individual coin varied in different colonies, Spanish dollars being worth four shillings sixpence in English money in one colonial market, five shillings in another, and five shillings sixpence in still another.

By way of adding to this confusion, the colony of Massachusetts Bay established a mint in 1652. Here the famous "Pine-tree shillings" were coined for a few years, until the British Government forbade further colonial coinage.

Toward the end of this period, in the majority of places this motley mass of currency was handled without relation to its face value, but by weight, as in the Middle Ages, when purchases were made with bags of gold and silver of varying sizes and weights.

By the middle of the seventeenth century it was clear that the growth of economic prosperity in colonial America necessitated some system of currency and some circulating medium. Without hope of obtaining financial support and regulation at the hands of England, the colonists naturally turned to that expedient which has always appealed strongly to a people without an adequate metallic currency: namely, the issuance of bills of credit.

The earliest appearance of paper money was an accident and had a distinctly humorous phase. In 1690, England being at war with France, Massachusetts undertook an expedition to capture Port Royal and Quebec. In line with the easy-going policy of those days, the Massachusetts governor enlisted the soldiers and sailors for this exploit upon the tacit understanding that they were to repay themselves for their martial labors with the indemnity they were expected to obtain from the captured French cities. The only flaw in this comprehensive plan of compensation was that the expedition was defeated, so that there was nothing to divide. With the rapidity that nearly always distinguishes a retreat, the conquered forces soon returned to the colony in a decidedly unpleasant mood. They promptly demanded payment of their back wages; and when the frightened governor and council sought to temporize with them they threatened mutiny.

At this point, some old colonial counsellor, long since forgotten, conceived the idea of paying off the troops with paper. His plan being adopted without a dissenting vote, the clang of the colonial printing presses began, and continued almost without interruption until the founding of the United States.

The original issue of 1690 amounted to only £7000, but the paper money so quickly relieved an untenable situation that it was promptly tried again, the second issue amounting to £40,000. Thereafter the other colonies followed suit. The Massachusetts idea was adopted in short order by New Hampshire, Rhode Island, Connecticut, New York, and New Jersey, and a little later Pennsylvania, Carolina, Maryland, Virginia, and Georgia printed large numbers of paper bills. In the beginning, each colony made a sincere effort to provide for the redemption at maturity of each issue of paper money; but, as time went by and the difficulties of redemption became more and more apparent, a spirit of laxity in this regard spread over the land, and with it, of course, the various bills of credit depreciated swiftly. By the time of the Revolution, bills of credit were in circulation all through the colonies, the value of which was, to say the least, extremely doubtful. As there was no uniform scale of depreciation, and as each colony made many issues of bills, a chaotic condition of conflicting values resulted which proved a great impediment to trade and to the imposition of taxes by either colonial or royal authority.[1]

---

[1] Documentary evidence regarding pre-Revolutionary depreciation is extremely difficult to find. However, the following example, taken from Rhode Island, and representing the culmination of a long process of colonial, Revolutionary, and post-

Although extremely complex in its various manifestations, the principal vice of an inflated paper currency may be explained simply. Paper differs from precious metals as a currency medium in that it has no inherent value—it merely represents value. But it is a convenient unit of exchange. If it represents a promise to pay in gold or its equivalent at some stated time, and if the people who use it believe that that promise will be honestly kept, it will circulate freely at a parity with gold. If, however, the general public does not believe that the promise behind the paper currency will be kept, it will depreciate in direct relation to the depth of distrust with which the promise to pay is regarded by the people. In considering the financial situation which existed during the Revolutionary War, we shall have occasion to observe that the bills of credit of that day depreciated in exact proportion to the popular loss of faith in the financial stability of the Revolutionary Government, and in the probable success of the colonial cause.

The period of paper money, or bills of credit, as they were commonly called, extended approximately from 1690 to 1751. The issues of different colonies were many and varied. Neither the amount of the issues nor the maturity of the bills was regulated by the colonies as a whole, or even by a single colony. Jealousies arose among the colonies over their respective paper bills, finally bringing about a mass of colonial legislation restricting and prohibiting the acceptance and usage of the paper money of other colonies. In this unsettled state of affairs, it was natural that the better-protected bills of the larger and

---

Revolutionary inflation, may be of interest. In this example, 6 specie shillings equalled the following amounts of paper shillings on the various dates listed below.

July 1, 1786................	9 shillings	April 1, 1788...............	38 shillings
August 1, 1786..............	10 "	July 1, 1788................	45 "
October 1, 1786..............	18 "	January 1, 1789.............	60 "
December 1, 1786............	21 "	April 1, 1789...............	72 "
January 1, 1787..............	24 "	July 1, 1789................	90 "
April 1, 1787................	34 "		

From Henry Phillips, "Historical Sketches of the Paper Currency of the American Colonies, 1863" (2 vols.), Vol. 1, p. 153.

richer colonies soon obtained a position of supremacy. The bills of Massachusetts circulated more freely and with better credit than those of Rhode Island, and the paper money of Pennsylvania was more valuable than that of the Carolinas. As time progressed, all the bills depreciated, with the result that the various colonial governments simply worked the printing presses more swiftly and increased the already heavy burden of paper which was choking the economic life of the people. It would be impossible to say how much paper currency was outstanding in the colonies about the middle of the eighteenth century, but it has been clearly shown that in Massachusetts alone in 1750 the paper bills in circulation amounted to approximately £1,800,000. The situation reflected by this figure was general throughout the colonies.

This development, of course, had a direct reflex action upon British merchants. It favored the export trade and made imports extremely difficult and hazardous. In fact, it affected their interests so adversely that the British Government, in 1751, passed an act forbidding any further issue of legal tender bills of credit by the colonies of New England. In 1764, this act was extended to cover all the colonies.

This restrictive legislation was a good thing, but it naturally irritated the colonials. From their point of view, the issuance of paper currency was the inevitable result of Great Britain's failure to provide a proper circulating medium; the Act of 1751 was a case of locking the stable door after the horse had been stolen. Further, they argued, it deprived them of their only currency—a poor and unsatisfactory currency, they freely admitted, but the only one they had. Some of the colonies did try to profit by the situation resulting from the Parliamentary prohibition, and some note issues were redeemed within the next few years. However, it was not possible for the colonies to reconstruct the situation without the help of Great Britain. In a short time they gave up the effort, and be-

gan to print notes again, evading the act of Parliament by issuing temporary treasury notes which were not legal tender, but
which nevertheless passed freely among the people. For additional currency, they turned to the notes issued by loan and
land banks, which, as we shall see, were a considerable feature
of financial operations in colonial days.

A colonial loan bank was in reality nothing more or less
than an agency established for the purpose of lending money
on the security of land. The money loaned was in the form
of paper notes secured by land as collateral. These banks had
none of the customary features of commercial banks of the
present day. They did not accept deposits, pay them out on
check, or make loans on the notes of firms or individuals. The
word "bank" was therefore in this instance used differently
from the way in which it is employed today, but it makes
little difference what they were called, the point is how they
functioned. As a matter of fact, throughout the latter part of
the eighteenth century they functioned quite well. Several
were established in New England about the year 1740, and in
1722 Pennsylvania established a loan office with four commissioners which operated on the same principle as had governed the private land banks. Under the Pennsylvania system, men were able to obtain bills of small denomination
in exchange for pledge of their land, and under the law they
were able to repay the loans made to them in twelve annual
installments with interest at 5 per cent. Of all the makeshift
methods employed by the colonists to supply the want of a
currency the loan banks were unquestionably the most conservative because the paper bills issued by these banks had a
real basic security in that land was pledged to support them.
It might be wild land, uninhabited and of problematic value,
but in most instances it was a better basis for the issue of paper
money than the shaky credit of the early colonial govern-

ments, whose promise to pay a note issue could always be taken in a highly "Pickwickian sense."[2]

We find, therefore, that toward the end of the eighteenth century the colonies suffered not only from taxation on the part of England without any opportunity to share in the legislation by which the taxes were imposed, but also from the evils which accompanied a swiftly increasing export and import business and thriving agricultural development in the face of an entire lack of any proper banking system, regulation of currency, and indeed of any adequate medium of exchange. It is little wonder, then, that the members of the Continental Congress found at the outset that it would be difficult in the extreme to make provisions for financing a new and weak federal government and for providing the necessary funds to prosecute the Revolutionary War.

[2] Beginning with 1681 and ended by law of Parliament in 1741, experiments were made with what our literature refers to as land banks. These were associations of merchants whose object appears to have been chiefly to supply for themselves and the community a sound bank currency, in view of the absence of other sound currency. The assets of the note-issuing association consisted of mortgages deposited by the members, who received notes of the association usable as money up to a certain percentage of the value of the mortgages. The notes were not redeemable on demand in specie; the bank had no specie reserve. The land banks during the period they were permitted to exist did furnish a good means of payment for the communities in which they existed. They did not do any commercial banking beyond the above-mentioned facts.

The first loan bank was started in 1712 in South Carolina. The idea spread rapidly and was continued to the end of the colonial period.

These were not banks in any of the modern uses of the word. The scheme was for the colony to print an issue of its bills of credit designed to be loaned out to the citizens of the colony at a rate of interest lower than the market rate. The citizen borrower gave mortgage security for the loan. This was a mere loan plan, not a banking plan. When overissuance of bills of credit was effected, these bills so issued depreciated along with the other issues of the colony. Pennsylvania refrained from overissue; Rhode Island is notorious for overissuance and depreciation.

See Horace White, "Money and Banking," Chapter 4.

CHAPTER II

REVOLUTIONARY FINANCE

THOUGHTLESS and uninformed critics have frequently condemned the Continental Congress for resorting to the issue of
bills of credit, but it should be remembered that Congress was
simply carrying on after a lapse of some fifteen years the same
policy which first had been adopted from necessity, almost a
century before, by the various colonial legislatures. The members of the Continental Congress had been grown men during
the time, then not long passed, when the colonial issues of
paper bills were the common media used to carry on trade.
Therefore, it was natural for them to return to the same method
of finance when the crisis caused by the war came upon them.

There is a direct connection between the early financial policies of the Continental Congress and the career and services
of Robert Morris as Superintendent of Finance. Had it not
been for the flood of paper money which Congress unloosed
upon the land and its rapid depreciation in value, a situation
would never have arisen so tragically desperate that Congress
voluntarily, though with exceeding bad grace, consented to
place almost dictatorial power in the hands of one man and
submit the finances of the entire country to his administration.

The Continental Congress loathed the idea of centralization
of power. All its members seemed to have been "state-minded."
From the beginning it performed its various duties through
the agency of committees. There were committees on everything—Foreign Affairs, the Army, the Navy, and the Finances.
Before the echoes of the muskets at Bunker Hill had died
away, the Committee on Finance had started in to work the

printing press assiduously for the purpose of making paper money.

On June 22, 1775, the Congress authorized the issue of bills of credit amounting to $2,000,000. The theory upon which such bills were issued was that Congress would authorize them and apportion each issue among the several states for payment, relying upon the patriotism of the state legislatures to live up to the obligations thus allocated to them. This was correct in theory, but did not work out in practice. In the first place, there was very little real money of any kind in the country, and when war came our infant commerce was so injuriously affected that the small inflow of money which had been obtained from abroad almost ceased. It is doubtful that the various colonies could have paid any considerable number of the bills of credit apportioned to them even if they had wished to. However, they never really tried to pay them.

The American people as a whole were fighting the Revolutionary War on the theory that they did not wish to be taxed by the English King, and their general dislike of taxation extended quite naturally from George III to their own government. After all, paying one's bills is largely an attitude of mind, and our ancestors did not have the proper attitude. It was a deal easier to keep on printing bills of credit without any certain maturity, than it was to limit the amount of money issued to the capacity of the nation to pay it when it was due. Therefore, the Continental Congress went gaily down the primrose path of fiat money, and the result was not astonishing although exceedingly disconcerting. Between 1775 and the fall of 1779, there were forty issues of paper money bills amounting to $241,552,780. Of this huge amount of credit instruments only a very small proportion was ever redeemed.

This was only a part of the national picture so far as easy finance was concerned. The issues above mentioned were put out by the Continental Congress, but the colonial legislatures did not allow such an attractive method of currency supply to escape their attention. The state governments on their own account during this period issued state bills of credit amounting to $209,524,776. Moreover, the states made most of these bills legal tender. They threatened anyone who refused to accept them with cancellation of the debts for which they were tendered, and added even further penalties to such unpatriotic refusal.

The colonies also indulged in no small degree in price-fixing legislation with the idea of bolstering up the falling values of these bills which were, indeed, one might say, works of fiction in the financial field. The ineffectiveness of price-fixing legislation was soon proved, but this did not deter the state legislatures from continued effort to force worthless paper upon the people.

In 1776 when the continental credit bills first came out, most people were inclined to take them seriously. It had been a number of years since there had been any such bills around, and people forgot that some fifteen years previously they had been one of the best jokes of the time. Also they were legally issued, and, in spite of what modern critics may say, the American people as a whole would like to obey their numerous laws. So for a while the citizens proceeded on the theory that the bills were real money and would be paid. However, it did not take long to convince everyone that these hopes were decidedly delusive. A few of the early issues were paid—very few indeed —and then a policy was adopted of extending the maturity of the various issues whenever they came due. This went along nicely for a while until the states got a better idea. They did not put any maturity date on the bills at all and so were saved the trouble of extending them.

The result was inevitable. The business world is cold-blooded and calculating. After the leading merchants became convinced that the credit bills were not to be paid, their commercial value decreased with alarming rapidity. From 1777 to 1779, it is true, the bills held up in value better than anybody had the least right to expect. This was due largely to the patriotism of the people, and to the fact that at the beginning of the war the British were none too successful in their military and naval operations. Real depreciation, however, set in during 1779, which both politically and in a military sense was a very bad year for the colonists. Credit bills depreciated from a ratio of eight to one in January, 1779, to thirty-eight and one-half to one in November. From then on matters went from bad to worse. Finally, in March, 1780, the Continental Congress was reluctantly compelled to acknowledge formally what everybody else knew to be a fact.[1]

Therefore, on March 18 a famous and useful measure was passed by the Congress. On that date an act was adopted which made provision for the acceptance of paper money in place of silver in the ratio of forty to one. In order to get rid of the mass of paper, this act contained a clever expedient. A tax of $15,-000,000 a month was imposed upon all the colonies for a period of thirteen months, and it was levied proportionately upon the various states. It was provided that this tax should be payable in bills of the old issues of paper money. When so paid these bills were to be destroyed and replaced by a new issue of paper bills in an amount not to exceed one-twentieth of the face value of the old issues. Six-tenths of these bills were to be paid to the states, and the remainder retained by the Government

---

[1] Number of paper dollars equal to one specie dollar: January, 1777-May, 1781.

1777:	January	$1.25	1779:	March	$10.00
	June	2.25		June	22.00
	December	4.00		December	45.00
1778:	March	5.00	1780:	February	55.00
	June	4.00		June	60.00
	December	6.00		December	100.00
			1781:	February	120.00
				May	500.00

On May 31, 1781, the paper ceased to circulate as money; but speculators dealt in it and it fell gradually to 1000 to 1.

From W. M. Gauge, "A Short History of Paper Money and Banking in the United States," Part 2, p. 26.

for national purposes. The new bills were to be redeemed in specie in five years, to bear interest at 5 per cent, and to be receivable for taxes.

This was the first piece of honest and conservative financial legislation that the Continental Congress passed, and even though they should have done something of the kind long before, nevertheless as it happened, they did it in time to save the financial honor of the country. Furthermore, the new law worked, which was the cause of surprise and congratulation.

Within a comparatively short period of time, under the operation of this act, $119,400,000 of old credit bills were paid in by the states and destroyed, while, on the other hand, only $4,400,000 new tenor notes were ever actually issued.

This Act of March, 1780, did not put an end to the depreciation of continental money. It was like opening a sluice gate when the creek has overflowed. It kept the cattle from drowning in the barnyard, but the poor beasts were very uncomfortable until the water was pumped out. Even after the act went into effect, there were several hundred millions of worthless paper bills in circulation, and although a quarter of them were surrendered and destroyed, the others survived to make a great deal of trouble. The chief virtue of the law was that it put an end to further issues of worthless credit bills.

Various efforts were made by the Congress and the states to control depreciation of the outstanding bills, but without any marked success. Depreciation continued and soon increased to such an extent that it became ridiculous. In January, 1781, it took $100 of paper money to equal $1 in silver, so that the evening clothes of a dignified citizen would have the book value of a small fortune. From that time on, the old bills of credit were really nothing more or less than a speculative commodity. People bought and sold them in bulk very much as Russian rubles were traded in during the war period and German marks during the reconstruction era succeeding the

World War. In a word, the system of continental currency had collapsed, and with it the whole financial structure of the young nation visibly tottered. We had no currency and no credit; and this fact was relied upon by England to defeat us as much as the military operations which at that time were not working out in our favor.

At this point it became evident to those in authority that there must be centralization of financial power if the country were to have any chance of successfully emerging from the impasse into which it had blundered. Therefore, after careful consideration and a good deal of argument, a new office was created—that of Superintendent of Finance— with almost absolute power, both supervisory and directive, over the finances of the continental government. This office was tendered to Robert Morris, who indeed was the only person seriously thought of in connection with the position. Since pre-revolutionary times he had not only been the leading merchant of Pennsylvania, but had shown such unusual ability in financial matters and had so succeeded in inspiring confidence in all classes of citizens that it was generally believed that, if anyone could pull us out of the deep hole in which we found ourselves, it would be Morris of Philadelphia.

CHAPTER III

ROBERT MORRIS, THE FINANCIER OF THE REVOLUTION

THIS is the story of a man and a period. The man is of outstanding personality—picturesque, dominating, able and colorful. But his vigorous and interesting life cannot be appreciated unless, in the first instance, we examine with considerable care the times in which he lived. Robert Morris is frequently referred to as the financier of the Revolution, and that he was. But he was far more. He was a leading citizen of Philadelphia and of the state of Pennsylvania long before the war of independence; a prominent merchant, a leader in society, a banker, and one of the principal exporters and importers of his day. Few men made such a deep impression upon the life of any colony as Robert Morris made upon that of Pennsylvania.

Morris was not a native of Pennsylvania but was born in Liverpool, England, on January 31, 1734. His father, also named Robert Morris, emigrated to America shortly after he was born and settled in Oxford, Maryland, as agent for a large firm of British merchants. At the age of thirteen, Robert Morris came out to join his father at Oxford, which was then an important town on the banks of the Chesapeake Bay. It was one of those settlements, of which we have had so many, that started out to be a big city and then apparently, for no good reason, stopped short in its career. Young Morris did not stay long in Oxford, however, but went to Philadelphia, then the largest city of the colonies, to seek his fortune. He soon attracted the attention of Charles and Edward Willing, successful merchants and able business men. They employed him and gave him his big chance in life. He took it and soon became a junior partner of the firm. Thus when his father died in 1750 he had already made a fine start in the world. From the time that he was admitted to the Willing firm in 1754 until the outbreak of the Revolution is a period of twenty-one years, and this hustling young colonial merchant made every year count in his favor. Though not the most showy period of his life, these years of preparation were probably the most valuable time of all. The intensive work of most successful lives takes place between twenty-one and fifty, and we should not forget that Robert Morris was twenty years old in 1754 and forty-one in 1775. At the latter date he had already laid the foundation of a successful career. He was not only known throughout the city and state as an energetic merchant with vision and personality, but he had become one of the most notable citizens of the largest town in colonial America. In 1765, when he was thirty, he had served as chairman of a committee formed to resist the hated "Stamp Act," and with strength and diplomacy he had seen to it that very few of the despised stamps were sold in Philadelphia. In 1769 he had married Miss Mary White, who was the daughter of Colonel Thomas White of Maryland, a man of prominence and wealth. As a result of this union, he had seven children—five sons and two daughters. Probably the greatest object in his life was to provide adequately for his numerous family, the tragic element in the situation being that in the end he failed utterly to do so.

Thus we find that in 1775, when hostilities began, Robert Morris was easily the most prominent merchant of Philadelphia. He was known and respected by everybody, and as a partner in the well-known Willing firm he had many ships on the sea and at all times a great quantity of goods coming and going from which he derived considerable profit. Briefly, he was a master of colonial trade and a leading citizen of his adopted city. He also had developed a flair for finance. In

ROBERT MORRIS

every gathering, men turned to him for advice as to the use of money and management of funds and credit. It was natural, therefore, that when the war actually began, he should in the first instance be elected to the Continental Congress and then almost immediately be placed upon an important committee whose duty it was "to suggest methods and provide measures for procuring money to prosecute the war." Throughout the dark years from 1776 to 1781 he was constantly in the public eye as a leader in colonial finance. In conjunction with other members he was always serving upon the committees which controlled the collection of income for the public treasury and also directed its expenditure.

In December, 1776, when Congress fled Philadelphia as the British forces drew near, Morris remained behind as representative of the Congress and for a short time was in command of most of the activities of the town. He assumed personal charge of the completion of several ships so that they should not fall into British hands, and he acted as food controller and general supervisor of all preparations for rationing and defense of the population. Meanwhile, he mobilized his private resources so that he might take advantage of the conditions caused by the war. He put his privateers to sea, and showed great shrewdness in the purchase and disposal of various supplies. In common with others, he lost by reason of the capture of some of his ships, but he gained far more than he lost in the high prices he was able to obtain when he got a cargo through. We should give Morris our unstinted admiration because though a man of much property he declined to take the apparently safe course and become a Tory. From the beginning of the contest Morris never wavered in his attachment to the colonial cause. True it is, that for a time he steadfastly opposed a definite break with England, and the promulgation of a declaration of independence. In the end, however, he bowed to the people's will, and together with his colleagues signed the great document. He was also strongly opposed from the outset to the uncontrolled issue of bills of credit. Had his advice been followed, much difficulty would have been avoided, and it might never have been necessary to enact the Repudiation Act of 1780. As an individual he did what he could to stem the financial tide. His firm issued its own notes, named "Bobbies" in compliment to him. No higher tribute could be paid to this remarkable man than that which his countrymen gave him when, in those troublous times, they preferred the paper money issued by his firm to that issued contemporaneously by the various state governments and the Continental Congress.

This brief outline of Robert Morris's early years brings us down to the day when he began his great financial service to his country as Superintendent of Finance. In order, however, to comprehend the crowded years when Morris acted as Superintendent, we should understand something of the character and peculiarities of the man as well as the bare facts of his career.

Morris was above all an intensely human person, and that perhaps constitutes his greatest appeal. He was never cold and austere as Albert Gallatin was, nor did he possess the dictatorial and intractable temper of Alexander Hamilton. He was a big man both mentally and physically, and he lived his life in a broad and expansive way.

He was forty-six years of age when he took office as Superintendent on May 14, 1781. Already he had accomplished much and his life had been one series of unbroken successes. Indeed, it was at about this time that he thought of retiring so that he might enjoy the good things of life before age crept upon him. Then of a sudden came this imperative call to serve his country, the acceptance of which placed him in the most difficult situation and subjected him to the greatest strain that he had ever experienced.

Morris had nothing of the recluse. He was no miser; he did

not love money for its own sake but merely because he must play an interesting game in order to get it, and its acquisition gave him power which he loved. He loved to make money, but he enjoyed spending it equally well. During his life he had a number of houses, all of them well located, spacious, and beautifully furnished. His town house at Fifth and Market Streets was the show place of Philadelphia. When Morris generously offered it to Congress as the presidential mansion during Washington's term of office it was gratefully accepted, and became the center of those splendid entertainments to which our first President invited the statesmen and the social leaders of the day.

Morris also had a hunting lodge in Montgomery County, and numerous farms. His most famous residence was one which he purchased as a country place, and is now included in Fairmount Park above the old waterworks. This residence was known as "Hills on Schuylkill" and had every advantage that a suburban house could have possessed during the latter part of the eighteenth century. For more than twenty years the leaders of the colonial world were entertained within its walls and on its wide verandas. Here came the dashing Lafayette and grumpy old Baron Von Steuben, and here also came beautiful Mrs. Bingham and Peggy Shippen, the ill-starred beauty for whose love Benedict Arnold surrendered everything a man should hold dear. Here also the Washingtons, Hamiltons, and the Jays were entertained by the merchant prince of his generation. It was, indeed, a brilliant group which constituted the social world during the early days of the republic, and Morris's openhanded hospitality set the keynote for the social affairs of the young and struggling country. Morris's dinners and wines were famous throughout the land, and formed a topic of conversation in London and Paris as well as in Philadelphia and New York.

Physically, Morris was a large man, weighing more than two

hundred pounds, with a ruddy complexion, light hair, and eyes of a peculiar shade of pale blue which looked intently and directly at anyone with whom he was conversing. A well-known portrait of him by Gilbert Stuart belongs to the permanent collection of the Academy of Fine Arts in Philadelphia. Morris's contemporaries have testified that the likeness obtained by Stuart was admirable. The pose is of absorbing interest. He sits in a large armchair clad in a blue velvet suit with ruffled shirt of lawn. One is impressed with the mental power which the painting reveals—a power essentially devoid of coldness and combined with geniality and a charitable outlook upon life. Indeed, it seems that the personality of Robert Morris is speaking to one across the century and a half which intervenes between his lifetime and the present day. As one studies the picture, one is deeply impressed with the unusual combination, force and kindness, energy and ability to play, optimism and intense practicality, vision and common sense—a most unusual combination of qualities valuable, and yet, in most instances, diverse. The conditions existing in this country in 1781 called for just this type of man to take the helm if success was to be achieved.

Optimism in finance is at times a dangerous factor, but at other times it is vitally necessary. After the collapse of the continental money in 1780, the only chance we had to pull through the quagmire in which we were engulfed was to obtain a leader of such outstanding and over-bearing personality and endurance, with so much self-confidence and faith in his own ability and in the future of the young nation, that he would be able not only to beat down tremendous obstacles himself, but also to inspire his assistants and the citizens of the entire country with the same faith and the same courage.

Nevertheless, in spite of his optimistic attitude toward life, he was a shrewd and competent man of business. He realized at the outset that he could never succeed in the tremendous

job which Congress placed upon his shoulders unless he had
an absolutely free hand and was allowed to be not merely the
financial leader of the country but actually its financial dictator.

He therefore informed Congress that he would not accept
the office of Superintendent of Finance except upon his own
terms, which were substantially as follows:

First, Congress must permit him to continue in his own private
commercial ventures.

Second, Congress must not expect him to recognize the old bills
of credit. He said very frankly that he could not take upon his
shoulders the added burden of the millions of worthless paper
money which both the central government and the states had issued
since the beginning of hostilities.

Third, he insisted that he must have absolute power to appoint
and remove all of the subordinate officers connected with his department.

These conditions proved a bitter pill for Congress to swallow.
They did not care much about the first one, although his private business affairs during his incumbency of office afterwards
formed one of the principal grounds for criticism of Morris's
administration. Nor were they too much disturbed by his insistence that the tons of paper money still floating about the
country should be thrown into the discard. But they did hate
to give him full authority to hire and fire within his own department, because this meant that a large part of their patronage would be lost to them permanently, and we must not forget that our political ancestors were politicians as well as statesmen, and that there were many mouths to feed among the loyal
supporters of the Revolutionary movement. Actually, there was
this feature in the situation which proved to be a determining
factor; Robert Morris did not need to be Superintendent of
Finance and indeed did not wish to be, because he knew that it
meant laboring night and day for years with much to lose and,

as he then thought, little to gain. On the other hand, the Continental Congress needed Morris as badly as a lame child needs a crutch.

A nation cannot become bankrupt in the ordinary sense, because there is no court to declare it so, but it can be insolvent, without a currency and with its credit practically ruined, and that was precisely the unenviable position which this country occupied when the Congress asked Robert Morris to rehabilitate its financial structure. Accordingly, after several months of hesitation, Congress capitulated and assented to all his demands.

Morris found himself Superintendent of Finance, with no real money to spend and with the country's credit in the worst possible condition. It was immediately necessary for him to formulate a series of policies in order to put the currency and credit in better shape.

The first problem was how to obtain the huge funds necessary for financing the war. The answer Morris devised to this was in one sense the only one available, namely, that he would rely as much as possible on loans, and to a very limited extent on taxation. He personally believed that the best form of taxation under the circumstances would be import duties, which we now call tariff duties.

This looked better on paper than in fact. We were not at that time a manufacturing nation, and our agricultural exports had been largely reduced not only by the British blockade of our coast but by the disruption of peaceful pursuits which war always entails.

On the other hand, the only kind of taxation which was possible, namely direct taxation, was extremely difficult to put into effect. America was then fighting a war largely because it resented years of taxation without representation by the British Government, and the hatred of taxation without representation could be easily extended to taxation under any conditions.

It is easy to criticize our forefathers for their refusal to pay adequate taxes, but if we put ourselves in the position which they occupied, we doubtless would be unwilling to pay taxes with any better grace. When a man pays taxes today he seldom does it with pleasure, but at least he knows that he is getting something definite in return. He is receiving from the Federal Government protection in time of war through the agency of a well-equipped army and an adequate navy; from the state and city governments he obtains police protection, fire protection, good schools for his children, and usable roads for his automobile.

What did people get for their taxes in 1781? Frankly, they did not get much, and they said so with emphasis. It may be added they did not need much. Each family in those days, at least in the country districts (and most families lived in the country), was an almost independent economic unit. The family raised its own food, produced its own meat animals and dairy cattle, spun its own clothes, taught its own children, and to a great extent fought its own battles. About the only things the average rural citizen had to buy were hats, shoes, gunpowder, muskets, the Holy Bible, quinine, and blue-mass. Under these conditions, can we wonder that the Revolutionary citizens did not want to pay any more taxes? As a matter of fact, they did not pay taxes, and even Robert Morris was unable to persuade them to do so.

This was one part of his administration where he failed. He could not be blamed for his failure, because popular opinion was against him and he had no legal authority. The Continental Congress possessed no power to tax the states, or to compel the states to tax their own people. All Congress could do was to determine that there ought to be a tax, and request the states to enforce it. Therefore, Robert Morris was reduced to pleading with the governors of the various commonwealths to see to it that the states paid their proportionate shares of the federal taxes.

Certainly Morris made every effort to get money out of the states. He wrote continually to the governors and leading officials of every state in the Union. Years later when his original copy-books were discovered under romantic circumstances on a dump heap in France, the world was startled to find how many hundreds of letters this persistent man had written in a vain effort to collect the taxes which should have been the life blood of war finance.

Finding he could obtain little but excuses and evasions from the different states, Morris, after a year or so, changed his policy and introduced a system of collecting taxes in kind which was known by the term "specifics." Under this system, the states which either could not or would not give money to support the Revolution contributed food, animals, grain, chickens, ducks, cloth, or anything they had which the continental army could use. In order to avail himself of such an arrangement, Morris had to establish a considerable number of warehouses and magazines throughout the states where these various "specific" contributions could be assembled, stored, and rendered available for use by the army. This meant that he had to establish a large corps of subordinate officials throughout the land, and also compelled him to rely on their honesty and attention to duty. As a matter of fact, he began to establish such a group of assistants as soon as he assumed office, because he soon found that the political appointees with which his department was filled when he took command were unreliable, and in many cases dishonest.

It is a fact that the system of "specifics" worked much better than Morris's efforts to obtain money from the states through the processes of ordinary taxation. But it was a makeshift at best, and extremely expensive to administer. Many food animals died in transit, the grain spoiled in the warehouses, and a great deal of graft and thievery was connected with the entire situation. Nevertheless, he actually did get a fair amount of food and some clothing in this way which could not have been otherwise obtained.

Another difficulty which affected the whole question of state taxation was the jealousy among the various commonwealths. All the states seemed to hang back in order to see what the others were willing to do, with the result that few did anything. Thus in April, 1782, when the first quarterly payment from the states came due, New Jersey was the only state to make any payment, and she gave only $5500, although the Government's budget for that year was $8,000,000.

Having been unable either to bully or coax money from the state treasuries, Morris started to work along another line and obtain money by means of domestic loans, similar in nature to the Liberty Loans of the World War. In this field he was somewhat more successful. During the war period, a series of public loans were floated, amounting, in paper money of various issues, to $63,289,000, of which, however, the specie value was only $7,684,000. It is probable that not nearly so much would have been raised by this method had it not been that in 1777 Congress used specie borrowed from France to pay the interest due on its domestic loans and in this way greatly increased their credit and popularity. Although Congress never did such a thing again, and indeed failed to pay any interest except in depreciated paper after 1782, nevertheless, the one touch of gold did much to save the entire situation.

State taxation proving ineffective, and domestic loans being of little real assistance, Morris was forced to place his principal dependence upon his ability to borrow money abroad. This is where his peculiar abilities were most thoroughly displayed. The various interesting and unusual methods he employed to obtain money from nations which were unwilling to lend it will long prove to be his greatest claim to fame as the financier of the Revolution.

The principle of relativity must be observed in connection with finance as well as in every other department of life. We must not judge past situations by present conditions. The amount of money borrowed by the United States from other nations during the war seems pitifully small today, but that is only because our country has grown so tremendously that we are now accustomed to the daily use of figures which would have astounded our ancestors. If we are to understand Revolutionary finance, we must never forget that what is small today was huge then.

With this in mind, it may be stated that between 1777 and 1783 the United States borrowed from France $6,352,500; Holland $1,304,000; Spain $174,017—making a total of $7,830,517.[1]

It will be observed readily from the table that the foreign loans of the United States increased greatly as soon as Robert Morris became Superintendent of Finance, and it would not be too much to say that without such an increase Morris could never have found the money necessary to win the war. These loans were his main dependence, and they proved sufficient.

Not all the credit for raising this money should go to Morris alone. It was team work that did it, and Morris had a great team. To accomplish his purpose, he relied upon our repre-

[1] These figures are quoted from the "Financial History of the United States" by Davis R. Dewey, reprinted by permission of Longmans, Green & Co., Publishers, as is also the following table which shows how these loans were made by years, viz.:

Year	France	Spain	Holland
1777	$ 181,500.00	$	$
1778	544,500.00		
1779	181,500.00		
1780	726,000.00		
1781	1,737,763.00	128,804.00	
1782	1,892,237.00	45,213.00	720,000.00
1783	1,089,000.00		584,000.00
Totals	$6,352,500.00	$ 174,017.00	$1,304,000.00

sentatives at the Courts of France, Spain, and Holland. In Paris we had one of our best men, Benjamin Franklin; in Madrid, John Jay, of New York, who later negotiated the Treaty of Peace with England; and at The Hague, John Adams, of Massachusetts, who was to succeed Washington as President, and who founded one of the famous families in America destined to continue eminent through many generations.

Again, we must think of Morris in terms of unremitting labor. The man's correspondence during his years in office was unbelievably voluminous. He knew no such thing as office hours, but worked all day and long into the night. Remember, he was subject to constant interruptions. It appeared that almost everybody was a creditor of the United States, and with a simple child-like faith, people of all classes seemed to believe that this great man was indeed a financial magician who could charm money from the very rocks themselves.

Beset as he was on all sides, it is difficult to understand where he found time to write as constantly as he did, not only to the governors and officials of the states, but to Franklin, Jay, Adams, and many others abroad. He bombarded these men with appeals for help, and their own writings testify that he not only drove them almost crazy with his insatiable demands, but he made them so angry that had it not been for the great cause to which they had all pledged their best energies, he would in all probability have lost their cooperation, and perhaps their personal regard. Spurred on by Morris's continual demands for cash, these men, particularly Franklin, went to the limit in their efforts to assist him.

Probably no more able diplomat ever was in the service of the United States than Benjamin Franklin. A democratic person of humble origin, he nevertheless achieved tremendous popularity with the French aristocracy in the most artificial period of Bourbon rule. Indeed, had it not been for his remarkable personality, he never could have succeeded in getting the loans that he did.

At this time, France was herself in a perilous financial condition. She had no money to spare, and it is to be doubted if she ever meant to support the Revolutionary movement in America to the extent to which she finally went. France hated the English nation, and when she saw that we were giving England considerable trouble, she thought it might pay to make a gesture in our behalf, and, at the most, to send her fleet over here with a small body of troops to help the cause along. In adopting this policy, however, she did not reckon upon the persuasive qualities of Benjamin Franklin or the indomitable energy of Robert Morris; before her statesmen realized where they were heading, she had loaned us several million dollars and from then on found herself faced by the disagreeable necessity of lending us more money, in order that we might eventually repay what we had already borrowed.

In lending us this money, France did all she could to protect herself. She made conditions that we should repay her at various times and in different ways. She was naturally anything but pleased that Morris, after promising anything he was asked to promise, seemed to forget all about the conditions of the loans as soon as he got the money. It is often asked if Morris cut some sharp corners and made some statements devoid of truth in connection with his work as Superintendent of Finance. The answer is that of course he did. He undoubtedly told some grand lies, and doubtless from time to time, especially where the French were concerned, he broke his word in a big way. It is probable that for years to come he will be criticized by hundreds of little men, none of whom would have been able to save a country when it was flat broke.

He did contribute more to the salvation of his country than any other man except Washington or Franklin, and in doing this he kept his word whenever possible and told the truth as much as he could. This is not an apology for Robert Morris— he had plenty of faults, but he also had many great and compensating virtues.

Soon after he entered the office of Superintendent, Morris decided that he could not rely upon France alone for financial support, and he began to develop a borrowing capacity with Spain and with Holland. Spain never lent us much money, but Holland furnished vitally needed help during the last two years of the struggle. Indeed, it was fortunate that these side lines were developed, because Morris and Franklin pushed the French so hard from 1781 onward that they almost overplayed their hand. Relations were so strained at one period that the Intendant of Finance would not permit Franklin to come to his house even for a social visit.

In working out a system to accomplish his purpose of wringing the last possible dollar from foreign lenders, Robert Morris employed a great many different schemes, some of which worked and some of which did not. Even at this distance of time, it is amusing and profitable to remember one of his devices, which might well be called "Triangulation."

Morris would frequently make a draft on Benjamin Franklin in Paris, and then if he could he would discount it. When he made the draft, Morris had no idea where the money was coming from to meet it, and he had a fairly clear idea that Franklin did not know where the money was to be obtained any better than he did. So, in order to give Franklin time to raise the necessary funds, Morris actually took advantage of the poor methods of communication which were then a feature of world finance. Knowing that business men in Cuba cleared their commercial paper through Madrid, he would send the draft to Cuba for discount. The paper merchants who bought it would then send it to their bankers in Madrid, and the Madrid bankers would send it to Paris for payment. All of this would take three or four months. Meanwhile, as soon as the draft was drawn, Morris would send word to Franklin that the draft had been made, but that it was coming along slowly through Havana and Madrid, so that if he hurried, he ought to be able to raise the money to pay it when it arrived. Morris was of such an optimistic turn of mind that he thought he was really doing Franklin a great favor by arranging matters in this way, and it never bothered him that Franklin was perplexed and worried by the succession of drafts which Morris kept sending him by this ingenious system.

It is as interesting to observe the methods which Morris used to spend the money he borrowed as it is to study the unusual and effective ways he employed to secure it. We must remember that when Morris was in supreme financial control, the Government owed large sums of money in all directions, and that there was very little cash or credit to meet the multiplicity of demands.

The private soldiers of the continental army were seldom paid their meager wages, and the officers were paid even less frequently, on the theory that most of them had some private means. The people who supplied the army with food and clothing and munitions had to engage in a constant contest to get even a part of their money. Everyone looked to Morris for payment. As he said, he could not walk along the street without being assailed from every side by creditors whose claims were just, and who were in no humor to be denied payment.

In this predicament, Morris gave many exhibitions of his ingenuity, boldness, and sense of humor. Wherever possible, he delayed payment or refused to pay on the ground that he did not want to pay an installment, when he had not the money to satisfy the entire debt. When this did not work, he would pay a little here and a little there, usually in unexpected places, and always where the payment would attract as much publicity as possible, and he would supplement every payment, no matter how small, with so many promises and congratulations that the debtor would usually leave in the highest spirits. Several times, Morris appears to have been in real danger of his life, notably on one occasion when he had to go into hiding to escape a band of Revolutionary soldiers who had not received their back pay, and were out to get it by any means, fair or foul. Indeed, it was the influence of Washington's great personality which prevented a disturbance which might have amounted to civil war at the time the army disbanded.

Many were the devices and schemes indulged in by Robert Morris in order to evade paying debts when he had not the money to do so. It is entirely probable that Morris's great friend and associate, Gouverneur Morris, would never have been appointed as Assistant Superintendent of Finance had it not been for the fact that he possessed the same name as Morris himself. To the fertile mind of the Superintendent this appealed as a real opportunity, and he was quick to take advantage of it. Gouverneur Morris lost a leg in early manhood, and for the rest of his life was a cripple. This situation suited Robert Morris and made his plan a complete success. In the office of finance at Fifth and Market Streets, Philadelphia, Gouverneur Morris was installed in a big, airy room on the first floor, and all the innumerable callers who inquired for Mr. Morris were shown in to him. He was dignified, with a gracious manner, and Robert Morris taught him all he knew with regard to small payments and attractive promises. If Gouverneur Morris succeeded in placating the debtors, well and good, but even if they became angry, none of them could possibly assault a man with one leg, so that much trouble was avoided in this way.

We must also remember that the great majority of the callers had never seen Robert Morris, and as the modern newspaper was not even thought of in those days, they had never seen a portrait of him. While all this discussion was going on below stairs, Robert Morris was working away in the third story back, his door being guarded by two tough but loyal citizens, who made it their particular business to see that he should not be interrupted against his will.

Shortly after Morris accepted office as Superintendent, he was called upon by General Washington to accomplish one of his most difficult tasks. Washington was preparing for the final campaign of the war, which resulted in the capture of Yorktown and the surrender of Lord Cornwallis. His army was in the north and had to be transported rapidly to the south, and properly fed while on the way. A number of regiments refused to move unless their pay was forthcoming. Also, no provision had been made to assemble boats and barges at the head of Chesapeake Bay to carry the troops to Virginia. Morris appreciated the importance of the situation as soon as it was presented to him, and he threw himself into the crisis with all the energy and ability that he possessed.

He wrote to the governors of the states most immediately affected. He coaxed reluctant individuals to help the army in this critical stage, and, as a final master stroke, he induced the French officials who accompanied the expeditionary forces, sent to our aid by Louis XVI, to put up a substantial sum in gold so that the hesitating regiments might at least be paid some real money on account. Perhaps no one act during Morris's administration did more to insure the success of the American arms than this magnificent and successful effort to transport Washington's army on its last victorious campaign.

Robert Morris, however, did far more for America than borrow money with difficulty and spend it with care.

Morris had a fine mind and a natural aptitude for finance.

Without much education, he was a graduate of the hard school of practical business experience, and in that school he seems to have mastered in a rough way the leading principles of economics and of financial management. He therefore realized as soon as he entered the office of Finance that it was vitally necessary for our Government to have some kind of a national bank, so that credit might be stabilized, taxes collected, and aid extended to the Congress through the lending capacity of the bank. Accordingly, in response to Morris's urging, the Bank of North America was established in 1782. It had an authorized capital of $10,000,000, but it was utterly impossible to obtain anything like that amount at that time. Seventy thousand dollars was finally raised from private citizens, although with great difficulty. The Government subscribed $200,000, which, following Morris's usual plan of putting money where it would do the most good, was diverted from a French loan which was intended for entirely different purposes.

Almost from the day it opened, the bank proved to be an invaluable aid to Morris's administration of the Department of Finance. Weak though it undoubtedly was, and insufficiently supplied with capital funds, it nevertheless provided a nucleus of credit which up to that time the country had never had.

After the institution opened, a loan of $100,000 was made to the Government. In February, March, and June, additional loans of $100,000 were made. Hence, in four months the bank loaned the Government $100,000 more than its paid-up capital. In addition to lending the Government money, the bank made collections of public funds, discounted notes of individuals who had claims which the Government had to pay, and by issuing its own notes helped to stabilize the weak and failing currency of the period.

Perhaps the greatest assistance which the bank rendered

to Morris was through its Government loans, but in addition
it created confidence, both at home and abroad. It was managed and directed by a number of the leading merchants of
the day, such men as Thomas Fitzsimmons, James Wilson,
and William Bingham being among its directors; its first president was Robert Morris's old partner, Thomas Willing, a man
whose name stood for the highest integrity, and whose reputation was an asset to any institution with which he was connected.

The year of 1783 was the last year of the Revolutionary War,
and with the close of hostilities, Morris felt that he could
gracefully retire from office. Never had he desired the superintendency of Finance. He had been forced to accept it
through official pressure and public clamor.

His great services were not generally recognized until long
after his death. Throughout his life, and especially during
the years he held office, he was constantly subjected to the
most cruel and false accusations. His honesty was questioned;
he was accused of having indulged in private trade, to his
own great enrichment, while at the same time he refused to
pay the legitimate debts of his country. It was said he had
used the power and privileges of his office to make much
money for himself while the soldiers starved, and people
cried for bread. Many believed that he had been guilty of
graft, and it was even said that he had sold Government property without legal authority and pocketed the proceeds. Indeed,
few public men have been called upon to withstand such a
storm of criticism and abuse.

Therefore, in the early summer of 1783, Morris began a
vigorous effort to relieve himself of the cares of office. He
wrote Congress tendering his resignation unless adequate provision should be made to care for the public debts. In the
course of this remarkable letter he expressed himself as follows: "To increase our debts, while the prospect of paying

them diminishes, does not consist with my idea of integrity. I must, therefore, quit a situation which becomes utterly insupportable. But lest the public measures be deranged by any precipitation, I will continue to serve until the end of May. If effectual measures are not taken by that period to make permanent provision for the public debts of every kind, Congress will be pleased to appoint some other man to be the Superintendent of their finances. I should be unworthy of the confidence reposed in me by my fellow citizens if I did not explicitly declare that I will never be the minister of injustice. I have the honor to be, etc., Robert Morris."

This letter caused a tremendous sensation throughout the country. Morris probably intended that it should. We shall never know whether Morris really wanted his resignation accepted at this time or not. It would seem that, in common with many other able men, he believed that Congress would never let him go, and he was playing his trump card, in order to compel them to fund the public debts and place the national currency on a sound basis.

If such was his belief, however, he was wrong. Congress was annoyed, worried, angry, and undoubtedly quite concerned, but Congress was unwilling to do the perintendent's will. Meanwhile, public opinion set in strongly against him. Even his closest friends and admirers, men like Washington, Hamilton, and Madison, failed to comprehend his point of view, and received his proffered resignation as an attempt to desert the cause in a critical hour.

Many negotiations were held with him in an attempt to straighten out his difficulties with Congress, but no adequate way was found, and finally, on November 1, 1784, eighteen months after his first resignation was to have taken effect, he laid down finally the duties of his office. He had been Superintendent of Finance for approximately three and a half years, and had carried the country through the crisis of the war. He had failed to raise taxes from the states, and it is quite true that he did collect pitifully little by way of domestic loans, but he had scored a great success in obtaining money from foreign governments, and he had done equally well in so arranging payments of the public indebtedness that, even though he never paid enough or nearly enough to satisfy claimants, he did pay enough to enable America to win the war.

If he did not always tell the truth while engaged in so doing, if he made a fortune for himself on the side, if he habitually promised far more than he could fulfill, and kept a large portion of the public in a state of violence and anger against him, such things should be forgiven.

Nearly a century and a half separates us from the Revolutionary epoch, and hence our judgment of the men and events of that time are far more reliable, just, and devoid of prejudice than if we had lived in those exciting days. Among all the great men of the period, three names stand out today, lustrous, untarnished, and unexcelled, and those three names are George Washington, Benjamin Franklin, and Robert Morris. With their aid the Republic of today became a fact; without them it would have been merely a dream.

Robert Morris's career after the Revolution is something which can give his true admirers little pleasure to dwell upon, and as it had little or nothing to do with American finance, it is not necessary to do more than summarize it here.

Had Mr. Morris returned to trade when he left his superintendency of Finance, he would, in all probability, have been successful. But the very optimism which made it possible for him to finance a war successfully in behalf of a practically bankrupt country urged him on into other fields of effort. After 1790 he appears to have completely abandoned his mercantile business, and from then on he indulged in all kinds of speculations in land. He was a man of florid and hopeful tem-

)erament, and the successful termination of the war seemed to him to ensure the immediate development of the entire country. That he was right in his belief regarding ultimate land values, time has abundantly proved, but he expected that those values would be attained in a few years rather than by slow degrees over more than a century.

Land was cheap; land was plentiful. Morris, although disliked by many, was considered a great financier. People flocked to him and gave him their savings with child-like trustfulness, which seems to have gone to his head. He bought huge quantities of land in all directions. At one time, he owned the greater part of New York State. He also bought the land on which the city of Washington now stands.

He operated individually and in association with partners, one of whom, Greenleaf by name, was a thorough scoundrel who aided greatly in Morris's ruin. Later on he did a land business through corporations, of which the best known was the North American Land Company. He became possessed of millions of acres of land, most of them in an utterly wild state. He strained his credit and that of his partners to make immense purchases, and then when over-extended, he suffered a series of blows which he could not withstand. From 1793 onward he was probably insolvent, but he made a gallant struggle and exercised all his well-known ingenuity to avert the inevitable result.

It is sad, indeed, to view the futile struggles of the great man as his creditors closed in about him. His optimism and faith in himself remained unimpaired almost to the last. In 1795 he wrote to his partner Nicholson as follows: "I am sadly plagued for want of money, but my health and spirits are as good as ever, and I hope to regain my position, but I have an arduous task to perform. It shall, however, be performed."

Unfortunately, fate ruled otherwise. In the latter part of 1796 his position became desperate. The Bank of Pennsylvania, the Bank of the United States, and his own creation—the Bank of North America—had entered judgments against him. He was pursued by constables and writ-servers, and was the object of numerous legal suits. The lands which he had bought with such bright hopes were sold in many states for the payment of taxes, and of course they went for a song. Finally after a period of self-incarceration at "The Hills," a particularly bitter creditor, George Eddy, bought up a mortgage on his property, and with its foreclosure obtained the right to enter the mansion, not only to take possession of it, but also of Morris himself, who had retreated there because it was his last legal refuge. Robert Morris was then lodged in jail, and from February 14, 1798, to August 26, 1801, he remained in the debtors prison at Sixth and Prune Streets.

It seems incredible today that a man like Morris who had done more to save his country than anyone but Washington himself should have been allowed to go to jail, by his fellow citizens. However, we must remember that human nature was much the same then as it is now. People in those days loved their country fully as much as we do, but they also loved themselves and their families. Patriotism was an abstraction, and although one might die for it, it did not interfere after the war was over with the general course of life. We admire and venerate Robert Morris at this time, and view with horror his incarceration for debt. Would we, however, have felt the same way about it had we been living in 1798? Particularly, would we have felt the injustice of the situation if we had happened to be among the many investors who had put their money with all faith in Mr. Morris's land schemes, and lost it to the last cent?

Nevertheless, Morris had firm friends even in his hour of humiliation and disgrace. One story about this period is pleasant to recount. When George Washington came to Philadelphia in 1798 to take command of the army, which was being assembled in preparation for war with France which was then imminent, he was met as usual by a large committee of leading citizens. After the customary welcome had been extended to him, General Washington looked about him and said wonderingly, "Where is my friend Mr. Morris?"

Amid considerable embarrassment, one of the gentlemen present replied, "Is it possible, Sir, that you have not heard? Mr. Morris cannot be present today. He is at Sixth and Prune Streets." Washington paused and looked greatly distressed. After a moment he said, "I never visited Philadelphia in the past that I did not receive the utmost hospitality from both Mr. and Mrs. Morris. I deplore the accident of fate which has placed him where he is, and I intend to visit him this evening."

Visit him he did, taking with him the best supper that money could buy, and these two old friends sat through that memorable night until, through the barred windows of Morris's little room, they saw the sun rise over the Delaware.

It is a human story, and a pleasant one, and it shows Washington great as always in every situation of life. So let us leave them, General and Financier, the saviours of the young Republic, bound by a friendship which neither the passage of time nor the coming of grief and disgrace could render less secure or binding.

America was indeed fortunate that when she needed them most she had two such men as George Washington and Robert Morris.

Chapter IV

ALEXANDER HAMILTON—RECONSTRUCTION
AFTER REVOLUTION

Shortly after midnight, on September 15, 1776, a column of weary men with jaded horses and lagging transport pushed its way along the Heights of Harlem, plodding steadily away from New York City, headed toward the East River, a heavy fog screening their movements from the enemy.

Part of this small force was a battery of artillery, and it might be observed that this battery bore itself rather better than the other units of the retreating army. The men sat erect on the limbers of the guns, the sergeants kept their proper positions on the flanks, there were no stragglers. It was observable, however, that no officer rode at the head of the battery, the captain was not in the place which the regulations dictated that he should occupy. Instead, behind the battery on foot, leading his tired horse, there marched a man who would have attracted attention in any group. He was below middle height, not more than five feet seven inches tall, and of sturdy build, but in spite of the fact that his continental uniform was spattered with mud, he wore it with an air which, though not exactly jaunty, was still filled with self-esteem and pride. His hair, showing red beneath the streaks in the powder caused by the rain, was gathered into a neat queue behind his massive head; his three-cornered hat surmounted his broad forehead at just the correct angle. The man was Captain Alexander Hamilton of the American Army, who in defiance of convention was obtaining a better marching order with his battery than anyone else by the simple expedient of marching behind it, instead of in front.

Through the night came a clatter of hoofs on the hard road, and a group of horsemen pressed forward led by a tall commanding figure, shrouded in a heavy greatcoat. The tall man noted the small officer on foot and reined in sharply.

"Who commands this battery?" Washington is said to have inquired.

"I do, Sir," Hamilton replied.

"Do you know where the officer in command should ride?" asked the General.

"Yes, Sir."

"Then why are you in the rear?"

"In order to bring this battery out of New York in proper order, Sir," the subordinate replied.

"Then you believe that you can improve the army regulations?"

"I can indeed, Sir, and should be pleased to undertake the task if you desire me to do so."

The only reply that Washington made at the moment was to give the short dry laugh in which he occasionally indulged, and then with a sharp order the Commanding General and his staff struck spurs to their horses and disappeared in the thick fog which hid the northern road.

Thus, at least legend has it, there met for the first time two of the greatest founders of this republic, and the chance meeting impressed itself indelibly upon the minds of both.

It was characteristic of Hamilton that he should see clearly through a faulty regulation, and also that with unbridled egotism he should inform the Commanding General that he was entirely confident of his ability to improve it.

It was characteristic of George Washington that he should overlook the conceit of the subordinate and remember the shrewd ability which had been the excuse for the conceit.

In a short time, Captain Hamilton left the artillery and took his place upon the staff. Washington needed brains to help him conquer the power of England with his little force of ragged continentals, backed by the uncertain support of an excited and distracted Congress, and he was taking those brains unto himself wherever he found them. In Hamilton he perceived immediately a clear, cold, and forceful intellect, joined with superb courage and a will to conquer.

It is hard to say just what were the relations of Washington and Hamilton, yet their names will go down the centuries in close conjunction. More than any other two men, they were responsible for the adoption of the Constitution and the organization of the Government of the United States. One would like to suppose that a bond of deep affection held their souls in close communion. One would like to believe that Washington regarded Hamilton in a paternal light which the younger man repaid by a similar affection as deep as it was sincere.

In fact, however, it is probable that no such tie existed. Spiritually, Washington was a far greater man, and his primary object was the salvation of his country. To further this great end he would suffer much, and he did suffer through his relations with Alexander Hamilton.

Hamilton, indeed, recognized Washington's essential greatness. He was far too intelligent not to do so; but his always flattering esteem of his own abilities led him on more than one occasion to compare himself with Washington, and we may believe that, to his own mind, he lost nothing by such a comparison.

Yet Washington owed many things to Hamilton. Even today the General's dispatches and war correspondence are models of pungent and epigrammatic English, and in many instances, the first drafts at least were penned by the brilliant young aide.

Then, too, in later years, when the first President, tired of the burdens of office, prepared to lay it down, it was Hamilton who wrote for his chief the famous farewell address, which is known in part at least to almost every American.

It was Hamilton who always was the first to volunteer for dangerous service, and whose horse was shot under him at the battle of Monmouth, when, as Washington said, "he seemed to be deliberately courting death."

It was Hamilton, however, who grew restive in playing a minor part in the great Revolutionary drama, even under such a leader as Washington. Thus it is related that one day when Washington sent an orderly to request Colonel Hamilton's immediate attendance, he dallied a little time to finish some brandied peaches in the dining room, and when he arrived tardily enough at the foot of the stairs, he found the General standing on the second floor landing in one of those cold white rages which swept over him at intervals.

Exactly what was said by Washington, we shall never know. He probably regretted it, and we may be sure that Hamilton's self-love would never permit him to repeat it, but the result was immediate. Hamilton resigned his staff position, saying that he could no longer serve in the military family of a man who had so chided him. Washington, after thanking him in a dignified way for his great services, granted his request for active duty and sent him back to the line. The war was almost over, and Hamilton was far from satisfied with his part in it. True, he had given every evidence of reckless bravery under fire, but we may imagine that he was deeply conscious of the taunts that officers of the assaulting columns always reserve for members of the staff, who, for the most part, are kept out of close contact with the enemy and live on the fat of the land. Of course, in the case of Washington's staff, there was very little fat to live on, but what there was they probably got.

Such being the case, we must not be surprised to find Colonel Hamilton again distinguishing himself in the last big
fight of the Revolution. Before Yorktown he commanded an
assaulting column, and dashing far ahead of his supports, he
mounted the redoubt first and alone. That the British troops
did not shoot or bayonet him is just one of the accidents of
fate. Indeed, it almost makes one believe in the force of destiny, because Hamilton's work was so obviously incomplete
at the time that his death would have been a great calamity.

He survived, however, and the war being over, returned to
his adopted state of New York, where in a short time he was
admitted to the bar and began the accumulation of one of the
best paying practices of that day. In this pursuit he was greatly
assisted by the statute which was soon adopted forbidding all
Tory lawyers to continue to practice their profession in New
York State. This hard regulation threw a large majority of
the ablest New York lawyers out of their livelihood and
opened the way for a few brilliant young patriots, among
whom Alexander Hamilton and Aaron Burr were most prominent.

And now it is time to ask ourselves a trifle more definitely
who this man Hamilton was, and how he came at so early
an age to occupy such a leading rôle on the stage of American
history. His youth furnishes an unusual example of pre-
cocious development. He was the illegitimate son of an unsuccessful Scotch planter on the Island of Nevis in the West
Indies, and was born on January 11, 1757. His mother, from
whom it is probable that he derived his great qualities, was of
French Huguenot descent, and beautiful.

His illegitimacy, when viewed according to the broader
standards of our day, was hardly a blot upon his scutcheon.
His mother had been married to a man of beastly character
who ill-treated her and then refused to divorce her. She was
helpless under the law to sever the bond, although today it

would be a matter of but a few months. Therefore, with the strength of a passionate nature she defied convention and lived faithfully with Hamilton's father until her death, which occurred when Hamilton was still a very small boy.

At the age of twelve, we find Alexander Hamilton managing a mercantile business in the West Indies, and already beginning to write whenever the opportunity presented itself. His description of a hurricane which struck the Island about that time was so accurately done that it caused much comment and led to a number of prominent citizens subscribing enough money to send the boy to America for an education. So, after a brief period at school in New Jersey, we find young Hamilton in Columbia College just before the outbreak of the Revolution. At this period he rose above mediocrity in the eyes of his new-found friends and compatriots by writing two remarkably able pamphlets favoring the Revolutionary cause, one of which, entitled "A Farmer Refuted," made a great stir.

The war breaking, the youth organized an artillery company, and becoming its captain, succeeded, as has been already related, in attracting Washington's attention by his soldierly conduct during the retreat from New York.

One way of looking at the Revolution induces us to believe that it ended in 1783, and so it did from a military standpoint. Nevertheless, if we consider the economic and financial conditions of the young country we will realize that the war period was not ended so soon nor so easily.

It is common knowledge that England firmly believed the American colonies could never stand alone, but in spite of their military success, must return perforce to the mother country. There was considerable ground for this view, for the infant Republic had no currency and was still flooded with millions of worthless paper bills. In addition, it owed relatively large sums to France, Spain, and Holland, which it apparently had no means of repaying, and more serious than either of these reasons was the fact that each of the thirteen colonies still remained almost supreme in its respective sphere. Under the Articles of Confederation there was lacking a strong central government, without which it was obvious to the rest of the world that the colonies could never hope to succeed as an independent nation.

The years from 1783 to 1787 constitute a period regarding which modern Americans can entertain small pride. However, these years had to be lived through in order that our fathers might realize how important it was to establish not a league but a country; not a group of free states, but one land, one people, and one flag. To the consummation of this new state of mind, Alexander Hamilton made a great contribution.

We shall never understand Hamilton's character and services unless we comprehend, in the first place, his utter disbelief in democratic government and his lack of faith in democracy as an institution. This unknown Scotch boy, handicapped by his irregular birth, and originally without friends or fortune, was nevertheless an aristocrat to his finger-tips. Little wonder that in later years his name was anathema to the friends of Thomas Jefferson, that vigorous leader of the people who devoted his life to the service of the common man.

It is but just to admit that, while Hamilton loved his American countrymen, he never believed that they ought to have much to say about their own government. Hence he became, even in the early days of the reconstruction period, convinced of the necessity of centralization of power; a distinguished and gallant leader in the cause of class control, and the proponent of the undoubted right of wealth and brains to govern the country with a degree of absolutism which would have been pleasing to Charles I or George III.

Confusion reigned supreme during those early reconstruction days, and it was some time before order began to emerge from chaos. When we examine the accounts of the time, there would seem to be little doubt that if the Constitution had been put to a popular vote it would have been overwhelmingly defeated. The reason is not hard to ascertain. There were two classes of citizens, creditors and debtors, and the debtors were far more numerous than the creditors. The country was very young and on the whole very poor. It was a pioneer land, peopled with small farmers, hunters, trappers, and the tradesmen and mechanics of the larger towns. These filled the ranks of the debtor population. To them a decentralized government was acceptable because it meant little insistence upon their obligations. Most of them raised almost all the food they needed, and for the rest, indulged in barter. Few of them wanted to pay their debts, and under the Articles of Confederation few of them had to.

On the other hand, few of them held any obligations of indebtedness on the part of others. These people were not the holders of foreign bonds, federal obligations, or state assignats, nor did they hold mortgages on land, ground rents, or land bank securities. The Revolution over, they came into a glorious open season, when, with little to stop them, they did about as they pleased. Fortunately, however, these classes, though constituting the numeric majority, did not form the entire citizenship of America. Nor were they, as the event proved, the most powerful and dominating class group. There were property holders in plenty, and they demanded a change in government.

Not only were the mercantile classes in the cities to be reckoned with, but the great manorial families, with their extensive holdings of land both in country and town, wielded a tremendous influence in the councils of those days; and the wealthy southern planters, urged on by a desire to protect their far-flung possessions, lined up for once in favor of a highly centralized national government.

It must not be supposed, however, that the country was

bankrupt or on the verge of ruin. We were then, as now, a land of tremendous resources. We had, however, a weak government without the power of levying taxes, and our financial condition went from bad to worse, thus adversely affecting the national credit, and the standing of the country among the family of nations.

Private business was hampered by the worthless paper bills still floating about the country, and while the men of property grew more and more rebellious over the situation, and more determined to effect such a change in government as would remedy their troubles, the great debtor class continued to clamor for cheap money and freedom from debt, evidencing such demands by outbreaks like Shay's Rebellion, and other wild demonstrations of a crude people.

In the following words, Dewey[1] has well summed up conditions existing at that time:

At heart the country was economically sound, but the national financial system was weak, and in 1786 it broke down completely; further borrowing at home or abroad was almost impossible; requisitions were of slight avail; domestic creditors were thoroughly alarmed, and when the efforts to secure unanimous consent for a national tax failed, it was agreed that, if a federated Republic were to continue, the Government, particularly in its relations to finance and commerce, must be remodeled. Every keen sighted statesman of the period recognized the necessity, although there was great variance of opinion as to the degree of readjustment.

The dissatisfaction resulted in the Convention of 1787, which framed a new Constitution.

The year before the Constitutional Convention, Hamilton had been instrumental in having another meeting called at Annapolis, Maryland. This was merely a convention intended to consider the trade and commercial systems of the United States, and make recommendations for their improvement. The

[1] Davis R. Dewey, "Financial History of the United States," pp. 58 and 59. Reprinted by permission of Longmans, Green & Co., Publishers.

call came originally from the Virginia Legislature, and although not all the states were represented, a sufficiently large number of delegates attended to make it possible for the convention before it adjourned to recommend the assembling of a larger convention the next year, for the purpose of studying our problems of government and finance, and adopting a new Constitution.

Hamilton took a leading part in obtaining the passage of this resolution by the Annapolis Convention, and was therefore largely responsible for the Constitutional Convention of 1787.

When the Convention assembled at Philadelphia, Washington was immediately chosen as its presiding officer, and there ensued that series of historic and epoch-making debates between the intellectual leaders of that day, from which emerged the Constitution of the United States.

In these fervid debates, hectic addresses, and momentous compromises, Hamilton took little part. More responsible than anyone else for the assemblage itself, the Constitution was not in any sense of his making. Instead it bears the stamp of Jefferson's genius, Madison's logic, and Washington's wisdom, combined with the shrewdness of Benjamin Franklin and Robert Morris, and the constructive thought of James Wilson.

Early in the Convention, Hamilton laid before the delegates his own plan of government, and in doing so he spoke for five hours with the fire, the eloquence, and the close reasoning that were always his. He must have known that his scheme had no chance of adoption. He advocated a president elected for life, a senate also elected for life, and a popular assembly with greatly restricted powers. He vested in the president of his creation a veto power which would have been highly satisfactory to Louis XIV. It was, indeed, a monarchial government which Hamilton recommended, thinly camouflaged by republican forms.

It was brilliant, futile, and utterly out-of-step with the spirit of the times. It had no chance of being translated into fact, and its author undoubtedly knew that it had none. Nevertheless, his speech in explanation and defense of his plans was a great forensic effort.

Gouverneur Morris, who had no sympathy with the plan, averred that he was never more stirred than by Hamilton's eloquence on this occasion. Nevertheless, with this speech Hamilton shot his bolt as far as the Constitutional Convention was concerned, and from that time on, he attended comparatively few of the sessions, devoting himself to his private affairs.

When the Convention finally closed and the Constitution became an accomplished fact, Hamilton returned to the fray and fought for the adoption of the great covenant to the very limit of his strength. To the minds of many thoughtful men, Hamilton's advocacy of an instrument of which he did not approve, constituted one of his greatest and most unselfish contributions to the national welfare.

Not only did he take a leading part in the sessions of the New York Legislature, at which the Constitution was discussed and eventually ratified, but he performed an even more important service. In conjunction with Madison and Jay, he was the author of those extremely able essays written in explanation and defense of the new Constitution, which the world will long remember as the "Letters of Junius," one of the ablest collections of political papers that has ever been penned.

It is quite clear that in spite of Hamilton's championship of the Constitution, and his unceasing and successful efforts to obtain its adoption by the states, he nevertheless had little faith in it or love for it. He regarded it as wrong in theory and weak in structure, but he sincerely believed. that it also represented a far better state of things than that which had existed under the Articles of Confederation. We may suppose that, even at that time, his active intellect was intrigued by the thought that after all a contract is very much what the parties to it choose to make it, and who can say but that even then the doctrine of the implied powers, with its far-reaching implications, rose for the first time in the brilliant mind of the "Little Leader."

As he strolled along Wall Street of an evening, we may imagine that Alexander Hamilton, erect, well-dressed, and strikingly handsome under his powdered wig, considered deeply how in the days to come he would, by the exercise of his imperious will and ingenious mind, supply the Constitution of the United States with ribs of steel.

In spite of the efforts of Hamilton and other patriots, it took a long time to get the Constitution adopted by the states. Finally, nearly two years after the Convention met, the new Government got under way, and thus the history of the United States as a nation dates from the spring of 1789.

The Government started slowly. On March 4, there was not a quorum present at either the Senate or the House of Representatives. Finally on April 6 a quorum was obtained, and George Washington was declared elected President of the new Republic.

On September 2, 1789, the law establishing the Treasury Department was adopted, and immediately the question arose as to who was to fill this vitally important post.

It was evident to all that the man selected must not only be well trained in finance, but must also have qualities of leadership and organization of a high order. The finances of the country were in a serious condition. Loans, both foreign and domestic, had remained unpaid since before the cessation of hostilities, and interest was running upon them; the exigencies of the confederation had compelled new and constant borrowings abroad, principally from Holland, which also remained unpaid even as to interest.

Furthermore, the internal debt of the United States was large and varied. Almost every kind of obligation was extant, from war bonds to the receipts of Revolutionary quartermasters. In addition, there were the debts of the various state governments, also relatively large and of every possible description.

That some form of funding these obligations must be adopted, everyone agreed, but the method which ought to be used to consolidate and regulate this ever-increasing mountain of debt was an enigma which seemed to defy solution.

At this juncture, all eyes turned to Hamilton. He was the friend of Washington. He had a reputation as a gallant soldier, and was a shrewd and successful lawyer. Since the war he had made himself a leader in New York politics, and had acquired national fame through his successful efforts to secure the adoption of the Constitution. He was young, handsome, and a leader of men.

Even today such qualities and such a reputation would be esteemed cogent arguments for his selection by political leaders; but fortunately, besides all the foregoing advantages, Hamilton possessed a mind which turned naturally towards the solution of financial problems. For many years he had suggested, both by written and spoken words, financial measures and expedients to his countrymen. He was already well known as a writer of ability on questions of finance, and so when it became necessary to choose a Secretary of the Treasury, no other name was seriously considered.

Robert Morris, the Superintendent of Finance, who had pulled us through the critical period from 1781 to 1784, strongly approved Hamilton's selection, and told Washington that he was undoubtedly the man for the place. Gouverneur

Morris, the able coadjutor of the former Superintendent and Hamilton's life-long friend, also added his indorsement. Indeed, the nomination of Hamilton met with almost universal applause, and he started upon his career in the Treasury with as fair a prospect of success as any public man could expect to have.

That Congress was eagerly awaiting the advent of a Moses to lead them out of the financial wilderness, there is ample proof. Hamilton had been in office only ten days when Congress by resolution directed him to prepare a report upon the public credit, which meant that, as soon as possible, he should submit a plan for extricating the country from the difficulties in which its credit and currency were involved.

The preparation of such a comprehensive plan was a Herculean task even to a strong and able man. Hamilton, however, faced the problem with enthusiasm. He was only thirty-two, and at the height of his intellectual powers. Against the advice of some of his closest friends, he had given up the sure prospect of an early fortune at the bar in order to serve his country at a salary of $3500 a year. He had, as many other great men, a capacity for hard work and unremitting concentration upon any matter which he had in hand. As we shall see subsequently, he did not confine himself to the formation of a financial plan, but during the first part of his official career, he completed a series of famous reports covering the establishment of a national bank, the reform of the currency, the installation of a mint, and the initiation of a system of moderate protection for the benefit of the manufacturing interests.

His first task, however, was to safeguard the public credit. To do this he studied the past and present financial systems of other nations, and if he seemed especially attracted by the methods employed by English statesmen, we must remember that he had been born a British subject, and that all his life he was mentally allied to the laws and constitution of the British Empire. This is no reflection upon his patriotism, for he had been a Revolutionist from his earliest manhood; but his hatred of Lord North and George III in no way detracted from his admiration of the great empire whose unworthy exponents he considered them to be.

In due course, Hamilton concluded his labors, and on January 14, 1790, he submitted to Congress his Report on the Public Credit, the most notable state document which he ever prepared.

In order to understand this epoch-making statement of policy which Congress, with little change quickly translated into law, we must separate the principal objects which Hamilton desired to attain, from the methods by which he expected to achieve them. In reading the report, one is apt to be confused by the complexity of the expedients the Secretary proposed, but these expedients, archaic and unnecessarily complicated as they seem to us today, are completely subordinate to the great purposes which more careful study will clearly reveal.

The basic idea, of course, was to fund and consolidate all the outstanding debts and obligations of the United States Government, and to provide for their gradual payment over a period of years.

In order to attain this end, Hamilton resorted to various plans, always having in mind that it would be well to pay as little in cash and currency as possible, because the country was so poor.

Hamilton divided the country's indebtedness into three parts: the foreign debt; the domestic debt; and the debts of the states, incurred in the prosecution of the Revolutionary War.

There was no discussion regarding the payment of the foreign debt, which amounted to approximately $12,000,000 and it was provided both in Hamilton's report and in the subsequent

Funding Act that this money would be forthcoming as soon as possible, and the debt liquidated. Little was gained there, except a decrease in interest rate, but the idea was to lighten the burden of the obligation and win the respect of the creditor nations.

The domestic debt raised by far the most complicated problems. It was so vague and various, and composed of so many different kinds of obligations, that it was difficult to decide upon its amount, and even more difficult to fund it.

The theory on which Hamilton proceeded, the main points of which are included in the Funding Act, was that while we must be meticulous in paying our foreign creditors at the earliest possible moment and in cash, we might, with justice, ask for a greater degree of consideration from our own people.

At this time the domestic debt amounted to $27,383,917.74, to which should be added the arrears of interest to December 31, 1790, of $13,030,168.20 and approximately $2,000,000 unliquidated debt, making a grand total of $42,414,085.94. This was a huge sum for those days and constituted nearly three-fourths of the entire national debt of $54,124,464.56.[2]

The plan recommended by Hamilton in his report and adopted in the Funding Act for the purpose of funding the domestic indebtedness is perhaps best described by Dr. Davis R. Dewey in his "Financial History of the United States"[3] as follows:

A loan to the full amount of the domestic debt was authorized, subscriptions to be received in any of the certificates of indebtedness which the government had previously issued during the Revolutionary War and the Confederation. No less than seven classes of obligations were defined by the statutes. These were as follows:

[2] Davis R. Dewey, "Financial History of the United States," p. 90; reprinted by permission of Longmans, Green & Co., Publishers. McMaster, "History of the People of the United States," Vol. I, p. 568.
[3] Davis R. Dewey, "Financial History of the United States," pp. 94-95. Reprinted by permission of Longmans, Green & Co., Publishers.

(1) Those issued by the register of the treasury.

(2) Those issued by the commissioners of loans according to the Act of Jan. 2, 1779, in exchange for bills of credit emitted May 20, 1777, and April 11, 1778.

(3) Those issued by commissioners to adjust the accounts of quartermasters and other supply officers.

(4) Those issued by commissioners to adjust accounts in different states.

(5) Those issued by the paymaster-general.

(6) Those issued by the payment of interest on loans, or indents.

(7) Bills of credit, at the rate of 100 to 1.

Subscribers to the principal of the new debt received two certificates, one for an amount equal to two-thirds of the subscription to bear 6 per cent interest; the other for the remaining third, beginning to bear interest after 1800. As the old indebtedness bore a uniform rate of 6 per cent interest, this legislation practically meant a reduction, until 1801, to 4 per cent. Holders of the old obligations were not obliged to convert; but, as it was probable that the market rate of interest would fall and the public credit would rise, it was expected that the government would speedily be in a position to extinguish the old debt, which was redeemable at pleasure, and thereby to terminate the interest. Conversion therefore appealed to the reason and interest of creditors rather than to their necessities. To clear off the arrears of interest, a 3 per cent loan was authorized dating from 1791.

The third portion of the national indebtedness was that incurred by the various states in connection with the Revolutionary War. These debts were difficult of exact ascertainment, but it was finally agreed that they amounted in round figures to $25,000,000.

Hamilton in his report strongly advocated that these debts should be assumed by the national Government. This recommendation was one of his principal objects, and it caused bitter and acrimonious debate in Congress.

In his report the Secretary had suggested a variety of methods by which the debt might be funded. He proposed to employ the English system of annuities, and to use extensively the vast tracts of land belonging to the nation to pay off domestic creditors. In the end, however, Congress failed to adopt most of Hamilton's more complicated suggestions as to method, but instead, the Funding Act of 1790, which was based upon his report, recognized his threefold division of the debt, and provided for the payment of each part, accompanying such provisions with the institution of a sinking fund and a sinking fund commission, also proposed by the Secretary, with the allocation to the sinking fund commissioners of all the profits derived from the operation of the postoffice.

We have now concluded a brief summary of the leading features of the report and the law which arose from it, so far as the methods of funding the debt are concerned. Let us now turn and examine with even greater attention, because of their superior importance, the great objects which Hamilton hoped to attain through the funding of the national debt.

The first important consideration that Hamilton apparently had in mind was to fund the debt in the form of long-term obligations which should be paid off gradually and by slow degrees. His thought was that such an arrangement would guarantee two desirable ends. There was at that time no national bank and no immediate prospect of one, and such currency as existed in addition to the tons of worthless paper with which the land was still afflicted, was of a varied, unregulated, and chaotic character, so that it seemed to Hamilton that Government stock, issued for debt-funding purposes, would serve excellently as a temporary form of currency and would pass from hand to hand in the course of trade, just as fifty and one hundred dollar bills do today.

His next purpose in this regard is more or less to be inferred, as for obvious reasons he did not state it with the same clarity as that just referred to; but we may readily conceive that he believed firmly that, so long as the American people were united in an effort to redeem gradually a large outstanding national debt, their very association in such a purpose would tend to draw them together and make them a united nation. This belief led him to favor long-term obligations.

The next object reflected by Hamilton's report arose in connection with the payment of the domestic debt. This presented as pretty a problem in law and ethics as could well be imagined. It must be remembered that since before the close of hostilities the various obligations constituting the domestic debt had been depreciating rapidly, and had been a fair subject of general speculation.

It will be recalled that during the World War it was a favorite practice of many people to buy Russian rubles and French francs at bargain prices, in the hope of making enormous gains when France and Russia eventually got on their financial feet again. This same situation also existed in connection with purchase of German marks during the early period of reconstruction. All of which goes to prove that we are much like our ancestors. They did precisely the same thing with the obligations of the federal and state governments issued during the Revolutionary War, and the prices they paid for them were in most cases exceedingly low.

The purchasers well knew they were taking a big chance, but they had faith in the United States and believed it would eventually pay its debts. The trouble arose primarily because, thanks to Hamilton's genius, the country paid its debts long before anyone expected that it would.

The principal question which Hamilton had to decide in submitting his report was whether the country, in funding its debts, should pay off its outstanding obligations at a sum represented by their face value, or on some other and lesser basis. It is difficult for us today to realize fully what a bitter issue this was in 1789.

Hamilton was faced by an ethical problem which would have seared the soul of a man less courageous than he. To do what he knew to be right was apparently to take sides with the wealthy against the poor, to champion the speculative profiteer against the poverty-stricken veterans of the Revolution who had parted with their evidences of indebtedness for a mere pittance and were now filled with rage at the thought that the purchasers would reap a reward out of all proportion to the sums they had paid.

In this crisis, Hamilton neither flinched nor hesitated, but stated unequivocally that it was neither right nor practically possible to differentiate between the holders of the country's debt. He stated with complete frankness that while recognizing the hardship to individuals which the decision involved, he was convinced that it was necessary, in order to vindicate the national honor, to pay every obligation according to its legal tenor, so that it might never be said that the United States had promised to pay one sum and in the end had paid another of less amount.

The battle over this question of liquidating the domestic debt was long and was fought with the greatest vigor. Already the two great political parties were beginning to form. On the one hand, Adams, Hamilton, and their followers represented the wealthy, property-holding class, or as we would say today the "big business" of the country; on the other hand, Thomas Jefferson, though Secretary of State, was beginning that series of alliances with the great mass of the common people which in the end made him their adored leader and the founder of the Anti-Federalists, the direct ancestors of the Democratic Party of today.

This was the time when James Madison, destined to be fourth President of the United States, a man of sincerity and in many ways an able statesman, was hesitating between his life-long friends and associates in the ranks of the Federalists, and the new, somewhat nebulous, group of eager contestants to whom in the end he gravitated, and one of whose chieftains he subsequently became.

Madison, never a very practical person, was deeply affected by the moral iniquity of paying the face value of the debt to speculative purchasers, and after many searchings of the spirit he lined up against Hamilton on this issue, and supplied the opposition with its most formidable arguments.

In spite of the efforts of Madison and his followers, Hamilton in the end triumphed, and fortunately for the credit of this country at home and abroad, the Funding Act eventually maintained the principle that the promise of the United States to pay at maturity should be maintained regardless of the hardships to individuals involved in such payments.

The last great object which Hamilton sought in his Report on the Public Credit was the assumption of the state debts, and over this proposition occurred the most violent controversy of all.

Hamilton had another primary object in his method of consolidating and funding the debts of the country. The debt of the United States was his principal concern, and many believed that it should be his only concern. The Secretary, however, never departed for an instant from his broad national viewpoint, and to his way of thinking, the debts contracted by the individual states in supporting the Revolution were just as much a part of the indebtedness of the country as those obligations which had been incurred directly by the Federal Government.

The state debts in 1789 amounted to approximately $25,000,-000 and were quite unevenly divided, some states having obligated themselves to a much greater extent than others. Hamilton felt sure that unless the payment of these debts was assumed by the national Government, they would be liquidated in a very irregular manner, and over varying periods, so that the credit of some of the states would probably be impaired, with the result that the credit of the country as a whole would suffer, especially in the eyes of other nations and of foreign merchants.

It is also probably true that Hamilton, in pursuance of his usual purpose to do everything possible to strengthen the power and prestige of the central Government, conceived the idea that the assumption of the state debts by the United States would form one more tie between the people and the Federal Government, and would make that Government stronger and tend to weaken the position of the states.

Hamilton's opponents, who by this time were numerous, were not deceived as to his purposes in advocating assumption, and the congressional struggle which ensued was long and bitter. After a period of intense debate, during which much eloquence was employed upon both sides of the question, the principle of assumption was carried in the Committee of the Whole, but the vote was so close that a short time thereafter, when the South Carolina delegation to the House of Representatives arrived, Madison's followers were able to have the whole question reopened, and on reconsideration the original action of the House was reversed.

The situation appeared to be desperate and might have been so considered by anyone less vigorous and determined than the Secretary of the Treasury. He refused to admit defeat, and cast about for some method by which his object might be attained. The way in which he "put it over" is illustrative of the resourcefulness and ingenuity of a facile and able intellect.

At that very moment another problem was disturbing the minds of our early politicians. They were trying to decide where the national capital was to be located. It is interesting at this length of time to review the various suggestions with regard to this important matter, and it is curious to realize that Harrisburg, Pennsylvania, and Germantown, now a suburb of Philadelphia, were at different times favored as the capital city of the country. History might have been considerably altered if either one of these cities had been chosen, and unquestionably the future of the one so selected would have differed materially from what it has proved to be.

In keeping with the widely different viewpoints of the eastern and southern statesmen, this particular problem seemed far more vital to the South than to the North. The North, because of its economic power and rapidly increasing population, even at that time, was fairly secure in its position. On the other hand, the southern states looked with jealous eyes upon the great commonwealths of the North, and were fearful that the location of the capital in any one of the big eastern states would be disadvantageous to the interests of their own section.

Hamilton therefore determined to arrange a trade—a political deal. He did not care particularly where the capital was to be located, and he had a shrewd suspicion that Thomas Jefferson cared a great deal.

As to the method adopted by Hamilton, we cannot be sure, but the report is that there was a little dinner, and at that dinner the two great antagonists of the early days of the Republic settled two momentous questions over the walnuts and wine. The result was that their supporters in Congress apparently ratified their wishes in short order.

The capital was placed in a small area carved from Virginia and Maryland, upon the upper reaches of the Potomac River, and the debts of the states were assumed by the Federal Government as a result of Jefferson's unexpected championship of such action. Years later, the third president found his behavior at this time returning to plague him, and his explanation was that Hamilton had duped him with regard to the matter. It does not seem probable, however, that Hamilton did anything of the kind. The Little Leader did not dupe people.

He had neither the patience nor the finesse. He did make a bargain with his opponent, a bargain which was in no way a corrupt one. If, in the long run, Hamilton profited more than Jefferson as a result of their agreement, that was Jefferson's fault, because he went into the deal with his eyes open, and if he failed to think the problem through, he had no one to blame but himself.

In spite of the jealous attitude of some states which felt that the assumption of the debts was unjust because the burden was an uneven one, and that some commonwealths profited more than others, within a short time after the decision was made, all parties seemed to be thoroughly content, and the credit of the country unquestionably was considerably improved by including all obligations, both state and national, in one great funding operation.

Hamilton's victory in forcing the assumption of the various state debts was the direct cause of one of the most serious difficulties that he was compelled to face, because it made it necessary to find new sources of national revenue in order to liquidate the combined obligations of the states and nation. In this dilemma, Hamilton filed his second Report on the Public Credit, in which he urged that Congress should levy an excise tax on spirituous liquors. He might have known that this plan would lead to a heated controversy, and he probably did know it, but he believed that there should be as little direct taxation as possible, and it was his policy, when he did levy direct taxes, to make them apply to luxuries rather than necessities. He evidently regarded hard liquor as a luxury. Unfortunately for him, many thousands of his fellow citizens regarded it as a necessity, and felt that any tax upon it was a direct invasion of their private rights.

The excise tax was a constant thorn in the side of the Federalist Party, and one of the first things that was done when Jefferson became President was to effect its repeal. Nevertheless, while it was in force it did supply sorely needed revenue with which to carry out the great object of liquidating the nation's indebtedness.

The two reports on the national credit, which constituted the greatest contribution of Alexander Hamilton towards the prosperity of his country, include only a part of his multifarious labors as Secretary of the Treasury. Never was a man so depended upon by the citizens of the entire country as was Alexander Hamilton between 1789 and 1795. The problems put up to him for solution covered almost all the questions connected with the organization of the new Government, and he met the demands upon him by the most unremitting study and by the intensive application of a brilliant intellect.

In furtherance of the policies which he was trying to initiate, he submitted to the Congress a number of other epoch-making reports, which it will be interesting to mention, although purposely the exact order in which they were presented will not be maintained. Thus we find that in due course he prepared a Report on the Establishment of a Mint, in which he discussed the whole question of coinage and currency. He advocated the maintenance of a double standard at a proper ratio between gold and silver, and this policy was promptly adopted by Congress.

Perhaps from the standpoint of future usefulness, his Report on Manufactures which was filed in 1791 was his most valuable effort for the benefit of posterity. It contained in brief a brilliant summary of the policy of protection; from the time it was written until the present, it has been a reservoir of arguments, and has been employed constantly and with the utmost confidence by all politicians and economists who believe in the fundamental correctness of a protective tariff. True it is that there is nothing in Hamilton's report which would in any way justify the high tariff policy which from time to time has been a feature of our national system. If he were alive today, the great Secretary would be a moderate protectionist and entirely out of sympathy with many of the "more orthodox" leaders of the Republican faith. He would probably be far separated in thought from the manufacturers of Pennsylvania and the sugar growers of Louisiana. Nevertheless, he was the first protectionist, and he sincerely believed in the doctrine of protection, though he did not believe in a tariff wall or in any favored commercial monopoly.

Another important report of Hamilton's was that dealing with the establishment of a national bank, which he filed with the Congress on December 13, 1790. Such an institution was properly a part of the Secretary's general plan for a strong federal government. There was little question that the country needed increased banking facilities; the only problem was as to the kind of banks that ought to be established.

Prior to this time, three banking institutions had been formed in the United States, viz.: the Bank of North America in 1781, and the Bank of New York and the Bank of Massachusetts in 1784. We have already seen that prior to the Revolution one of the greatest defects in England's colonial policy was her failure to give the colonies any banking facilities whatever.

Hamilton's report was a lucid and forceful document. He dilated upon the numerous advantages to be derived from a national bank, stressing the increase in the currency to be attained by means of issuing the bank's notes, and also showing that through mobilization of the wealth of individual citizens collected in the form of deposits, the bank would acquire a lending capacity which should be of inestimable service to the government of a young country. He then took up a number of so-called economic disadvantages which opponents of the bank had adduced as reasons for refusing a charter to such an institution, and disposed of them in his usual clear-cut and downright manner.

Today the language of his report seems curiously strained, and the subjects dealt with are far removed from the economic life of the present; but we must remember that all this happened nearly a century and a half ago and that at that time such problems as the danger of a bank lending fictitious credit to bankrupts, or causing a tendency to over-trade resulting in banishing gold and silver from the land, seemed entirely reasonable to our forefathers, although to us they appear to be both archaic and illusory. In concluding his report, Hamilton proposed a general plan for the institution of the kind of bank he had in mind, and he strongly urged that Congress take immediate action to make such a bank a reality.

As a result of this report, a bill establishing a national bank was presented to the Senate in December, 1790, and after having been vigorously debated for a month it was passed and sent to the House for consideration. There another fierce debate ensued, which, even when read today, displays the utmost forensic ability and legal acumen on the part of those who participated in it. Never in his long career of public service, did James Madison make a more brilliant argument than he did in the course of this debate, when he assumed and maintained with great ability the position that Congress was without power to charter such an institution, because there was no direct authority for such action in the Constitution of the United States. His eloquence, however, was without avail, and after a week of argument, the House passed the Bank Bill by a vote of 39 to 19, and it was then submitted to Washington for approval.

When this occurred, it seems clear that the President was greatly troubled as to the proper course to pursue and hesitated between the two opinions, both of which had been so ably presented during the debate in the House. At this juncture, being in real doubt as to what he ought to do, Washington called upon three members of his Cabinet to submit their views in writing upon the constitutionality of the Bank Bill. Written opinions were received in consequence of this request, and among them those of Jefferson and Hamilton stand out preeminently.

Jefferson, of course, opposed the bank on the theory that the Government of the United States was one of strictly delegated powers, and no power not specifically contained in the Constitution should be assumed to exist. Hamilton countered with an opinion, displaying great ability, in which for the first time he enunciated the doctrine of the implied powers which was later to be adopted by John Marshall, Chief Justice of the United States, and made the keystone of his policy as the first great judicial exponent of the Constitution.

Hamilton argued that where an end to be obtained was a necessary supplement or corollary of a specific constitutional provision, it was not necessary that it should itself be specifically covered by the language of the Constitution. Thus he contended that under such a clause as Article I, Section VIII, Paragraph II, which provides that "Congress shall have power to borrow money on the credit of the United States," there existed an implied power to institute a national bank in order that the power to borrow might thus be facilitated and made effective.

We have seen that in his Reports upon the Public Credit, Manufactures, the Founding of a National Bank, and the Establishment of a Mint, Hamilton completed a comprehensive plan of organization and operation for the Government of the United States, and performed a signal service to his country which posterity has always been proud to recognize. If we desire, however, to fully understand Hamilton's brilliant though stormy career, we must appreciate the fact that his great services were only partly recognized when they were rendered, even by his followers and supporters, and that moreover there was a large group who not only disagreed with him as to his policies and methods, but were violently opposed to him on personal and political grounds, and consequently did all that they possibly could to defeat and disgrace him. He accomplished his all too brief span of life in a whirlwind of opposition, and he was always in the thick of a fight.

George Washington is generally supposed to have been a non-partisan President, a man elected by universal acclamation, and even during his lifetime removed from the dust of political conflict by the purity of his purposes and the greatness of his character. Nothing could be further from the truth. Washington was not a man without a party, although he sincerely strove to be non-partisan in the administration of his high office. Speaking frankly, he was a Federalist, and he was a Federalist for definite reasons. He was a man of good family and owned considerable property. Indeed, he was a rich man, as wealth was counted in those days. He had farms and slaves, and he was always conscious of the dignity of his position both as a private citizen and as the head of the Government. If there was anything democratic about Washington, history fails to reveal it. He was an aristocrat to his finger-tips, and his wife was even more aristocratic than he. During his administration, he lived in Philadelphia in what might be considered semi-regal style. The levées of Madame Washington were not very different in character from the garden fêtes at Buckingham Palace, and those who attended them included such people as the Tilghmans, Chews, Morrises, and Binghams, representing the proudest families of the old colonial aristocracy. Even on the Fourth of July, a poorly dressed farmer or a horny-handed mechanic might have found it impossible to make his way into the presidential presence.

Alexander Hamilton was the active leader of this party of aristocratic democrats who had succeeded in winning the

Revolutionary War, and were now proceeding to found the new republic. More than any other man of his party, he sincerely disbelieved in the feasibility of a purely democratic government. He stood for aristocratic control under the form of republicanism, and he never departed from this fundamental belief.

On the other hand, America at that time was in a very crude state socially. It was largely populated by small farmers, and in the cities by tradesmen and laborers; hunters, trappers, and other pioneers formed the social group which dominated the outlying districts. Numerically, these people far outnumbered the aristocratic element, representing the manorial families and the successful city merchants, who had gained control of the Continental Congress, fought the Revolutionary War to a successful termination, and were now proceeding to organize a republican form of government. But the mechanics, tradesmen, and farmers lacked effective leadership, so that their numerical strength was of very little use to them.

Gradually, however, beginning during Washington's first administration, the nebulous opposition to the aristocratic control began to consolidate, and leaders of ability and vision rose to prominence and power.

At first the new party of opposition lacked even a name, then it was tentatively known as the Anti-Federalist Party, a negative title which was more of a liability than an asset. A little while later, the name Republican was adopted, and finally, though not for many years, the more appropriate title of Democrats was assumed by the political adherents of the faith of Jefferson, Madison, and Andrew Jackson.

We are discussing, however, at this time, the effect of party strife upon Hamilton's career. There seems to be no doubt that Hamilton believed himself to be in effect Washington's Prime Minister. He acknowledged no primacy in the Cabinet so far as the Secretary of State was concerned, and not unnaturally maintained that as Congress had invited him to do all the spade work necessary to form the Government, he should be considered the leading member of the Cabinet and should rank directly after the President of the United States.

Needless to say, Jefferson never conceded Hamilton's contention in any way, and from the beginning of the administration, he was in constant opposition to the Secretary of the Treasury on almost every question that arose in the council room.

No two men could have been more different in character or in methods of operation than Alexander Hamilton and Thomas Jefferson.

Hamilton was brilliant, passionate, eloquent, often tactless, frequently ill-tempered, but forceful and sincere. He had little humor and could not get along with a great many men. He was too dictatorial and nearly always averse to compromise.

Jefferson, on the other hand, was shrewd, secretive, and suave, and his mind was as good in quality as that of Hamilton though less constructive and more philosophical. He was an excellent judge of men, and got along with his supporters better than almost any other political general in the history of our country. He was revered and highly esteemed by his followers, who served him with a faithfulness and degree of enthusiasm seldom equalled. Jefferson had an ingenious and somewhat Italian type of intellect. He seemed to prefer to gain his objects by indirection rather than by frontal attack; in this respect also he differed from Hamilton, to whom the sledge-hammer style of fighting strongly appealed.

It is unnecessary to examine with care the kaleidoscopic political struggles which occurred with increasing intensity during the five years that Hamilton headed the Treasury. We may note, however, that during this time Hamilton and Jefferson both indulged in bitter personal attacks upon one another which greatly distressed the President and which, when viewed calmly in retrospect, reflect little credit upon either statesman.

Jefferson, through his friends in the new Anti-Federalist group, had a series of resolutions adopted in the fall and winter of 1792-93[4] which called upon the Secretary of the Treasury to submit a detailed report showing every item of expenditure made during his service as Secretary. It was fully believed by the Jeffersonians that, owing to the chaotic conditions under which Hamilton had entered office, and the difficulties involved in organizing and operating the Treasury Department, it would be impossible for him to submit an itemized account which would be satisfactory to his congressional critics. In this, however, they were sorely mistaken, for in spite of the tremendous labor involved in the preparation of his famous reports, Hamilton had so well organized his department that when suddenly called upon to give a full account of his financial operations, he was able to do it with the

[4] The first set of resolutions was introduced in Congress on November 21, 1792, by followers of Madison and Jefferson and contained the following requests: (1) that the Secretary lay before Congress an account of the moneys borrowed at Antwerp and Amsterdam; (2) a resolution, also aimed primarily at Hamilton, requesting the President to send down a statement of the loans made by his authority, the terms, what use had been made of them, and how large the balance was, if any remained; (3) a resolution requesting information regarding all persons employed by the various Government departments and their pay. That these were forthcoming readily did not satisfy Madison and Jefferson, so with the former drawing them up and the latter supplying the ideas, a set of five additional requests were presented to Congress by a satellite of the pair by the name of William B. Giles of Virginia. These demanded: (1) all copies of papers authorizing foreign loans to be made; (2) the names of the persons to whom and by whom the French debt had been paid; (3) a statement of the balances between the United States and the bank; (4) an account of the Sinking Fund; and (5) the unexpended revenue at the close of the year of 1792. These resolutions were answered by Hamilton in three exhaustive reports which momentarily abashed his persecutors, but on February 27 they returned to the hunt with nine more shameful resolutions, the net effect of which was to charge Hamilton with having violated the law of the land and of having far exceeded his authority in the exercise of his office. The debate raged the following day, and finally, late on the night of February 28, the resolutions were voted down by a fair majority. See McMaster, "History of the People of the United States," Vol. II, pp. 115-117.

utmost exactitude, confusing his critics and greatly increasing his own reputation.

Nevertheless, he did it at great cost to himself, for it involved months of highly concentrated labor, most of which was performed at night, and contemporary accounts tell us that throughout one long winter the candles burned from dusk to dawn almost every night of the week in the office of the Secretary. It is not easy to forgive such an assault upon one's personal honor, especially when it involves such exhaustive labor in order to prepare an effective defense, and Hamilton did not forgive Jefferson and his followers, but hated them with a straightforward manly hatred which was very human and can be appreciated by all of us who read the story of those exciting days.

Hamilton himself was not without fault in all this welter of political animosity. He attacked Jefferson through a series of anonymous letters which he gave to the public press while he and Jefferson were members of the same Cabinet. This was something he never should have done, and he probably realized it long before he died.

Political conditions were bad in those days, and the country was crude, young, strong, and rough. Men loved, hated, and fought with wholehearted intensity which can hardly be appreciated today.

Finding that they could not succeed in an attack upon Hamilton's honesty, the Anti-Federalists looked searchingly about for some weak spot in his armor, and they found it. Hamilton's weakness was women. This also, of course, was closely connected with his lack of humor and personal vanity. It is also true that many men of intense natures have sought such an outlet for their passions. Hamilton probably had many affairs of the heart, but only one of them has come down to us in very tangible form. During his secretaryship, he became entangled with a certain Mrs. Reynolds, a woman of unusual beauty, but coarse, underbred, and in no way his equal. She happened to have a husband who was a thorough blackguard. Knowing of her relations with Hamilton, he was low enough to profit by them and accept money to keep his mouth shut. It is believed that, not getting all he wanted, he told the drab story to some of the Anti-Federalist leaders. The news was received by them with unrestrained pleasure. They used it almost immediately in the guise of political blackmail. In other words, they threatened Hamilton with exposure if he did not concede several political issues which they put up to him.

In this crisis, Hamilton as usual acted in a big way. He told the gentlemen who conferred with him that they could go to the devil, that he would never fail to do what he thought right in order to save his own reputation, and then, to the utter surprise of all his friends and opponents, he wrote a pamphlet in which he told the whole miserable story of his relations with Mrs. Reynolds, and published it at his own expense.

In the light of succeeding years, it seems a pity that the great man should have so humbled himself. It is hardly probable that even his bitterest political opponents would have really used this story against him or given it any actual publicity. However, they bluffed him into the idea that that was exactly what they intended to do, and in return he did the one thing that could save his political at the expense of his personal reputation, and the one thing that could actually discredit his opponents and put them in an impossible position. It required great moral courage for Hamilton to tell the story of Mrs. Reynolds to the world, and it is significant that his wife stood by him with loyalty and faith. She knew her Hamilton, and she was probably not much astonished when she heard of the affair. She could have had little doubt of his deep love for her, and she was a big enough woman to regard his weakness as merely a passing phase.

There is little to add to the account that has already been given of Hamilton's services as Secretary of the Treasury. The famous Whiskey Rebellion, which arose in western Pennsylvania in 1793, was a vigorous protest against his excise policy, and characteristically he took up the gage of battle and went in person at the head of a body of troops to put down the insurrection. This he succeeded in doing in a very short space of time.

It is also unnecessary in this study to deal with Hamilton's attitude on the issue of a war with France. He deeply resented the attitude of the French Government, and he did all in his power to prepare this country for what he believed to be an unavoidable and righteous war. Fortunately, however, calmer counsels prevailed and the conflict was averted.

Finally, in 1795, Hamilton decided that his work was done. He had organized the Treasury Department and made it successful and respected by all who dealt with it. He had funded the foreign and domestic debts of the United States. He had laid the basis for the protective tariff soon to become an outstanding policy of the American people. He had directed the organization of the judicial system of the country. He had founded the First National Bank, organized the mint, dictated the character of the currency, and established the double standard as a method of maintaining parity between silver and gold.

Many other things he had done within these few years during which he had occupied the position of financial dictator to the American people, and as he looked over his work, even though still a comparatively young man, he may have felt a degree of lassitude, and he must have sensed that his life was to be brief in years, though full of achievement. At any rate, he thought that the time had come to lay the crushing burden down, and so he resigned and retired once more to practice law in his home city of New York, with the praise of Washington ringing in his ears.[5]

A few short years passed, during which he still maintained his active interest in politics and during which he functioned as the leader of the Federalist Party. He soon came to a parting of the ways with John Adams, who succeeded Washington, and essayed the difficult task of carrying on the presidency immediately after the retirement of the great man.

Hamilton became even more bitter and opinionated as time went on, and the constant factional fighting in which he was involved did not help to mellow him or improve his attitude of mind. It is probable that a letter of bitter criticism which he wrote about John Adams just before the President came up for reelection contributed not a little to his defeat, and resulted in Hamilton's greatest opponent, Thomas Jefferson, being elevated to the presidential office. Still, it is a tribute to Hamilton's utter sincerity of purpose and fundamental honesty that, when faced with the question of either supporting Jefferson for election in the House of Representatives or allowing his friends to turn in for Aaron Burr, he never hesitated a second, but threw the weight of his influence in favor of his old political enemy, because, as he said, although he had been opposed to him for years, he believed him to be an honest and patriotic man, while he considered Burr utterly unworthy of respect either as a statesman or as a candidate for office.

The result of this action on Hamilton's part was not immediate, but undoubtedly it was the cause of that fatal meeting on the morning of July 11, 1804, when on the Heights of Weehawken, overlooking the Hudson and just across the river from the great city of his adoption, Hamilton faced Aaron Burr in accordance with the code of honor of that day. It was a cruel ending to so great a career, for Hamilton was only forty-two years old. He knew that he would probably not survive the meeting; he wrote a pathetic letter to his wife the night before which makes it very clear that his spirit was at rest and he was prepared to die. Hamilton did not believe in dueling, and was not particularly expert with the pistol. Burr, on the other hand, was a crack shot, and had engaged in several duels. When the command to fire was given, Burr coolly shot Hamilton through the body while Hamilton fired in the air. Both men were hurried from the field by their seconds, and Hamilton was taken to a nearby residence where he lingered in great agony for two days, finally dying as the result of an infection of his wound.

There have been many men of whom the United States has had a right to feel proud, but only a few may be considered to have been the founders of the Republic. Among this small group Hamilton stands out, and as the years pass, his primacy will become even greater than it now seems. Of all the constructive intellects to which the Government of the United States owes its being, none played a greater part in its formation than that of Alexander Hamilton, soldier, patriot, and financier.

Chapter V

ALBERT GALLATIN—REPUBLICAN FINANCE, RE-
DUCTION OF THE NATIONAL DEBT, AND
FINANCIAL PROVISIONS FOR THE
WAR OF 1812

In 1789 when George Washington was inaugurated as the
first President of the United States, there were no political
parties in the country as we now understand such agencies of
government. It is true that there had been a sharp division of
sentiment both before and after the adoption of the Constitution by the Convention of 1787, and it is also true that this
division of sentiment in a general way had ranged on one
side those who believed in a strong central or federal government, and on the other those who believed with equal earnestness in strong state governments based on the original colonial
governments. This division of sentiment was hardly geographical at this time because Rhode Island was in favor of state's
rights, while Virginia with equal earnestness espoused the
federal cause. It is probably true, however, that viewing the
states as a whole, the Federal attitude had its stronghold in
the North and the Anti-Federal or state's rights doctrine, even
at that early period, found its greatest number of supporters
in the South. It was too soon, however, for party lines to be
drawn with any degree of strictness, and we must not forget
that the popular veneration for President Washington had
much to do with the apparent unanimity of political sentiment
that prevailed during the early years of the Republic.

As time went by, however, conditions changed greatly, and
the rise of a strong opposition party might readily be termed,

in the words of the late President Harding, "a step towards normalcy." Perhaps the solidification of Anti-Federalist sentiment was due in no slight extent to the forceful yet overbearing character of Alexander Hamilton, who, as we have seen, was generally regarded as the Federalist leader—because even in those days George Washington was so revered and his innate sense of justice was so universally recognized that, except among the most irresponsible of citizens, he was regarded as head and shoulders above party turmoil and partisan opinion.

Hamilton, on the other hand, was a fighter, a born combatant, a man who adhered to his friends and hated his enemies with equal intensity. It is from such affection and such hatred that party strife grows. In spite of the esteem of the measures he introduced, in spite of his unquestionable patriotism, his brilliancy, and his energetic and unselfish devotion to the public business, it was not long before the able yet dictatorial course which Hamilton pursued raised about him a cloud of opponents, some of them as energetic, as eager, and almost as able as he.

Hamilton, as we know, became Secretary of the Treasury in 1789, and within about two years placed the finances of America on an unassailable foundation as the result of his masterly efforts with regard to the funding of the national debt, the founding of a national bank, the establishment of the mint, and the tariff. His epoch-making reports, however, were not adopted without bitter struggles which brought together, in opposition to their talented author, the ablest minds holding opinions contrary to his. The result was that by 1792 there existed in America a strong minority party under the able leadership of Thomas Jefferson, James Monroe, and Albert Gallatin. This group was known at the outset as the Anti-Federalist Party. Later, seeking to claim a title which would be more than a mere negation, they first chose the name of Democrat-Republican Party, and a short time thereafter shortened this somewhat unwieldy designation to the Republican Party. By 1793, this group, though still a trifle hesitant in its opposition because not yet free from the dominating character and great reputation of Washington, whose sentiments were known to be Federalistic, nevertheless, was month by month growing more daring and more determined in its conflict with the leadership and doctrine of Hamilton and his associates.

By 1796, when Washington delivered his farewell address and retired to the peace which Mount Vernon afforded him, the Republican Party had gained such strength that it controlled the House of Representatives and had obtained very nearly equal representation in the Senate. Nevertheless, when John Adams was elected to the presidency as Washington's successor, he found a strong supporting party behind him; the Federalists were still in control of the Government and apparently represented the majority of the voting population of the young country. Adams, however, possessed an unfortunate personality. He was sincere, upright, and more than ordinarily able, but he did not have the genius for making friends and was conspicuously lacking in tact. Furthermore, it must be admitted that it was extraordinarily difficult for any man to succeed George Washington as President of the United States. Comparisons are inevitable in life, and there was no man in the country at that time capable in any degree of filling the place left vacant by the national hero, who of his own accord, had so unselfishly retired to private life.

Adams certainly could not fill Washington's shoes, and it is a serious question whether the innate consciousness of his inability did not constitute a deep and controlling irritation which stayed with him during his entire term as President. Though not exactly a quarrelsome man, Adams found it impossible to get along with the leaders of his party, and one after another his supporters dropped away until, just at the end of his term, he had a deep and fundamental difference with Alexander Hamilton, who although a private citizen since 1795, had nevertheless continued prominent in the Federalist Party and in the great State of New York was its almost undisputed leader.

Nero, watching the Imperial City burn at his feet, saw no greater destruction of his patrimony than Adams might have observed during his brief term in office had he noticed the continuous and fatal disintegration of the great party which had elected him to the presidency.

All this time the little group of brilliant men constituting the leadership of the new Republican Party were quick to take advantage of the mistakes of their opponents. When the new century dawned and the elections of 1800 came around, they made a brief, bitter, successful campaign, and, taking advantage of their opponents' weakness and with Hamilton sulking in his tent, were swept into office on a tidal wave of popular opinion. Thus began the first reform administration in the history of the country, and with it the leadership of that strangely gifted visionary and philosopher, that able politician, Thomas Jefferson, was firmly established.

The young Republican Party was a party of the people as opposed to the Federalists who were admittedly recruited from the property-holding class. It is well to remember also that, from the time of its birth, the Republican Party was deeply affected by the incidence and progress of the French Revolution. Hamilton and his followers had always been admirers of the British Constitution and the British system of government. They had always been conservative in thought and practice, and while not monarchists, though freely accused of such sentiments by the Republicans, they undoubtedly preferred a limited monarchy to a revolutionary republic. On the other hand, Thomas Jefferson had returned to this country fresh from his service as minister to the Court of France, where he had been present during the early period of the

French people's struggle for liberty. Naturally democratic in thought and principle, he had sympathized from the first with the French proletariat and believed that, horrible though the necessity might be, the agonizing revolutionary experiment of France was justified by centuries of oppression, and certain to result in deep and lasting good.

We, therefore, find the two American political parties of the day in opposition on a question of foreign policy, indeed hardly a question of policy, as it was in no way connected with the immediate affairs of America but rather a question of ethics as to which they conscientiously differed.

It is difficult today to picture to ourselves the bitterness of the period, the enthusiasm on the part of many for the cause of France, and the detestation of others for the crimes and excesses committed by the French rabble in the name of liberty, especially when these excesses were made to include the murder of the king and queen and the exile of many of the best and noblest men and women in the kingdom to foreign shores. The streets of New York and Philadelphia were filled with the adherents of both parties, the French sympathizers wearing in their hats the tricolored cockade, many even adopting the red cap of liberty, while their opponents were equally willing to show their adherence to the contrary opinion by the display of other symbols. Genet, that pestiferous meddler sent to America by the French Government for the special purpose of causing trouble, was able by his undiplomatic and illegal actions greatly to increase the ill-feeling which already existed, and hence a foreign revolution had much to do with the growth of political parties in the United States.

Thomas Jefferson, third President of the United States and leader and founder of the new Republican Party, was born in Albemarle County, Virginia, in 1743, and lived until 1826. His long life spanned the end of the colonial era and lasted

well into the beginning of the new Republic. Probably no
man in American history has left such a deep personal impress on so many people. Perhaps this personal impress was
one of Jefferson's most distinguishing characteristics. In spite
of his greatness, Washington left most men cold. Hamilton
loved the United States far more deeply than his fellow men.
Yet, it has often been said that Alexander Hamilton paid
far more attention to his enemies than he ever did to his
friends. Jefferson, however, was a different type. He frequently
disagreed with his most loyal supporters, he was often at odds
with Madison and on occasion would rebuke Gallatin with
pointedness and asperity, but he was a natural leader and a
born politician, and besides he was a great human philosopher
with a sincere belief in the inherent goodness of mankind
and a deep affection for his fellow citizens. It is said of Jefferson that in the neighborhood of Monticello where he lived
and near which one of his greatest monuments, the University
of Virginia, now stands, it is not unusual to hear him still
spoken of in the present tense. After one hundred and forty
years the citizens of that locality still say, not "Mr. Jefferson
was," but "Mr. Jefferson is"; not "Mr. Jefferson said," but
"Mr. Jefferson says." Surely eulogy could add nothing to this
tribute.

Thomas Jefferson's greatest contribution to his country's history and policy was a firm belief in freedom of opportunity
and opinion for the common man, the average citizen. Jefferson was sincerely opposed to class privilege. He deprecated
extravagance in government, and favored strengthening the
power of the states and cultivating the doctrine of home rule.
It is characteristic that on the morning of his inauguration
he went unattended to the Capitol to be sworn in as President of the United States because he would not give counte-
nance by any act of his to what he regarded as the useless
pomp and circumstance of office. He has often been accused

of posing, but this was no pose. It was as sincere an act as ever was performed by any public man.

Next to Jefferson among the leaders of the new party was James Madison, who succeeded him as President of the United States, an eminent Virginian with a large acquaintance among the public men of his day. A ready and able debater, and a man of wit and resource, Madison early made a deep impression upon his contemporaries. Originally a Federalist, he separated from that party rather early, and definitely took his place among the opponents of Federalist doctrines when he made his able constitutional argument against Hamilton's proposition to establish the First National Bank. This argument in favor of a strict construction of the Constitution and against the so-called doctrine of the implied powers, was referred to for many years as a model of logic and expression by the leading exponents of the strict construction idea. When the new administration came into being, Madison assumed the position of floor leader for the Republicans in the House of Representatives. During Jefferson's administration, Madison was his right-hand man upon the floor of Congress, and today would be called the spokesman of the administration.

Among the other brilliant men in the Republican Party at that day may be noted William B. Giles, of Virginia, resourceful in debate and bold in action; John Nicholas, also of Virginia; and Edward Livingstone of New York, a scion of one of the first families of the Empire State, and one of the young men who in that remarkable time came to a quick and useful maturity. There was also Albert Gallatin, of whom we shall say much more presently. There were likewise many able men among the Federalists led by Dayton of New Jersey, speaker of the House, and Fisher Ames, the greatest orator of the day.

As one reads the yellow pages of the old reports, one is struck with the remarkable learning and ability displayed by those young giants of debate upon the floor of the Federal

Congress. It was a critical time—a new Government dedicated to freedom was being born. Precedents were few. New men and new measures were constantly being brought forward. A new land, undeveloped, imperial in extent and unbounded in promise, was just being discovered and thrown open to a brave and adventurous people. It was indeed a time of youth; America was young, and she was being made and developed by young men. Never again, perhaps, will such a situation present itself. Never again, perhaps, will so many young intellectual giants make their names and reputations in the service of a new land.

Albert Gallatin has just been mentioned among the leaders of the Republican Party. In many ways he made a more lasting contribution to his adopted country than any of his associates. Gallatin was a Swiss, born in Geneva on January 29, 1761. He came of a noble family, and his parents dying during his infancy, he was brought up by a friend of his mother's, a maiden lady, Mademoiselle Pictet. He was, however, on excellent terms with his relatives, and his life was considerably influenced by his grandmother, Madam Gallatin-Vaudenet, who seems to have been a woman of great strength of character and dictatorial spirit. After Gallatin graduated from the Academy of Geneva in 1779, his grandmother commanded him to take service in the military forces of her intimate friend, the Landgrave of Hesse. Had he done so, he most certainly would have been shipped to America and taken part in the Revolution as an enemy of those people who were subsequently to become his fellow countrymen. Gallatin, however, even in early youth had acquired certain radical democratic ideas, and when invited by his grandmother to accept the commission of lieutenant-colonel in the army of the Landgrave, he told her flatly that he would never serve a tyrant, whereupon the old lady gave him a severe box on the ears, which little tribute of affection seems to have affected his entire career. He immediately began to plan a journey to America, and finally on April 1, 1780, he and his friend Henri Serre left Geneva and came to the new world.

They landed at Boston on July 14 and from there wandered about the country. Finally, after various adventures, Gallatin went to New Jersey in February, 1784, and from there to Fayette County, Pennsylvania, about four miles north of the Virginia line, where he built a log hut, opened a country store, and remained until nearly the end of the year. Subsequently he spent considerable time in Richmond, but always returned to western Pennsylvania, with which part of the country he was to be identified throughout the rest of his life. At this time Pennsylvania, in the neighborhood of Pittsburgh, was very far west indeed. The country was wild in the extreme, and although hilly, wooded, and beautiful, was still the hunting ground of numerous Indian tribes and supported much game. It was sparsely settled by a race of hardy pioneers of Scotch Presbyterian ancestry, and these were the people who formed Gallatin's first constituency and elected him in 1790 a member of the Pennsylvania Assembly. He was re-elected in 1791 and 1792 without opposition. As a member of the legislature, Gallatin showed unusual industry and took a leading part in the deliberations of that body. During the session of 1791 to 1792 he served on thirty-five committees, prepared their reports and drew their bills. He was especially prominent in the cause of better roads and improvements in education. He earnestly endeavored, though without success, to establish the equivalent of a high school in every county of the state.

In 1791 the attempt of Alexander Hamilton to institute an excise tax upon distilled spirits created an amount of bitterness which it is hard for us to understand at this day. We must recollect, however, that the colonists fought Great Britain because of their opposition to taxation, and that in a new

country where there was little currency, and the people were
on the whole poor, any direct tax was sure to excite vehement
opposition. It was also true that in the outlying districts the
farmers could not market their grain, and were therefore compelled, or thought they were compelled, to operate stills and
turn it into liquor to keep it from spoiling. Thus they naturally
regarded a tax of this character as a direct attack upon one
of their vital interests. Farmers like these formed the greater
part of Gallatin's constituency, so it is not to be wondered at
that he took a leading part in the various remonstrances, public meetings, and agitations which led up to the famous
Whiskey Rebellion which convulsed the western counties of
Pennsylvania in 1794. This is one of the events of Gallatin's
life in which he never took any pride, and rightly so, for it
came as near sedition and treason as it was possible to come
without entailing the larger guilt.

In 1793 Gallatin was elected to the United States Senate
from Pennsylvania, but served only from the time he took his
seat, December 2, 1793, until February 28, 1794. His seat was
then declared void on the ground that contrary to Article I,
Section 3, of the Constitution he had not been a citizen of the
United States for nine years at the time of his election to the
office of senator. The decision was rather technical and involved a strict party vote, and it is interesting to note as indica-
tive of the growing strength of the Republicans in Congress,
that Gallatin lost his seat in the Senate by a vote of only 14
to 12. Although only a member of the Senate on this occasion
for a period of two months, Gallatin took positive stand in
vindication of his party's actions, with the result that, before
he left the Senate, he had gained the bitter enmity of Alexander Hamilton. This was due to the fact that while a member
of that body he introduced a resolution calling upon the
Secretary of the Treasury for an elaborate and itemized statement of the national debt as of January 1, 1794. The items

in question were to be segregated under distinct heads including the balance to creditor states, a statement of loans—domestic and foreign—contracted from the beginning of the Government, statements of exports and imports, and finally a summary statement of the receipts and expenditures to the last day of December, 1793, distinguishing the moneys received under each branch of the revenue and the moneys expended under each of the appropriations, and stating the balance of each branch of the revenue remaining unexpended on that day. Similar and separate statements for the years 1791, 1792, and 1793 were called for also. It is curious to note that in spite of the fact that the Federalists controlled the Senate, this resolution of Gallatin's was finally adopted and Hamilton was obliged to reply that it was impossible for him to make any such detailed statement of the country's finances without engaging a large force of additional clerks or else completely dislocating the routine business of his department. Even the Secretary's friends did not pretend that his letter of reply was a sufficient answer to the resolution as adopted, but evidently Gallatin was unable to command the votes necessary to require a more specific reply from the head of the Treasury.

It is safe to say that when Gallatin left the Senate a feeling of relief animated the Federalist majority, and a grim determination arose among them to keep this man from ever coming back again.

It has never been proved that Gallatin was responsible in any degree for the whiskey insurrection. On the other hand, it seems quite clear that he used his full influence to counsel moderation and submission to the Federal Government, although in the very beginning of the movement, he did take part in some seditious meetings. It is also pretty generally admitted that although Hamilton was anxious to secure an indictment against Gallatin for criminal participation in the whiskey uprising, there never was any evidence which would justify such action. Consequently it never took place. In 1795 Gallatin was elected a member of the Fourth Congress of the United States, which met at Philadelphia on Monday, December 7. This was just at the close of Washington's second term, and the once strong Federalist Government had been greatly weakened. Jefferson had gone, and Hamilton was a private citizen engaged in law practice in New York City. Edmund Randolph was Secretary of State, Adolph Pickering the Secretary of War, and Alfred Wolcott, Jr., had succeeded Hamilton as Secretary of the Treasury. From the beginning of the session, Gallatin took a leading part in the legislative battles which quickly began to rage. Almost at once the antipathy of the Republicans towards the administration was made manifest. Even the usual commendation of President Washington was amended by them so as to greatly qualify the expression of confidence and affection which the Federalist majority in the Senate had originally proposed.

Gallatin's first constructive work was to secure the appointment of a Standing Committee of Business as a check upon the administration of the Treasury Department, which committee in a short time became the Ways and Means Committee of the House of Representatives—from that period until today the most important committee of the House. There were many measures in the Fourth Congress upon which Gallatin spoke eloquently and well, but as they were devoid of financial features they are not within our view at this time.

It is remembered that he interested himself in the sale of western lands, and endeavored to have the proceeds constitute a fund for the payment of the public debt, thus foreshadowing one of his greatest services to his country. He spoke in favor of direct taxes, and again laid stress upon the necessity of reducing the public debt at an early day, and then, as later, he opposed the expenditure of any considerable amount for the maintenance of the military and naval forces of the United States. His principal aim, however, was to check and control the operation of the Treasury. Day in and day out he bombarded Hamilton and Wolcott with demands for accounting after accounting, explanation after explanation. He did develop the fact that enormous lump sum appropriations had been made which had been expended by the administration in certain instances not in accordance with the purposes of the appropriations. He never proved anything in the least derogatory to the integrity of either Hamilton or Wolcott, but he did show looseness of administration and laxity in bookkeeping, and he threw into bold relief, as a result of his constant questioning, the dictatorial and assured attitude of Alexander Hamilton, who, conscious of his own rectitude, bothered little about details of expenditure, and who, when certain that the end was worthy, worried not at all regarding the means. Gallatin charged at one time that the debt of the United States was much larger than the administration stated it to be, but this assertion was never proved.

Whom the gods destroy they first make mad, and this seems to have been true of the policy of the Federalist Party during the last part of John Adams's term as President. Increasing political bitterness led to the adoption of the famous Alien and Sedition Laws which gave into the hands of the executive a degree of power which if unscrupulously exercised might readily have amounted to grave persecution. This was the last straw, and from the time these laws were adopted, it became highly probable that the next national election in 1800 would bring about a change in administration. Moreover, the grave danger of a French war, although it had no direct effect on the situation, yet greatly increased party bitterness.

Then came the famous presidential election of 1800, probably the most bitter and hotly contested in the history of the United States, with the possible exception of the Tilden-Hayes

election in 1876. The original vote was so close that the election
was thrown into the House. Jefferson and Burr were tied on the
first ballot with an equal number of votes, and when the tie
was finally broken, Jefferson was elected President and Burr
in accordance with the law of that day became Vice-President.
Shortly after Mr. Jefferson came into power he satisfied public
opinion and did precisely what was expected of him by ap-
pointing Albert Gallatin Secretary of the Treasury. From that
time the young, dignified, and able Swiss began a career as
the head of his country's financial department, second only
to that of his great opponent and predecessor.

The appointment of Gallatin as Secretary of the Treasury
was no haphazard matter. If a political party is to be successful
it must contain financial critics of a high order because a
party always begins as an opposition group, and in handling
the government, one of the most important functions is the
competent management of the public finances. In the early
days of his service in the Pennsylvania Legislature Gallatin's
mind had turned naturally towards financial matters. He it was
who almost alone drew up the able report of the Committee of
Ways and Means of the Pennsylvania Legislature during the
session of 1790 to 1791, in which report the committee recommended the immediate reimbursement and extinction of the
state paper money, the immediate payment in specie of all the
current expenses or warrants on the Treasury, and the discharge without default or repudiation of every debt or engage-
ment previously recognized by the state. Such a policy, based
upon honesty and a due realization of state obligations, was
unusual and refreshing in that disordered time, and the reasons advanced by Gallatin in support of such a policy were
recognized the country over because of their moral and financial soundness.

In November, 1796, Gallatin published his sketch of the
finances of the United States in which he dealt under sepa-

ALBERT GALLATIN

rate headings with the revenues, the expenses and the debts of the Government, supported by statistics gathered through his own efforts, entailing a vast amount of labor. Even at this early period the difference between Gallatin's mode of thought and that of Alexander Hamilton was acute and interesting. Hamilton believed that a fairly large national debt was a good thing, but Gallatin vigorously opposed any such policy and reverted to the homely principle that a debt should be paid at least at maturity, and that ordinarily if payment could anticipate maturity a better result would be obtained.

During 1800 Gallatin published a treatise entitled "Views of the Public Debt, Receipts and Expenditures of the United States" which was in fact a critical examination and analysis of the financial operations of the United States since the adoption of the Constitution. The partisan nature of this pamphlet is undoubted, as a good deal of space was devoted by Gallatin to a vigorous attack upon the assumption of the debts of the states by the national Government. However, in spite of its partisan character a great many able arguments were introduced by him to the effect that for a young government the fiscal policy of the United States displayed considerable extravagance, and that economy in administration and reduction of the national debt were objects which the entire nation should make every effort to attain.

Thus, in carefully framing his personal financial policy over a period of ten years, Gallatin also succeeded in outlining a popular program which met with the approval of the Anti-Federalists or Republicans just then becoming so powerful. It was only a question of time before they would succeed in taking over the Government of the United States with all the responsibilities and opportunities which its assumption entailed.

Just as there was no reasonable doubt in 1789 as to the man who should be chosen as first Secretary of the Treasury, so

there was little question in 1800 who should be chosen to
occupy that great and important office. Just as Hamilton
brought to his work a mature and well-thought-out policy, so
Gallatin, his able successor, was ready to carry on when his
time came because he had fitted himself by close application
and constant observation to initiate and carry forward his
own financial policies which, while resembling those of his
predecessor in the inherent honesty and purity of motive
which always characterized them, nevertheless sharply differed
in principle and in detail from those of Hamilton and his immediate successors.

Gallatin was appointed Secretary of the Treasury on May
14, 1801. As soon as he took office he began a personal study
of the administration of the department, at the same time
laboring diligently to reduce the amount of business which
had piled up since the retirement of Secretary Wolcott. As
has been said, his two principal policies upon assuming office
were to institute drastic economies in the financial operations
of the Government and to take steps to reduce the public debt.
In a communication to President Jefferson drafted during
1801, Gallatin outlined his initial plans as follows:

There is but one subject not mentioned in the message which I
feel extremely anxious to see recommended. It is generally agreed
that Congress should adopt such measures as will effectively guard
against misapplications of public moneys by making specific appropriations whenever practicable; by providing against the application of moneys drawn from the treasury under an appropriation
to any other object or to any greater amount than that for which
they have been drawn; by limiting power in the application of that
money whether by heads of departments or by other agents; and by
rendering every person who receives public moneys from the
treasury as immediately, promptly, and effectually accountable to
the accounting office (the comptroller) as practicable. The great
characteristic of the old administration has been total disregard of

laws and application of public moneys by the department to objects for which they were not appropriated.

We may thus observe that in spirit at least Gallatin was the father of budgetary finance, and the great movement towards universal budget systems of the present day would have found in him a sincere and earnest advocate. The practical problems, however, which presented themselves for solution were difficult in the extreme. It is evident that Gallatin failed to appreciate the many objects of legitimate expense with which even a new government had to reckon. Moreover, having gone to the country upon an alluring program of tax reduction, the Republican Party was expected by the American people immediately to initiate a system of sweeping tax reform, and at the same time to run the Government not merely as well as the Federalists, but infinitely better.

Like many another financial officer before and since, Gallatin therefore looked over the field of national finance in an effort to find an answer to the insistent question "Where to cut?" and though no pacifist, he soon determined that the two departments where expenses could be reduced most readily and least annoyingly were the Army and the Navy. He also took a fling at the diplomatic and customs service. Thus whereas under the administration of President Adams for the four years ending December 31, 1800, the expenditures for the military establishment had amounted to $8,076,750.71, the record for similar expenditures during Jefferson's first administration ending December 31, 1804, showed an expenditure of $4,549,572.11; during his second administration for a like period ending December 31, 1808, the expenditures amounted to $6,126,656.97. The expenses of the Navy Department under Adams were $8,070,777.52; during Jefferson's first administration they amounted to $5,432,049.15, and during his second administration $6,853,673.79. These figures are quite persuasive and show the effect of careful and sustained economy.

Considering the grand total of receipts and expenditures of the two periods, we find that the receipts of the Federal Government under John Adams amounted to $42,040,630.45 and the expenditures totalled $40,306,413.88, making a net surplus for the Adams administration of $1,734,216.57. Under Thomas Jefferson, however, for a period twice as long as Adams's incumbency, we find that the receipts amounted to $113,605,626.18 and the expenditures were $106,288,077.29, or a net surplus accumulated during Gallatin's administration of $7,317,584.89. This excess of receipts over expenditures was accumulated notwithstanding the Louisiana purchase, an unexpected and costly item, and various payments which were made during the same period in reduction of the principal and interest of the national debt.

This remarkable reduction in expenditures was also accompanied by a very considerable decrease in the national revenues, which made its accomplishment even more difficult. The excise duties which had always been a sore spot with the people were repealed in 1802, and though a popular measure, a net loss of over $600,000 annually was involved. Subsequently, in 1807 the tax on salt was repealed, which meant a loss of about a half million dollars a year. In spite of these reductions in revenue, the remarkable saving referred to above was made under Gallatin's direction in the course of eight years.

At the same time that the Secretary of the Treasury was busying himself with the difficult task of putting the country's house in order and carrying on its business with less revenue and much greater economy, he began a vigorous effort to reduce the debt of the United States which on January 1, 1801, amounted to $80,161,207.60. Shortly after taking office,

Gallatin suggested that by the annual payment of $7,300,000
the principal and interest of the national debt might by January 1, 1810, be reduced to the extent of $32,289,000, leaving
a balance of $45,592,739, and that by continuing payments in
like amount on an annual basis the entire debt would be discharged by the year 1817. The Secretary further stated that
such an allocation of the country's revenues might safely be
made without in any way interfering with the just payment
of all current expenses.

When this prediction was made, Gallatin could not anticipate the extraordinary drain upon the Treasury caused by the
warfare against the Barbary pirates and by the Louisiana purchase, and it is a remarkable tribute to his energy, ability, and
foresight that, in spite of these unusual and unexpected expenses which cropped up to modify and interfere with his
program of debt reduction, he did succeed by the year 1810 in
making a net reduction in the national debt amounting to
$27,540,329.93, or roughly, within $7,000,000 of the ideal he had
set before the country some nine years previously.

To accomplish this reduction in the national debt, Gallatin
made use of the sinking fund already provided for by law,
though it would be incorrect to say that he was ever fascinated
by it as a financial device, believing that fiscal operations were
ordinarily far more complex than necessary, and that in finance
as in law, the most simple methods are always the most effective.

Let us now consider the "x" in the equation which rendered
Gallatin's policy of retrenchment and of debt reduction so
difficult of accomplishment.

Thomas Jefferson was no financier, and it is probable that
secretly at least he was not in thorough accord with Gallatin's
severe principles and undeviating determination to keep the
party's pledges of strict economy and elimination of debt. Jef-

ferson was a greater man than Gallatin, and he took a wider view than was possible for Gallatin's single-track mind; he was extremely anxious to leave behind him, as he did, a brilliant and attractive record for the benefit of posterity. Therefore when the opportunity arose to purchase from France the imperial province of Louisiana, which then included the whole of the western half of the Mississippi Valley and the territory now included in the states of Louisiana, Arkansas, Oklahoma, Missouri, Iowa, Minnesota, Kansas, Nebraska, the Dakotas, and a large portion of Wyoming, Montana, and Colorado, he did not hesitate to consummate the deal, although he knew very well that in doing so he might well jeopardize the record of his administration for fiscal economy. He realized also that the acquisition of this mighty empire was a distinct departure from the settled principles of the Republican Party, and constituted an exception to that doctrine of state sovereignty which he had hitherto espoused, and which he had, in season and out of season, forced upon his party followers as a fundamental article of political faith.

Jefferson saw that all objections to the acquisition of Louisiana were trivial compared with the limitless future of that great domain. He perceived clearly that, added to our young country, this new territory would constitute an element of potential growth and strength for a thousand years to come, and he wisely foresaw that his reputation as a politician and even as a philosopher would be secondary a hundred years later to his reputation as a far-seeing statesman if he acquired for his country the woods, fields, and rivers of this rich and almost unknown land. Dominated by this brilliant idea of peaceful conquest, Jefferson turned naturally enough to his overworked Secretary of the Treasury and told him it was his business to pay for it.

Gallatin's private feelings on this point have not come down to us, and perhaps it is just as well. Parodying the well-known lines of Tennyson, it was "his not to reason why, his not to make reply, his but to do and die, etc., etc.," and while he did not die in carrying out his orders, his policies were sadly hampered.

The purchase price of Louisiana was $15,000,000, a relatively small sum today but a large one in 1803. Of this amount $3,750,000 was to be paid in specie to American citizens having claims of a certain description upon the French Government, and $11,250,000 was to be paid directly to France in a Government stock or obligation bearing interest at 6 per cent payable in Europe, the principal of the obligations to be paid at the United States Treasury.

It is characteristic of Gallatin that, although probably greatly disappointed by the inevitable dislocation of his chosen policies of economy and tax reduction, he quickly rearranged his plans so that under his advice the only alteration in the financial provisions he had initiated which was necessary to carry out the Louisiana purchase, was an increase in the sum allocated to the sinking fund from $7,300,000 to $8,000,000 annually, which increase was sufficient to fund the Louisiana purchase and make the provision already pledged towards the annual reduction of the national debt.

Another important feature of Gallatin's service in the Treasury consisted of the preparation he made for financing the second war with England, commonly known as the War of 1812. We must always remember that, when he took office, Gallatin's main policy was to conduct the Treasury with the utmost economy consistent with effective government, and just as Jefferson's unexpected purchase of Louisiana was a disturbing element so far as this policy was concerned, so the second war with England was even more completely upsetting. Indeed, it is remarkable that the Secretary was able to adhere to his program of economy in any degree, in view of the great strains and stresses which the War of 1812 placed upon the Treasury.

It is true that the war did not come upon us with undue suddenness. It was easily predictable after 1807 when the Orders in Council passed by the British Government practically forced all neutral nations either to give up their foreign commerce, or to carry it on subject to the supervision and veto of the British.

Jefferson's retaliatory policy expressed by the Embargo and Non-intercourse Acts was weak, ineffective, and from the standpoint of political economy very prejudicial to American interests. Furthermore, bad as the Orders in Council were, the decrees with which Napoleon replied to them were even worse. It soon became evident that America was caught between two contending forces, and that the infantile commerce of our young country was completely at the mercy of both France and Great Britain and might not survive. The right of search and seizure being arbitrarily enforced against us by Great Britain, a situation arose between 1807 and 1811 so humiliating to our national pride, that it was quite clear that neither President Madison nor the Congress would longer bear the injustice and insults which the English were constantly heaping upon us.

It seems pitiful that after ten years of able and self-sacrificing work resulting in wonderful accomplishment in the interest of national economy, Gallatin was forced to stand helplessly by, and see the structure which he had erected with so much labor and painstaking effort razed within an hour.

The public debt on January 1, 1812, amounted to $45,154,-463. In less than eleven years the United States had paid for the purchase of Louisiana, reduced the national debt to an extent never dreamed of during the earlier administrations, and, with a continuance of prosperous and peaceful conditions, would undoubtedly have been able to wipe out the entire debt within a few more years. However, fate had willed that the event was to be entirely different from that for which Gallatin had fought and striven so earnestly. During January, 1812, the Ways and Means Committee of the House of Representatives asked Gallatin to prepare a plan of war finance; this he did by suggesting a series of special loans for war purposes, rather unfortunately failing to provide a comprehensive scheme of special taxes as a part of his program of war finance. Also, for the first time—Gallatin initiated issues of Treasury notes or short-term Government obligations receivable in payment of all duties, taxes, or debts due the United States. And thus the War of 1812 was financed on a basis of borrowed money, some of it borrowed on long and some on short credit, but the distinguishing point of Gallatin's policy seems to have been a careful avoidance of internal taxation for the purpose of obtaining funds with which to defray the expenses of the war. Undoubtedly, a great deal of politics was mixed up in the Secretary's program of war finance, and we can readily believe that Gallatin was far too good an economist to have resorted to the expedients he did resort to except as a matter of necessity. Ever since the inauguration of Thomas Jefferson and the rise to power of the Republican Party, economy had been its watchword, and taxation had been reduced and limited in every possible way. The people had been deliberately educated to resent the theory and practice of direct taxation. The excise taxes for which Hamilton had sacrificed so much had been swept away by Gallatin and his friends. Therefore, when suddenly the dark war clouds descended upon the land and, as always under such circumstances, large funds became an immediate necessity, Gallatin was afraid to tax his public; he felt constrained to incur a burden of debt for posterity and mortgage the future of the United States rather than to take the safe and sane course of compelling the generation which fought the war to pay at least a considerable part of the expense connected with it.

Unfortunately, the vice of this mistake was not confined to the War of 1812, but remained as a precedent and a governing principle to rise again and plague us during the Civil War, which was financed by Salmon P. Chase, then Secretary of the Treasury, in a manner quite similar to that adopted by Gallatin fifty years before.

Even the policy of special loans and Treasury notes was not successfully carried out. The Embargo and Non-intercourse Acts had deeply offended the merchants of New England. Their commerce had been destroyed, their ships lay rotting at their docks, their infant manufactures were paralyzed and in many instances ruined, and not unnaturally they laid all these calamities at the door of the administration. When war followed a few years later they adopted an attitude of sullen neutrality and so far as they could refused to participate in the conflict. As a consequence of this sectional policy they declined to subscribe to the war loans, thereby endangering their country's success and seriously injuring its credit.

The first loan was opened March 14, 1812, for $11,000,000 at 6 per cent, and by strenuous efforts it was put over. But when the second loan was issued on February 8, 1813, this time for $16,000,000, a very serious situation developed. No better way of indicating the state of affairs presents itself than by itemizing the location of the subscriptions to the second loan:[1]

States east of New York.................. 486,700
State of New York.....................5,720,000
Philadelphia, Pa........................6,858,400

[1] D. R. Dewey, "Financial History of the United States," p. 133. Reprinted by permission of Longmans, Green & Co., Publishers.

Baltimore and District of Columbia......2,393,900
State of Virginia....................... 187,000
Charleston, S. C....................... 354,000

From the above table it may readily be seen that almost the entire burden of the loan was borne by New York and Philadelphia with some assistance from Maryland and Virginia. The New England and southern states might really have been counted out of the picture, and this constituted a serious menace to the unity of the United States. Undoubtedly Great Britain believed that one of the results of this war would be the separation of Federalist New England from the rest of the young country, but in this she was fortunately disappointed.

The inside story of the way in which this critical situation was retrieved and the way in which this loan was finally put over the top is romantic and interesting. From the moment the subscription lists were opened, the disaffection of New England and the South became daily more evident and alarming, and popular fear and distrust in the financial ability of the United States spread from man to man with all the rapidity of a contagious disease. At this zero hour three prominent and wealthy men stepped into the breach and performed a public service which should never be forgotten as long as our country survives. These men were David Parrish, Stephen Girard, and John Jacob Astor. Curiously enough, all were foreign born, but all were prominent and successful merchants in their day and generation, and Girard and Astor have remained in our history as two of the greatest names in American private finance. Gallatin knew all of them well. They were his personal friends, and realizing the delicacy and danger of the situation which he then faced, they voluntarily offered to take up $8,000,000 of the loan at the rate of $88 for a certificate of $100 bearing interest at 6 per cent, redeemable before December 31, 1825, they to receive ¼ per cent commission on the amount accepted. In the case of a further Government loan for the year 1813 they also were to be placed on an equal footing with the takers of that loan. Astor then made a further offer to take for himself and associates $2,560,000 additional on similar conditions. Gallatin promptly accepted the offer as made, and the loan was an accomplished fact.

In order to appreciate the patriotism involved in the assumption of this large participation by the gentlemen just mentioned, we must put ourselves back in thought to the day when it was made. The United States was a young and a weak nation engaged in an unpopular and dubious contest with a great world power. The people of the United States were by no means a unit as to the advisability or necessity of waging this war. Had this loan failed, it is highly probable that the credit of the country would have received a shock from which it never would have recovered. If there was ever an example of patriotic gambling it was furnished by the action of Parrish, Girard, and Astor at this time. These men were reputed to be hard dealers—to use a colloquialism of today they were "hard boiled"—but they had a deep sense of gratitude to the land which had given them opportunity, and having realized their ambitions and accumulated what in those days amounted to great wealth, they were impelled to take the joint action which was so effective in upholding the country's credit and which undoubtedly resulted in winning the war.

The negotiation of this loan practically ended Gallatin's service with the Treasury, as shortly therafter he was sent to Russia to endeavor to secure the mediation of that government between the United States and Great Britain; from Russia he proceeded to Ghent as one of the commissioners to negotiate the peace. However, the policy initiated by him was continued, and Treasury notes and additional loans were issued between 1813 and 1815 in the following amounts:

LOANS AND NOTE ISSUES
1813 to 1815

February 8, 1813, to February 24, 1815[2]

February 8, 1813, Loan	$16,000,000
February 25, 1813, Treasury notes	5,000,000
August 8, 1813, Loan	7,500,000
March 4, 1814, Treasury notes	10,000,000
March 24, 1814, Loan[3]	25,000,000
November 15, 1814, Loan	3,000,000
December 26, 1814, Treasury notes	10,500,000
February 24, 1815, Treasury notes	25,000,000
	$102,000,000

It is to be noted that this system of rapid increase of Government credit obligations quickly resulted in depreciation and impaired credit. In the sale of the war loans between 1812 and 1816 it has been estimated that the Government lost in the neighborhood of $46,000,000, and the loss on the Treasury notes was correspondingly great. In the end Congress appeared to realize the necessity for direct taxation, and in 1814 direct taxes to produce at least $6,000,000 annually were levied. These taxes included duties on carriages, taxes to be paid by distillers of spirituous liquors and taxes on distilled spirits themselves, taxes on auction sales, wine dealers' licenses, import taxes in the nature of tariff duties and higher postage rates, and luxury taxes; but as usual this program of direct taxation was adopted too late to do more than alleviate the dangerous situation which had been brought about by the initial mistakes of the Treasury and the Congress.

Summarizing Gallatin's conduct of the Treasury during the war period, we must frankly admit that his principal policy was opportunistic and economically unsound; but on the other

---

[2] Compiled from "Financial History of the United States" by D. R. Dewey, p. 132. Reprinted by permission of Longmans, Green & Co., Publishers.
[3] Followed five months later, August, by suspension of specie payments.

hand, we must give him full credit for the energy and ability with which until the end of his service he endeavored to make the best out of a bad business, and we must further admit that it was largely due to his efforts and to the friendly confidence which they reposed in him that the patriotic syndicate subscription of Parrish, Girard, and Astor which undoubtedly saved the country's credit in 1813 was brought about.

We now turn to another phase of Gallatin's financial activities, namely, his relation to the first Bank of the United States. When the First National Bank of the United States was chartered in 1791, the Anti-Federalists, among whom Gallatin was even then a leader, bitterly opposed it. Indeed, the greatest forensic effort of Madison's career was his speech in the Congress against the proposed bank in which he endeavored to prove that nowhere in the Constitution did authority exist which would enable the Federal Government to create such an institution.

When Gallatin became Secretary of the Treasury he had at least no predisposition in favor of a national bank. It is, nevertheless, interesting to know that as he went on with his work, he became more and more convinced that the bank was of the greatest value to the conduct of the early financial operations of the United States.

Perhaps no other situation during Gallatin's long tenure of office affords such an excellent illustration of the way in which his mind slowly diverged from the mass opinion of the rank and file of the Republican Party. Public office always tends to increase the sense of responsibility held by the incumbent, and radical theories together with the ideas of youth fall away before the acid test of practically applying general principles in the execution of the duties of a particular position. Hence it is not surprising to realize that as Gallatin went on with his work as Secretary of the Treasury, he became more conservative in his ideas and policies, and more thoroughly appreciative of the value of the bank. In thus altering his opinions, he undoubtedly must have been aware that he was running counter to the ideas and prejudices of his fellow Republicans. Jefferson, who was not in any sense a financier, never understood the bank and consequently never liked it. In fact, he was afraid of it. Madison had long before taken such a definite stand that he could not change, while a great number of influential Republicans were intent upon founding a large number of uncontrolled and flimsy state banking institutions which they could readily perceive would have great opportunities to make money in that era of unregulated promotion and chaotic economic conditions.

The pinch came in 1809 when the stockholders of the bank petitioned for a renewal of its charter, which was due to expire by limitation of time on March 4, 1811. This issue was put directly to Gallatin, and he was obliged to take sides for or against the renewal of the bank's charter. In this crisis, consistent with his well-known sincerity and courage, he did not hesitate. He sent a report to the Congress on March 9, 1809, in which he reviewed with particular care and great ability the operation of the bank during its lifetime of a score of years. He showed that even though 18,000 shares of the bank stock were held abroad and only 7,000 shares in the United States, nevertheless little real harm was done thereby because the foreign stockholders had no vote. He further showed that during its career the bank had averaged 8⅜ per cent per year in dividends, and he stated without qualification that in his opinion the affairs of the bank of the United States had been well and honestly managed during its entire history. Gallatin then went on to describe what he considered to be the principal advantages of the bank so far as the United States Government was concerned. He enlarged upon the value of the institution in the collection and transmission of public funds and in the safe-keeping of Government deposits. He also emphasized the great possibilities of its lending power when the Government funds stood in need of help and adjustment. He recognized the objection raised by the bank's critics on the ground of foreign ownership of a large proportion of its capital, and he made a number of suggestions looking towards the modification of this admittedly unattractive feature. Gallatin showed clearly that because of the obviously large number of foreign stockholders, more than $7,000,000 would have to be sent abroad within a brief period if the charter were not renewed, whereas, if the charter were renewed, only 8⅜ per cent of its capital in the form of dividends would have to be shipped out of the country.

In spite of the advocacy of the Secretary of the Treasury, Congress refused to recharter the bank, and although another earnest effort was made by the stockholders to obtain a renewal of the charter three months before it expired, it was impossible to convince the Congress of the wisdom of continuing a financial institution which had already abundantly proved its usefulness to the Government and to the country as a whole.

The discussion of recharter came up again in Congress for final decision and a debate ensued. The question became a political issue, and the Republicans (Gallatin's own party) lined up almost solidly against it. When a vote was taken in the House of Representatives it was moved to postpone renewal indefinitely, and so close were the factions that this resolution was carried by a single vote. In the Senate the same question resulted in a tie of 17 to 17. The deciding vote then lay with Vice-President Clinton, who for years had been one of Gallatin's most bitter enemies. One can imagine the smile of satisfaction with which that now-forgotten statesman sealed the fate of the bank, and thus discomfited his eminent opponent in the Treasury.

The result of the refusal to recharter the bank of the United

States was precisely what Secretary Gallatin had predicted it would be. It was indeed worse than he thought, for no one had realized that our second war with England was so close at hand. Not only was the United States compelled to enter a war period without the aid of a national banking institution, but long before the declaration of war, scores of unreliable state banks had sprung into being and had begun to affect injuriously the credit of our country both at home and abroad. This was naturally so because there was no adequate system of financial control to which state banking institutions were compelled to submit. Also, the country was in a period of early development of great resources with insufficient capital, and the time was one of fatuous optimism and unwillingness on the part of an ill-educated public to face the simplest facts of finance whether public or private. So distressing was the result of the refusal of Congress to renew the charter of the bank that a very few years later on, March 3, 1816, to be exact, the second bank of the United States was chartered by the Congress.

Probably no event in Gallatin's entire incumbency as Secretary of the Treasury grieved him more deeply or called for a greater display of moral courage on his part than the issue raised by the petition to renew the charter of the Bank of the United States. In this trying situation he showed, as he did on every other occasion during his career, the high qualities of character which always distinguished him, coupled with a breadth of view and a dogged courage which were as admirable as they were unusual.

More than any other one thing Gallatin's championship of the bank operated to divorce him from the position of leadership which he had long held in the counsels of the Republican Party. In spite of the fact that he followed, perhaps erroneously, Republican principles in his arrangements for financing the War of 1812, he was never again popular with the rank and file of the party and he was doubtless "persona non grata" with its chieftain after the fight over the bank had taken place. However, his talents were so considerable and his reputation so international, that when he retired from office as Secretary of the Treasury in 1813 he was appointed first Peace Commissioner to negotiate a treaty of peace with England, and subsequently Ambassador to France. In both of these capacities he rendered invaluable service to the United States. Nevertheless, one cannot but suppose that from the standpoint of the practical politicians of his period, these honorable appointments were considered an excellent method of getting him out of the way or, as the English put it "kicking him upstairs." He retired from diplomacy in 1827 and established himself in the City of New York, where he was interested in banking. There he lived the life of a prominent and respected citizen for many years.

He died on August 12, 1849, bequeathing to his family an imperishable reputation as one of the really great minds responsible for the organization of the Government of the United States. He was a true man, distinguished by dignity, ability, and courage. If he had little humor and his nature was rather somber, it was doubtless because from his youth upward he had given the best that was in him to the task of founding on a firm basis the complicated financial system of a young and struggling country, and of protecting the vital interests of an infant and economically inexperienced nation soon to be among the greatest of the world.

STEPHEN GIRARD

CHAPTER VI

STEPHEN GIRARD—RISE OF PRIVATE FINANCE AND FOREIGN TRADE

COULD we transport ourselves backwards along the avenue of the years, and take our place under the leafy trees which then so thickly lined Chestnut Street in the City of Philadelphia, we might observe among the hurrying crowd of pedestrians a short stocky man, walking along with bowed head and hands loosely clasped behind him.

We should notice immediately that this man's progress had a peculiar effect upon all those in his vicinity. Young and old, rich and poor, stepped aside for him and gave him room, yet he never appeared to take the slightest notice of them but continued his stroll, apparently regardless of all about him—indeed, lost in thought.

Upon gazing more closely, we should see that this man had but one eye, and that his face was set, deeply lined, and somber beneath bushy brows. We also should notice that his clothes, though plain, were of the finest broadcloth and his linen of the best quality.

Any street urchin could tell us immediately who this gentleman was. He would inform us eagerly that his name was Stephen Girard, the wealthiest citizen of Philadelphia, a great merchant, a leading banker, a great miser, and a man to shun. I do not think we would be satisfied with this contemporaneous account of Girard, because we would be entirely unaffected by the prejudices of the time, and we could not but be impressed by the strong, if reserved, personality before us, which seemed, it is true, to convey the impression of strength and power, but by no means a feeling of the nearness of evil.

Let us then return to our own century, and with the advantage which such disassociation from personal bias always gives, consider in some detail the career of Stephen Girard, who himself summed up his life in the words, "Merchant and Mariner."

Stephen Girard was born of fairly well-to-do parents on May 20, 1750, at Bordeaux, France. In early youth he left home to sail as a cabin-boy on a vessel in which his father had a financial interest. For more than twenty years he followed the sea, learning the profession of sea captain in a school of extremely hard experience. In early youth he lost the sight of his right eye, and through the rest of his life this was to be a sinister and distinguishing characteristic. He obtained his captain's license in 1773, and shortly thereafter engaged in a venture which was to plague him for many years, and to remain forever as something of a blot upon his reputation. It was when he commanded the ship *La Julie* that he became obsessed with the desire to engage in profitable trade. He therefore bought a cargo of merchandise from Bordeaux merchants on credit, and sailed to San Domingo with the highest hopes of a successful voyage. Unfortunately, everything went wrong, and when his cargo was disposed of at a loss, he was unwilling to return to Bordeaux and pay a pittance to his old friends. This was what he probably should have done, but instead he took what little money he had and started for America with a fresh cargo. He did not return to Bordeaux for many years, but eventually he paid all his creditors with interest.

Stephen Girard will always be associated with Philadelphia, and life being as it was, it is not strange that his coming to that city was purely accidental. He sailed up the Delaware in 1776 intending to leave in a few days, but when the time came to depart, he found the harbor blockaded by the British

Fleet. So he sold his ship and settled in the city whose greatest citizen he was to become.

Girard's earliest activities in Philadelphia were not unusual or particularly profitable, for he sailed a small vessel up and down the Delaware selling various kinds of goods to the townspeople along the stream. These, however, were years of preparation; he was accumulating his first store of wealth and doubtless was already planning intricate commercial ventures and dreaming a young man's dreams.

Then in June, 1777, occurred an event which vitally affected Girard's entire career. He married Mary Lum, the daughter of a ship-builder, who, though uneducated, apparently possessed beauty and common sense. With her he lived happily for some twelve years, when she became hopelessly insane and had to be confined in the Pennsylvania Hospital, where she remained for a period of twenty-five years until her death in 1815. To add to the horror of the situation, Mrs. Girard, who while sane had always longed for children but had never had them, became a mother in 1791, a short time after she had been admitted to the hospital. Fortunately the child died soon after birth. No one who seeks to form an accurate estimate of Stephen Girard's character can fail to observe the effect which this over-shadowing domestic tragedy had upon his mind and disposition.

Girard was a proud man, reserved, unsociable, but intensely devoted to a few people. He loved his wife and he longed for children. Her living death seems to have changed his whole outlook on life. Such a man would never sink beneath a blow, no matter how heavy it might be. Nor would he seek solace in study or literary pursuits, for his lack of education closed these paths to him. A man like Girard would do exactly what he did. He would throw himself mentally and physically into a course of life which entailed the most unremitting labor. From the rising of the sun to the going down of the same,

Girard occupied himself with constant work, until the shadows lengthened and the final message came. He was a man of action, a courageous and constant worker, and we must always remember that he worked to forget.

To study the life of Stephen Girard is to view the rise of mercantile enterprise in the new Republic. Girard became a man of substance, and a successful ship-owner, at about the time that Washington was sworn in as first President of the United States. From that time for more than forty years he was actively engaged in import and export trade.

To understand his labors, we must, therefore, have a clear idea of the conditions existing during that period relating to trade and commerce.

The United States was the unwanted infant among the family of nations. It was neither liked nor respected. The French Revolution brought forward Napoleon Bonaparte, and his unrestrained ambition almost immediately forced France into collision with England. England was the greatest maritime power in the world; France for many years was the greatest military power on the continent of Europe. Both countries found that the control of the seas was vital to success. England forbade neutrals to trade with France, and France pursued the same policy with regard to England.

America, caught between the two contending parties, was a victim of each. Throughout the period of the Napoleonic Wars, we were in constant trouble with both England and France. Our ships were captured, our cargoes were confiscated, our sailors were impressed.

The merchants of that day were subjected to constant injustice and the severest losses. To be a successful merchant during the first quarter of the nineteenth century required more than ordinary ability, courage, and resourcefulness.

There was, however, another side to the picture. The very difficulty of bringing cargoes into port made these cargoes tremendously valuable when once they were landed. People will always pay well for luxuries. In those days tea, silks, fur, rum, and bolts of fine cloth were much desired. The man who could run the gauntlet of the British and French warsnips and supply the well-to-do citizens of any country with the goods they most desired, was sure to make a great deal of money. Indeed, he could well afford to lose a rich cargo now and then, if he was generally successful in evading the blockade.

Girard was a merchant of this type. Contrary to public belief, he never owned a large number of ships at any one time, seldom more than six. During his whole career he never owned more than eighteen ships. He was, therefore, able to concentrate his attention upon a small number of vessels, and by intense application and much forethought, he could and did guide them, on the whole, with great success.

Those were days when letter-writing was still considered to be an art, and Girard wrote letters continuously for more than forty years. He was a master of detail, and at the same time he possessed extraordinary vision. He was also self-reliant, and considered it his job to plan a voyage with such thoroughness that every reasonable contingency was taken into consideration. Not only did he instruct his agents what to do should certain events occur, but frequently he even furnished them with minute instructions along several alternative lines.

True, he had partners from time to time—his brother Jean in the early days and Baldesqui somewhat later. But he did not work well in double harness, and his achievements were really due to his own ability. His is a lonely figure, but a strong and capable one.

It is clear, however, that Stephen Girard could never have guided his ships with such uncanny foresight and preeminent ability had he not possessed encyclopedic knowledge of the world commerce of his day.

He was no youth when he began his career as a merchant,

but a man forty years of age with an unusual background of experience to help him in his work. Since boyhood he had sailed the seven seas. He knew the treacherous tides of the English Channel, and the tricky storms of the China Coast. He was at home in Mozambique, and the dangerous tides off Cape Hatteras held no terrors for him. His knowledge, however, was by no means only geographical; he was acquainted with the products of every land and with the markets as well. Thus he was able to instruct his captains and his supercargoes where to go, what to do, when to buy, and how to sell in every quarter of the known world.

He constantly added to this great store of knowledge by personal contact with mariners and traders from every port. People considered him a mean and unsociable man, yet he lived well. A constant stream of interesting visitors passed through his counting-house and oftentimes his residence on the waterfront. We can readily imagine that such topics as the current price of beaver pelts in London and the latest quotation on the best China teas at Hong-Kong were often discussed by Girard and his friends over their walnuts and wine.

Girard possessed an inquiring mind, unaffected by traditional beliefs. Although he always remained, at least nominally, a Catholic, he must have read many a book which was on the Index. His reading is reflected in the names he chose for his ships. In 1796 he launched the *Voltaire*, and in 1801 the *Rousseau* and the *Liberty*. Later on we find among his vessels such names as *Helvetius, Montesquieu*, and *North America*. He also had ships with the more plebeian titles of *Good Friends*, the *Kitty*, the *Sally*, and *Two Brothers*.

Probably at no time between 1790 and 1816 was Stephen Girard free from constant danger of having his ships captured and their cargoes confiscated. His principal contribution to the development of private finance in this country lay in his ability to overcome such obstacles and to make a huge fortune in spite of them.

Nor was he interfered with by foreign nations alone; some shrewd blows were dealt him by the Government of his own country. In 1807 an embargo was placed upon all American ships, and while it lasted not a vessel was allowed to leave port. This was in reprisal for the Orders in Council of England and the decrees of Napoleon. Although this embargo was lifted in 1809, the situation was not greatly improved, because the Non-intercourse Act took its place, by the terms of which American ships were forbidden to trade with England or France.

In one way the War of 1812 was of advantage to Girard, for his ships were not in more danger than they were during so-called peace times, and on the other hand he was free to trade and even to do a little privateering on the side. Of course, he had some losses during the war. The *Montesquieu* was captured, but so great was the demand for her cargo that Girard was able to buy her back from the British for $180,000 in cash, and then after paying $149,682.09 in duties he was still able to sell the cargo at a good profit. This was doubtless an extreme case, but generally speaking Girard showed such wisdom in his commercial ventures that his occasional losses, though huge at times, had no serious effect upon his fast-accumulating fortune.

He had a touch of genius when it came to trade. During the embargo, he bought and sold cotton with great profit, and later dealt successfully in coffee and sugar. He constantly studied the markets of the world, docketing every available scrap of information which came to him through his captains or his innumerable correspondents, so that he might always be able to dispatch his ships to ports where certain goods were at that time to be purchased cheaply, and then immediately send his vessels forward to other destinations where the same goods were in demand. The resulting profit was not to be accounted for by any element of luck, but was a tribute to the man's sagacity and intimate knowledge of the economic conditions of the world.

Subsequent to the War of 1812, there is little of interest to recount in connection with Girard's mercantile career. For over fifteen more years he was active as a merchant and constantly added to his manifold possessions, but the romance of the trade had departed. No more captures, no more press gangs, no more confiscations, and no longer any necessity for such ingenious expedients as sending a ship to sea with two captains, one English and one French, neither of whom was the real commander; three flags and three sets of papers, one real and two faked, so that no matter what kind of a warship she might meet, she could be all things to all men.

Yet there were other interesting features in the career of this many-sided man, and one of them, at least, had a considerable effect upon the financial history of his country.

The first Bank of the United States passed out of existence in 1811, because of the refusal of Congress to recharter it. Stephen Girard had always staunchly supported the bank, and indeed had been a member of a committee of Philadelphia merchants who had appealed to Congress in favor of a new charter. However, when he saw that an adverse decision was inevitable, he immediately made provision to avail himself of an opportunity which he visioned long before anyone else was aware of it. Prior to the closing of the bank, Girard purchased a large number of shares of the bank's stock from English holders, and when the bank was closed, he made a big profit. He also bought the physical assets of the bank when it went out of business, including its building in Philadelphia, and the cashier's residence nearby. He then immediately opened his own bank in the same quarters, under the title, the "Bank of Stephen Girard." He started this enterprise with a capital of $1,300,000, and from the beginning he did a general banking business in a successful way.

His entrance into this field was not a source of pleasure to the other bankers of the city, state, and nation. Indeed, Girard always claimed that he was a victim of a well-thought-out conspiracy on the part of the other Philadelphia banks. They refused to take his notes, and in every way tried to interfere with his banking operations and hamper his success. He countered by accumulating some $300,000 of notes of the Bank of Pennsylvania, which he presented one day with a demand that they be paid by the bank in specie. As may well be imagined, this caused a great stir in the banking circles of Philadelphia, and the conspiracy died right there. A compromise was arranged, and the Bank of Pennsylvania was able to avoid considerable inconvenience by agreeing to accept the notes of Mr. Girard's bank in the future. This incident would seem to show that Stephen Girard was by no means devoid of a sense of humor.

Although the banks were forced to adopt a policy of cold civility towards Girard and his bank, neverthless the trouble was not over, and did not end for a good many years. Both in Congress and in the Pennsylvania legislature, effort after effort was made to pass legislation hostile to Girard and his interests, his bank being the chief object of attack. However, the canny old merchant was never found sleeping. In one way or another he managed to defeat all his enemies, and to the end of his life remained a banker, and a very successful one.

As a banker, Stephen Girard came into frequent contact with Albert J. Gallatin, Secretary of the Treasury under Jefferson and Madison, and this association led to one of the principal events of his life, an event which constituted his greatest service to the United States.

In 1813 the second war with England was in full swing. It was an unpopular war, particularly with New England, whose shipping interests had been much hurt by the embargo. It was all very well for the United States Government to declare war against England, but when it came to paying for it, that was another story.

In 1812 a loan of $11,000,000 was negotiated with considerable difficulty, but by February, 1813, the need of further funds was urgent. A loan of $16,000,000 was authorized and its flotation immediately was attempted by Gallatin. By March the situation began to look very serious as only $6,000,000 had been subscribed. At this point, a syndicate was formed, consisting of Stephen Girard, David Parrish, and John Jacob Astor, and these three men subscribed for the remaining $10,000,000 of the loan. The subscription was on the basis of $88 for every $100 certificate, and in the end the subscribers doubtless made a fair profit.

The effect of the action of this syndicate was immediate and remarkable. The evanescent quality of confidence was aroused in the public mind. If Astor and Girard, the two richest men in America, thought enough of the Republic in its hour of greatest need to venture such a large portion of their fortunes in its defense, it was proof positive to their fellow citizens that the country was going to win the war.

It may seriously be questioned whether this patriotic deed did not turn the tide and ensure our success in the War of 1812.

It has undoubtedly been worth while to examine the life story of America's first great merchant, in order to ascertain the effect of his deeds in developing the commerce of the young country and contributing to the early financial structure of the land. If we stop, however, without going further, we shall not appreciate the many valuable qualities of this great and frequently misunderstood character.

In the slang of today, Stephen Girard's contemporaries undoubtedly considered him "hard-boiled," and doubtless in a certain sense he was. He probably never forgot the brutality from which he had suffered as a cabin-boy, and he certainly never forgot beautiful Mary Lum.

Constant work was his creed, his ideal, his vocation, and his play. He engaged in the great game of business with assiduity and devotion. He surpassed other men because he had acquired greater experience, worked longer hours and much harder than they, and in the last analysis, he had a touch of business genius. Such a man is never popular while he lives.

He kept the rules of the game, but he held others to them with severity. He did not, however, foreclose numerous mortgages and turn hundreds of poor people out of house and home, as did his great contemporary John Jacob Astor. He walked the streets a simple, silent, reserved, and lonely man. He must have known what people thought of him, and I do not believe that he did not care, yet he made no sign. Men must have asked many times, "What is he saving for?" The answer was in his will, and this they never read until he had passed beyond.

He did, however, during his lifetime give proof of his unselfishness and kindness of heart, which, indeed, was remarked by some. In 1793, and again in 1797 and 1798, Philadelphia was visited by a plague so dreadful that the chronicles of that time refer to its ravages with awe and horror. It was the yellow fever, brought to the port by immigrants or sea-farers, and so rapid was it in its attack and so unprepared were the medical authorities of that day to cope with it, that the people, especially the poor who could not flee from the city, died by hundreds, and an atmosphere of hopeless terror descended upon the stricken town.

In this critical hour, Stephen Girard stepped forward to help. Judging from his past history and his apparently selfish devotion to personal gain, we might suppose that this help consisted at best in liberal donations of money with which to fight the disease. His method, however, was far more personal, and fraught with great danger to himself. He volunteered to serve as overseer of the city Pest House, where the poor were dumped on beds of straw, and where the scenes of suffering and death were horrible beyond the power of words to describe. In such surroundings during the winter of 1792-93, Girard and his friend Peter Helm labored incessantly to relieve the sufferings of the poor and the afflicted. Girard with his own hands performed the most menial and disgusting services for the poor people who were the victims of the dread disease.

Characteristically, he made little of it, and when it was over he returned to his counting-house and resumed his ordinary occupations. Philadelphia, however, did not forget, and the city Councils passed a resolution of thanks in appreciation of the devoted work of this inscrutable man.

When it comes to the essential qualities of the spirit, there is little ground for comparison between Astor and Girard. Girard's charitable labors, however, did not suffice greatly to increase his popularity. He was a hard man and a millionaire, and once the yellow fever had passed, that was all that many remembered.

So we come at last to that bitter winter night, December 26, 1831, when alone in his residence on the waterfront, Stephen Girard lay dying. He had said a month previously, "When Death comes for me, he will find me busy, unless I am asleep. If I thought I was going to die tomorrow, I should plant a tree nevertheless today." No man could have better summarized the philosophy of his life.

As the night wore on, the world of the flesh must have receded from that intrepid soul and the world of the spirit must have drawn very near. Finally, however, the veil began to lift, but with a flicker of the old vitality, Girard rose from his bed with a final exertion of fast-fading strength and tottered across the room; supporting himself by a bureau, he raised his hand to his head, and with the exclamation, "How violent is this disorder! How extraordinary it is!" the great man died.

At least, he died physically, but there is probably no man more alive than Stephen Girard is today in the city of his adoption. In his will, for the first time, he showed to the world the controlling purpose of his later years—the motivating reason for his ceaseless labor to accumulate the millions he bequeathed. In Philadelphia the white walls of the college he founded still house hundreds of orphan boys, whose education and success in life are a tribute to his vision and unremitting labors.

Truly, he was a great man, not merely a great merchant, or mariner, as he himself said, but a supreme embodiment of labor, charity, and love.

There let us leave him, an inspiration and a benediction. It is certain he did not live in vain.

Chapter VII

LAND SPECULATION

Hitherto we have adhered almost entirely to periods connected with the rise of public and private finance in America. In each one of these there has been a dominating character whose life has given color to the whole period. Now we come to the point where it is not a question of one man's life, or of one period, but rather one of a number of economic factors which affect many men and many periods. The final results of these have a direct general effect on the history of American finance both public and private, and have been very contributive to the development of private finance.

The three things with which we deal in this way are: land, tariff, and silver. Land, with which we are concerned principally in this chapter, never was a great national issue from the standpoint of party politics as were the tariff and silver. But although it was not a party fetish, it did have a great influence on the development of finance in this country.

As a background to this subject, the student must realize that business corporations primarily interested in profits to be derived from the rise in the values of land were chiefly instrumental in colonizing North America. It is this fact, of the colonizing initiative being taken by business corporations rather than by the Crown in North America, which has been of profound influence in making the social and economic history of British North America very different from that of Spanish America, where the Crown directed all colonization.

The business corporation's opportunity for the exploitation of North America came with the weakening of Spanish colonial enterprise at the end of the sixteenth century. The Spanish credit had been steadily ruined by bad judgment. For example, in 1596, Philip of Spain repudiated a debt of 14,500,000 ducats owed to European financiers, which sum had been wasted in religious wars in Europe. Meantime the Dutch and other north Europeans, by meeting all their obligations, kept their credit good, and as Spain weakened, they were able to finance a venture—by way of poaching, of a sort—not only into the Far East, but also into North America.

The first business corporation actually to achieve anything in North America was the Virginia Company, incorporated in 1606. It founded Jamestown in 1607 and guided its promotion until its bankruptcy in 1624, when the King took charge of Virginian affairs. The company's charter was revoked in 1632.

In 1606, likewise, the Plymouth Company had been organized and incorporated, with a view to promotion north of the Delaware. It was inactive, and was, therefore, reorganized in 1620, the reorganized company being popularly known by the title of "The Council for New England." During the period of its control of New England, several lesser joint stock companies, unincorporated as well as incorporated, settled Plymouth Colony, Massachusetts Bay Colony, and lesser colonies. The Pilgrims had come over as the local representatives of an unchartered joint stock company financed by profit-seeking London capitalists. Masachusetts Bay Colony, settled by the incorporated joint stock company known as "The Governor and Company of Massachusetts Bay in New England," was governed under the charter of incorporation of the company until 1684, when the charter was revoked and the King took charge of the colony.

The New Netherlands was founded, exploited, and governed by the Dutch West India Company; New Sweden on the Delaware by the Swedish New Sweden Company; France and Russia also largely used the business corporation in North American exploitation.

In later days, in British colonization, the Carolinas were developed by the six proprietors organized as a joint stock company; Georgia, by a trust company; and the East and West Jerseys (New Jersey), between 1664 and 1702, by joint stock companies for the most part, and for a time by trustees.

These colonizing corporations, of course, had objects in addition to the special one of realizing on the increase in land values. Sometimes there were religious motives; always an eagerness to profit in trade between this colony and the mother country. But everything which increased settlement and trade increased land values, and the increase of land values was an important inducement for prospective investors to put their money into the stock of these early colonial corporations chartered in London.

Towards the middle of the eighteenth century the swarming population of the English colonies, increased by a steady immigration of Scotch-Irish, French, German, and English indentured servants, released criminals, and dissident religionists, of all sorts—some of them of the finest racial stock and some of them of the worst—had flooded westward to the Appalachians.

Land speculators, companies, and individuals anticipated the overflow to the fertile fields over the mountains and the Ohio, and were always busy trying to get grants of land which they could subdivide among settlers at a profit. By 1749, there was a population of about 1,000,000 in the English colonies, and scarcely 80,000 in French North America. The population of Spanish Florida at this time was negligible. The 1,000,000 British had a large birth-rate and a low death-rate, and tens of thousands of persons desiring Indian lands to farm were beginning to push against the Ohio River and the Appalachian borders of the already occupied coasts. The French were eager to check the possibility of the overflowing of this human reservoir beyond the natural barriers referred to, desiring to reserve the West for their fur trade.

The clash between the French and British came when a Virginian company, called the Ohio Company, chartered in 1747, planned to colonize the Ohio Valley in order to appreciate the value of lands granted to it. In 1754 it sent out young George Washington as surveyor. Then occurred an overt act by French officers in the Ohio Valley which precipitated war.

The Revolutionary War looms big in history, and justly so. The French and Indian wars, however, were more costly to Great Britain than the War of the Revolution. As a matter of fact, the British Government sent to America in the French and Indian War a large number of soldiers and sailors, and spent more blood and treasure in defending the colonies and in wresting North America from the French for the colonists' benefit than she spent in attempting to suppress their rebellion.

Although in the various attempts at the reduction of Canada, no large armies, like those of Burgoyne or Cornwallis, were lost by surrender, yet the number of men slaughtered in siege and battle was greater, and the expeditions, being in the wilderness, were more costly.

The first clash, in 1754, between Virginia and colonial French troops was the opening of the first war in North America which was not a mere colonial reflex of war between the parent states in Europe. In this case it was war in the colonies which led to war between the parent nations in Europe.

If the colonies, French and English, had been left to fight out the issue themselves, it is evident that the tremendous superiority of the English colonies in point of numbers and ability to raise militia for military operations would have eventually overwhelmed the resistance of the 80,000 French fur traders and farmers and their Indian allies. Colonial affairs, however, were not to be decided merely by military operations in the colonies. The war which was to decide the issue in North America was to be a world-wide war. It ended in the acquisition of Canada and the Ohio Valley by Great Britain.

After the war Virginia continued her interest in Ohio Valley settlement, and particularly was eager to get a land bonus for the soldiers who fought in the French and Indian Wars. Another center of westward development was instituted in Philadelphia, though here the purpose was not so altruistic as in Virginia. In Philadelphia it was mostly a question of commercial prosperity, of making money out of the situation. One of the men who early took an interest in the affair was Benjamin Franklin. He entered the land business because he saw there was a chance of making a great deal of money, and also he saw that, if the country was ever to become a strong nation, it must take care of its potential power in land. So Franklin became interested in this proposition and wrote several pamphlets on it. He drew up a plan for settling the Ohio Valley, but although it was discussed a good deal, no important result ensued. A man named Hazard also made out an elaborate plan for the settlement of the Ohio Valley based on Franklin's pamphlets, likewise without results.

Other schemes were numerous. There was, for example, the Mississippi Company, founded in 1763. It was not a financial success in a big way. Then there was the Carolina plan. This was a new scheme by Benjamin Franklin and some of his friends, also not as successful as some had hoped it would be. But out of all these schemes the country was settled, and this after all was the main point. It does not make any difference to us that the promoters did not make much money. But as a result of their planning there did come a very swift settlement of a great empire by an adventurous and pioneering people. It was at that time that the great lines of covered wagons first started across the continent and never halted until they crossed the Mississippi.

We now come to one of the most interesting of the situations, namely, the effort of Samuel Wharton and Benjamin Franklin to incorporate a company for the exploitation of the Ohio Valley and for the settlement of the country west of the Alleghenies. They conceived this idea about 1764 or 1765, but the main efforts we shall notice were concentrated between 1768 and 1774, and the principal figure in the situation was Samuel Wharton acting with the full knowledge and consent of Benjamin Franklin and his associates.

We have an idea that the Revolution was caused largely by the taxes of Great Britain, and that it can be allocated to the question of taxation without representation. Although that is true, one is forced to the opinion after reading Alvord's[1] study of the Mississippi Valley in British politics, that another factor was the failure of the British ministers to adopt a consistent system of land expansion. From the time the French and Indian War ended in 1763, there was an opportunity for the British Government to come to terms with its colonies and to support a big western movement, but it failed to do so.

In those days in London there was staged, first before the Board of the Treasury and then before the Board of Trade, one of the greatest political rows that ever occurred, and it never came to any settlement. The colonial agents were using every effort to obtain land grants from an indifferent and recalcitrant privy council. The principal figure in the situation was Lord Hillsboro. He shifted the responsibility for obtaining the new grants to Samuel Wharton, and Wharton could not get anywhere. When he finally did secure a grant the war came along and he could not use it. But because of this effort to get the land in the West, the covered wagons were moving

[1] C. W. Alvord, "Mississippi Valley."

and the country was being settled, whether the land was actually granted or not.

The Revolution came on and the land question was held in abeyance until 1787 when a new land fever developed. After the Revolution a new group of politicians had arisen. People no longer attacked the Board of Trade in London. They dealt with the new government in this country, and the man who led them was Patrick Henry.

The South Carolina Company was the first company to be incorporated by Thomas Jefferson. Then the settlers wanted to go to the Mississippi, and began to make land settlements in that direction. The company was mismanaged, and, naturally, nobody made any money out of it, but at the same time another slice of the West was settled.

We now come to Patrick Henry and the Virginia Company. All this time Patrick Henry had been an admirer and follower of Thomas Jefferson. When the Virginia Company was organized to buy these far western lands, it was part of the deal that such lands could be paid for in paper currency, so, to accomplish the purchase, Patrick Henry bought up huge amounts of outstanding depreciated paper money. Then there came along that other citizen whom Patrick Henry always opposed, Alexander Hamilton, with his plan for assuming the debts of the states and his Funding Act. Patrick Henry should have opposed it with all his oratory, but he did not. He left Jefferson and turned to Alexander Hamilton. Thus Patrick Henry's company was paid for with Alexander Hamilton's money, and that part of the country was settled.

Robert Morris then staged the biggest land speculation of all, culminating in his North American Land Company. Through this company Robert Morris and his partners became land poor. They had discounted the growth of the country by a hundred years, and Robert Morris went to jail. Still the country was being settled.

After the end of Morris's great speculation, in the beginning of the first decade of the 1800's, the day of the great business corporation form of organization for land speculation was about over. Big business had carried on the work since the settlement of Virginia in 1607; now the lands on the other or western side of the Mississippi River and in the fertile "Old Southwest"—Alabama and Mississippi, soon to be desired for cotton after the invention of the cotton-gin—were to be dealt in mostly by individual speculators who were organized into temporary associations or partnerships.

The first real craze for speculation came just after the War of 1812, induced largely by the bargain made by the Treasury Department with western banks. The agreement was that the banks were to receive and reissue the Treasury notes, and in turn the Treasury would receive the notes of the banks in payment for land. The result was a rage for land, encouraged by the fact that bank-notes were cheap and easily obtained. The credit system permitted the purchaser to go in debt for the major part of the price, and the prospect of making subsequent payments with cheap money seemed good. Everybody bought land. Then came an order of the Treasury refusing to take depreciated money in payment, with the result that great numbers of purchasers were unable to pay at all, and the land was forfeited. In many instances leniency on the part of the Government was all that prevented wholesale for-feiture.

Speculation in the Southwest was at times accompanied by fraud. For example, in 1819 a group of about forty men in Alabama agreed among themselves not to bid above the mini-mum price for a certain township of land. They got the land at $2 an acre and immediately offered it at auction realizing $19 per acre for it—not a bad day's work.

The next great wave of speculation preceded the panic of 1837. The years 1831 and 1832 were years of phenomenal growth in trade, industry, and internal improvements. "The introduction of the new means of intercourse," says Sumner, "produced a development of industry so great as to amount to a revolution, so sudden as to create a convulsion." In 1825 the Erie Canal was completed, and in 1828 the Baltimore and Ohio Railroad was begun. But the effect upon business produced by these means of communication, though large, was not comparable to that resulting from the extensive application of steam to water transportation. By 1825, steamboats were found everywhere from the Hudson to the Mississippi. The result was a considerable reduction in the cost of transportation, a large increase in the volume of production, and a marked diminution in the price of and demand for the commodities transported. The American industry most affected was the cultivation of cotton, a commodity much used after 1824. The demand for cotton led to brisk speculation in southern and especially southwestern real estate and, to some extent, also in western lands.

Emigration pushed west and southwest as the demand increased for the products of lands in those regions, and as cheap transportation to market became available. Up to 1820, the Government's selling price of land had been $2 per acre. A law of April 24, of that year, lowered it to $1.25. In 1818, public lands to the amount of nearly $2,000,000 had been sold. In 1819, sales amounted to $3,270,000. During the next ten years it never exceeded this amount. But, beginning with 1829, a rise set in in the volume of sales, and in 1834 nearly $5,000,000 worth was sold. Speculation now began to run wild. In one year, sales jumped from $4,800,000 to $14,700,000. In 1837, the increase was to $24,800,000. McGrane, in his study of the panic of this year, observes concerning this development,[2]

That speculation threw itself with peculiar intensity on the public lands, was owing to the nature of the given circumstances. Ap-

[2] R. M. McGrane, "The Panic of 1837," p. 43. Reprinted by permission of the author and the University of Chicago Press, Publishers.

parently, it bore, more than any other kind of speculation, the character of a solid investment of capital; for land was, and remained, a tangible object, and not simply a sign of value, like bank stock, which might be turned into a piece of waste paper in a night. Neither did it, like the products of industry, lose, in course of time, the qualities on which its capacity of being realized upon depended. That its value would some time be much greater than the price now paid for it, it was impossible to doubt. The mistake in the calculation of the speculators was that they thought they would be able to sell it with advantage the day after they had bought it, whereas, from the very fact that speculation had obtained control of it, it would necessarily soon become unsalable for a long time. Besides, the supply of the Government was unlimited, and the price so low that it was possible to engage in very large speculations with comparatively small means, but it is to be noted, especially, that the price of the public lands remained the same, while all other prices were rising greatly.

McGrane[3] also points out something of the relation of foreign funds and the institution of slavery to this speculative development. Foreign funds in the South, loaned through the state banks, at 8 per cent, were used in considerable part in the expansion of cotton and the concomitant expansion of the institution of slavery. Not only the plantations, but also the slaves and their posterity, served as security for such loans—the plantations in Florida, for instance, at the rate of $8 an acre, and the slaves at $350 each. It is not necessary to say that the borrowed money was not used in the improvement of plantations already under cultivation, that is, in more thoroughly farming them. A real exodus of slaveholders and their slaves took place. Planters without any means, and the sons of large planters, moved away with from twenty to thirty slaves, began to grub up large tracts of virgin soil, and laid the foundation of new plantations, without any capital except the sums borrowed from the banks on the security of the

[3] R. M. McGrane, "The Panic of 1837," pp. 26-27. Reprinted by permission of the author and the University of Chicago Press, Publishers.

mortgaged land and slaves. Of the public lands which were sold in the ten years beginning with 1830, 20,132,240 acres were from the young slave states and slave territories, Alabama, Florida, Arkansas, Louisiana, Mississippi, and Tennessee. This, therefore, meant a great shifting of the slave population. While its increase from 1830 to 1840 in the old slave states amounted to 86,393, in the new slave territories it was 391,920, so that in the latter their number nearly doubled. The aggregate increase of the slave population amounted to 24 per cent, but it was only 5½ per cent in the old slave states, and in three old border states and the District of Columbia there was even a decrease of 26,288. The center of gravity of the slaveholding interest began to be transferred in the direction of the Southwest. The capital under the stimulating influence of which this process was accomplished came from the free states and from Europe. The security for this capital was not only the land of the plantations, but also the slaves, with their yet unborn posterity. The cause of the whole, in the last analysis, was the demand for cotton, which was increasing in immense proportions. The price of cotton had risen rapidly from 6 to 8 and 10 cents per pound; maintained itself, between 1833 and 1834, steadily between the limits 11 1/3 and 11 3/4 cents; and in 1835, between 14 cents, its lowest price, and 20 cents, its highest; fluctuated during the last months of 1836 between 12 and 20; fell, in April, 1837, to 11 and 15, and finally, in May, to 8 and 12. This enormous enhancement of price, while production increased steadily and rapidly, might well turn people's heads. The cotton crop of the United States between 1833 and 1837 was increased from 1,070,438 bales to 1,422,968 bales, chiefly from the new slave states.

During this period, not only was the business of the state banks booming, but the great central bank, the Second Bank of the United States, was doing a larger and larger share of its business in the speculative West and Southwest. On May

1, 1828, the discount and exchange dealings of the bank in those sections of the country had been $13,697,000 out of a total of $39,352,000; on May 1, 1832, the sum was $36,419,000 out of a total of $70,000,000. In other words, the western and southwestern loans had increased from a little over one-third of the whole to over one-half of the whole, the number of offices doing this enormous business being 9 out of a total of 26, established almost exclusively in cities of moderate size.

In the midst of the heated land speculation of 1836 came Jackson's "Specie Circular." This helped prick the bubble of inflation floated by the local banks of West and Southwest. As market values of lands had risen above the Government's fixed selling price, there had been an eager contest on the part of those who could borrow money to buy for speedy resale at an advanced price. The local banks were all too ready to lend. The borrowers bought from the Government's sales agency. Frequently the Government then deposited the purchase price in the bank which had lent it. Here it once more served as a loan to another, or even to the same land speculator. Bank-notes served as the medium of this pyramiding of credit, the notes constituting the equivalent of a deposit credited to a borrower, and usable as a means of payment for lands.

The actual farmers of the West, upon whose votes Jackson relied considerably, began to protest against the Government's policy of permitting a facilitation of the land speculation, which skyrocketed land prices beyond reason and yielded enormous profits not to the tillers of the soil but to professional speculators.

The President, taking notice of their protests, in the circular of July 11, 1836, ordered that all payments for public lands henceforth must be made not in bank-notes, but in specie. The disastrous effects of draining specie from the legitimate business of the East to speculation in the West we shall consider in connection with the panic of 1837. Here we may merely note that it was one of the factors which served to deflate bank credit in the West and prick the bubble of inflated land prices.

The foreign demand on our specie ensuing upon the financial difficulties in London in January, 1837, made for the disappearance of specie even in the West, and shortly caused suspension of specie payments by banks everywhere. There was nothing with which to buy Government lands. The inflated values of landed property disappeared. The boom was over, and most of those who were caught with land purchased at the inflated prices were ruined.

Another lull followed, with a new craze of speculation in the years just preceding 1857. Thereafter came the Civil War, and in due time the Homestead laws providing for sale of public lands direct to settlers. One cannot neglect the fact that even then speculation in a less direct way took place, through large land grants to railroads in their promotion period which were often mere plums for speculators who were only incidentally interested in railroading.

In the period from 1803 to the Civil War, not only the speculator proper speculated in land. It was also the practice for a real farmer to buy up more land than he could ever use, farming a part of it, and holding the rest as a speculation.

The original speculators probably rendered the greatest public service. It was the practice for such men to prospect far beyond the line of settlement, seeking out sections of land most suited for farm purposes. These they would buy from the Government at, let us say, $1.25 per acre. They then aroused an interest in emigration and directed the prospective settlers to their land, which might be resold at $2.50 or $3.00 an acre. There is no doubt that settlement was stimulated and advanced by these prospector-speculators, and that they rendered invaluable service not only to the emigrants who sought good land, but to the entire nation, for it was largely as a result of their speculative enterprise that the country was settled.

Chapter VIII

JOHN JACOB ASTOR—THE ADVENTURE OF
THE FUR TRADE

IF AN interested observer had been stationed on the snow-covered banks of Chesapeake Bay at the end of January, 1784, he might have seen an old-fashioned ship locked in the ice at some distance from shore. It was no unusual thing for vessels to be held up in those days for long periods when within sight of their destination, and this was what had happened to the good ship commanded by Captain Jacob Stout, upon which a German lad of twenty was a passenger.

I shall venture to say that no one at that time paid much attention to the youngster, and certainly no one realized that within a comparatively few years he would become the richest man in the new country and would definitely establish a world-wide business with its roots fixed firmly in the virgin land. The boy was John Jacob Astor, who, after serving a short apprenticeship to a brother engaged in the musical instrument business in London, was seeking his fortune in America.

The Revolutionary War was over, but the worst part of the period of reconstruction was in full swing, and economic conditions in the new land were chaotic and unsettled.

Astor had brought with him a collection of cheap flutes and other musical instruments in which he had invested the savings he had been able to accumulate while apprenticed to his brother in England, and it was undoubtedly his intention to continue in the same line of business after he reached this shore. However, fate decided otherwise for him, and his involuntary detention on the ice-bound frigate off the capes of the Chesapeake had much to do with changing his decision regarding his life work. On board the ship with him at that time was an old hunter, and this worthy man lightened the hours of waiting by recounting to the impressionable boy many of his adventures as a fur trader—a vocation which had carried him from the eternal snows of Canada to the foothills of the Rockies, which were then known to Indians and trappers as "The Shining Mountains." We need not doubt that the hunter's tale was a dramatic story and lost none of its effect upon the lad because it was told in halting sentences and uncouth English.

When after a long period of delay Astor finally landed in America, he made his way to New York City, where his older brother, Heinrich, had for several years been a prosperous butcher—the same business, by the way, which Astor's father followed in the little town of Waldorf, Germany.

Declining Heinrich's offer to engage with him in the butcher business, Astor started to work for a baker until he was able to procure a job with a fur merchant, Robert Browne by name. Within a year, however, we find him engaged in the fur business, and he soon began to buy skins from the farmers and traders in the vicinity of New York travelling up the Hudson to the neighborhood of Peekskill and Albany, and dealing at times with the Iroquois Indians, who still clung tenaciously to their former hunting grounds. Slowly we find Astor extending his trips throughout the northern frontier. We can picture to ourselves his short, stocky figure, his fair complexion, and his determined face, as he trudged through the wilderness from post to post and from one tiny settlement to another, with his pack strapped to his shoulders containing the gaudy ornaments and cutlery which he used for trading purposes and the beaver skins which he acquired by barter from the farmers, Indians, and trappers. If ever a man learned a business from the ground up that man was Astor. It is but fair to state that, although during his later years he travelled little and sat in New York City like a great spider spinning a web of greed and acquisitiveness over the whole continent, nevertheless he probably never asked any of his men to take bigger risks or to endure hardships more severe than he had himself encountered in early youth.

The years went by, and Astor prospered. He left his Quaker employer and branched out 'for himself. After awhile he became known throughout the East as a shrewd and successful trader in furs. Always he seemed to have the ability to make other men work for him in ways extremely profitable to himself, and within a comparatively short time he set up his own organization of traders and trappers which, using New York as a center, covered the country from the Canadian line to the Missouri River. At this point we may inquire as to the extent of the opportunities which existed then in the fur trade. The answer will be interesting.

America in those days was economically an undeveloped land. The thirteen states of the Union held tenaciously to the Atlantic seaboard hemmed in on the westward by the peaks of the Appalachian Mountains. Until after the War of 1812 very little manufacturing was carried on, and that of the crudest kind. This was a farming country, and each family formed an independent unit—the members of each group making practically everything they used or consumed except hats, shoes, flintlock muskets, and gunpowder. The parents of those days based their production of large families upon the moral precepts of the Holy Bible. But we may be pardoned today if in the light of history we believe that the huge families of that time were really brought about more by economic conditions than by such outstanding examples as the "begats" in the Book of Genesis. In those days every healthy child was an asset and increased the welfare of the family group.

The necessity which faced each community of consuming practically all its home products and meat animals greatly limited the field of trade. Human nature being as it is, the people of the country desired to trade and earnestly sought some medium of exchange which would enable them to purchase from abroad some of the luxuries of life. The answer to this problem was found in furs.

Apparently the number of fur-bearing animals in the land was limitless. Every tumbling stream of the back country abounded in beaver dams, and wild deer roamed at will where we now find the dusty streets of many cities. The bear, the fox, the marten, and the otter were to be found in countless numbers in the East, and in the West beyond the Mississippi River the plains were black with herds of buffalo.

It would have been of little use, however, to slaughter these animals if there had been no market for their pelts. The determining factor in the colossal growth of the fur trade was that such a market existed—many markets in fact.

In London and on the continent of Europe, men of substance wore tall hats made of beaver skins, and fur coats were in constant demand. The European supply of skins was inadequate to meet the needs of the people, and the American furs were greatly desired. Also American goods were in many cases of a quality superior to those obtainable abroad. At that same time, in far-away China, there was a steady demand for fur garments and robes, and young Astor was one of the first to sense the possibility of exchanging furs for tea and silks. In that way, products of the Orient most desired in America were brought to our shores, where they were greedily purchased at high prices, thus establishing a circulation in trade which meant huge profits to those responsible for its institution.

We must not suppose, however, that Astor founded the fur trade; he did nothing of the kind. He organized and centralized it, and he extended it to a remarkable degree, but he did not found it. From the earliest days there had been fur trade on the American continent. The first colonists exchanged bright-colored cloth, beads, and cutlery for the pelts which the Indians brought them. Gradually a number of important trading companies sprang up, and when Astor began his business career these companies, all of English inception, constituted the biggest factors in the fur trade. The business of each company was limited by certain rather vague geographical lines. North of the St. Lawrence River in Canada the Hudson Bay Company conducted its operations. This was the oldest corporation and possessed the greatest vitality, for it is still conducting its business at the present time. Further to the south and east, was the territory of the Northwest Company which for years was Astor's greatest competitor. This company traded along the Great Lakes and on the Assiniboine, Saskatchewan, and Athabaska Rivers. West of the Great Lakes and as far south as the Missouri and the Mississippi Rivers constituted the sphere of influence of the Mackinaw Company. South of St. Louis and throughout the territory which later became the Louisiana purchase the Missouri Company was predominant. Shortly after the nineteenth century opened, Astor himself had become dominant from the St. Lawrence Valley along the Great Lakes and down the Hudson. He looked, however, for new worlds to conquer.

The profits in the fur trade of those days were great, and the business was shamefully carried on. The machinery of the trade was uncomplicated, but called for courage, shrewdness, and willingness to exploit trappers and aborigines, together with a certain amount of working capital, which was not necessarily large, considering the volume of profits to be gained. All the fur companies traded in the same way, and their methods should be described.

The directing heads of the trade were agents or partners (as in the case of the Northwest Company) in the field. These men occupied, as bases, a considerable number of trading posts established at strategic points along the Great Lakes and the principal rivers. Under them worked the traders and trappers—the real heroes of the trade. The term "hero" must be qualified, however, because it would not be well to unduly exalt these hard-boiled children of the forest; they were probably among the toughest individuals which this country has ever known. Even the bad men of a later day and the California miners of '49 could scarcely rival them in viciousness and general depravity. They were, nevertheless, fearless, bold, energetic, and industrious, and without them there would have been no fur trade on the American continent nor would the new territories have been opened as soon as they were.

It was the purpose of each one of the great fur companies to keep its group of trappers and traders in constant debt to it and, therefore, in complete subjection to its will. For continuous risk of life and health, for exposure to the snows of winter and the broiling heat of summer, on an unexplored and savage frontier, these trappers received on the average a salary equivalent to $150 a year in addition to their food and support while on the company's business. When they received their paltry wages, they almost invariably gravitated to some trading post where they got gloriously drunk and stayed drunk until their wages vanished, after which they went to work again. The evil of intoxication was in no way restricted, and the intemperance of the traders and trappers probably made the greatest blot upon the record of the fur-trading corporations. The North American Indian, though barbarous and at times extremely brutal, possessed many outstanding virtues until he became intimately acquainted with the Christian subjects of European countries. The use of liquor as an instrument of trade did more to ruin and debauch the Indian character than any other single thing. For nearly a century the trading companies and their agents supplied the Indians with gin, whiskey, brandy, and rum in an effort to obtain from them the skins of fur-bearing animals for the lowest possible price. In this they were successful, but at the cost of the moral and physical welfare of the Indian race. It may be readily imagined, however, that the profits of the fur trade were enormous. It has been reliably estimated that during the fifteen years between 1815 and 1830 the expenses of the American Fur Company (Astor's company) were $2,100,000, of which total $1,500,000 represented merchandise, $450,000 went for wages for two hundred trappers at $150 a year, and $150,000 went for wages for twenty clerks at $500 a year. The receipts of the business were estimated at $3,750,000, divided as follows:

26,000 buffalo skins per year at $3	$1,170,000
25,000 lb. beaver skins per year at $4 per lb.	1,500,000
4,000 otter skins per year at $3	180,000
12,000 coon skins per year at $.25	45,000
150,000 lb. of deer skins per year at $.33 per lb.	742,000
37,000 muskrat skins per year at $.20 per lb.	112,500
Total	$3,750,000[1]

It has been stated previously that Astor looked for new worlds to conquer. Great though his winnings had been in the Hudson Valley, he already dreamed of a gigantic corporation (today we would call it a trust) which should dominate the fur trade of the American continent. The first step was to establish a line of trading posts all the way across the country. Such an idea at that time could have been possessed only

[1] See "John Jacob Astor," by Arthur D. Howden Smith, J. B. Lippincott Company, 1929, p. 222.

by a man of extraordinary vision, and Astor was such a man. Unquestionably he had a remarkable mind and could see the future more clearly than almost any of his contemporaries. He displayed this faculty not only in connection with the fur trade, but also in his appreciation of the future development of real estate in New York City, which by shrewd investment and unbounded faith he made the substantial basis of his colossal fortune.

Already the finer spirit of the race had begun the conquest of the far western country. In 1793 Alexander Mackenzie, a dour Scotchman of flint-like spirit, pushed his way, despite severe hardships, across the plains and mountains of the Northwest as far as the upper reaches of the Columbia River and then down that river to the Pacific shore. In 1806 came the Expedition of Lewis and Clark—one of the most romantic adventures of early American pioneers. After that it was only a question of time when "The Shining Mountains" and the desert land beyond would cease to hold back the eager hordes of a hardy race—and the conquest of the West had definitely begun. As always the first comers were the hunters and the trappers; after them the farmers; and last of all the men who made the cities.

It was in the fall of 1810 that Astor initiated his great scheme for extending the fur trade across the continent. Already he had prepared a system of distribution which would be strong enough and sufficiently world-wide to market any quantity of furs, however large. Ever since the turn of the century Astor had been carrying on a constantly increasing shipping business as a means of transferring his furs to profitable markets. In this way he had particularly developed the China trade, and it was one of his pet projects to facilitate his contact with the Flowery Kingdom by securing a base port in the Pacific Ocean at the mouth of the Columbia River.

On September 8, 1810, Astor dispatched the ship *Tonquin*

from the port of New York with instructions to make the long trip around Cape Horn and then to sail up the west coast to the mouth of the Columbia. There it was to meet an expedition under Hunt and Mackenzie, two of Astor's trusted lieutenants, which meanwhile would have travelled over land across the continent to the place of rendezvous. Both expeditions were well planned with Astor's usual foresight, and yet in spite of the fact that each reached its objective, the enterprise as a whole was a dismal failure. In a sense, it constituted one of the greatest tragedies of Astor's career because, more than any other public performance of his, it displayed the weak points of an otherwise great character.

Astor, though possessing a mentality which was probably quite equal to that of Benjamin Franklin or Robert Morris, was entirely devoid of their patriotism and devotion to public service. Indeed, his greatest fault was complete selfishness. Had he planned and executed his western expeditions with some thought to the interest and welfare of his adopted country, they might have been successful, and the map of Canada might be much less extensive than it is today. However, he characteristically sought men to use as instruments who would in his judgment be less independent and more subservient to his interests than the American-born trappers upon whose loyalty he could have relied. The result was that his chief representative on the *Tonquin* was a Scotch-Canadian by the name of MacDougal. When the mouth of the Columbia had been reached and the trading post established after untold hardships and much loss of life, MacDougal made a deal with the representatives of the Northwest Company as soon as the news arrived that the War of 1812 had begun. He not only betrayed Astor and sold him out, but at the same time he surrendered an imperial territory which otherwise would in all probability have been held for the United States.

True it is that Astor lost more than $100,000—an immense

JOHN JACOB ASTOR

amount in those days—on these expeditions, and he lost the money courageously and without undue complaint. Nevertheless, he might have saved himself a fortune and his country an empire if he had not been so enslaved by avarice.

The War of 1812, however, was by no means an unmixed evil so far as John Jacob Astor was concerned. Indeed, he would never have acquired the control of the fur trade which was his in later years if the war had not occurred.

To say that Astor was enraged as a result of the collapse of the ill-fated expeditions to the Columbia is to under-state the case. He was wild with anger, and his enmity towards the British was unbounded. His fury was all the more dangerous because he gave very little external evidence of it. He was cold, reserved, self-contained, and highly unsentimental. Therefore, when he went out for revenge he was a man to avoid. If he had any natural human affection, and there is reason to believe he had, it seems to have been restricted to his own family circle. Outside of his clan he was cold-blooded, calculating, and intensely selfish. Consequently, in planning his revenge, he took full account of the effect of the war upon the public mind, and used it for his own purposes. He had many friends in the Congress and in the higher positions of the Government service, and as soon as the war was over, he began a successful agitation to obtain legislation which would make him supreme in the kingdom of fur. Without doubt the Act of 1816, known as the Exclusion of Aliens Act, was passed primarily as the result of his constant agitation in its behalf. This law prohibited aliens from hunting or trapping within the borders of the United States, and as soon as it was passed it placed the Northwest Company and similar corporations completely at Astor's mercy—and mercy was a quality he did not possess.

Eight years before, Astor had consolidated all his interests in the American Fur Company, and this corporation grew so rapidly and became so strong that it served as a definite measure of its master's greatness. Indeed, for more than half a century it received the compliment of being known throughout America merely as "The Company"—no one having any doubt as to which company was meant when the phrase was used.

After the War of 1812, backed by the prohibitive legislation above referred to, Astor had little to fear from his Canadian rivals, and the rest of his long career in the trade, which extended until 1836, was devoted to ceaseless warfare against the independent companies. Some partnerships and individual traders had the temerity to challenge his supremacy and to seek for themselves a place in the sun. For some seven years after the war the American Fur Company contented itself with consolidating its gains and controlling the fur trade throughout the eastern part of the United States. In 1822, however, the company turned its attention towards one of its principal rivals, the Missouri Fur Company, which for many years had dominated the trade throughout the valley of the Missouri. This was the company led and controlled by the romantic Spaniard, Manuel Lisa, and it had enjoyed a long, interesting, and profitable career. The battle that ensued was bitter and lasted a considerable time. The traders and trappers of the competing corporations used strong-arm methods and even resorted to murder to eliminate their rivals from the field. Finally the American Fur Company triumphed, and St. Louis became its western headquarters. Gradually its operations were extended not only by expansion of the business but through the same kind of absorption of competing firms which in later years was to be a distinguishing characteristic of the Standard Oil Company. In this way Bernard Pratt and Company and Bostwick and Company were merged with Astor's monopoly. Later on, the Columbia Fur Company was likewise benevolently assimilated by the octopus of the fur trade. Year by year the operations of the American Fur Company extended far to the west; year by year its rivals became fewer, and year by year its policies, as dictated by the now fast-aging German in New York City, became more ruthless.

The last stand against the Astors, for by this time William Astor, the worthy son of his father, had become a partner in the schemes of the older man, was made by the independent hunters of "The Shining Mountains." There in the inaccessible vastness of the Rockies, final resistance to the mighty company which Astor had made was carried through to the usual conclusion about the middle of the thirties.

From 1836 onward, Astor, though officially retired, was really in practical control of the American fur trade, and he reached the zenith of his dominance at just about the time when the fur trade itself was beginning to change and to become less important. This was due to the steady influx of settlers throughout the country and the consequent deforestation of large areas of land. As the farms increased, it was not only the Indians who withdrew further and further to the west, but the wild fur-bearing animals of the land were also compelled to seek other haunts, so that by the middle of the last century the fur trade as a dominant economic factor of American commerce was but a shadow of its former self. The great early adventure of American trade was over.

The remainder of Astor's life, and he lived to be a very old man, is of little interest to us in connection with this study. How he schemed and plotted in order to become the greatest landed proprietor of his day is a story of surpassing interest, but it cannot be told here. In all probability he was the most unpopular man of his generation, for his acquisitive methods were not those likely to endear a man to his fellow citizens. He bought mortgages by the wholesale and foreclosed them without pity. He purchased great tracts of land for ridiculously small amounts of money and then leased them on what are now known as improvement leases usually for twenty years, at the end of which time he reacquired the land with all the houses and other buildings which the tenants had erected upon them in the intervening period. His was a curious character, like those of most great men. He was a combination of admirable traits and unworthy motives. That he was brave, industrious, efficient, in his business, far-sighted in his plans there is no room for doubt, but that he was selfish, cruel, remorseless, and devoted solely to the upbuilding of a colossal personal fortune there can, also, be no question.

As has been said before, he did not found the fur trade in America, but without him it would never have become the great controlling factor of the country's economic life. Always a leader of rare parts, he visioned the wilderness of the West in a way which no other man of his age or generation ever succeeded in doing. He could not be controlled or hindered by difficulties which seemed insuperable to lesser men. He refused early in life to recognize the Rocky Mountains as the geographical limit of his adopted land. While still a young man he made his great though unsuccessful attempt to conquer the Pacific coast, and although he failed in this, the country certainly acquired the great territory of Oregon largely as the result of his efforts. But when all is said, it must be admitted that his chief vice of unrestrained greed prevented him from attaining the success which with his remarkable ability should have been his. He promoted and organized the greatest corporation of his day, and through it, for nearly half a century, he reigned as czar of the fur trade, then the chief field of commerce in our youthful country. For all this he will long be remembered and duly respected. But he will likewise be remembered as a man without conscience as to the methods he employed, as one who deliberately debauched the Indians and his own employees, and as one who stamped upon the entire commerce in furs a symbol of cynical materialism which even today is the thing that most deeply impresses the student. We can never forget the romance, the tragedy, the failures, and the successes of those interesting and vital years.

CHAPTER IX

MADISON, HAMILTON, AND THE FIRST NATIONAL BANK

IN SEVERAL preceding chapters two aspects of early American financial history have been presented. On the one hand, we have seen Girard and Astor amassing huge personal fortunes, and while so engaged incidentally rendering important service to their country. On the other hand, there has been depicted the great drama of land—the opening of the West, inspired largely by unfounded estimates of gain to be secured from land speculation, and, though unsuccessful financially, nevertheless of tremendous value in the economic development of the country. Now it becomes necessary to revisit the field of public finance, and in so doing to retrace our steps to the closing decade of the eighteenth century.

In the course of his report submitted to the House of Representatives of the National Congress on December 14, 1790, Alexander Hamilton, then Secretary of the Treasury, wrote as follows:

It is a fact well understood that public banks have found admission and patronage among the principal and more enlightened commercial nations. They have successively obtained in Italy, Germany, Holland, England and France, as well as in the United States. And it is a circumstance which can not but have considerable weight in a candid extent, of their tendency, that after an experience of centuries there exists not a question about their utility in the countries in which they have been so long established. Theorists and millions of people unite in the acknowledgment of it.

Undoubtedly, Hamilton sincerely believed these words when he wrote them, but there was no such unanimity of opinion regarding the utility of a national bank in the United States at the time he proposed it as he alleged existed in foreign countries. The difficulty was that from its very inception the question of a national bank in this country constituted a political issue, and therefore it could not be treated in a dispassionate and logical manner by either side to the controversy which it immediately caused.

The agricultural commonwealths of the South feared from the beginning that the establishment of a national bank was a measure adopted by the Federalist North to strengthen the central Government. They felt that, if this Government were supported with deposits obtained from the wealthy class, an alliance would be created between the rich merchants of the country and its political rulers which would be adverse to the states which were struggling even at that time to construe the Constitution as a League of Nations rather than as a purely governmental instrument adopted as the legal basis of a single state.

The first attack upon Hamilton's plan was attempted by James Madison, later President of the United States, and those men who were subsequently to form the Anti-Federalists and leaders of the Republican Party. This battle of giants has been reviewed carefully in the chapter devoted to Alexander Hamilton and the reconstruction period. It is enough to say at this point that the fight over the bank brought up for the first time the method to be employed in interpreting the Constitution, the South taking the position of strict construction, whereas the North championed a liberal interpretation of the great instrument. Hamilton, with such a policy in mind, defended the establishment of a national bank on the theory that although it was not specifically authorized in the Constitution, there was an implied power to establish such an institution in order to exercise effectively the borrowing capacity granted to the United States.

After some hesitation, Washington signed the bill on February 25, 1791. It provided for a bank of the United States situated at Philadelphia. The capital was $10,000,000, divided into 25,000 shares with a par value of $400 each. It was also provided that the subscriptions, both private and public, should not be paid entirely in specie, because it was realized that the amount of currency in the country at that time was quite limited. The act therefore made provision for the use of United States bonds, then known as United States Stock, and each subscriber was allowed to make payment of three-fourths of his subscription in United States Stock bearing 6 per cent interest.

The government was to subscribe one-fifth of the total capital of the bank, but the device adopted to bring this about, though highly ingenious, was a contradiction in terms and constitutes one of the few blots upon Hamilton's record as a financier. It was not dishonest, but it was not frank, and economically it was far from sound. The scheme was that the Government should subscribe to $2,000,000 of the bank stock, and as soon as the subscription was made the bank would lend the Government $2,000,000, which the Government would agree to repay in ten annual installments. In this way the Government would become a stockholder without putting up any money, and would then borrow back the full amount of its stock subscription and have ten years to pay the subscription in yearly sums on the installment plan. Meanwhile, it would get any dividends that were coming its way. The scheme did not work satisfactorily, and no one with any common sense would have thought that it would.

It was further set forth in the Bank Bill that the bank should not contract debts in excess of $10,000,000 more than its deposits. It was also given permission to issue its own notes within certain limits, and these notes were made legal tender for all debts due to the United States.

The Secretary of the Treasury was empowered to demand periodic statements of the bank's condition, but could not demand such statements more frequently than once a week.

Twenty-five directors were to be elected in such a manner that not more than three-fourths of them would be eligible for reelection in any succeeding year. It was also provided that the stockholders could not be elected directors unless they were citizens of the United States.

Shortly after the bill was signed by the President, arrangements began to be made for establishing the bank in fact as well as in theory. By supplementary legislation, adopted March 20, 1791, it was provided that stock subscription books should be opened on the first Monday of June, and commissioners were duly appointed to receive subscriptions to the stock of the bank. When the books were opened on June 4, 1791, there was a rush to subscribe and no difficulty was experienced in getting together the original capital. Indeed, the records of those days show that the entire capital of 25,000 shares was subscribed within two hours and additional applications for 4,000 shares were in hand.

A great deal of detail work seems to have been necessary before the bank could actually commence business, and it was not until the fall of 1791 that the stockholders got to the point of electing directors. On October 21, 1791, a general meeting of stockholders was held at Philadelphia at which the directors were chosen. There were twenty-five directors in all, and Thomas Willing, the former partner of Robert Morris, was elected first president.

It was natural that the majority of the first board of directors should have been Federalists in politics, and that a considerable number of them should have been residents of Philadelphia; but these facts did not endear the management to the great mass of citizens. Rightly or wrongly the poorer classes of that day regarded Chestnut Street, Philadelphia, in the same light that the farmers of the West now look upon Wall Street, New York. Hence from its inception the National Bank was considered to be the exponent of the wealthy and privileged classes, and a great mass of unsympathetic opinion piled up against it among the great body of the people.

Another difficulty that soon arose was attached to the policy, adopted against Hamilton's advice, of establishing branches in various states throughout the country. Thus within a short time branch banks were opened in New York, Boston, Baltimore, and Charleston. Although each branch was supposed to be independent, the actual fact was that the independence of all the branches was more theoretical than real. They elected their own presidents and most of their subordinate officers, but they were really controlled by the central bank at Philadelphia. The branch cashiers were appointed by the officials of the central bank and owed their first loyalty to it. The directors of the branch banks also were elected by the directors of the main bank. The capital of the bank was divided between the parent bank and its branches, $4,700,000 being retained in Philadelphia while the balance, a total of $5,300,000, was distributed in various amounts among the branches.

From the beginning, the bank was highly successful in rendering the principal services which its friends had claimed it would be able to perform. It was of great assistance in collecting and safeguarding the revenues of the Government, and it transmitted the funds of the United States from one part of the country to another with safety and rapidity at a time when under any other system it would have been impossible to transport physically large amounts of money through rough country, over bad roads, with the danger of robbery and the certainty of delay.

The judicious employment of its notes also increased the currency of the country in a proper manner, and stabilized it more thoroughly than was thought to be possible.

The greatest service which the bank rendered, however, was in the exercise of its loaning capacity for the benefit of the Government. The country was young and poor, and the administration frequently needed financial assistance. The establishment of a national bank created a focal point where the individual wealth of the country could be concentrated, with the result that when the nation needed cash the bank usually had it in hand.

Thus it may be noted that the earliest loans by the bank to the Government were in anticipation of revenues which had not been collected, and in this way the Government was enabled to keep going without distress, pending the receipt of taxes from sources both domestic and foreign.

On March 20, 1794, an initial loan was made. It was of a somewhat unusual nature and was known as the Algerian loan. The reason for this loan was the necessity of defeating the Barbary pirates who at that time constantly preyed upon the commerce of the country. The loan was for $1,000,000 and was split between the Bank of the United States which took $800,000 and the Bank of New York which subscribed for $200,000. The Government pledged uncollected tariff duties in payment of the loan.

Again in 1794, two other loans were negotiated for extraordinary purposes. A war with France was expected, and $3,000,000 at 5 per cent was borrowed from the bank in anticipation of the coming struggle, which fortunately failed to materialize.

It will be noted that the lending capacity of the bank was almost constantly called upon by Hamilton and to a lesser extent by his successor Wolcott. However, the loans were large and frequent enough throughout this entire period to establish thoroughly the usefulness of the bank as a source of supply to the Government of a young and needy country.

Meanwhile, the other side of the picture was not so promising. It was one thing for the United States to borrow from the National Bank, and quite another matter to pay back the sums which had been borrowed. In 1792, the United States owed the bank $2,536,595.56, and in 1798, some six years later, the Government's indebtedness had increased to approximately $6,200,000. In short, the Government was shockingly bad pay.

This situation could readily have been cured had Congress been willing to levy taxes large enough to take care of the debt, but the politicians of one hundred and thirty years ago were not radically different in their outlook from the politicians of today, and they showed the same willingness to let the future take care of itself and pass the burden to their descendants whenever it was possible to do so. Already the Excise Tax was proving to be an encumberance for the Federalist Party, and Congress was afraid to add to the tax burden of a pioneer people who on general principles resented all taxes.

In 1794, Hamilton resigned his secretaryship, and was succeeded at the head of the Treasury by Oliver Wolcott, of Connecticut. Wolcott had been a close adherent of Hamilton since Hamilton first took office, and hence there was no change in policy when he assumed control. He was, however, apparently much disturbed by the growing debt of the United States to the bank, and he endeavored to fund the various loans and provide a systematic scheme for their repayment within a reasonable space of time. But he was opposed in every particular by the Anti-Federalist majority in Congress, which was becoming more bitter in its opposition from day to day.

Finally as a last resort it was found necessary to sell the Government's stock in the National Bank in order to meet its debt to the institution. Of the 5000 shares of bank stock held by the Government, 2160 were sold for $500 a share, netting $1,080,000. The sum of $120,000 was obtained from the sale of new Government stock, and a little later 620 shares more were sold for $304,260. As a result of these sales the Government made a good profit but lost its participation in its own bank. It is a reliable statement that the Government realized a profit of $671,860 from the sale of its bank stock, in addition to which it had received dividends of somewhat more then 8 per cent for a number of years, or approximately $1,101,720.

All this time, or to be more exact, during the first ten years of the bank's existence, a considerable feeling of opposition to the institution had been growing up. This had several basic causes. In the first place, as has been said, the bank was a political issue between the two great parties, and the Anti-Federalists were opposed to it on principle, believing that it was unconstitutional and formed an important part of the machinery devised by Hamilton to strengthen the Federalist Party.

This idea that the bank was unconstitutional was wide-spread, and was maintained for many years after the Supreme Court had definitely held that it was constitutionally justified. Thomas Jefferson never believed in the constitutionality of the bank, and a generation later, Andrew Jackson, in his first message, questioned the constitutionality of the Second National Bank which had been instituted upon the same general theory as the first.

The opposition to the bank was based also on an excellent economic reason which arose out of its power and competitive features with relation to the various state banks that began to be chartered about this time throughout the different commonwealths. Private enterprise was just getting started, and the field of private banking appeared to offer brilliant rewards to the clever and courageous entrepreneurs of that day.

Comparatively little cash capital was needed to start a state bank, and no adequate system of supervision existed to fetter the directors or cause them undue annoyance. Without being in any way dishonest, a small amount of capital employed in a state institution might with good luck be made to yield large returns. As long, however, as the Government supported one big national bank, the opportunities of state banks were bound to be considerably curtailed. The national institution would undoubtedly exercise a dominating influence in the entire banking field. If capably managed it might be able through its note issues to control the currency and through its lending policy, it could unquestionably enlarge or restrict the credit facilities of the country almost at will.

It is not hard to see, therefore, why so many people became more and more opposed to the Bank of the United States, and it is not to be wondered at that, with this popular sentiment constantly increasing, the Anti-Federalist Party, which had never been favorable to the bank, became vigorously and actively opposed to it.

Thomas Jefferson became President in 1802, and with his inauguration the Anti-Federalist Party took over the administration of the United States. Albert J. Gallatin, the financial genius of the new party, was selected by Jefferson as his Secretary of the Treasury, and he went into office pledged to carry out a policy of strict economy and to pay off the national debt as rapidly as possible. Gallatin was Secretary of the Treasury not only during the two terms of President Jefferson, but throughout most of the incumbency of President Madison. As a result of his experience in that highly responsible office, we may note a decided change in his attitude towards the Bank of the United States and in his policy with regard to it.

Official responsibility tends to sober any man and make him more conservative than ever before, and Gallatin was no exception to the general rule. It was not long before his former political opposition to the bank faded away, and in its place came realization of the service it rendered to the government;

this service he immediately sought to employ for the common good.

Jefferson viewed Gallatin's growing appreciation of the bank with considerable distrust, and he is said to have indicated very plainly to his Secretary that so far as it was possible to do so, he wanted him to favor the various state banks with Government deposits. Gallatin, however, though never disloyal to his chief, was stubbornly unwilling to sacrifice what he considered to be the best interests of the United States to the exigencies of local politics.

It is to Gallatin's credit that while he risked his own standing with his party to defend the Bank of the United States, as Secretary of the Treasury he borrowed less from that institution than any of his predecessors. To him the pledge of economy which he had made to the people was no light promise, and throughout his long career in the Treasury, he steadfastly endeavored to make his pledge good. The wonder is, however, that he succeeded in doing so to the extent that he did. The records show that only once did Gallatin apply to the bank for a loan.

The agitation against the bank increased by leaps and bounds after Jefferson became President. Finally, three years before the bank's charter would expire by limitation of law, its friends determined that the thing to do was to put the question of renewal squarely before Congress without delay, so that if the bank was not to be rechartered the general business of the country would be as little affected as possible by the refusal.

Accordingly, a petition for a renewal of the charter was presented to the House of Representatives on March 6, 1808, and referred to the Committee of the Whole. In the Senate the petition came up on April 20, 1808, and was referred to Gallatin as Secretary of the Treasury for consideration and report. This reference put Gallatin in a very delicate situa-

tion, one in which a man who possessed less moral courage
than he would have been inclined to equivocate. It was clear
to Gallatin that if he strongly favored a renewal of the bank's
charter he would antagonize most of the leaders and practically all of the rank and file of his own political party,
whereas if he failed to do so, he would be lacking in his
sworn duty as Secretary of the Treasury of the United States.
In this critical juncture, Gallatin did not hesitate, but on March
3, 1809, submitted his report to the Senate, which strongly
advocated a renewal of the bank's charter and gave the Secretary's reasons for such a recommendation.

In this report Gallatin laid great stress on the usefulness
of the bank to the Government by reason of its lending capacity and upon its further usefulness in caring for the public
moneys and transmitting them throughout the country, as
well as the services rendered by it in collecting the federal
revenue and stabilizing the currency.

Notwithstanding the favorable report of the Secretary, the
bank's opponents continued their campaign against its recharter. It was vigorously urged that most of the bank's capital was held abroad, and that its profits benefited foreigners
instead of citizens of the United States. It was further urged
that the bank was constantly growing in power and would
soon become a financial colossus which would dominate the
country and crush the poor in the interests of the wealthy.
Gallatin pointed out that the very fact that so much of the
capital was held abroad was an argument in favor of renewing the charter, because if it were not renewed more than
$7,000,000 must be sent abroad almost immediately, which
would prove a serious strain for a country in the financial position which the United States then occupied.

The trouble was that Congress was in the control of the
Anti-Federalist Party, and the question of the bank's recharter had become a strictly party issue, which meant that neither

party was capable of dealing with it without intense passion and prejudice, so that the outcome was a foregone conclusion. On April 17, 1810, a bill was introduced providing for a renewal of the bank's charter. This bill, however, never got past the Committee of the Whole in the House. Nothing further was done, although a good deal of talk was indulged in by both sides, until finally, three months before the expiration of the charter, another petition was submitted to Congress by the stockholders, asking for a renewal. This was on December 18, 1810, and a bitter debate immediately ensued.

Gallatin almost alone of the Anti-Federalists leaders continued his loyal support of the bank. The Federalists, of course, fought for it as hard as they could, and there was also a thorough mobilization of sentiment on the part of the merchants and the business men of the country in favor of a recharter. However, the bank's friends were unable to save it, although the vote in Congress was as close as it well could be.

The bill providing for a renewal of the charter was defeated in the House because a motion to postpone the renewal indefinitely was carried by one vote; in the Senate the vote was tied 17 to 17. This left the deciding vote to Clinton, who was the Vice-President and one of Gallatin's personal enemies. Without hesitation, the Vice-President voted against the renewal, and the First Bank of the United States passed from the stage of history.

The result showed how unfortunate and ill-timed the action of Congress was. The charter of the bank expired in 1811; the next year the country was engulfed by the War of 1812, when it needed the national bank more desperately than at any time since the Revolution.

As Secretary of the Treasury, Gallatin was expected to find the funds with which to win the war, and he had no national bank to aid him in borrowing the large sums needed to carry on the conflict. Moreover, no banking institution was sufficiently powerful to maintain the credit of the country during the war period, or to prevent the stringency in the currency which almost immediately followed. In August, 1814, the leading banks of the country suspended specie payments, and thereafter conditions were chaotic until some time after the close of the war.

Between 1811 and 1816 the state banks increased from 88 to 246. It was a wide open season of unsupervised banking. Loans were unduly expanded, credit was strained. In addition, the war, which was extremely unpopular in New England, disrupted the credit situation and created a condition of affairs with which even the strongest state banks were utterly unable to cope. The credit demands of the war period and of the reconstruction era which followed it, caused a tremendous expansion of the notes of the state banking institutions, and the wide sales of public land in the South and West brought with them a pyramiding of loans which was detrimental to credit and paved the way for eventual disaster.

It is therefore little to be wondered at that, when the conservative citizens of the country took stock of the situation sometime after the close of the War of 1812, a new and insistent demand for the reestablishment of a national bank became evident on all sides.

The outcome was that in 1816 a bill providing for the chartering of a new bank of the United States was put through Congress with little opposition, and with a general belief that it was high time to return to an institution which had so thoroughly proved its value and which had been so greatly missed.

CHAPTER X

ANDREW JACKSON AND NICHOLAS BIDDLE— THE FIGHT OVER THE BANK

IF THE career of the First National Bank was stormy, that of its successor was marked by a series of battles from the beginning to the end of its existence.

The only time when the Second National Bank enjoyed comparative tranquillity was at the start, when the lessons of the War of 1812 were still fresh in the minds of all, and a genuine desire for a strong central banking institution pervaded all classes of society. Even Henry Clay, who in 1811 had opposed the bank, now supported the application for a new charter as highly necessary under existing conditions.

Accordingly, on April 10, 1816, the Second National Bank Act was passed, the provisions of which were as follows: the capital of the bank was to be $35,000,000, one-fifth of which was to be subscribed by the Government, which was to pay for it in coin or in 5 per cent stock. Other subscriptions were payable one-fourth in coin and the remainder in coin or "stock" of the United States. There were to be twenty-five directors, five of them to be appointed by the President and the others elected by the stockholders. The bank was to keep the public money and to aid the Government without charge in negotiating its loans.

Branches could be established and notes issued in any denomination not below five dollars. These notes were to be receivable for all payments due to the United States. No other bank outside the District of Columbia was to be established by Congress during the continuance of the charter. In con-

169

sideration of the exclusive privileges and benefits conferred, the bank was required to pay a bonus to the Government of $500,000 annually for three years beginning after the end of the second year of its existence. Under its charter the bank was to continue for twenty years.

When it started, the bank incurred a difficulty which the First National Bank did not have to face. It had to overcome a great many bad banking habits which had been contracted by the people of this country during the five-year interregnum between the two national banks. Business men had become accustomed to unreliable and insecure state currency, and they were used to injudicious loans. Money had been easy, and no one liked to settle in specie. The tendency was to consider anything like conservative banking in the nature of business persecution, and hence we must not blame the management of the Second National Bank too severely if in the beginning it failed to conduct its affairs as strictly and carefully as it should have done.

The bank really went through several distinct periods during the twenty years of its existence. The first period ran from 1816 to 1818, during which time an undistinguished person by the name of Jones was president of the bank. Then ensued another two-year period when a far more notable individual, Langdon Cheves, of South Carolina, assumed the presidency, and did much to initiate a conservative policy. The third period ran from 1822 to 1836, and covered the presidency of Nicholas Biddle.

From 1822 to 1829, Biddle, much more progressive than Cheves, ruled the bank with honesty and conservatism, and owing largely to his efforts, the reputation of the institution was established and its business much expanded. But the period from 1829 to 1836 was the stormiest of the bank's career. It was during these closing years, for the charter expired in 1836, that the Democratic Party under the lead of Andrew

Jackson, one of the most picturesque of all our Presidents, attacked the bank in full force and eventually succeeded in preventing its recharter.

The earliest days of the bank were marked by a deplorable gambling in its capital stock. The charter allowed stock subscriptions to be paid in installments, which made it possible for speculators to deal extensively in the stock of the institution. From April, 1817, to December 1 of the same year, the price of the bank stock fluctuated continuously and with a wide range. For instance, on April 1, 1817, it was quoted at $118; on July 10, $154; and on December 1, $114; about two years later, in July, 1819, it had fallen to $92.50.

This speculative arrangement was much aided by the directors of the bank, who adopted a resolution allowing stockholders to discount their personal notes on the security of the bank stock. In this way no specie was actually paid in as required by the charter, but by bookkeeping entries the bank lent the purchasers the money with which to pay for its own stock.

It was not long before the policy of establishing numerous branches at strategic points throughout the country was in full swing. In all, twenty-nine branch banks were established, and although in theory each one of the branches enjoyed a certain degree of autonomy, yet as a matter of fact, especially under the presidency of Biddle, the branches were rather strictly controlled by the central bank at Philadelphia, particularly on the question of note issues and branch drafts. Although Biddle never admitted the fact, the parent bank at no time was able entirely to control the branches with regard to these matters, and eventually this led to a condition of inflation which gave the bank's enemies one of their strongest arguments against it.

Another feature of this early period was the initiation of the so-called "Race Horse Bills." These were bills sent from one branch to another for collection, and owing to general indisposition to pay would not be settled but instead the debtor would meet the obligation by drawing a bill on another branch bank. In this way the debt would be passed from branch to branch, in some cases almost indefinitely. In addition to such grotesque performances, the bank during the first three years of its existence continually over-issued its notes and loaned large sums of money on insufficient security. As a matter of fact, in its early days the principal distinction between the Bank of the United States and the more reputable state banks was one of size, because the national bank was as speculative in its policy as the state banks themselves.

In 1819 it was realized by the private stockholders and the officials of the Government that drastic action would have to be taken if the bank was to be saved and kept in a solvent condition. It was at this difficult time that Langdon Cheves of South Carolina, a man of good standing and a banker of ability, was chosen president. It cannot be said that Cheves rendered distinguished service to the bank, but at least he had the sense and the courage to apply the brakes. The trouble was that he put on the brakes too hard. His cautious and even timorous policy resulted in a too rapid contraction of the bank's notes in circulation, and such a reduction in loans that the volume of business was cut down, to the detriment of legitimate borrowers and against the interests of the bank's depositors.

In 1819 the country experienced a serious financial and industrial depression. It was not caused by the national bank or the state banks, although the loose manner in which they had been conducted certainly contributed towards it. The seeds of the trouble were to be found, however, in the rapid growth of the country, especially in the manufacturing industries which had sprung up like mushrooms from the time of the Embargo and Non-intercourse Acts, and particularly after the War of 1812. Moreover, there had been much speculation in lands, and the optimism of a pioneer people had led to over-confidence and consequently to over-extension of all types of enterprise. It was the same old story which has been told many times since in the history of our country. The result was a period of great hardship, with many factories closed, farms abandoned, and people out of work. This of course was immediately reflected in the condition of all the banks of the country, and the Bank of the United States felt the hard times with special rigor, because of the mistakes it had made in the recent past.

It was at this time that a new and commanding figure appeared upon the scene. The old City of Philadelphia has given many able men to the Republic, but she never produced a more elegant or romantic figure than Nicholas Biddle, or "Czar Nicholas," as he was known to his friends and contemporaries.

Mr. Biddle was born in Philadelphia, January 8, 1786, springing from one of the most distinguished families in the community. He was educated at the University of Pennsylvania and at Princeton, graduating from the latter institution in 1801 at the head of his class. He studied law, but did not practice it long. In 1804, General Armstrong, then Minister to France, made him his private secretary, and from that year until 1807, he was in the diplomatic service abroad. Thereafter he travelled extensively throughout Europe, and on his return to Philadelphia he resumed the practice of law, although he devoted himself more particularly to literary pursuits. He was elected to the state legislature and distinguished himself in that body. In 1819 he was appointed a Government director of the Bank of the United States by President Monroe, and in 1822 he was elected president of the bank.

When Biddle became connected with the great institution which was to constitute his claim to a place in history, in

1819, he was but thirty-three years of age. Nevertheless he had given early promise of a brilliant career; he was well educated according to the standards of those days, and he had won the confidence of the President through an acquaintance which had begun some years before when Monroe was our Minister to England, and young Biddle was attached to the French embassy.

Biddle's letter to Monroe upon receiving the news of his appointment is interesting and worth quoting in full:

PHILA., Jan. 31, 1819.

My Dear Sir,

I have received by this day's mail your letter of the 29th announcing your having nominated me one of the directors of the Bank of the U. S. I need not say that I consider this remembrance a proof of that uniform kindness and friendship on your part which I value so highly, and as such I beg you to accept my thanks for it. I have, however, little concern with Banks & have hitherto declined sharing in the management of the institution when it was proposed to me by the stockholders. Yet I am unwilling to avoid any duty by which you think I can be of service. The truth is, that with all its faults, the Bank is of vital importance to the finance of the Govt. and an object of great interest to the community. That it has been perverted to selfish purposes can not be doubted— that it may—& must—be renovated is equally certain. But they who undertake to reform abuses & particularly of that description, must encounter much hostility & submit to much labor. To these the hope of being useful can alone reconcile me—and if I should undertake the task I shall endeavor to persevere till the character of the institution is re-established.[1]

These brave words of youth were indeed prophetic and seem pathetic when read today. Biddle did indeed encounter much hostility and submitted to the greatest labor in his long years of service as president of the bank.

If he was over-bearing and opinionated, he was honest and

[1] Reginald C. McGrane, "The Correspondence of Nicholas Biddle," p. 12.

NICHOLAS BIDDLE

courageous; if he allowed the bank to become the football
of party politics, at least he never intended to do so; and if
he brought down upon his head the disapprobation of the
multitude, it was because he believed in the righteousness of
his cause and fearlessly faced a popular idol in the presidency,
a man whose character was as strong as his own and who
was equally fearless in any contest—Andrew Jackson, as picturesque as Roosevelt, as patriotic as Lincoln.

When Biddle became president, he found the bank's affairs
in a very chaotic condition. The methods of banking employed
were very loose, and one of the worst features was the free and
unrestricted issue of notes by the various state banks. Even
during the administration of Cheves, the national bank had
been accustomed, when making discounts, to reissue the notes
of the state banks instead of presenting them for collection.
Biddle changed all this and insisted on a weekly settlement of
all bank balances by the state banks, and instead of reissuing
the state banks' notes, issued instead notes of the Bank of the
United States.

Such a policy was fundamentally conservative. For the first
time it compelled the state banks to guard their note issues
with sedulous care, knowing that they must be settled for in
cash at frequent intervals. Of course, such a policy made its
author unpopular with all who were interested in the numerous state banks, but Biddle had a man's job to perform and
he intended to do it. It was his purpose to reform the United
States Bank from top to bottom, or as he put it in his letter to
Monroe, to "renovate" it, and this he did with courage and
expedition.

One result was that the inner differences in credit standing
between the various branches and the parent bank were
speedily ironed out, and within a short time the notes of one
branch were accepted without question by the other branches
and the parent bank. This in itself was a great step forward,

as in the early days there had been astonishing variations in the financial reliability of the branch banks.

We must remember that at this period, economic and financial conditions in the country were by no means stable and differed greatly between the different sections. The New England states and the East in general constituted the wealthy area. It had been settled the longest, and it contained almost all the manufacturing industries and nearly all the largest cities. On the other hand, the southern states and the great undeveloped western territory were filled with hustling pioneers who were busily engaged in building roads, digging canals, establishing towns, and in brief, planning a civilization in the forest and on the plains. Naturally, the branch banks in the North and East differed materially from those in the South and West, and the whole scope of business changed when this territory was left and the other invaded.

Thus from the beginning of Biddle's term there was a difficult problem which he had to solve. It was his task to afford banking facilities to the entire country, and the country's necessities and business methods differed greatly from one region to another. He must be all things to all men; he must endeavor to satisfy the conservative merchants of New York and Philadelphia, and at the same time be sufficiently progressive to extend credit and furnish a currency to the rough traders of Kentucky, and the planters of the Carolinas.

From the first, Biddle was troubled by the difficulty of supplying a well-regulated and stable currency. He could not trust this fundamental duty to any other agency than the Bank of the United States, and the law was so framed that it was very difficult for the bank to meet this vital need. Under the charter all the notes of the bank had to be signed by the president and countersigned by the cashier. Obviously the framers of the charter had never visioned the growth of the country, or believed that within a few short years it would be impossible for two officials to attempt to sign personally the great bulk of the paper money used by the people, yet this is exactly what occurred. With the curtailment of the state bank-notes, Biddle desired to initiate a policy of purchasing bills of domestic exchange with the notes of the bank, and in this way substitute the credit instruments of the institution for the obligations of individuals. The idea was excellent, but in order to accomplish it, it was apparent that Biddle and his cashier would be obliged to do nothing but sign bank-notes day and night.

Congress was appealed to upon several occasions, but for some reason which is difficult to ascertain, it stubbornly refused to allow anyone except the president and cashier of the bank to sign the notes. In 1818 the bank first requested remedial legislation in this regard, and the Senate passed a bill authorizing the appointment of a vice-president and deputy cashier for the purpose of signing the notes of the bank. The bill, however, was lost in the House. Once again in February, 1821, the Senate passed a similar bill and again the House refused to adopt it. Two more unsuccessful attempts were made, but Congress never consented to permit any change of this character in the original charter.

It is said, however, that there is no law so carefully drawn that it cannot be evaded in some way, and as Congress refused to give aid, a most ingenious method was evolved by which the language of the charter might be circumvented. The instrument employed to effect this result was known as the "branch draft." Just who was responsible does not appear, but whoever suggested it Biddle was quick to take advantage of the plan. First, however, he submitted the proposal to the ablest lawyers of that day, Daniel Webster and Horace Binney, and both of them agreed that branch drafts were entirely legal.

The machinery of the branch draft was by no means complicated. A branch bank would issue a draft, signed by its president or cashier, drawn on the cashier of the Philadelphia bank and made payable to some officer of the branch bank or his order. The officer in question then endorsed the draft payable to bearer, and in that way it became freely negotiable and could be used as currency all over the United States. The drafts were printed so that they closely resembled ordinary bank-notes, and during the period when they were current throughout the country few people ever realized the difference. They were credit instruments, based upon good security, and though somewhat informal, they were in effect money, and were universally so regarded. This ingenious system enabled Biddle to get around the narrow-minded and obstinate pose assumed by Congress, and furnished him with the means of giving to the country a substantial and sustainable currency, made and controlled by the Bank of the United States and its various branches.

During the early years of his administration, Nicholas Biddle administered the business of the bank with unusual ability and along strictly conservative lines. He insisted upon short-term loans, usually on good two-name paper, and he granted few extensions, kept his funds as liquid as possible, and restricted the loan period as far as he could to sixty or ninety days. That he was able to enforce such a policy throughout the many branches of the bank is extremely doubtful. It is certain, however, that he sincerely tried to do so.

The economic differences between the various parts of the country have already been explained, and early in his presidency Biddle was faced by the problem of controlling the bumptious and speculative tendencies of the southern and western branches. One of his principal methods of effecting such control was through the branch cashiers. These men were chosen and trained by the parent bank in Philadelphia, and were always kept in close touch with the central institution. They were made to feel that their first allegiance was to the big bank, and they acted as liaison officers between the bank itself and the officers and directors of the branches.

Gradually Biddle's policies were crowned with success, and after five or six years he was able to report a much-improved state of affairs. The currency had been stabilized and amplified by the judicious employment of the bank's notes and the drafts of its branches, and the chaotic credit condition which had existed by reason of the uncontrolled practices of the state banks was a thing of the past. Furthermore, the loans of the bank had been put on an excellent basis and had become far more liquid than they had ever been before, while on the other hand the legitimate business needs of the country were promptly met from the constantly increasing deposits for which the great bank had become the focal point. In brief, it had been a triumph for conservative and far-sighted banking practices, and Biddle had every right to feel just pride in the result of his early years in the office of president

Another side to the bank's business, however, was not as attractive in its characteristics. After a few years in the presidency, Biddle became less conservative than he had originally intended to be. This was not so much his fault as the fault of the times. Towards the close of the first quarter of the last century, the United States was expanding with rapidity and this expansion movement was principally towards the South and West. As usual, the resources of the East were called upon to finance the expansion, and great pressure was brought to bear upon Biddle and his officers to supply the necessary funds to develop the new territory which was being so quickly peopled by enterprising pioneers.

Biddle's plan for rendering aid was to work through the branches already established in the southern and western states, and so far as possible to allow these branches to do the business upon their own resources, merely supporting them from time to time as such assistance might actually be required. The plan was good, but its execution was faulty. Biddle apparently forgot that the officers of the branch banks were citizens of the new states and territories and imbued with the progressive and unconservative ideals which were held by all their neighbors. It seemed impossible to teach them that inflation was unwise, and that the pyramiding of loans was sure to result in disaster. Moreover, after 1830, a tremendous increase took place in transportation facilities, and this inevitably brought additional population and larger business opportunities in its train. This was the period when the earliest railroads were constructed, and a network of canals began to crisscross the more thickly settled parts of the country.

The bank would have been criticized severely if it had not done its share in promoting the wonderful rise of industry in the United States, especially as coincident with the prosperity of the country, and in a sense because of it, the bank at this time had more free money to lend than ever before in its history. By 1831 the Government had paid for its stock in the bank, and Biddle was looking around for good places to put the institution's funds. The result was that in spite of the careful methods adopted by Biddle when he first became president, and the conservatism of his general administration of the bank's affairs, he gradually allowed the bank and its branches to become heavily involved in southern and western loans, so that by 1832 the bank's lending capacity was severely taxed to support the volume of business which was being transacted by it in the South and West.

Meanwhile the institution was becoming more and more powerful, and acquiring yearly a large number of critical friends and out-spoken enemies. We must not forget in this connection that the bank had never been popular with the

Democratic Party.[2] Its predecessor, the First National Bank, had been strongly opposed by Thomas Jefferson and James Madison, the Democratic leaders of that day. Their successors in the party had no greater love for a corporation which they sincerely believed, in spite of the decision of the Supreme Court, to be without Constitutional warrant. At the time the leading case was decided, John Marshall had for some time been Chief Justice, and the Jeffersonians always had regarded him as the head devil of the Federalist Party, and never had put the least faith in anything he said, even when he spoke officially on behalf of the Supreme Court. It may be said that so far as the Democrats were concerned, Marshall may have silenced them but he never convinced them.

Besides doubting the constitutionality of the bank, the Democrats regarded it as a soulless monopoly and a particular instrument of the wealthy classes. They believed that through its more than a score of branches it was reaching out over the land like a gigantic spider, endeavoring to catch all the poor people in its mighty net, and hence they were against it and entertained a strong desire to get rid of it. It mattered not to them that it frequently aided the Government by substantial loans, and that it was also of great assistance in transmitting the Government's money and collecting its import duties. The fact that it controlled and stabilized the currency, and indeed through its notes furnished a great deal of the better type of currency which the people enjoyed, left them cold. They argued that state banks under proper supervision could accomplish every end attained by the Bank of the United States with less expense and much less danger to the poorer citizens of the country, and they refused to concede that the

[2] It should be remembered that by now the Anti-Federalist or Republican Party had changed its name to that of Democratic Party, which it was to retain up to the present day. There was to be no Republican Party, as far as name was concerned, until the descendants of the Whigs were to espouse the name in the election of Abraham Lincoln to the office of chief executive.

national bank was really a valuable aid in administering the financial affairs of the United States.

This general feeling against the bank did not occur suddenly but, rising from small beginnings, gradually increased until, by the time the bank had become about fifteen years old, it represented the deep-seated opinion of a numerical majority of the inhabitants of most of the states. It did not include the professional and merchant classes, and therefore did not represent the public opinion of the ruling groups, but it was nevertheless the belief held by the great masses of the people and at that time these masses were struggling mightily to control the machinery of government, in which attempt they were destined before long to succeed.

In 1828 a real dyed-in-the-wool Democrat was elected President of the United States for the first time in its history. This is said with due appreciation of the fact that Thomas Jefferson founded the party. Nevertheless it must be remembered that Jefferson was a man of good family, who, starting life as a Federalist, developed his Democratic theories during his later years, whereas Jackson was the son of a poor tenant farmer, had no educational advantages, and fought his own way from the time he was a small boy, without help or assistance from any persons of standing in the community.

Of all the picturesque characters that have enriched our country's history, Andrew Jackson is probably the most unique and colorful. He captured the imagination of his contemporaries, just as did his eminent successor, Theodore Roosevelt, more than half a century later.

Jackson was an old man when he was elected President. He was sixty-one, and he had led a life of constant hardship and turmoil. Born practically on the dividing line between North and South Carolina, he emigrated to Tennessee while still a young man, and having studied law in the incomplete and desultory manner which was characteristic of those days,

Underwood & Underwood

ANDREW JACKSON

he became prosecuting attorney and subsequently judge of the Superior Court of Tennessee. This was in Jackson's youth, and Tennessee at that time was a frontier state, inhabited by the roughest and toughest kind of frontiersmen. It may not mean much today to say that a man has been prosecuting attorney and judge, but in those days such offices could be successfully administered only by men of tried courage and strong personality.

In 1802 while still a judge in Tennessee, Jackson was elected major-general of the state militia, and thus began his military career. He had had no previous military experience so far as is known, but his life had been one of constant combat. He was always engaged in some kind of a brawl, and his turbulent character and violent temper, added to his ability to shoot straight and with uncanny accuracy, made him a foe to be feared. He fought several duels, the most famous of which was with Charles Dickenson, a prominent man who had insulted his wife. This occurred on May 30, 1806. Although badly wounded himself he managed to kill Dickenson.

Subsequently in 1813 came the Creek War, which was really the foundation of Jackson's military fame. He was forty-seven years old at the time, in poor health, and he had led a rough, hard life from his earliest years. The Creek campaign became a series of quarrels with other officers, battles with the enemy, and finally triumphs on the part of Jackson. The Creeks were a brave tribe and put up a good fight, but Jackson pursued them from one place to another, reducing their strongholds, and driving them back with relentless eagerness, until at last he wiped out all armed opposition. As a result of this campaign, he was made major-general in the regular army, and placed in command of the Department of the South.

Meanwhile, the War of 1812 came on, and Jackson was in a splendid position to reap great benefit from it. On January 8, 1815, the Battle of New Orleans was fought. It was a hot fight, and Jackson won a complete victory. The British General Pakenham was killed, and their losses were very heavy, amounting to two thousand killed and wounded, whereas of Jackson's forces only seven were killed and six wounded. Curiously enough the battle was fought three weeks after the Treaty of Peace had been signed, but communication was so poor in those days that no one knew about it.

Nothing could have been more fortunate for Jackson's future than the Battle of New Orleans. It came at the end of an unfortunate and unpopular war. Almost all the American victories had been at sea. Washington had been burned, Hull had surrendered, and the people as a whole were disgusted with the military result of the struggle. Then after it was over, along came General Jackson, and in a post-mortem fight, so to speak, gave the British a terrible drubbing and restored everyone's self-respect. It was a great day for a great man, and the General's future was assured. It made no difference that he was ignorant of economics and statescraft, that he quarrelled constantly, and was obstinate, violent, and self-willed. Indeed, nothing made any difference except that he had defeated the British in the most signal victory of the War of 1812, and was already regarded as a national hero. He continued his military operations in 1818 by putting down the Seminole insurrection in Florida. In 1823 he was elected to the Senate of the United States by the Legislature of Tennessee.

He seems to have made little impression during his brief service in the Senate, but his place in the affections of the people was already secure. He was a serious contender for the presidential nomination in 1825, seven states voting for him, thirteen for Adams, and four for Crawford. After that election he exhibited the greatest rancor when Henry Clay was made Secretary of State by John Quincy Adams, claiming that the appointment was evidence of a corrupt bargain between the two men which had resulted in his own defeat for the presidency. Like many other theories of the General, there is good reason to doubt its accuracy. Nevertheless, by this time Jackson was a national character and a popular leader. He had gathered around him the great mass of the poorer people in the country, and he was their hero, almost their god. The very characteristics which repelled the educated classes constituted his strongest claims to the loyalty and affections of the lower orders of society. So it was that at the end of John Quincy Adams's term, Jackson found the great opportunity of his life, and with the enthusiastic backing of the common people he was triumphantly elected President of the United States.

Andrew Jackson gave the country many surprises during his two terms as President, but he seldom caused a greater stir than when in the course of his first message to Congress in December, 1829, he made the bald statement that many people doubted the constitutionality and expediency of the law creating the Bank of the United States, and went on to say that the bank had failed in its principal purpose, which was to establish a uniform and sound currency. He then vaguely suggested that it would be far better to have a national bank as a branch of the Treasury Department, which should be empowered to accept public and private deposits, but would not be authorized to make loans or purchase property. In this way, he indicated, the bank would retain its principal advantages without having the power to oppress the people.[3]

Looking backward, it seems clear that at this particular time Jackson was not as hostile to the bank as he appeared to be. Indeed, we can now perceive quite well the reasons which impelled him to raise the issue in his first message. In those days, however, public men were not distinguished by

[3] Davis R. Dewey, "Financial History of the United States," p. 200.

any considerable sense of humor and they made the mistake of taking the old Indian fighter far too seriously.

The reference to the bank included in the President's message caused an inquiry to be made into the affairs of the institution in both Houses of Congress, and the committees of both the House and the Senate made reports highly favorable to the bank in which they discussed in great detail its constitutionality, expediency, and value to the country, thereby calling attention to the attack upon it by the President, and lending a great deal of dignity to what it is probable Jackson intended to be nothing more than a smoke screen.

In order to understand the President's point of view, we must recall the political situation which existed in 1828. At that time and for many years thereafter, the huge western territory which was fast filling up with emigrants and from which new states and territories were constantly being formed, constituted the balance of power between the older commonwealths of the North and South. These two groups of the original states were hopelessly divided on almost all political and economic questions. They never had agreed on such issues, and as the country was then in its fourth decade, their leaders had decided that they probably never would agree. It was not only the question of slavery which divided them, although that was the issue over which they eventually went to war. They did not agree about the tariff; they were at odds over the bank; they were divided upon the question as to how far the Federal Government ought to go in promoting and financing internal improvements in the states—and in fact they were opposed to each other on almost every point which came up for decision by the Congress. Such being the case, both North and South wooed the West, and the West was coy.

The great need in the new states was for internal improvements, and these they kept demanding constantly from Congress. Generally speaking, the North was opposed to the expenditure of much money by the Government for such a purpose, while the South was willing to support such a policy. The North, however, strongly advocated a protective tariff to which the South was bitterly opposed, even to the point in some instances of nullification. In certain parts of the West there was considerable sympathy with a protective-tariff policy, and taken as a whole, the West was nationalistic in spirit and ready to support the North against the South on this issue.

It may be seen therefore that when Jackson became President the biggest issue before the country was that of the tariff, and the question of federal aid in the internal improvements of the states was only secondary to it in importance and vital interest.

Jackson, when elected, represented no organized party. His strength was largely personal and was due to his war record and his picturesque personal qualities which appealed strongly to the rough-and-ready citizens of that day. The very fact that he had drawn support from so many different groups of men was certain to cause him embarrassment as soon as he entered the presidential office and found it necessary to formulate and maintain a consistent policy therein. Jackson was no fool, and in spite of his ill temper and manifold prejudices, he possessed one of the keenest minds of any of our presidents. He usually knew what he wanted, and he also knew how to obtain it. He was a great bluffer and played to the galleries constantly and with consummate art. Even his violent temper was largely assumed. Indeed, he told his intimate friends that he was seldom as angry as he appeared to be, but he found it very useful to make people think he was. He went on the principle that it was far better to be feared than loved, and it must be admitted that he "got away with it."

Jackson knew very well that if he took a strong position on the tariff or with regard to internal improvements, he would alienate a large body of his followers, no matter which view he chose to advocate. He came from Tennessee, and many of his supporters lived in the southwest and were bitterly opposed to a tariff of even moderate proportions. On the other hand, he was idolized by the great mass of voters in the manufacturing state of Pennsylvania, and they all believed in the tariff as though it were an article of religion. The same situation existed in a general way with regard to the question of internal improvements. Faced therefore by this diversity of opinion among his own followers, Jackson looked around to find some issue upon which he could take a bold stand in agreement with the great mass of his party, and he believed that in attacking the bank he had found just the issue that he desired. So far as he knew, nobody cared much for the bank except the wealthy merchants of the North and East and the members of the professional class. Inasmuch as all these people had always disliked him intensely, and voted against him whenever they had the opportunity, the old man thought that it was perfectly fair to attack them through their beloved bank, and in doing so announce a firm policy which would cause a big stir and divert attention from the tariff and internal improvements which he was afraid to touch.

That he ever intended to go much further in attacking the greatest financial institution in the country, there is certainly room to doubt. It is true that he did not like banks because on one occasion he had acted as an accommodation endorser and signed a number of promissory notes to aid a friend, without in all probability understanding the legal consequence of such an act. The friend became bankrupt and Jackson had to pay all the notes, for which he had never received a cent in return. This little incident in his past would seem to account for his general hatred of banks and banking. He never understood what a bank was or its purpose in the economic scheme, but he did understand that if it had not been for a bank he would never have had to pay a large sum of money, which in his opinion he did not owe, and it was impossible to argue a man of Jackson's meager education out of such an attitude of mind.

However, he was far too canny to initiate a serious fight against the Bank of the United States unless he was really forced to do so. He knew the tremendous power which the institution had acquired during a period of thirteen years, and he also knew that the business interests of the country would rally solidly behind it in case of an assault. Therefore it is highly probable that had Jackson's reference to the bank in his first message been ignored by the bank's friends, nothing further would have come of the matter.

It was not ignored, however, and for an excellent reason which was also political—Henry Clay, the great Whig leader, was consumed with ambition to be President, and he believed that in attacking the national bank, Andrew Jackson had put himself completely in his power.

What of Nicholas Biddle, however, the high-bred and forceful president of the institution, and his group of smug, self-satisfied directors? Did they not have something to say about what should be done at such a critical hour? Yes, they had a great deal to say about it, but they were in the hands of the Philistines.

Had they rested content with the favorable congressional reports regarding the bank which were submitted in the spring of 1830 and bided their time for several years, there is little doubt that they could have obtained a new charter without exciting the strenuous opposition of the President or his friends. True it is that certain individual members of the Senate and the House kept up a campaign of sniping at the bank which was irritating although not dangerous. In 1831, Thomas Benton, the able representative of Missouri in the Senate, introduced a resolution prohibiting the recharter of the bank and supported it with a brilliant address. This need not have unduly disturbed its friends, however, or its officials. Benton had always opposed the bank, and in his attack upon it represented no large number of his party associates.

All this time, however, Henry Clay had been casting about for some issue upon which he could defeat Jackson and his mongrel horde of ragged supporters, for so he regarded the crude, strong, and young Democracy. Clay was a brilliant man, but egotistical and very selfish. He was a born leader, and he gathered to himself the ablest Whigs in the Senate and the House, compelling them to serve his ends with unswerving devotion. He was a martinet when it came to party discipline, and cracked the whip whenever he deemed it necessary to bring his followers into line.

Clay had associated with him in his venture, Daniel Webster, the greatest orator of the day. Though Webster originally had opposed Clay in 1816 on the question of the reestablishment of the national bank, he since then had come to realize the important services which it rendered to the country. Moreover, he disliked Jackson even more than he did the political chicanery of the great compromiser. Consequently these two men, Clay and Webster, with many others of the same faction, brought great pressure to bear upon Nicholas Biddle and his associates, in order to induce them to petition Congress for a recharter so that the bank issue might be squarely before that body prior to the presidential election of 1832.

Biddle's correspondence and numerous other contemporary records show that the directors of the bank and Biddle himself were in doubt as to the proper course to pursue at this time. They must have known that they were taking a long chance in allowing the recharter of the bank to become a partisan question and a leading political issue, but unquestionably they feared that, if they refused to obey Clay's command, he and his Whig friends would withdraw their support from the

bank, or at least cease to back it with the enthusiasm which
they had hitherto shown.

It was an ugly situation and a hard position to occupy. It
was indeed a problem for Biddle to make up his mind what
was best to do. In this dilemma he sent Mr. Thomas Cad-
wallader, one of his most trusted lieutenants and a director
of the bank, to Washington, and kept him there for some
time in order to feel out congressional sentiment and keep
him informed with regard to the progress of the affair. Cad-
wallader apparently reported that the only course to pursue
was to petition for a recharter, so finally, with misgivings, a
petition for a recharter was introduced in Congress during
January, 1832, and was favorably reported upon by committees
of the Senate and the House of Representatives. Another committee of investigation was appointed, and although on this
occasion, because of the political nature of the question, there
was a strong minority report, nevertheless the majority of
the committee reported in favor of renewing the charter, and
in due course the bill granting a renewal was passed by both
houses of Congress.

Henry Clay was delighted at the result. He reasoned that,
if President Jackson failed to veto the bill for a recharter, he
would be inconsistent with the policy he had already strongly
outlined, whereas, if he did veto the measure, he would place
himself in opposition to all the conservative and wealthy citizens of the United States. He would antagonize the professional men and the large and powerful mercantile class and
would ensure his defeat at the coming election.

Undoubtedly Jackson was just as fully aware of the trap
which Clay had laid for him as was that gentleman himself,
but the good old fighter never flinched when put to the test.
It was not likely that the man who had emerged unscathed
from a dozen duels and rough-and-tumble fights and who
had defeated the British at New Orleans from behind a flimsy

barricade of cotton bales, would show any lack of courage when faced with a moral issue, even though failure to gauge the public mind with regard to it would entail the loss of the presidency.

On July 10, 1832, President Jackson vetoed the bill providing for a recharter of the Bank of the United States. In the course of his veto message, which was a strong and ably written state paper, he commented upon the growing power of the bank in opposition to the rights of the people and seriously adverted to the existence of a large body of foreign stockholders, whose very existence might prove a serious danger to the country in time of war. He painted the national bank as a huge, grasping, unprincipled monopoly of money which was already a crushing weight upon the honest but ambitious poor, and which would in time be a weapon of the favored classes to be used in defeating the will of the common people.

Of course, most of Jackson's statements were nonsense, but they were highly effective in the places where they were intended to be read, namely, in the homes of the great majority of the voting public.

The campaign of 1832 was an extremely bitter one, and was fought with the most unrelenting vigor by both sides. Clay attempted to foster a third party by taking advantage of a sporadic movement against Masonry. Accordingly, his friend William Wirt was nominated by the Anti-Masonic party, the idea being that he would draw largely from the Jackson vote in certain states. Clay might have saved himself this trouble, however, for when the election was held, it resulted in an overwhelming victory for the hero of New Orleans, or "Old Hickory" as by that time he was affectionately called by his adoring followers.

In the electoral college, Jackson got 219 votes, Clay 49, Wirt 7, and Floyd of South Carolina obtained the 11 votes of that state. The popular vote was 707,217 for Andrew Jackson against 328,561 for Henry Clay, and 254,720 for William Wirt. Jackson's total majority, leaving out South Carolina which practically cast a blank by voting for Floyd, was 123,936. These figures, although they appear small at the present time, were surprisingly large in 1832.

The event proved that Clay and the Whigs had completely under-estimated Jackson's strength with the people. They fell into the error of believing that the prominent classes were the controlling group in a democracy. This can never be the case where manhood suffrage exists and the people are intelligent and courageous. The citizens of the country in 1832 did not really care a pin what Andrew Jackson's position was with regard to the Bank of the United States. They did not understand the bank any better than he did, but they did understand him. They knew he was honest, fearless, and sincere. The fact that he had no social graces, had enjoyed little education, and was sneered at by the landed aristocrats, were all arguments in his favor with almost all those who voted for him. He was a popular idol, and nothing he did was wrong. If he did not want the bank, they did not want it. If he did want it, let him have it. The result was not surprising to any man who knew the temper of the American people in 1832.

Henry Clay did not know it, and he failed in his highest ambition as a result. Andrew Jackson was fully aware of it, and he entered his second term with a glow of satisfaction and imbued with the firm belief that the American people had given him written instructions to wipe the bank off the face of the earth. It was a great misfortune for the country, and incidentally for Biddle and his friends, that the old man in the White House should have felt as he did after the election of 1832, but it was something that could not be helped because the die had been cast.

Jackson's next move in his war against the bank was not

long delayed. He made up his mind that the bank and its managers were unworthy of any confidence, and he conceived the idea that it was his duty as President to see to it that the deposits of the funds of the United States were removed from the bank as quickly as possible. In arriving at this conclusion, the President was not entirely without justification.

True it is that from time to time in the course of his numerous messages and attacks upon the institution he brought forward many baseless accusations and indeed made a number of ridiculous statements in an effort to undermine the institution and place it in a poor position before the country. On the other hand, several things had occurred since the beginning of the bank war which, when fairly examined, reflected but little credit upon Nicholas Biddle and his fellow directors.

In the first place, it was entirely true that the bank had favored a good many politicians with loans and various other financial accommodations. It was also a fact that the bank had spent a great deal of money in written propaganda in support of its petition for a recharter, even going so far at one time as to have printed thirty thousand copies of a pamphlet which were distributed broadcast throughout the country. Obviously it was no sin for the bank to state its case in the best possible manner to the public, but there was a real question as to the extent to which the funds of the bank should be expended for such a purpose. It may readily be believed that Andrew Jackson made the most of this seemingly political activity on the part of the institution when he began his efforts to remove the public deposits.

Another incident connected with the bank also greatly enraged the President. One of the cardinal issues in Jackson's conduct of foreign relations was to compel France to pay the debt it had owed to the United States for a good many years as a result of injuries to our commerce during the period of

the Napoleonic Wars. As a result of his well-thought-out
scheme to make France pay, Jackson, acting through his Secretary of the Treasury, drew a draft upon France through the
Bank of the United States for nearly a million dollars on account. This draft was dishonored, since France refused to pay
it, and Biddle immediately claimed damages in the amount
of $15,000 for the injury to the bank involved in the protest
of the draft. This greatly angered the President, who refused
to pay any damages whatever, and his refusal resulted in a
long-drawn out law suit which the bank eventually lost.

Then came the trouble over the 3 per cents. In 1832, the Secretary of the Treasury informed the bank that it was the
purpose of the Government to pay off a large portion of its
remaining debt amounting to approximately $6,000,000, which
was outstanding in the form of 3 per cent Government bonds.
Biddle opposed such action and even went so far as to swallow his pride and interview the President personally on the
subject. This interview really frightened Jackson more than
anything Biddle had ever done, for soon afterwards he said
to a friend: "I tell you, sir, she's broke. Mr. Biddle is a proud
man and he never would have come on to Washington to ask
me for a postponement if the bank had had the money. Therefore, sir, the bank's broke, and Biddle knows it." Of course,
the fact was that the bank was not "broke" at all, but Biddle
was strongly opposed to realizing enough cash from its resources to make such a large payment, which he regarded as
unnecessary and unwise. In stating his position, however, Biddle made the mistake of adding a very foolish reason to some
pretty good ones. It was all right to state that $9,000,000 of duty
bonds would be payable on July 1, and as six millions additional cash had to be raised in the same month, business conditions would be greatly disturbed. That was true. But to
go on to state that an epidemic of cholera was feared and
that the people would need ready cash to combat such a

national affliction was so silly that even schoolboys could hardly be expected to believe it. Jackson certainly did not, and he went ahead with his efforts to pay off the national debt with the added belief that the bank was in actual danger of financial collapse.

This was not all of the story, however, and the rest was considerable. The Treasury finally agreed to defer payment of $5,000,000 of the 3 per cent bonds until October 1, if the bank would pay the interest for the three months intervening. Biddle jumped at the offer, and immediately sent an emissary to England who worked in connection with Baring Brothers, the fiscal agent of the Bank of England, and started a campaign to extend as many of the 3 per cent bonds held abroad as possible, and to arrange to pay off only those holders who insisted upon it. This effort of Biddle's to retain the Government money for the bank's profit, because the Government bonds paid only 3 per cent and Biddle could make 7 per cent with the funds devoted to their payment, created a bad impression in the country as a whole, and many people who had up to that time been loyal adherents of the bank began to fail in their support.[4]

The time was therefore ripe for the action which Jackson had in mind. In order to carry it out the President was obliged to obtain the cooperation of his Secretary of the Treasury. This was necessary because, in the original act under which the bank was chartered, it was provided that the Government

[4] On March 24 Biddle was informally notified by the then acting Secretary of the Treasury that the Government would probably wish to use part of its deposits to retire the 3 per cents which were a remnant of the old funded revolutionary debt; and on July 25 the Secretary of the Treasury so notified Biddle formally.

But meanwhile Biddle had arranged secretly with Barings to extend as many of the bonds as possible and to buy up the rest, for the Second United States Bank. This was a violation of the charter of the United States Bank, which was prohibited from purchasing public securities. It was also a violation of the understanding with the Treasury. By this deal Biddle aimed to make the difference between 7 per cent, which was what deposit money was worth to the bank, and the 3 per cent payable on the bonds. See Horace White, "Money and Banking," pp. 284-285.

funds should be deposited with the bank by the Secretary of the Treasury, who could remove them for cause if he submitted his reasons to Congress in writing. Thus it will be perceived that contrary to the usual practice in the United States the Secretary of the Treasury was as to this matter given a degree of power and independence which in most other matters he did not possess.

The Secretary of the Treasury at this time was Louis McLane of Delaware, a man of conservative tendencies and one who appreciated the value of the services rendered by a national bank. He was unwilling to go along with Jackson on the question of removing the deposits, but he had been loyal to the President on other issues, and Jackson had no desire to humiliate him by removing him from office. Therefore in 1833 Jackson appointed Livingston, who had been Secretary of State, Minister to France, and promoted McLane from Secretary of the Treasury to Secretary of State. This left open what to Jackson's mind was the key position of his Cabinet, and in the full belief that he was selecting a man after his own heart he appointed William J. Duane of Pennsylvania to the Treasury in January, 1833. Duane's chief recommendation as far as Jackson was concerned, was that his father had been editor of a strong pro-Jackson paper and, as the President said, he believed that the son was a "chip off the old block."

It appeared he was right in holding this view, but the result was highly unsatisfactory to him. Duane was an able lawyer and apparently had not sought or desired public office. He was an honest man, but extremely stubborn, and a voluminous letter-writer. Whether he intended it or not, he was adept when it came to enraging the old soldier in the White House. Jackson's friends also claimed that Duane knew exactly what he was put in for, namely, to remove the deposits. Duane asserted quite as vehemently that he never had any idea that the President wanted to do anything quite so foolish.

The fact probably is that Duane's old clients and friends in
Philadelphia, most of whom were tied up with the bank in
one way or another, exerted so much pressure upon him that
his backbone was stiffened to the point of refusing to obey
the President's wishes. After all, he knew as well as anyone
that within a few years at the most he would have to return
to Philadelphia and would probably want to live there the
rest of his life, and he had no intention of alienating his best
friends in order to please "Old Hickory."

As a matter of fact, the Cabinet was badly split over the
question of removing the public funds from the national bank.
Most of the President's constitutional advisers were opposed
to any such drastic action, believing that the best plan was
to let the bank alone for the rest of its brief career, knowing
full well that in the absence of a renewal of its charter it
would pass from the picture in 1836. Not so the President or
his Attorney-General, Roger B. Taney, of Maryland, or perhaps more important than either of them, the members of the
"Kitchen Cabinet."

We have not attempted in this story to cover the entire history of the Jackson administration, or long before this we
should have described the surprising power and influence of
the small group of men who from the very first surrounded
Andrew Jackson and to a great extent controlled his political
actions—not because the President was a weak man, but because he was an uneducated one and had little regard for
a majority of the members of his Cabinet.

Jackson had originally been elected as a result of a political
coalition, and the general understanding was that John C.
Calhoun of South Carolina, the southern leader, was to succeed him at the end of one term. Calhoun was strong, able,
and powerful; he represented the South which, in conjunction
with the new West, had made Jackson President. Therefore
three members of the Cabinet were Calhoun men: Ingham,

Branch, and Berrien. Of the others, Martin Van Buren, at first Secretary of State and later Vice-President, was the only one on whose advice Jackson seemed to depend. It is probable that the existence of the different factions had much to do with the President's attitude towards his Cabinet. In contrast to his predecessors, Jackson seldom held meetings of the Cabinet, but dealt with each Secretary individually and in his own way. He did, however, have close advisers, and they have gone down in history as the real Jacksonian Cabinet which ruled the country during eight turbulent years. They were all bright men and in their own way patriotic. Authors differ as to the exact constitution of this group, but a majority among historians are willing to admit that at all times it consisted of William P. Lewis, Frank P. Blair, and Amos Kendall, and it is admitted that from time to time a few other men, notable among whom were Isaac Hill and James A. Hamilton, the son of Alexander Hamilton, whose politics were entirely different from those of his eminent father, also were added to its councils.

Of the three individuals closest to Jackson, Amos Kendall was by far the most able and the most interesting, and it is he who appears to have been the moving force in connection with the removal of the deposits.

William P. Lewis was an old friend and neighbor of Jackson's in Tennessee. Having little personal ambition, he was the "gum-shoe man" of the administration. He was always around, padding softly from one committee room to another, and his job was to keep the President fully informed about what was going on in Congress.

Frank P. Blair was a dashing two-handed fighter whose pet duty was to praise the President's views on any occasion through the columns of his newspaper, and to lead in the attacks on the old man's enemies. He was a prolific and forceful writer, and of great aid to the President during most of his administration.

Amos Kendall, the brainiest of the lot, was really the "Colonel House" of Jackson's era. He was a man of great intelligence, brave and unselfish, and with a political acumen and an ability to estimate popular sentiment on any occasion which was almost uncanny in its accuracy. He was a lank little man, modest, retiring, and seldom seen in public; but long before Jackson retired from office he was generally admitted to be the valiant, inscrutable guide of the presidential policies, and he has left many traces of his genius in some of the ablest state papers of the era.

It was this group, so much condemned at the time, which really kept the President firm in his purpose to remove the deposits from the bank and furnished him with the means of translating that purpose into fact.

The idea, of course, was to transfer the Government money from the Bank of the United States to various state institutions, but in the course of his objections to the removal, Secretary Duane had raised the point that the state banks might be unwilling to receive the Government's money under such conditions. To meet these objections, Jackson had Amos Kendall travel about the country and interview officials of the leading state institutions, and after a time Kendall reported that he had received assurances from a sufficient number of state banks that such a transfer would be entirely agreeable to them and to their stockholders. Acting upon this information, Jackson renewed his efforts to induce Secretary Duane to issue an order for the removal of the deposits. Duane persisted in his refusal to do anything of the kind. Jackson, supported in his attitude by his Attorney-General and the "Kitchen Cabinet," called a meeting of his official Cabinet during September, 1833, and went over the whole case with them. He did not succeed in obtaining their support, however, nor did he overcome Duane's continued refusal to sign the order. He then indicated to Duane that he would be willing to receive his resignation, but Duane, apparently by this time in thorough accord with the friends of the bank, refused to resign. Not only that, but he wrote Jackson several long involved letters defending his attitude, which letters drove the old man wild. Finally on September 23, 1833, Jackson issued a brief order removing Duane as Secretary of the Treasury and immediately thereafter appointed Taney as head of that department. This settled the question, for on September 26, Secretary Taney issued an order that thereafter the public money should be deposited in certain state banks. Also in accordance with the Bank Act, Taney, on December 3, 1833, presented to the Senate his reasons for the removal of the deposits. These reasons were not particularly well presented, and were mostly political in character. They were really weaker than they might have been. The main point stressed, was that the bank's charter would soon expire, and that it was unwise and unsafe to keep the public money in the bank during the brief interim before it went out of business.

It might be concluded that with the removal of the Government deposits the story of the Second National Bank had reached an end, but such was not the case. As the President said, Nicholas Biddle was a proud man and he was as intelligent as Amos Kendall, as bold as Blair, and as stubborn as Duane. It is probable that about this time Biddle realized that so far as the renewal of the bank's charter was concerned the game was up, but there was one thing left and that was revenge. He was still president of the most powerful financial institution in the country. It would appear that he conceived the idea that in the time that was still left to him he would exercise that power in a way that Andrew Jackson and his supporters would never forget, so that they would rue the day on which they had locked horns with him over the recharter

of the bank to which he had devoted the best years of his
life, and whose success was inevitably entwined with his personal reputation and the achievement of his life's ambition.

The bank was through, perhaps, but Nicholas Biddle was
not, and there is much of romance and vital interest in the
story of what he did during the last three years of the bank's
existence. It is only fair to Biddle to recognize the fact that
he and his friends denied vigorously that there was any element of revenge in the policy adopted by the bank after the
refusal of Congress to recharter it and the removal of the
Government's deposits.

Like most debatable questions, there are two sides to this
one. Duane was dismissed September 23, 1833, and the removal of the deposits was ordered by Taney a few days thereafter. In spite of all the furor occasioned by this governmental
action, the bank was really not materially harmed by it. Reading from the annual report we find that on January 1, 1833,
the bank's assets amounted to $80,800,000, while its liabilities
were $37,800,000, leaving a balance of $43,000,000 and a capitalization of only $35,000,000. The Government's deposits at
this time amounted to some $9,800,000. The loss of them from
a monetary standpoint did not constitute a severe blow to
the bank, but it unquestionably did affect the prestige of the
institution. Furthermore, it helped to increase the power and
standing of the various state banks which the Government
then selected as depositories.

What actually happened was that just about the time the
Federal Government sought to withdraw its funds from the
Bank of the United States, the bank began to reduce its loans
and contract its note issues. The reason for such action, according to President Biddle, was that the general warfare against
the institution and the encouragement which the removal
of the deposits had given to the state banks made it necessary
for the national bank to pursue a policy of extreme con-

servatism, and keep its resources as liquid as possible. Biddle did not say so, but it was probably true also that the result of Kendall's swinging the circle to ascertain whether the state banks would be willing to receive the deposits was that the leading state institutions immediately began to clean house in order to get themselves in proper shape to receive the deposits when the Government should be ready to hand them over. In order to do this, they contracted their own note issues and called loans quite as freely as did the national bank.

The inevitable result was that during the winter of 1833-34 money was tight, and business was in distress. Jackson and his friends, aided by the "Kitchen Cabinet," blamed it all on Nicholas Biddle, but as has been said before, it does not seem that they were right in doing so.

On the other hand, to aver that Biddle had no ulterior motive in planning a stringent policy of loan reductions and note contractions would be to credit him with a more saintly disposition than we are justified in believing he possessed. In the light of after events, it would seem to be true that Biddle and his friends were not responsible for the period of depression which existed in 1833-34. At least they were not primarily responsible for it. Many other factors existed in connection with the situation. It is quite possible that the national shock to business which occurred when it was known positively that the national bank must close its doors, and when the Government some years in advance of that event took the public money away from the institution, had much to do with starting the depression.

Business is a delicate instrument that is easily affected by the mental attitude of the public. Nevertheless, though the policy of the national bank was a strong factor in the situation, it is also a fact that the restrictive policies of the various state banks had much to do with it as well.

No matter what the causes were, it is undoubtedly true that

the people of the United States suffered greatly during the depression of 1833-34. Interest rates were up to from 1½ to 3 per cent a month, and foreign exchange was selling at high premiums. Furthermore, as is usually the case, manufacturing production throughout the entire country was slowed up and orders fell off alarmingly. Instead of regarding the situation from an economic point of view and endeavoring to cure it, Andrew Jackson, whose second term was drawing to its close, showed the worst possible temper regarding the matter and indulged in a series of violent outbursts against Biddle and the bank. He blamed the entire situation on Biddle's attempt to secure revenge against him personally, and his only panacea seemed to be an impracticable scheme to replace bank-notes with hard metal.

As a method of reprisal, Taney's successor, Woodbury, informed the Bank of the United States on November 5, 1834, that branch drafts would not be received by the Treasury after January 1, 1835. This of course meant not only great inconvenience to the bank, but also serious loss to the public who for years had regarded branch drafts as the equivalent of bank-notes and had been quite justified in doing so. However, the country recovered from the depression of 1833-34 quite rapidly because the depression was not due to any real lack of prosperity, but was caused entirely by unnecessary dislocation of the country's financial machinery.

During all the time that this depressed business situation had existed, a running fight had been kept up in Congress by the President and his allies against the friends of the bank. In the winter of 1834, Henry Clay had managed to have the President severely censured by the Senate for his actions in connection with the national bank. This greatly angered the old man, and his friends returned to the battle with renewed ferocity. Throughout that long winter the debates were carried on by both sides with the utmost animosity and ill-feeling.

It is probably true that Biddle and his friends believed that the business depression to which they had contributed would eventually compel President Jackson to restore the deposits to the bank; if they ever believed this, however, they showed a complete lack of understanding of Andrew Jackson's character. The more angry the President became, the more determined he was that the Government's deposits should never be restored. He was entirely honest in this determination for he sincerely believed that the bank was on the verge of bankruptcy, and that it was his sworn duty to protect the public money as much as he could.

After a battle in Congress lasting more than two years, Jackson's friends managed to get the resolution of censure expunged from the journal of the Senate on January 16, 1837. This was after the bank had passed out of existence, but nevertheless it was to Andrew Jackson one of the most pleasing events in his long and belligerent career.

From 1824 to 1836 there were a number of attempts to investigate the affairs of the bank. These attempts were often quite evidently without any practical purpose but merely a means to annoy and harass the officers and directors of the institution. Nothing definite came of them, however, and the bank passed out of existence under the terms of the act creating it in 1836. Before the institution ceased to exist as a federal bank, Nicholas Biddle obtained a banking charter from the State of Pennsylvania, and the business of the bank was carried on without apparent interruption, although after 1836 it became a state bank.

It is interesting to note that the bank was heavily involved in the financial panic of 1837, because it had pursued a policy of buying commercial paper with too much freedom and indulged in a considerable amount of speculation. The result was that the United States Bank failed in 1838 and again in 1841. Notwithstanding its inability to continue successfully in business, the bank ultimately paid all its creditors, although the investments of the stockholders proved to be a total loss.

We thus come to the end of one of the most interesting financial epics in the history of the United States. It will be worth while briefly to review the tragic affair and endeavor to summarize the principal facts connected with it and draw a few definite conclusions regarding them.

We must recognize in the first instance that the question of continuing the Bank of the United States became highly controversial, and in the end a vital political issue. This made it difficult if not impossible for most men alive in 1833 to obtain a clear and unbiased view of the situation. There is no reason, however, why we cannot obtain such a view today.

From 1816 to 1822 the Bank of the United States was mismanaged in many ways and failed to obtain the confidence of the public. In 1822, however, with the coming of Nicholas Biddle to the presidency we find a new and improved situation, characterized by Biddle's conservative policies which emphasized the necessity of a sound currency and liquid short-term loans. Then in the late twenties, we have the change in the bank's business caused by the tremendous expansion of the South and West, resulting in a call for capital which Biddle could not ignore but was unable to supply in accordance with the conservative principles that had governed the early years of his administration.

Nothing, however, in the bank's history up to 1828 would seem to justify the opposition to it displayed by Andrew Jackson from the moment he became President of the United States. The causes for this opposition must be sought elsewhere and have been indicated in this chapter. The bank was not a monster. It was not unconstitutional, nor was it badly managed, nor an instrument of the wealthy to oppress the poor.

It was, however, a powerful instrument of finance, controlled and operated by the wealthy business men of the United States. It was not in sympathy with the crude hordes who were settling the South and the West, nor did it appreciate the tremendous potential power which even then existed in the crowds of city mechanics and tradesmen, who were just beginning to realize that this was their country and that they had a good deal to say as to how it should be run.

Undoubtedly the worst mistake made in connection with the bank was the injection of the question of its recharter into the presidential campaign of 1832 in response to the dictatorial demands of Henry Clay. Such action on the part of Biddle and his friends irrevocably joined them to the fortunes of Clay and his Whig Party. Accordingly, when Clay and his supporters went down to ignominious defeat the Bank of the United States went with them. From November, 1832, the bank never had any real chance of obtaining a new charter.

It is not to be wondered that such an antagonist as General Jackson, with the plaudits of a vast majority of his countrymen ringing in his ears, should have believed that he had a special mandate from the people to put the national bank out of business as soon as possible. This belief accounts for his ill-advised and stubborn attitude regarding the removal of the Government's deposits and for his bitter refusal to restore them in spite of the serious business depression of 1833-34.

All these years the governing class of the country had been in a state of constant ferment over the question of the bank. It was an interesting and colorful period. It was a time when the United States had been in existence some thirty years and was in the hands of a second generation. Nearly all the Revolutionary soldiers had joined the great majority. George Wash-

ington had already become something of the beneficent myth
which he remained for many generations. Hamilton was a
memory; Jefferson an old man retired and waiting the last
call. The original thirteen states no longer represented anything like the entire country. Already interminable lines of
covered wagons were pushing westward from the Virginias
across the Alleghenies, and from New England around the
borders of the Great Lakes down into the fertile plains of
Illinois, Indiana, and Ohio. The nation was like a young
giant just beginning to realize its strength and to rejoice in its
power.

The men of those days were crude, rough, violent, but intelligent and vastly interesting. They lied, fought, and drank
hard, and it is impossible to read the history of the times without seeing clearly that the United States of those days, under
the conditions which then existed, was certain to divide into
strong and entirely different groups which would contest
every policy with the utmost bitterness but at the same time
with earnestness and ability.

It is not merely because all this happened so long ago that
the men of those days seem to us of more than ordinary
stature. Henry Clay would have been successful in almost
any vocation or any country. He was a natural leader of men,
and he possessed great personal charm in addition to political
sagacity and a mentality of the highest order.

Daniel Webster has never been excelled as an orator and
seldom equalled as a lawyer. In the whole library of political
orations there is probably no greater example of emotional
address than his famous reply to Senator Haine of South Carolina on the question of tariff and nullification. On the other
side of the Senate, Thomas Benton of Missouri was a strong
figure, while McDuffy, Dallas, Sargent, and Horace Binney
were all men of ability so outstanding that they would have
been ornaments to any legislative assembly in any age.

Into this stately group projects the gaunt, unusual figure of Andrew Jackson—his piercing black eyes shrouded by matted eyebrows and crowned with a great bushy mass of snow-white hair brushed straight back from his high forehead. Never was there a man of greater personal courage, nor a statesman who loved his country more devotedly than he. He did not know the meaning of the word compromise, but he did know his objectives, and he pursued them with a tenacity of purpose and a courageous willingness to venture even life itself in the quest, which made him the adored leader of the mass of the people.

Let us call to mind this strong, picturesque President, and using the best information that has come to us endeavor to picture him and his associates as they must have appeared to their contemporaries. About him we see grouped as curious a Cabinet as any President ever had. Here is the pale, high-bred face of John C. Calhoun, stately, dignified, but without a trace of humor. Beside him appears the suave, well-dressed figure of the sinuous Van Buren, shrewd, impassive, and withal showing capacity for leadership. There we also see the red-faced, portly Eaton, the fragile reputation of whose beautiful wife probably lost the presidency to Calhoun, and undoubtedly split the Cabinet and changed the whole progress of the administration. Then there is McLane, the courteous, honest, and conservative head of the Treasury, and later on the small, poorly balanced face of Duane, with all the stubbornness of a weak character. Last, but not least, we may note the tall, commanding figure of Roger B. Taney, with the cold, steel-like glance of the fanatic, and the strength of a commanding purpose.

It is not enough that we should read the facts and figures connected with the turbulent career of the Second National Bank. In order to appreciate the thrilling quality of events which disturbed its life's history, in order to comprehend the tragedy which its rise and fall held for many of the leading men of that distant day, and in order to understand the great leaders at that vitally interesting time, we must endeavor to go back in thought for more then a hundred years, and in the light of those hectic days to visualize the human structure of our country a century ago. If we do this we will be not merely reading history, but living it, and we can in such a way appreciate the cold, dry facts of one of the most interesting periods in the annals of the United States.

CHAPTER XI

MARTIN VAN BUREN AND THE PANIC OF 1837

IT IS doubtful if any president ever came into office with a fairer prospect of peace and prosperity before him than did Martin Van Buren. On March 4, 1837, he rode from the White House to the Capitol side by side with Andrew Jackson, his illustrious predecessor. It was one of those rare March days of brilliant sunshine, and the incoming executive must have felt at peace with the world and have experienced the gratification which would be natural to anyone who had just attained a life-long ambition. It was fortunate that Van Buren could not look into the future, for if he could have done so, the splendor of the day would have been spoiled. Could he have realized that in six months the entire complexion of affairs would be changed, that a financial crisis unprecedented in severity would be upon the country, and that he would be held personally responsible for much of the distress which his countrymen would have to experience, he would have been greatly sobered and probably disheartened.

There never was a greater contrast between two men than between Andrew Jackson and Martin Van Buren. If we look backward we can see them as they sat together in that elaborate carriage upon Inauguration Day. Jackson, old, gaunt, with bushy eyebrows and straight, harsh white hair brushed upright from his forehead, fronted the world with a look of command and of severity; Van Buren, many years his junior, handsome, dapper, immaculately dressed, with the side whiskers which were popular at that time, gave an impression of breeding and geniality, but no suspicion of the force of character which was really his. As a matter of fact, the casual observer upon that Inauguration Day would have said that the good-looking, vain little man was about to step into the shoes of a giant. The observer, however, would have been wrong. In spite of a some-what foppish appearance and a suavity which was part of his political stock-in-trade, President Van Buren was no weak character, but a man of ability, decision, and courage. His career had been a long and honorable one in his native state. He had been a member of the State Senate, Attorney-General of New York, Governor of the State, and United States Senator. Also, for a brief period he had been Minister to England, and since 1833 he had presided over the Senate as Vice-President of the United States. It is true that he was a practical politician, one of the first indeed in our country's history. He might even be termed a boss, according to the understanding of that term in our day, but it should be remembered that real political bosses are never weak characters, and Van Buren was no exception to the rule.

It would seem that many people have misunderstood Van Buren and misinterpreted his career because of his relationship to Andrew Jackson, the most picturesque and violent of our presidents. Van Buren, during all of Jackson's incumbency, was one of the old man's favorites, and it is probable that from an early day he planned and schemed to succeed Jackson in the presidency. It must have seemed at first a most dif-ficult thing to bring about. John C. Calhoun, a great statesman and a man of iron will, had led a vitally necessary group of southern Democrats who had contributed a support without which Jackson could never have been elected. In return, it was generally understood that Calhoun was to succeed to the presidential office after the Old Warrior had served one full term. This understanding was nullified by a number of violent disagreements between the two men, beginning with the famous social war over the status of Mrs. Eaton, the pretty

wife of the Secretary of War. In this imbroglio, Van Buren
sided with the President—and was fortunate because he was
a widower and therefore did not have to endeavor to convert
his wife to a realization of Mrs. Eaton's innocence and charm.
From this time onward, Calhoun and Jackson drew farther
and farther apart until, in the great dispute over nullification,
their paths diverged forever. Van Buren meanwhile became
closer and closer to the old leader. Van Buren was an experienced politician and he had great personal charm of manner
and an unusual amount of tact. A number of times he was
placed in very delicate and difficult positions by the violent
attitude Jackson assumed toward certain public questions, but
he always managed to compose his difficulties with the chief,
and it is fair to say that next to the members of that curious
and wholly extra-legal body, the "Kitchen Cabinet," Van
Buren was regarded with a greater degree of affection by
Jackson than any other man in American public life. At the
same time we must not suppose that Van Buren gave merely
lip service to either Jackson or his principles. Indeed, he proved
his mettle when he adhered to these principles during his own
presidency at a time when to depart from them would have
greatly increased his popularity and might have resulted in
his reelection.

Our primary object, however, is not to discuss in detail the
administration of Martin Van Buren, but only such part of
it as is concerned with the first great financial panic experienced by this country. We must in the first instance survey the
economic condition of the United States at the close of General Jackson's second term so as to understand the causes of the
financial depression so soon to occur. The period from 1820
to 1837 was one of peace and constructive progress. The
Napoleonic Wars kept Europe in a state of constant turmoil
from the middle of the last decade of the eighteenth century
until the Emperor's final departure for Saint Helena in 1815.

With Napoleon at last safely chained, Europe set about to reconstruct the civilization which had been so greatly menaced. Immediately international trade began to improve, and, as the close of the Napoleonic period was also practically coincident with the end of the War of 1812, our own country shared in the general era of improving trade and unaccustomed security.

This was the time when our pioneer forefathers began in sober earnest greatly to extend the frontier. There have been many waves of emigration; the paths to the West have been trodden many times by all kinds of people and over a period extending from the earliest colonial times to the final settlement of Oklahoma and Indian territory—events well within the memory of men comparatively young today. However, there probably never was a time when the westward movement was more vigorous or more romantic than during the three or four decades which succeeded the War of 1812. It was then that manufacturing was just beginning to be an important factor in the life of New England, with the result that the foreign-born were invading the old commonwealths of the most ancient part of the country where today they form such a large and important part of the population. The descendants of the original settlers, nearly all of whom were farmers, were deserting the relatively barren fields and rocky pastures of the north, and pushing westward along the margin of the Great Lakes into the fertile plains where today we find the great states of Ohio, Illinois, Indiana, and Michigan. Meanwhile, far to the south the inhabitants of Virginia and the Carolinas were also pushing westward their long lines of covered wagons across the Alleghenies and descending into a land of promise where today lie the states of Tennessee, Kentucky, and Missouri.

Not only was the country greatly enlarged by this westward movement of a considerable portion of its population, but in the settled regions of the East the enterprise of the people was

shown in a series of internal improvements. Among these were
the completion of a national system of trunk roads, and the
building of a number of long canals which were to serve for
years as important highways of commerce. Thus by aiding in
the transportation of goods the people greatly facilitated both
the import and export trade.

At this time, owing to the general prosperity of the country
and the love of luxuries which naturally followed in its wake,
the imports of the United States considerably exceeded the
exports. Yet, in spite of that fact, specie continued to be plentiful in this country—a situation which could have but one
meaning, namely, that foreign investors were willing to
keep their money here in order that they might indulge in
speculation while lending it to American enterprisers for the
purpose of developing our young and potentially wealthy
land.

The most interesting feature of the entire situation was that
as far as we were concerned it had never happened before. In
colonial days, America had been a small agricultural country
whose trade had been severely restricted by England and
whose prosperity was greatly limited by that and other factors.
Life here in the early days was hard. The country was undeveloped, the Government was largely ineffective, economic
conditions were bad, and everything was necessarily on a
small scale. After the Revolution, it took twenty years for
the young country to get on its feet, fund its debts, and establish a stable Government worthy of international respect.
Then came the political overturn which brought in Thomas
Jefferson; shortly thereafter the difficulties with England commenced which eventuated in the War of 1812 with all its
attendant misery and loss. It was not until after 1815 that the
United States really began to be prosperous in a big way.

Like everything in the world to which people are not accustomed, it proved to be a situation difficult to control. The

Americans of that day were not greatly different from Americans at the present time except that they had less knowledge of government and economics and were handicapped by poor communications and a good deal of inexperience in the business world. It is not surprising under such conditions that the wonderful progress which the country made during the twenties and thirties went to the heads of its inhabitants like champagne, and, not content with the blessings which Providence freely vouchsafed to them, they endeavored in a short space of time to discount the progress which the country would normally achieve during the century that was to come.

It is well that we should appreciate this general situation before going into the details of the panic of 1837, for it will enable us to disabuse our minds of the political prejudices which so greatly complicate a correct understanding of the economic phenomena of that terrible time. Most of the business leaders of that day were members of the Whig Party and had bitterly opposed Andrew Jackson for eight long and riotous years. They were therefore mentally disposed to lay the blame for everything at the door of Old Hickory, and it was indeed possible to blame him for some of the undoubted causes of the panic without doing him the least injustice. On the other hand, it would be equally futile to place the entire blame upon either Andrew Jackson or the Democratic Party. Neither Jackson nor his followers should be saddled with the major portion of the blame. The roots of the panic of 1837 are to be found in the era of inflation, undue luxury, and speculation which immediately preceded it. Although there is no doubt that some things which President Jackson did, helped the panic conditions along and probably hastened them, nevertheless, the principal causes of the panic were those which have just been mentioned.

Let us now review the economic and financial situation of the United States at the beginning of 1837 so that we may

WALL STREET, 1845

have a better appreciation of the basic reasons for the panic
conditions which so rapidly ensued. We should first observe
that there was no national bank, and it will be remembered
that one of the great objectives of Andrew Jackson's administration was the destruction of the national banking system.
The bank war, as it is still called, raged throughout both of
Jackson's terms of office. It was the principal issue upon which
he was reelected President in 1832, and he naturally considered
that his election at that time constituted a mandate from the
people to rid them of what he used to call "the monster."
Not content with vetoing the bill to recharter the bank, he
went much further and withdrew from the institution the
deposits of Government money amounting in all to about
$9,800,000. Even though this did not seriously cripple the bank
itself, the transfer of the Government funds to state banks
was undoubtedly instrumental in stimulating the growth of
a large number of these unconservative banking institutions,
and such a growth, especially at that time, was unfortunate
and baneful in its results.

It is true that the Second United States Bank, particularly in
its early days, made many mistakes and at times encouraged
speculation, but after Nicholas Biddle became its president it
was conducted for a long time along sane and conservative
lines. It succeeded in stabilizing the currency, and, by compelling the state banks to settle their debts in specie, it unquestionably prevented a period of dangerous inflation and perhaps
deferred panic conditions for many years. It is probably true
that Andrew Jackson's personal dislike of Nicholas Biddle, as
much as any other single cause, impelled him to withdraw the
Government deposits. No matter what his reasons were for
doing as he did, it is now quite clear that the economic results
contributed definitely to the panic of 1837.

The state banks selected to receive the Government's funds
immediately began to extend their loans, even before they

actually became governmental depositories; and the mere hope of obtaining a portion of the Government deposits led to the creation of hundreds of new state banks. There was no system of supervision such as exists today, no controller of the currency, no national bank examiners; and, the Bank of the United States having lost its charter, even the salutary restraint which that great institution formally exercised over its branches and through them upon the state banks themselves, was lost to the country.[1] The result was a period of free borrowing such as the young nation had never experienced before. As has been said, the period was one of intense business activity. Commerce was active, trade was increasing, manufactures were beginning to be a real factor in national affairs, and everything was on the up road. This of itself meant that money was needed in large amounts to develop the fast-multiplying opportunities for business enterprise, and unquestionably there was a real demand for funds which was justified, and which, if it had been the only cause for the expansion of credit and increase of loans, would have been no detriment to the country's welfare, but an actual benefit.

This, however, was by no means the only factor in the situation. Often in connection with the demands of legitimate economic enterprise, the American people over-estimated their business chances, and discounted success with that optimism and abandon which has always been one of our national characteristics. Furthermore, the banks themselves encouraged men to borrow money from them, and no reasonable limita-

[1] While it is true that there was no federal supervision over state banks as we now understand "supervision," there was important indirect federal control in that by Act of Congress, June 23, 1836, no state bank could receive federal deposits unless it made weekly returns of its condition, submitted to examination at any time, redeemed its notes in specie on demand, and refrained from the issue of notes of less than $5. The act under which this supervision was exerted was one "regulating the deposits of Government money." On November 1, 1836, 89 banks were so regulated, and had governmental deposits to the amount of some $49,378,-000. D. R. Dewey, "Financial History of the United States," pp. 209-210.

tion was placed upon the amounts so freely lent or the kind of business selected to receive such liberal support.

Yet there was an even more dangerous feature in the situation, namely, the element of speculation. It seems as though, from time immemorial, unusual prosperity has always brought with it an era of speculation and in the end a period of inflation; 1837 was no exception to the rule. It is quite true, though, that however willing men may be to speculate, they must have something to speculate with and ways in which to accomplish the object which they have in view.

Today, speculation is a relatively simple matter. All one has to do is to lift the telephone instrument off its hook, get a broker on the wire and give an order to buy stocks on margin or sell them short, and the deed is done. It will be remembered, however, that in 1837 the Stock Exchange was very rudimentary in form and there were very few corporations, so that speculation as it is understood today was not available to the gamblers of the period. Nevertheless, they speculated just the same. They had something which lent itself readily to speculative processes, and, with the aid of the numerous and unsupervised state banks, they readily evolved a technique of speculation which they found efficient and quite capable of making a few people rich and causing the ruin of many others.

The thing in which they speculated was land, preferably land belonging to the Government of the United States. The public lands of the country at that time were so great in extent that it seemed as though they would never be exhausted. Until 1820 the price at which these lands had been sold was $2.00 an acre. By an act of April 24, 1820, the price of public land was reduced to $1.25 an acre, and from that time onward, purchase of such lands increased in volume, and speculation in them became general and profitable. There was no great public movement, however, in this direction until 1834, during which year nearly $5,000,000 of public lands were sold. In 1835 the value of land sold was $14,700,000; in 1836 it grew to $24,800,000. This huge increase in the sale of public lands was the direct result of the employment of state banks as credit agencies. From 1836 onward, the entire country indulged in a riot of land speculation. Moneys were borrowed from banks and invested in land. The land was then mortgaged and the same money, which had been deposited meanwhile by the vendor, was borrowed again to purchase other land, the loan being secured by a mortgage of the land originally bought; and so the loans mounted ceaselessly until the whole credit structure became topheavy and tottered dangerously.

President Jackson was no economist, and it was a long time before he realized the true meaning of this enormous return from sales of Government lands. As late as December, 1835, he told Congress in his annual message that the increasing sales of public lands was an evidence of prosperity and cause for national congratulation. The sales during 1836, however, brought the President to his senses; too late to do more than increase the fast-multiplying evils of the situation, he endeavored to put on the brakes.

His method was revealed by the famous "Specie Circular" of July 11, 1836, in which Woodbury, then Secretary of the Treasury, ordered that thereafter all public lands must be paid for in specie.

This order was by no means indefensible theoretically, and it was entirely consistent with the hard money views which Jackson had proposed for many years. Had it been issued at an earlier date, before the great wave of land speculation had reached its height, it might have been extremely helpful and would probably have been an active factor in reducing and indeed preventing inflation. Coming, however, when it did, it was a flagrant example of shutting the stable door after the horses were stolen, and undoubtedly it was instrumental in precipitating a national panic, though it was not one of the primary causes.

Just why President Jackson influenced Secretary Woodbury to issue the specie circular will always be a question. The President's admirers have always stoutly maintained that it was his hatred of paper money as the ideal tool of the capitalistic interest which controlled his mind and dictated his action. Admitting the general truth of such a statement, it would seem that in this instance "Old Hickory" was affected by a more opportunistic reason.

For more than five years eastern speculators armed with eastern cash had been invading the western area and buying up the choicest farming lands at prices too high for the citizens of those states to match. It is true that these early sons of Wall Street used very little actual cash in their maneuvers; instead they employed the notes of various state banks, and from the viewpoint of the western farmers they were using unreal money to deprive them of real land in their native states.

Flushed with anger at what they considered unfair competitive buying the westerners appealed to the old man in the White House, who had never been known to turn a deaf ear to the poor and the oppressed. Undoubtedly this plea for aid, coming at a time when Jackson had just realized that something was radically wrong with the land situation, had a powerful effect, particularly since it was directly in line with his long-cherished ideas in favor of coin and against even a moderate use of bank paper.

The specie circular was the result. The effect of the circular was immediate and injurious. Perhaps the worst result was a moral one. Instantly the whole country, especially the business community, became convinced that the Government had lost faith in bank paper and indeed in the general credit structure. What other reason could there be, said many, for such a drastic requirement as cash payment for public lands in a time of unexampled prosperity? The result was general contraction at a time when easy money with a gradual reduction of inflated conditions would have been an alleviation if not a cure. Then too, the change in policy denuded the East of specie just when it was most needed and caused it to be taken westward where it did no great amount of good. In effect, hard money disappeared from the great states of the Atlantic Seaboard at a most critical moment, leaving the leading banking institutions of the young country without that basis of credit which is the life blood of national finance.

The specie circular, however, did not cause the panic in spite of the firm belief, long held by the eastern bankers and the powerful Whig Party, that it did. It was merely a contributing cause, and there were others.

One of these was that curious device for handing over to the states the excess of national income, known as "the distribution of the surplus." This statute was the result of a peculiar economic and political situation never since duplicated in our history. The Whigs, representing the industrial East, were wedded to a protective tariff; the Democrats, representing the agricultural states of the South and West, were divided between a low tariff and free trade. From about 1820 for a period of fifteen years the country had enjoyed remarkable prosperity and increased its population, resources, and national wealth. In 1835, the national debt was liquidated, and the national income continuing to flow into the Treasury without interruption, its disposition became a question of vital import to the whole country.

For once the two great parties were in substantial agreement as to the desired end, though for entirely different reasons.

For years the southern and western commonwealths had been besieging Congress for funds with which to pay for internal improvements, despite the fact that liberality along this line was contrary to the basic doctrine of state's rights. Some progress had been made so far as road building was concerned, and the great Cumberland road which for a long period was one of the main highways to the western frontier, was financed by federal appropriations. However, such grants were secured with difficulty because of the antagonistic attitude of the strict constructionists, among whom was Andrew Jackson. Hence it seemed to be good policy to use the national surplus for internal improvements in an indirect manner, if some practical way could be found to do it.

Ordinarily the Whigs would have been lukewarm to such an idea, but it seemed to them to be a good way of avoiding an embarrassing situation which they feared would soon arise.

The theory on which the tariff system was founded was the necessity of obtaining sufficient revenue for governmental needs through the protection of infant industries by import duties. In 1835, even the high tariff adherents had little idea of the extremes to which this policy would be carried during and after the Civil War, so that rates then considered high would now appear ridiculously low. The whole tariff structure was so tentatively and insecurely established that a drastic reduction in national financial needs such as was likely to result from the extinguishment of the national debt, might conceivably imperil not merely specific rates but the protective tariff as a whole. For this reason, the Whig Party lent an attentive ear to the suggestion of surplus distribution.

The only real question, and it was a serious one, was as to how it should be done. State pride and adherence to the principles of strict construction were found to be too strong to permit of an outright gift, hence the statesmen of that day resorted to what we should term camouflage. By the Act of June 23, 1836, it was provided that all the money in the Treasury of the United States on January 1, 1837, with the exception of $5,000,000 (which apparently was retained as working capital) should be deposited with the states in proportion to their respective representation in the Senate and House of Representatives. Technically the transaction was in the nature of a loan, as the Government received certificates from each state in return for the deposit and elaborate provisions were made for interest and redemption, which, however, were taken seriously by no one. Henry Clay, then the acknowledged leader of the Whig Party, unequivocably stated that he did not believe that, at the time the surplus was distributed, a single member of the House or Senate thought that a single dollar would ever be demanded or repaid.

The amount for distribution on January 1, 1837, was $37,000,000; it was to be paid to the states in four installments three months apart and the first payment of $9,367,000 was made on the above date. Even though the country was still highly prosperous at that time, the sum involved was too large relatively not to cause considerable disturbance in the field of finance. In order to get such a large sum in cash the various state banks from which it was withdrawn had to call loans, and refuse credit to general business for lack of liquid funds. The next payment on April 1, 1837, came just before the crash and greatly increased the difficulties of the bankers at that critical time. The third installment, although paid in theory, was really made by means of notes and credit obligations of extremely doubtful value; and the final installment, owing to the exigencies of the Treasury, was never paid at all. The total surplus distribution amounted to $28,101,644, and there would seem to be no doubt that it was a contributing cause to the panic conditions with which it was largely coincident. It caused contraction at a bad time, it reduced the loanable funds of the banks and thus adversely affected business; and it involved the physical removal of large amounts of currency from the East to the West and South, thereby dislocating the nation's financial machine at a critical moment.

The stage is now set for the tragedy about to be described. In the spring of 1837, we may vision a young people engaged in the pleasant task of developing a rich and fertile continent, still agricultural in the main, but with an efficient merchant marine and a rapidly growing manufacturing interest. To this people, after the hardships of the revolution and the troubled years which preceded the war of 1812, there suddenly came the undreamed-of opportunities which the long peace succeeding the Napoleonic Wars brought in its train. Is it strange that an energetic and imaginative race over-shot the mark? Is it to be wondered at that in a few years desire exceeded performance, and a flimsy credit structure was reared to help in discounting the success which it was sincerely believed the immediate future held in store? Was it contrary to human experience that, with millions of square miles of virgin land waiting the ax of the pioneer and the plow of the farmer, our fathers should speculate wildly in a medium so certain to increase in value, where the only x in the equation was the element of time?

Thus, in the spring of the fateful year, we find our country at its highest point of prosperity, its wealthy class indulging in all the luxuries of the day, and yet, in spite of the excess of imports over exports, with no return of funds abroad because the investing class of Europe was abetting our promotive efforts by lending us their money to develop our young and flourishing land. Prices were inflated, speculation was rampant, credit was over-extended, and hope was high. The sun shone brilliantly on this the best of all possible worlds—but conditions were ripe for a tempest, and it was not long in arriving.

As in the case of other panics, the first downward movement started abroad. Money became tight in England, partly because of local conditions and partly because of disturbed conditions in the United States immediately brought about by the specie circular and the deposit of the surplus. Great Britain had lent immense sums to us, and anything tending to lessen confidence in her lusty young creditor was sufficient to give her a case of financial nerves.

In our inflated and over-extended condition, the British upheaval proved as contagious as scarlet fever. After the event men always wonder how the thing started. It is always difficult and seldom profitable to trace a panic to its sources. When the time is ripe it just happens, and it happens quickly. In this case the whirlwind passed in less than thirty days, but its effect was far-reaching and the depression it caused long-drawn-out.

The panic began in earnest in the early winter of 1837 and progressed with unprecedented force and rapidity. It very rapidly assumed overwhelming proportions, and was believed to threaten seriously the entire financial structure of the young country. Naturally, the Atlantic Seaboard was the worst seat of the trouble, because then, as now, the funds of the country were largely held and managed there. Throughout the dreary winter of the panic year there was a succession of business failures on the part of firms, corporations, and individuals, which, though general throughout the United States, was felt to a greater extent in the cities of New York and Philadelphia than elsewhere. Everything seemed to come to a head at once. We were then a nation of farmers, and the crop failures, which at this period were bad, lessened the purchasing power of the people and immediately affected the merchant class. This additional contributing cause assisted in a final result which was unfortunate beyond the expectation of the greatest pessimists of that day. Then for the first time were observed the various symptoms of financial dislocation and commercial distress which since then have come to be regarded as standard indicia of panic conditions. Old established firms assigned for the benefit of creditors; corporations became bankrupt. Banks closed, often with no assets worthy of the name. Business halted in its stride and staggered along at a pace which daily became slower and more uncertain. Thousands were discharged from employment. Trade was stagnant because the people had no money to buy the necessities of life and luxuries were out of the question. Indeed, in less than six months, the great bubble of national prosperity which had been swelling steadily for fifteen years exploded, and the people were back to hard pan, with nothing to remind them of the dreams of wealth they had enjoyed other than worthless securities and deeds to land which would not fulfill their expectations in less than three generations. It is a sad story to relate even at the distance of nearly a century. And yet it was not different essentially from the depressions of the recent past; its manifestations were different but its fundamental causes were the same.

In a time such as we have been describing, the stronger banks usually hold on for a considerable time after panic conditions take effect. It was not until May that the banks of New York City suspended specie payment, and the other banks throughout the country followed their example within a very brief space of time. Such action, however, was notice to all that drastic measures must be taken to relieve the situation, and President Van Buren, by a proclamation issued May 15, called an extra session of Congress to meet on September 4 to consider the state of the nation.

Meanwhile vigorous efforts were made to induce Van Buren to rescind the specie circular of 1836. He was waited upon by numerous committees of bankers and other citizens and he was told in plain language that, if he wished to escape personal responsibility for the sad condition of the country, he must repeal the Jackson circular and repeal it in short order. He was told that the country had been normal and healthy until this executive order had dislocated our national finance by making such a demand upon the specie of the country that, in our then inflated condition, it was impossible to meet the demand without causing a panic. It was argued forcibly to him that the specie circular was not merely unwise from an economic point of view, but that it constituted an actual breach of faith on the part of the Government with the people, because the national policy had been to encourage all citizens to buy Government land on credit, and the Government itself had accepted all kinds of bank-notes and paper obligations without dissent or criticism until suddenly, like a bolt from the blue, the word had come that thereafter Government agents might accept only gold or silver in payment for land.

The committee of New York bankers urged that in six months New York real estate had depreciated to the extent of more than $40,000,000, that in two months there had been more than 250 business failures in New York City alone, and that inventories on the shelves of New York merchants had depreciated more than 30 per cent within the same period. This tale of woe was merely representative and was parallelled by many other complaints of a similar nature from every state in the union.

Perhaps there never was a time, except during a war, when a President was so generally assailed by citizens of every class and every type and occupation, and when day and night importunate appeals were made to him to take action in a way which was earnestly desired by a majority of his fellow citizens. There comes to mind only one other President who occupied a situation similar to Van Buren's in embarrassment and importunity; it was many years later that Grover Cleveland stood almost alone, deserted by the leaders of his party, but rugged and determined in his intention to preserve the gold standard unimpaired and to protect the financial honor of the

United States against the fanatical forces which seemed intent upon dragging it in the mire.

It is interesting at this point again to consider the man who was President of the United States in 1837. Martin Van Buren even today is imperfectly understood. He was one of those men who, starting from unattractive beginnings, improve with age. He was a country boy of New York State, with few advantages, but great ambition and determination of character. In early youth he was considerably influenced by Aaron Burr, whose erratic career is still remembered as an example of the misapplication of a brilliant mind and a fervent character.

Van Buren was a good lawyer, but the law was not his real vocation. He was a politician and a diplomat. He had a touch of genius when it came to handling men, and it was his misfortune that throughout his long career his personal appearance always belied his real ability. He was below the average in height, inclined to stoutness, not to say rotundity, and he was always so perfectly attired that the word "dapper" might have been fittingly applied to him. Everyone will realize that it is unfortunate for a statesman to present such an appearance. Our greatest Republican leaders have never conformed to a model of this kind. Henry Clay was careless, even slovenly in dress, but withal a singularly handsome man. Andrew Jackson was most comfortable in his old dressing gown and carpet slippers, and the gaunt and ungainly figure of Abraham Lincoln still fills the page of history to the exclusion of lesser men.

Van Buren, however, was a dapper man, and besides the sartorial perfection of his appearance he wore a pair of bushy and well-trimmed side-whiskers, which in the portraits that remain to us still successfully mitigate the effect of a strong and uncompromising chin.

Admittedly there was much of the courtier in Van Buren.

He was an experienced politician when he joined the Jackson Cabinet as Secretary of State. He had been Governor of New York and Senator as well. He knew men—and what was quite as useful, he knew women also. It is not too much to say that his kindly tolerance and courteous attention to the beautiful Peggy Eaton, the wife of Jackson's first War Secretary, was the factor which established him firmly in the affections of his chief and at the same time caused a lasting breach between President Jackson and Vice-President Calhoun. However, fate played a hand in this game, for it was Mrs. Calhoun who refused to call on Mrs. Eaton, whereas Van Buren by lucky chance was a widower and in social matters could call on whom he pleased.

Nevertheless, as years passed by and Van Buren by close adherence to Jacksonian dogma won increasing favor with the old leader, the people of the country became convinced that he was nothing more than Jackson's "yes man," a sycophant and a flatterer who would let nothing stand in the way of his overweening desire to succeed a greater man in the presidency. The people forgot, or perhaps they never knew, that before he ever entered the Cabinet he had been the shrewd and masterful boss of his party organization in New York State, the first real political boss in the history of the country.

Therefore, we may readily believe that when, in that chaotic and dismal winter of 1837, the delegations, deputations, and committees descended upon the White House like a flight of seventeen-year locusts, they anticipated little trouble in moulding this weak and dependent character to their way of thinking; they believed that by the threat of holding him responsible for Jackson's errors they could easily compel him to rescind the specie circular and bring relief to a tortured people.

In this, as the event proved, they were wrong, and they

were greatly astonished when they found it out. Instead of a weak man, unable to stand on his own feet and seriously at loss for want of his predecessor's experience and guidance, they were met by a short, thick-set gentleman with a quiet smile and steely eyes. He listened to them in silence, dismissed them with courtesy, and rejected their requests with politeness and finality, stating publicly at that time and subsequently in his official communications to the Congress that he was absolutely determined not to rescind the specie circular, because he had long been convinced that a hard money policy was best for the country, and he and President Jackson had agreed upon this point for many years. He also said, and in the light of after events we must concede that he spoke truly, that even if he did rescind the specie circular it would have little effect upon the situation. He maintained, quite correctly, that the specie circular had not caused the panic but was merely a contributing factor. He made it entirely clear that in his judgment the people had brought the storm upon themselves by over-indulgence in speculation, particularly in land, over-production of goods, inflation of credits, and general laxity in business practice.

Van Buren, however, did far more at this juncture than merely refuse to interfere with the Jacksonian policy of hard money. When the Congress convened in special session in September, 1837, the President addressed to it a message which was eminently statesman-like because it was inherently constructive. Van Buren first suggested liberal issues of Treasury notes in order to lessen the stress of the existing situation, and this method, which was promptly adopted by Congress, proved effective in bringing the country back to a normal condition. Van Buren also suggested a new departure along the line of national credit which will long be associated with his name. Though not the inventor, he will always be regarded as the father of the sub-treasury system of the United States. This system, which he proposed in his special message of September, 1837, provided for the establishment of a number of sub-treasuries throughout the country, into which the public revenues should be paid directly by the United States collectors of customs, and which should exercise those duties of a national bank directly connected with the collection and transmission of Government taxes, thus providing a rapid and effective method of collecting and dispersing the revenue of the country. It was in effect a clever way of divorcing the ministerial duties of a national bank from its purely banking functions, and it was entirely consistent with Van Buren's sincere belief that a national bank was unnecessary to the welfare of the government but that certain of its functions should be performed by the Government itself through some agency particularly designed to accomplish the work involved with economy and expedition.

It may readily be realized that any such plan coming from the President at such a time was unlikely to meet the approval of Congress. So far as his suggestion that the country issue Treasury notes was concerned, that was an entirely different matter, because every one realized that there was a dire need of additional currency and credit, and Congress was glad to adopt this suggestion regardless of who made it. The sub-treasury idea, however, was a different proposition. Coming from an unpopular President in a time of deplorable business depression, it met a whirlwind of opposition from the popular representatives. A bill was introduced containing most of the President's ideas, but without a hard money clause satisfactory to the President. This was corrected, but nevertheless the bill failed in the House, although it passed the Senate. It was reintroduced the next year and failed again. It failed for a third time in 1839, but was finally passed and signed by the President on July 4, 1840. When it finally went into effect, it proved a useful method of doing important Government work in the absence of a national bank. The fact that it was continued over many years, indeed, until the time of the Federal Reserve system, is a sufficient proof of its fundamental wisdom and workability.

As we review the past, and consider dispassionately the stirring events which filled Van Buren's term, it is not astonishing that he failed of reelection. He was one of those unfortunate men who come into office just in time to reap the reward of their predecessor's mistakes. The panic of 1837 was no worse than many other panics which have swept this land at various times in its history. It was probably not as severe as the panics of 1873, 1893, and 1929, but it was the first big panic we ever had, and it made an impression of a deep and lasting character as much from the fact of its novelty as from the intensity of its effect. Panics and depressions are not pleasant subjects to write about, but they are profitable to reflect upon. It is interesting to observe that no matter how they may differ from one another in superficial ways, they appear strikingly alike when we delve deep enough to discover and analyze their fundamental causes. As we leave this subject, let us not forget that the panic of 1837 probably did Martin Van Buren a lasting favor, for without it he would have been misjudged to eternity by a majority of Americans. It took the stress and strain of that panic year to bring to light the integrity, the courage, and the unflinching determination of this unusual man—a worthy, but greatly misunderstood President of the United States.

CHAPTER XII

SALMON P. CHASE AND JAY COOKE—
FINANCING THE CIVIL WAR

THE great conflict between the states was brewing for a long time, but like a severe thunderstorm when it finally came it arrived with astounding rapidity. It was the election of Abraham Lincoln to the presidency which precipitated armed conflict. It is important to remember, therefore, that there was a great difference between the outlook of even experienced statesmen during the first part of that fateful year and the last quarter of it. Lincoln was elected President in November. South Carolina seceded from the union on the twentieth of December. A confederacy was formed on February 4, 1861, a month before Lincoln took office. Only a little more than a month after he became President, on April 12, 1861, Fort Sumter was fired upon. This was really the starting point of the war, as President Lincoln called for troops three days later. Immediately both North and South found themselves faced with the certainty of devastating fraternal conflict, and both sides became aware, for the first time, of the vital necessity of raising funds for the prosecution of the war.

If we would understand the situation as it existed in the North at that time, we must not only realize the rapidity with which the war finally broke, but we must also understand that in the North it was firmly believed that the war would be of short duration. Undoubtedly, there was reason for this view. Two-thirds of the entire population of the United States resided in the states which remained loyal to the Union, and two-thirds in value of the real and personal property in the United States was in possession of the northern commonwealths, so that, both from the standpoint of wealth and man power, it appeared that the North had a safe preponderance.

One important factor, however, was seemingly overlooked. The North was the center of the manufacturing industries and contained the great majority of the city dwellers of the country; considered as a district it represented industry and business rather than agriculture and leisure. The result of this fundamental difference between the two sections was that there were many more intelligent officers in the United States army at the beginning of the war who claimed southern states as their birthplace than officers who came from the great industrial centers of the North. In the South at that time (and the same thing is true to a considerable extent today), the army and the navy were considered to represent professions to which any bright young man might be proud to belong, in spite of the fact that they offered very little in the way of material reward. Thus we find that when the war began and the southern officers resigned and returned to their home states, the Confederacy was able to put in the field, almost immediately, armies commanded by such men as Johnson, Stonewall Jackson, J. E. B. Stuart, and Robert E. Lee, whereas the North had to depend in the beginning on old General Winfield Scott, the hero of the war with Mexico, and General George B. McClellan, who though undoubtedly a great organizer, failed lamentably as a commander in the field. In addition, Lincoln spent some two years in vain search for a general who could win battles, and was not successful until he found at long last Ulysses S. Grant and gave him supreme command of the Federal forces.

The program in the North in 1861 was simple, and if it had been possible of execution, would have been thoroughly effective. Almost everyone believed that all the North had to do was to dispatch a strong army from the neighborhood of Washington, march a short distance, lay siege to Richmond, capture the city, scatter its defenders, and then spend a month or two in rounding up the fugitive troops of the Confederacy, after which peace would be declared and everyone would go home. The only trouble with this scheme was that nobody could be found who was able to carry it out. McClellan, Burnside, Polk, and many others tried to execute the general plan of operations, only to meet defeat after defeat from armies which were smaller than their own, but much more intelligently commanded. "Jeb" Stuart, the dashing cavalry commander of the Confederacy, actually rode circles around McClellan, cut off his supplies, destroyed his railroads, and captured his rear guards without anyone being able to stop him. And so the war which was to have been gloriously concluded with a grand review and parade down Pennsylvania Avenue sometime in the fall of 1861, went on and on and on until 1862 was a memory and half of 1863 had also passed. It was not until General Meade decisively defeated Lee at Gettysburg in July of 1863—a battle by the way which Lee had not wished to fight but which he had been forced to engage in for political reasons—that the tide of the war began to turn, and at last the greater wealth, resources, and man power of the North made themselves felt in a way which could no longer be denied.

It may reasonably be asked what all this has to do with finance, even if it is war finance. It has a great deal to do with it. Even today men who are not in any sense financial experts, are able to perceive that the Federal Government committed a long series of mistakes in financing the Civil War, and our generation is prone to reproach the statesmen of that day in no uncertain terms for the stupidity and lack of foresight which characterized the financial arrangements of the war between the States.

It is impossible to deny that the financial policy of our country during the Civil War was ineffective, lacking in wise policy, and much botched in execution. But on the other hand, it should never be forgotten that the financial plan adopted by the Government was intended to cover one short, sharp, victorious campaign, and that this plan had to be revised while still in operation so that it would be adequate to supply funds for a long-drawn-out conflict of nearly four years' duration, the eventual outcome of which, during almost half that time, was extremely doubtful.

Unquestionably, the war finance of the sixties was distinguished by a long succession of mistakes in spite of which it finally supported the nation to a successful issue, and these mistakes began before the fight started. The first and perhaps the greatest mistake of all was Lincoln's appointment of Salmon P. Chase as Secretary of the Treasury. Chase knew very little about finance, and he proceeded to prove his ignorance. No one, however, should blame President Lincoln too severely for making this appointment. It was strictly in line with precedent, as Chase had been one of the leading contenders for the presidential nomination, and furthermore represented the great and powerful state of Ohio, so that, by placing him at the head of the Treasury, the President brought one of his leading opponents into his own group in a position subordinate to himself, thereby going a long way towards eliminating him in any contest which might arise concerning the nomination four years thereafter. At the same time he greatly pleased the citizens of a powerful state. Also it is fair to say that at that time President Lincoln probably did not believe that war was imminent, and thought that Chase, who possessed considerable ability, would make a fine figure as head of the Treasury during a time of somewhat troubled peace, while the real work of the Department could be satisfactorily discharged by his subordinates. This plan, however, was destined to be no more workable than the ninety-day campaign against Richmond. Within thirty days after Secretary Chase took the oath of office, he was engaged in the unfamiliar task of financing the United States to fight a great Civil War.

Since the financial program of the war period was deeply affected by the personality of the Secretary of the Treasury, it will be profitable to review briefly the history and characteristics of this remarkable man. First let us recollect his personal appearance, and the effect which it created. He was tall, broad-shouldered, handsome, dignified, and egotistical to a degree which it is difficult for many to understand. He may have had a ray of humor in his cradle but it probably vanished when he began to toddle about the room. One can never imagine the infant Chase laughing at himself when he fell down in rompers. He was an earnest man and industrious. He was not a native of Ohio, but lived a great part of his life as a hard-working lawyer in the City of Cincinnati. From the beginning, he was an uncompromising Abolitionist in a town which was only across the river from slave-holding Kentucky, and for commercial reasons, the great majority of people in his own class were by no means opposed to slavery as an institution, though they happened to live in a free state. Chase had the courage of his convictions. More than that, he was willing to risk his social standing and his lucrative law practice in order to champion the rights of many poor friendless fugitive slaves. For this he deserved reward, and by a curious irony of fate the reward he got was to be elevated to a position for which he was thoroughly unfit, and in which his many good qualities were hidden and his weaknesses were glaringly exposed.

He was, however, far more than a lawyer Abolitionist of persistence and ability. He was a fine speaker in the florid style of the day, and he was a shrewd politician. Unquestionably, he possessed elements of leadership. He gathered about him a majority of the citizens in his district who, though they lacked social distinction and were on the whole plain people, mostly farmers, nevertheless possessed the power of numbers and were inspired by a sincere enthusiasm to drive the curse of slavery from the land. These plain people elected Salmon P. Chase Governor of Ohio in 1856, and in 1860 they were solidly behind him in the Republican convention and made a determined though unsuccessful attempt to nominate him for the presidential office. So we can readily perceive that when Abraham Lincoln selected Chase as his Secretary of the Treasury he had excellent grounds for doing so, and although his principal motive may have been political, he had no reason to feel that he was placing an inexperienced and unfit man in a great office, always admitting, however, that Chase's experience and fitness could not be said to be connected in any way with finance.

Let us now see what the new Secretary did when the war cloud broke. Certainly he was compelled to start with very little in the way of funds, for curiously enough, although the general condition of the country at the close of Buchanan's administration was excellent, there was very little actual money left in the Treasury. Indeed there was only $1,716,000. The Secretary's first task was to estimate the financial needs of the United States during the fiscal year of 1861-62. In his first report to Congress, Chase estimated that the sum needed for the succeeding year was approximately $320,000,000. The mere estimation of probable expenses, however, was the easiest part of the Secretary's task, for having stated the sum which must be produced, it then became his duty to suggest to the Congress ways and means for raising it. At this point Chase made his initial and perhaps most serious error. It was, however, an error for which there was abundant precedent, and it was also caused in great degree by the fact that, in common with the great majority of the other northern leaders, Secretary Chase sincerely believed that the war would be of short

duration. In an earlier chapter of this book, attention was
called to the financial program conceived by Albert J. Gallatin
for the purpose of supplying the funds necessary to win the
war of 1812, and it was then shown that Gallatin adopted a
policy of raising the ordinary expenses of the Government
during the war period by means of taxation, and producing
the additional and much larger amount of money required
for war expenditures by means of loans—the thought being
that a war is fought by one generation but not for the benefit
of that generation alone, and that further succeeding generations should bear a just proportion of the expenses. There
is a great deal in this theory that is appealing, and to a considerable extent just, but, if the final welfare of the nation is
the result chiefly desired, such a policy is illusory and ineffective. Carried to its logical conclusion, it means that for several generations a country must struggle against a large
national debt, during all of which time its credit and prestige
are adversely affected. A far better system is the one adopted
by the Wilson administration during the World War and
regularly pursued by Secretary Mellon during the post-war
administrations of Harding, Coolidge, and Hoover. Such a
plan of war finance makes national prestige the main objective. From the beginning of the war period, it places a heavy
burden of taxation upon the generation carrying on the war,
but at the same time permits an extensive borrowing policy.
Then, the war over, the taxation program is continued in a
gradually diminishing ratio, with the purpose of discharging
the burden of borrowed debt during the lifetime of the young-
est generation of the war period. The theory is that such a plan
of operations, though undoubtedly burdensome to the generations alive during the period of conflict and the twenty years
succeeding, nevertheless is calculated to bring the nation itself
back to a normal financial state at a much earlier date than
nations which employ the Gallatin plan, thus giving to the

people a strong and improved position which can result only in international leadership and greatly augmented national power. It is fair to say, however, that no financier of Secretary Chase's time had ever tried to finance a war in accordance with the methods of McAdoo and Mellon. The theory of Gallatin represented the standard plan of war finance, and for a political-minded and inexperienced secretary it was certainly the easiest way out of a difficult situation.

On the other hand, one is prone to believe that moderation was as much a virtue then as it is now, and the great trouble with Secretary Chase was that in arranging his program of war finance he showed very little moderation in his methods. He pursued a policy of extensive borrowing and neglected the opportunity to impose war taxes to an extent which was not warranted by the Gallatin theory. Undoubtedly Chase acted as he did because he thought that the war would soon be won, and he feared to impose taxes upon the people because he was afraid that such taxes would be resented by the electorate, would be difficult to repeal when once imposed, and would react most unfavorably to the Republican Party at the next presidential election.

In taking this position, however, the Secretary and his associates showed that they were not in touch with the fundamental spirit of the nation. Many wars have been fought from motives of greed or aggression, but every really great war involves a moral principle of a highly controversial nature. In the Civil War the issue was slavery, and our fathers had a feeling in regard to that institution which, as the years go by, it is increasingly difficult for us to understand.

The people of the North believed that slavery was a relic of barbarism, and that it was unjust, immoral, debasing, and vile. The people of the South believed that it was a patriarchal institution ordained by God, fortified by Holy Writ, beneficial to the slaves, and from an economic point of view vital to the welfare of the southern states, which, in this way only, could develop their resources and maintain supremacy in agriculture.

There was no middle ground to the sincere and upright minds of either side, and the result was a war horrible and devastating. Old friends were separated, families were divided, and it was more than forty years after the fighting was over before the bitterness of the conflict was completely assuaged.

Under these conditions the people of both North and South were willing to be taxed from the very beginning. In fact, many of them demanded it, and only the political leaders failed to appreciate that at this crucial time taxation was not regarded as a curse, but as a blessing and a crown of principle.

Instead, therefore, of sensing the true situation and beginning his administration with a demand for an extensive program of taxation, Chase entered at once upon a financial policy the chief characteristic of which was reliance upon Government loans. It is true that he found the Treasury surprisingly depleted; indeed, it was astonishing that in a time of prosperity the only available funds in the Treasury should amount to $1,716,000 and that $18,000,000 of new debt should have been incurred during the latter part of the previous administration. However, such was the case, and Chase was quite justified in making new loans to meet this unexpected and unhappy situation. Thus, during April, 1861, he sold $8,000,000 worth of 6 per cent bonds at prices between 94 and par, and during May he placed on the market $7,000,000 of 6 per cent bonds at lower levels. This financing, however, was clearly intended to meet inherited obligations and should not have seriously interfered with the initiation of a new and stronger policy.

The first opportunity Chase had to outline a plan of war finance occurred when Congress met in July, 1861. At that time he made suggestions which in the light of later events were to seem pitifully inadequate. He recommended that approximately $30,000,000 of additional funds should be raised by taxation. He advocated a direct tax, an income tax of 3 per cent, and a policy of confiscation of rebel property upon which he relied to a much greater extent than he should have done. Congress itself seemed to realize that the Secretary's financial program would prove inadequate, and during its earliest session after the capture of Fort Sumter it provided for the issue of $250,000,000 of Government obligations. It was upon the basis of this blanket authority, that Chase negotiated the first big loan of the war, namely, $150,000,000 three-year Treasury notes bearing interest at the rate of 7 3/10 per cent. This loan was marketed through a coalition of eastern bankers, and it resulted in a series of misunderstandings between Secretary Chase and the financial leaders of the East which hastened if indeed it did not cause the suspension of specie payments by the northern banks, and the Government itself on December 30, 1861.

It is difficult to speak justly of this situation when more than seventy years have intervened since it occurred, and yet perhaps the very passage of time enables us to obtain a better perspective than would have been possible at an earlier date. Let us see in the first place what the chief mistakes were which the Secretary made at this juncture, and then endeavor to understand the motives which led him to make them.

In the fall of 1861, the country had been at war since the preceding April; also it was a civil war, and the entire financial and commercial structure of the land was much more disorganized than it would have been had we been facing a foreign opponent as a united people. We had no national bank, no system of supervision over state banking institutions, no national banking system, and no scientific method of conserving specie. There was unquestionably drastic need of some kind of currency with which to carry on business, and if large amounts of Government bonds were to be sold for coin, it was inevitable that specie would be withdrawn from business at least temporarily, and there must be some substitute to take its place. The only substitutes then existing were the notes of the state banks and the notes issued by the Government itself. The bankers requested—indeed almost demanded —that as they sold the $150,000,000 of the new Government loan, they should be allowed to retain the proceeds instead of being compelled to settle with the Government in coin; that the Treasury should accept from them their own notes in settlement of the bond sales, and furthermore, should, so far as possible, allow the proceeds from the bond sales to remain with the various banks on deposit, and only check upon them as occasion might arise. They further requested that the Treasury should, so far as possible, refrain from issuing demand notes of the Government during this period, for the inevitable result of large issues of Government notes would be that they would enter into immediate competition with the state banknotes as currency, thereby making the transactions of the bankers more difficult, and tending toward a general depreciation which would extend to both the notes of the banks and those issued by the Government.

It does not seem that this was an unreasonable series of suggestions on the part of the northern bankers who were unquestionably using their best efforts to market the first big war loan which the Government had issued. It is a fact, however, that the Secretary of the Treasury positively refused to accede to any of the requests. Mr. Chase claimed that he was legally obliged to insist that only coin should be received by the Treasury in payment for the bonds. This position was strongly controverted at the time and it seems foolish now. Under any circumstances, he was most unwise in not endeavoring to have Congress immediately rectify the situation— which Congress would have been quite willing to do. He also declined to cease or even to moderate the rapid issue of additional notes by the Government, claiming that the country needed currency of some kind so badly that he had no choice but to proceed as he was doing.

These mistakes were fundamental ones, and, occurring early in the administration, probably had more to do with Chase's continued financial difficulties than any other factors. The immediate result of the position assumed by the Secretary was that the whole powerful banking fraternity of the North was alienated, and led to adopt a poor opinion of the Secretary's ability and temperament. Unquestionably, the general agreement among the banks to suspend specie payments on December 30, 1861, was the direct result of the Secretary's refusal to cooperate with the banks in connection with the first loan. To go a step further, it was the suspension of specie payments and the lack of a well-thought-out and practicable financial plan for carrying on the war which led to the issue of more than $400,000,000 legal tender notes, an action which is generally believed to have been the most unwise move made by the United States during the entire war period.

Many critics of Lincoln's administration have declined to go behind the record of events and give consideration to the causes which led to them, and such critics have unhesitatingly condemned not only Salmon P. Chase but the President himself for the halting, procrastinating, and unwise financial measures which were employed in the early days of the war. Let us, however, be more charitable, and let us take a broad view of the situation in the hope of ascertaining the underlying motives which actuated Chase in making his unfortunate decisions.

We must realize that, in spite of the events of President Buchanan's administration which should have constituted a distinct warning to all concerned, the Civil War came upon the North as a great surprise. Furthermore, the people of the loyal states sincerely believed that the war would be of short duration, and that with a fair amount of luck it ought to be ended before Christmas of 1861. The political leaders visioned a rapid assembling of volunteers, a brief training period, a victorious march down the peninsula ending with the capture of Richmond, and then a glorious review of all the troops on Pennsylvania Avenue in plenty of time to enable the boys in blue to get back home before Christmas. It seems ridiculous that any sane men should have seriously believed anything like this, but the fact is that most of them did, and starting with such a premise, we are much better able to comprehend the improvident financial policy of Secretary Chase than if we consider the Civil War from the standpoint of the trials and tribulations that actually filled four long, bloody years. Chase suggested few taxes because he thought he would not need them. He issued Government notes with a free hand and insisted upon Treasury settlement in coin, because he never dreamed that the war period would last more than a year.

Then, too, we must remember that Salmon P. Chase was not a banker in any sense of the word. He was a lawyer, an orator, a former Governor and Senator of Ohio; his contact with finance had been very limited, and his human relations included no bankers or financial leaders of any degree of prominence. It is probable that when he walked into the first great gathering of influential financiers which had been called to assist the United States in marketing its first war loan, he was unknown personally to more than 80 per cent of those present. This in itself was a handicap, and a severe one. Chase was not a good mixer, and he was essentially mid-Victorian. He was tall, broad-shouldered, indeed a fine figure of a man, but his deep-set eyes glowed with the fanaticism of the early Abolitionists, and were lit with no ray of humor. He was undoubtedly one of the great Republican leaders of his day. But men respected and feared him—they did not like him. Thus, by the irony of fate, the task of conciliating the worried and over-strained bankers of the North descended upon shoulders broad, it is true, but unbending and incapable of reasonable adjustment to meet a difficult and unexpected series of trying situations.

We must, however, continue our study of Chase in his human relationships if we are to understand the Government's increasing load of financial worries during the years 1861 and 1862. If the Secretary was unable to cooperate with the leading bankers of the United States, he was even more inept when it came to dealing with Congress. No man occupying a high Cabinet position was ever more out of touch with the prevailing sentiments held by the national Legislature than was Secretary Chase.

The Congress of the United States in 1861 was a legislative body obviously unbalanced politically because of the withdrawal of the southern members, and under the domination of a few leaders whose discretion and good judgment had been much affected by the war-time conditions, and whose main object in life was to preserve the Union regardless of the sacrifices necessary to do so. There were very few men in this Congress who had had much financial experience. In the Senate, Fessenden, who was later to succeed Chase in the Treasury Department, was the only outstanding financier, and he had had little practical experience. In the House the influence of Thaddeus Stevens was dominating, and in wielding it, he was assisted by E. G. Spalding of New York and Representative Morrill whose main interest was in the formulation of a tariff policy. Even within the confines of his own political party, Chase can hardly be said to have been popular. He was out of touch with the powerful eastern faction, and for years had been one of the greatest rivals of Seward, who was then Secretary of State and leader of the party in New York. Chase had been Governor of Ohio during the late fifties, and consequently had not been in Washington at a time when he might have formed friendships and alliances which would have been invaluable to him during his term as Secretary of the Treasury.

Therefore, when in December, 1861, Secretary Chase submitted his first regular report on the finances to the Congress, his suggestions came before a group of men who were not his friends and only in a general way his allies, who obviously did not regard him as a financier of ability, and who did not feel in any way obliged to accept his leadership in matters financial unless the measures he proposed seemed to them to be both adequate and just.

As a matter of fact, Chase's report was decidedly tentative and incomplete in that it did not strongly propose a definite and comprehensive program by which necessary funds could be raised to pay the cost of the war. Chase attempted to continue the policy he had outlined in the preceding July of taxing the people as lightly as possible, and paying the unusual expenses of the war period by means of Government loans. Hence he missed a golden opportunity to insist upon a drastic program of taxation, contenting himself with suggesting a slightly higher scale of internal revenue duties and an income tax to yield approximately $30,000,000. At the same time, he was obliged to admit that he had made a wrong estimate of the amount which the taxation he had already advocated would probably yield, and he also indicated that there would have to be at least $214,000,000 additional funds raised for war purposes. He asked Congress for blanket authority to make further loans of $200,000,000. In this connection he brought before Congress for the first time his pet theory of a national banking system. This was undoubtedly a splendid plan and, in the end, when he got it adopted, was of the greatest benefit to the United States. However, it was ill-timed to meet the desperate situation which existed in 1861, and the leaders of the Republican party in Congress were probably right in believing that it would not be effective to do the

work which Chase expected of it, although they eventually
realized that, entirely apart from the demands of war finance,
a national banking system was a desirable thing. When finally
instituted, it remained for many years an outstanding monument to the wisdom of its creator. Indeed, in the light of after
events, it is not too much to say that it constitutes Chase's
greatest contribution to the financial policy of the United
States.

We must, however, keep our minds focused upon the year
1861, and try to understand why Secretary Chase brought
out his national banking idea at that time and just what
he hoped to accomplish by it. As far as anyone can tell now,
Chase was strongly influenced in his advocacy of a system
of national banks by a strong dislike of state banking institutions, and an almost complete distrust of their methods of
operation and control. Whether or not the Secretary had a
further animus in this regard because of his recent controversy with the bankers who had assisted him in connection
with the first Government loan, it is of course impossible to
say, but it is by no means unlikely that he had such a feeling.
Chase did not like state banks. He not unreasonably believed
that their notes constituted an unreliable currency which was
frequently competitive with Government notes, and he thought
that it was high time that Congress should exercise control
over the credit circulation of the country. He believed that,
by means of a national banking system Government notes
could be made a reliable basis of the national currency, and
that, particularly in war-time, they could be kept in a reasonably safe condition, and as little inflated as the unsettled conditions prevailing at the time would allow.

There was reason in Chase's argument for his system of
national banking, but the x in the equation was the element of
time. Evidently the Secretary did not realize that it would
take a good many months to organize a chain of national

banks, and replace state bank-notes with a national bank-note currency. He also failed to understand that in time of war it would be doubly hard to put such a system into effect. Meanwhile the war was going on, and it was going none too well for the North. Expenses were rising to unparalleled heights. Gold was being drained from the country, and hoarded by individuals, firms, and corporations to an extent unprecedented up to that time. It was clear to every thoughtful man in Congress that something must be done to give the country a currency which would be adequate to the needs of business and war finance, even though it might be without definite maturity, unsecured, based entirely upon the national credit, and in a sense nothing more than a definite promise on the part of the United States to stand back of it eventually, if, as, and when it should be possible to do so. Also, there was nothing new in this situation. It was reminiscent of the bills of credit of the early colonies and the paper money of the revolutionary period. Many countries had adopted a similar type of paper bills under the stress of war and other conditions of economic crisis. In brief, the Secretary of the Treasury proposed to Congress a conservative and on the whole worthy system for establishing a national currency of Government bank-notes without, however, suggesting any efficient method of putting it into effect in time to give the country a currency which was desperately needed within a brief period. Congress, on the other hand, appreciating far better than the Secretary the vital need of the people, swept his whole ambitious plan into the discard, and substituted for it an entirely different scheme of operations which was embodied in the famous Act of February 25, 1862.

This act provided for a number of important legislative remedies in connection with the situation which then existed. It is unnecessary to try to describe it in detail. It will suffice to say that its two most important features were the provision

for the issue of $500,000,000 Government bonds bearing 6
per cent interest payable in twenty years and redeemable after
five years. These bonds were to be sold at market value for
coin or treasury notes. In the common parlance of the day
they were known as "Five-Twenties," and with the first large
issue of bonds, sold broadly through the country. The other
important provision of the bill was the authorization of the
issue of $150,000,000 of legal tender United States notes in
various denominations with a minimum of not less than $5.00.

In considering this epoch-making measure, we must segre-
gate for consideration the two leading features of the bill, and
by dealing with each in turn, endeavor to develop the further
history, first of the Government loans during the war period,
and second, the various issues of so-called "legal tender" notes.
We will then first discuss the fate of the "Five-Twenties" and
subsequent Government bond issues in an effort to discover
the policy which governed the Treasury and the Congress with
relation to the authorization and sale of Government loan
bonds. It should be remembered that the United States Senate,
a body which has frequently been less wise than the House of
Representatives, rendered valuable service in connection with
the Act of February, 1862, by amending the House bill so that
a sinking fund was established for the retirement of the Government debt, and that the bond interest should be payable in
coin. Undoubtedly these conservative after-thoughts had much
to do with the subsequent sale of the bonds. It was, however,
much easier to authorize a large bond issue than to dispose of
it, particularly during the years 1862 and 1863 when the North
was just beginning to realize that it had a real fight on its
hands and the southern generals were riding circles around
McClellan, Burnside, Polk, Hooker, and other Union com-
manders. We should never forget that just as the financial
standing of an individual is directly dependent upon his economic condition and general reputation for honesty and pros-

perity, so the financial standing and credit of a nation are directly dependent upon its reputation for successful operation, and in the event of war, for military and naval victories. This was clearly exemplified during the Civil War by the decrease in sales resistance to bond issues which occurred during 1864 and 1865 when the Union armies were in the ascendant, as compared with the dark days of the first two years of the war when the Confederacy won many victories, and until the defeat of Lee on the field of Gettysburg, seemed to have an excellent chance of attaining independence.

Chase's policy, if he really ever had one of a fixed and definite variety, was to issue as few big loans as he could get along with, to put them out at the lowest interest rates he thought practicable, and to make them as short in term as the bankers and investors would permit. There is no question that, in adopting such a policy, the Secretary was actuated by the purest patriotic motives, but it is also beyond doubt that on a number of occasions his adherence to these guiding principles led him into serious error. Thus, it was commendable for Chase to reduce the interest rate to 6 per cent, but when in the Loan Act of March 3, 1864, with the war not yet won, he cut the rate of interest from 6 to 5 per cent, he practically killed his market and left the country gasping for financial breath at a most critical period.

The Act of February, 1862, was followed by many others; a study of the various loan bills from 1862 to 1865 develops a complicated and bewildering state of affairs which it is unnecessary to understand fully in order to get a clear idea of loan policy of Chase and the bond situation during that troubled era. There were a few outstanding Government loan bills, the one already referred to and the Act of March 3, 1863, being among the most notable. The Act of 1863 authorized an issue which was known as the "Ten-Forty" bonds. The authorization was for $900,000,000, but only $75,000,000 were sold. It was obvious that this big new issue had been brought out much too soon after the Five-Twenties of the previous year, and there is no doubt that the two types of bonds competed with each other for popular favor in a very unprofitable way.

Again, the situation was complicated by the stubborn quality of Secretary Chase's mind. As has already been mentioned, the Act of 1862 provided that the bonds issued under it should be sold at market value, and this, for reasons best known to himself, the Secretary construed as meaning that they should be sold for par or better. No one else in the Treasury seems to have believed that this was the meaning of Congress, but Chase insisted that such was the case, and defied common sense and economics for a long time in a hopeless effort to make people pay more for the bonds than they were actually worth. Finally the matter was clarified in the Loan Act of 1863 and the Secretary's conscience was appeased, but this was long after the mischief had been done.

The bonds issued in 1863 were payable in not less than ten or more than forty years and bore 6 per cent interest. They were a good security even in the doubtful times during which they appeared. Their worth, however, would never have been sufficient to accomplish their disposal. This was brought about by an interesting succession of events in which the colorful personality of Jay Cooke, a Philadelphia banker, was first brought to the attention of the American people. Just as the Revolutionary War was brought to a successful issue not merely by the victories of Washington and his generals but also by the stupendous efforts of Robert Morris, so the Civil War would quite likely have come to an inglorious close for the North had it not been for the resistless energy, the flair for publicity, and the super-salesmanship of Jay Cooke.

Cooke sold the bonds of a struggling Government direct to the people when the market was glutted with them and

Confederate victories were of frequent occurrence. Cooke assembled in a brief time more than twenty-five hundred assistants and drilled them into the most efficient sales force which had ever existed up to that time. Cooke filled the war-time newspapers with patriotic appeals and alluring advertisements which not only called upon the people to buy the obligations of their country as a matter of duty, but showed them clearly that they could be patriotic and still serve their own pecuniary interests at one and the same time. Of all the interesting characters of that vital period in our history, there is none which has a stronger appeal than that of Jay Cooke. The author well remembers meeting Cooke while attending a fraternity convention at Put-in-Bay, Lake Erie, more than twenty-five years ago. Mr. Cooke at that time was a very old man, and on a sunny day in July he was found sitting on a pile of rocks on a little island in Lake Erie engaged in his favorite sport of fishing. At the distance of over a quarter of a century his image is still clear and his piercing glance is well remembered. He was a small man, spare of figure, but with a fine head and unusual eyes—deep, piercing, intelligent, and even in age full of fire. It is a privilege to have met personally so great a man.

Cooke had had an interesting and successful career before the War. Since 1844 he had been a member of the well-known firm of E. W. Clark and Company in Philadelphia, a financial house of established reputation. This firm had much to do with the early railroad finance of the United States, having been engaged in the organization and operation of such early roads as the Pennsylvania, Northern Central, the Philadelphia and Erie, and the Pittsburgh, Fort Wayne and Chicago Railroad. It had also had a great deal to do with the financing of the Mexican War, so that, when the Civil War came, Jay Cooke was no neophyte but was well able to become a leader in the important and delicate work of marketing the Government's bonds. It is difficult today to realize how vitally important it was to dispose of these bonds rapidly, but our forefathers realized this fact to the fullest. The Civil War soon after it began cost the country about a million dollars a day, which soon increased to a million and a half dollars a day and so it went on increasing until the end. Someone had to sell the bonds, and the bankers of the country, after disposing of the first war loan, became deadlocked with Secretary Chase, and after the suspension of specie payments were unwilling to enter into any further engagements to sell Government securities under his direction.

In this situation Chase naturally looked about him for a deliverer, and fortunately for him he found Jay Cooke. Sitting in his office at Third and Chestnut Streets, Philadelphia, Mr. Cooke resembled a great general on the battle-field. Men who were associated with him at that time have told the author that his tremendous personality dominated the entire scene. This beady-eyed little man for several years worked night and day, and in the end was completely successful. Singlehanded he flooded the country with sales literature and loan propaganda; single-handed he directed his army of salesmen and agents spread like a fine net throughout the loyal states; single-handed by hook and by crook he placed this huge mass of Government bonds of varying types and different maturities and interest yields in the hands of all the people. He called to them with a clarion note to serve their country in her hour of need, and he did not call in vain. It is interesting at this point to quote from a personal letter written by Cooke to Chase during the most intense period of his sales campaign. The letter was written on September 7, 1862 and said in part:

This has been a hard day. I have been at it from 8 A.M. until after 5—a continual stream, clergy, draymen, merchants, girls, boys and all kinds of men and women. Some of our citizens who came in— I mean those of mark—went out almost with tears in their eyes so overjoyed at the patriotic scene. We gave the day almost exclusively to smaller subscribers. 106 subscribed today and it is no small job to explain to so many ignorant people the why's and wherefore's. I am glad to say that they all went away happy and delighted and we bagged over $70,000 as the day's work.

There is no doubt that our country owes much of the success of the war to the efforts which Jay Cooke put forth to merchandise the Government loans and secure the funds with which to fight it, and perhaps no single individual ever owed more to another than Salmon P. Chase owed to Cooke. When Chase found Cooke he was almost at the end of his resources. He had antagonized the leading bankers of the country, he had failed to impress Congress with his national banking scheme, and he was frankly at odds with the leaders of his party both in and out of the national legislature. Had he not been able to sell the obligations of the United States directly to the people, he would almost certainly have been driven from office within a very short time—a thoroughly discredited man. However, he found Cooke, and Cooke saved him; also, which is far more important, he saved the North by raising the money with which to pay for the war.

The last great loan act was that of March 3, 1864, which authorized an issue of $200,000,000 of bonds with interest at not more than 6 per cent and redeemable at not less than five and not more than forty years within the discretion of the Government. A ruling was made that the minimum redemption period should be ten years, and thereafter the bonds of this loan were known to the people as the "Ten-Forties." This was the loan where Secretary Chase, with his usual ability to make patriotic mistakes, reduced the interest yield from 6 to 5 per cent and hence made it difficult to sell the bonds. This was the last loan issued during Chase's incumbency. Senator Fessenden who succeeded him proceeded under the Act of June 3, 1864, and during 1864 and 1865 issued more

than $800,000,000 bonds with interest at 7.3 per cent, and with
the aid of Jay Cooke, once more brought forward by Chase's
successor, he was able to market a large number of these
obligations in order to clean up the great final expenses of
the war.

This brief review of the chief Government loans does not,
however, include even a majority of the acts under which Government obligations were issued during this strenuous time.
Secretary Chase was never particularly enthusiastic so far
as the big loans were concerned. He did not like them, perhaps because he did not understand them, or at least failed
to comprehend their probable results. On the other hand, he
had a distinct affection for short-term loans and he put out
quantities of them. There were, for instance, the Treasury
notes of 1861, the "Seven-Thirties" of the same year, the one-
and two-year notes of 1863, the compound interest notes, and
many other short-term loans with varying and often conflicting characteristics. Chase was able to sell many of these short-
term obligations to banks and bankers, and he liked to do
this because it cost nothing in comparison with the larger
loans where he had to pay a selling commission, although Jay
Cooke defrayed his expenses out of his commission of ½ and
later ⅜ of 1 per cent and he got much quicker results, which,
of course, was what he was principally after. During 1863
and 1864, Chase was able to market through the bankers of
the eastern seaboard states, notably New York and Philadelphia, one-year notes amounting to $44,520,000 and two-year
notes in the sum of $166,480,000. Obviously, although the
Secretary could not obtain sufficient funds in this way to
finance even a considerable part of the war expenses, they
were of great assistance in putting through the general scheme,
and had a distinct effect in helping the currency situation, for
even in spite of the fact that many of them were coupon notes,

they did circulate to an unexpected extent among business people who in those years were hard put to it for currency.

It is now time that we turn back to the first great loan law of February, 1862, and develop its other important provision, namely, that providing for the issue of legal tender notes, and trace the development of that idea through the years which immediately followed. It has already been stated that in the Act of February 25, 1862, the issue of $150,000,000 of legal tender United States notes in denominations of not less than $5.00 was duly authorized. This was fiat money and the camouflage was slight. It not only meant that the Government was printing and issuing hundreds of millions of dollars in paper money which it was unwilling to state when it would redeem, but it meant that this paper currency was by legislative decree required to be accepted as legal tender for taxes, debts, and demands of all kinds due to the United States except duties on imports which had to be paid in coin and interest on Government bonds which was also declared to be payable in the same medium. This action by the Government was clearly a return to the fatal policy of paper bills which had been such a blot upon the history of colonial America and had resulted so disastrously during the Revolutionary War, making necessary the Act of Repudiation of March, 1780. It was frankly a type of legislation which could be justified only by the most dire necessity, of opportunistic character which was apparent to the most casual onlooker, and well calculated to reduce instantly the financial standing of the United States in the eyes of the entire world.

Such being the case, why was such a policy ever adopted? The question is a legitimate one; the answer by no means easy. It was certainly not suggested by Secretary Chase in his report of December, 1861. With all his blundering, he must be absolved of responsibility for this policy. The blame for its initiation is certainly not his. Indeed he objected to it vigorously at the time of its inception, and although he protested less and less as time went on and finally was brought to a state of almost complete acquiescence, it was only because he stood in desperate need of currency and saw no other method by which it could be obtained. As a matter of fact, the Secretary thought his national banking system would supply all necessary currency, and that was why he vigorously urged its adoption. Congress, however, with more common sense than Chase showed, realized the impossibility of establishing a system of national banks during war-time rapidly enough to meet the needs of a disappearing currency medium, and hence, under the leadership of Spalding and Morrill, substituted for the banking idea the policy of issuing legal tender notes.

Chase was by no means alone, however, in his opposition to this type of currency legislation. The leading bankers of the country interposed serious objection, and sought to suggest other plans which were, however, far too complicated to make them appeal to a somewhat radical Congress which was intent only on winning the war in the quickest possible time. Then, too, we must once more recollect that the idea in 1861 was that the war would be of brief duration, and probably no one supposed that the first issue of legal tenders would have to be greatly enlarged. But as time went on, and peace seemed to fade farther and farther into the background, the Finance Committees of the Senate and House felt compelled to start up the printing press again, and largely increase the volume of legal tender notes. The reason, of course, was the constantly increasing cost of the war which bore more and more heavily upon the northern states. Thus on July 11, 1862, another $150,000,000 of legal tenders were authorized, and on January 17, 1863, $100,000,000 more were put out, and again in March of the same year $150,000,000. Thus on June 30, 1864, there were actually issued and outstanding $431,000,000 legal tender irredeemable United States notes—which was the high-water mark of the legal tender flood.

There were very real distinctions between legal tender notes of different issues, one of which should be thoroughly emphasized. When first put out, the legal tender notes contained a saving clause which gave them whatever respectability they possessed. This was the provision which made the first and second issues convertible within five years at the option of the holders into 6 per cent Government bonds. Thus, by providing a method of turning a Government obligation without maturity into a Government gold bond with a known maturity date and a regular interest-yield, the worst feature of the legal tenders was made capable of elimination at the will of the holder. This provision, however, naturally operated to limit the sale of Government bonds, and this brought it into disfavor with the Secretary of the Treasury with the result that, at his urgent request, the Act of March 3, 1863, made no such provision in connection with legal tender notes issued thereafter, and in addition limited the right of prior holders of legal tender notes belonging to the first two issues to exchange these notes for Government bonds by stating that the option to this effect contained in the legal tenders must be exercised on or before July 1, 1863.

Of all the mistakes which Secretary Chase made, this was probably one of the very worst. It led somewhat indirectly to his resignation, because as soon as the Act of 1863 began to operate, the price of gold began to rise as the relation between the legal tender notes and Government bonds had come to an end and the great mass of paper currency was left with no barometer of value. Gold then became a commodity and almost instantly was seized upon by financial gamblers as a favorite medium for their operations. A gold exchange was formed, and the price of the precious metal was played with by the Wall Street brokers as though it were some gilded football of enormous proportions. So flagrant did the situation become and so desperate were the gambling operations of the gold ring, that both the administration and Congress felt that some drastic method must be employed to alleviate the situation. Again Secretary Chase displayed his lack of intelligence when an economic issue was involved and strongly advocated the passage of a bill to put an end to gambling in gold. The result was that the famous "Gold Bill" of June 17, 1864, was passed. This act made it illegal for anyone to contract to purchase or sell gold to be delivered on any day subsequent to the making of the contract; it also prohibited the purchase or sale of foreign exchange to be delivered at any time more than ten days subsequent to the making of such a contract, and further prohibited the making of any contract for the sale and delivery of any gold, coin, or bullion of which the person making such contract was not at the time of making the contract in actual possession.

The result of this unusual piece of legislation was just what the economists of that day expected and prophesied. It would not and could not work, and a bad situation was made intolerable. Between June 18 and July 5, 1864, the price of gold see-sawed between 95 and 185. Finally on July 2, fifteen days after its adoption, this law was repealed by Congress. Meanwhile, on June 29, 1864, Chase had sent his resignation as Secretary of the Treasury to President Lincoln. It is but fair to say that it is hardly likely that Chase resigned solely because of the repeal of the gold bill. There had been difficulties over patronage, and for some time Chase had felt that his presence in the Cabinet was becoming embarrassing to the President, and that his advice was not being followed. It is probable that he supposed that Lincoln would refuse to accept his resignation and beg him to reconsider, but the wise war President had by this time apparently become weary of his masterful and obstinate Cabinet officer, and had doubtless calculated that it would be a good thing to allow him to resign while their personal relations were still relatively unimpaired.

We have now reviewed the loan policies and the legal tender issues of the Civil War period, and there remains for consideration one other important feature of the time, namely, the various attempts which were made to raise funds for the prosecution of the war by means of taxation.

This was, of course, the weakest point in Civil War finance. Had the need for greatly increased taxes been adequately met during 1861 and 1862, many of the untoward events which occurred then and later would very likely have been averted. But in the beginning the North was completely deluded with the idea that the war would be a short, sharp, victorious conflict costing little in lives and money, and almost everyone failed to realize the necessity for providing through taxation for a long and dubious struggle. The result was a fatal mistake in policy which in the end was partially, but only partially, rectified.

Thus, at the beginning of the war, the tariff of 1860 was really a peace measure, and the tariff of 1861 showed only a slight increase in rates on such articles as sugar, tea, coffee, hemp, hides, rubber, and silk. Meanwhile almost two years passed away without the construction of a systematic plan of internal revenue, the proceeds to be devoted to the winning of the war. The Act of July 1, 1862, was the first comprehensive law which imposed a well-thought-out series of internal revenue taxes. Even in that act the policy adopted was to tax many things lightly and few things heavily. Thus taxes were placed upon nearly all luxuries such as wines, tobacco, carriages, yachts, plate, and other articles used by the wealthy; occupations were also taxed, checks bore internal revenue stamps, and tickets, steam-boat fares and all other payments in the same category paid similar tribute. It was indeed a general and inclusive law, and it served to make the people as a whole realize the existence and importance of the war without at the same time seriously annoying them. No sooner had the policy of internal taxation been adopted, however, than immediate steps were taken to raise the tariff as compensation to the merchants of the country who were compelled to pay unusual amounts in war taxes under the provisions of the internal revenue acts. This, of course, was the genesis of the high protective tariff policy which, beginning in the war-time tariffs of the sixties, reached its apogee during the next decade, in the end bringing defeat to the Republican Party which had so enthusiastically sponsored it, and so loyally protected it against the assaults of its critics and defamers.

The real upward movement in internal taxation, however, did not take place until 1864, when for the first time a serious effort was made to make the people as a whole pay a considerable share of the expense of the war. Thus, internal revenue taxes in 1863-64 produced $109,741,000; and in 1865, $209,464,000. This was real taxation. It meant that the people were paying until it hurt; it was sound conservative finance, the only trouble being that it should have been adopted two or three years previously. The fact that the tariff was raised in proportion to the imposition of internal taxes did not detract from the value of the changed policy though it introduced a complication which was to bring trouble in the future. At the same time the income tax, which in 1861 had been ·fixed at the low rate of 3 per cent on all incomes over $800, was increased until in 1865 it stood at 5 per cent on incomes under $5000 and 10 per cent on incomes above that level.

Contrary to all the expectations of practical politicians, there was very little grumbling during the latter part of the war because of the rapid and heavy additions to the tax program of the country. Indeed, the politicians had all along completely misunderstood the hearts and minds of the American people. The answer lay in the nature of the struggle which was being waged. It was not a war of selfish aggrandizement. It was a war of principle backed by altruistic emotion, and a sincere desire to help the down-trodden and oppressed. The people of the North and of the South as well responded to their leaders without reservation whenever they were called upon to do so and made their sacrifices of money, goods, and even life itself in order to maintain the ideals in which they so firmly believed. The Civil War was a tremendously unfortunate incident in the life of the nation. It stopped the natural progress of the United States for more than two generations. It was equivalent to the elimination of twenty years in the natural progress and up-building of the country, and its actual money cost as well, was huge, indeed astounding. It did, however, serve a vitally useful purpose because it definitely settled an issue which had so divided the people of the United States that it became impossible for them to develop the country with unity of spirit or with effective utilization of their unparallelled economic and natural resources. In other words, it was a necessary though evil event, and in the end it was paid for, as all great wars are paid for, by generations which were either unborn or in the cradle at the time that it was waged.

In concluding this brief review of the general financial policies which prevailed during the great struggle, it is but fair to say that although these policies were administered by Salmon P. Chase as Secretary of the Treasury, they were not his policies—with the exception of the national banking system which in the end proved a monument to his memory— and he is not to be solely blamed for the many errors which occurred in putting these policies into effect, nor should he be over-praised for some of the beneficial results which flowed from them. Secretary Chase, however inexperienced in finance, and cursed with an inflexible mind and stubborn nature, was a pure-minded citizen with statesmanlike qualities and a judicial temperament which in the end won the respect, if not the affection, of his fellow countrymen. He stands before us today as one of the leaders of a troubled time. He is perhaps at his best as the friend of the slave, the unselfish and courageous advocate of an oppressed race. He had no humor, he had little grace of mind, and he was not blessed with any genial qualities which would endear him to his generation; but he was a man of courage with constructive thoughts, a broad intellect, and great energy. He was fortunate in his associates, among whom we must never forget his greatest aide and collaborator Jay Cooke, the Philadelphia banker.

Chapter XIII

JOHN SHERMAN—THE RESUMPTION OF
SPECIE PAYMENTS

Just as the personality of Salmon P. Chase is interwoven with every part of the period devoted to Civil War finance, so the character of John Sherman and his manifold accomplishments as Congressman, Senator, and Secretary of the Treasury are inevitably connected with the years immediately following the war, when the debts of the struggle were refunded and the bitter conflict over the currency was waged. He was the great compromiser of the reconstruction period; his suggestions were largely followed in financial matters from the close of the war until 1875, when the Republican Party lost the congressional elections for the first time since the war. It was also as a result of his domination of Congress that the Resumption Act was passed just before the control of that body passed to the Democrats. By a curious turn of fortune's wheel, it was fated that in the administration of President Hayes, which began in 1876, he should be the Secretary of the Treasury whose duty it was to prepare the country for the operation of the Act which he had originally constructed. Thus it was as the result of his careful planning, that on January 1, 1879, after nineteen years of suspension, the United States should resume specie payment—and what is more, continue successfully to carry out redemption in spite of the warnings and misgivings of perhaps the majority of the leading statesmen and financiers of that day.

Since Sherman was so prominent during this vital time we should review briefly his long and interesting career. He came of a family prominent in American annals. The fame of his brother, General William T. Sherman, is known to every schoolboy and for a century to come will be connected with the old army song "Marching through Georgia." John Sherman, the younger brother, was born at Lancaster, Ohio, on May 10, 1823. In his early years he practiced law at Mansfield. He did not come into prominence until he was elected to Congress in 1854. He was then an Anti-slavery Whig, and shortly thereafter became active as one of the founders of the Republican Party. He served in the House of Representatives until 1861, and was then elected to the Senate. By a curious co-incidence, he took the seat made vacant by the resignation of Salmon P. Chase, who left Congress to become Lincoln's Secretary of the Treasury. Sherman's service in the Senate was long and honorable and lasted until 1897. It was not continuous, however, as he resigned in 1877 to become Secretary of the Treasury in the administration of President Hayes, returning to the Senate at the conclusion of Hayes's administration. In 1897 he again resigned to become Secretary of State under McKinley, but left office in 1898 owing to the unusual burdens placed upon his shoulders by the Spanish War, which at his advanced age he felt unable to bear. He passed away at Washington on October 22, 1900.

This brief summary of so important a life is nothing more than a framework which is presented at this point so that the reader may visualize the length of Mr. Sherman's career and the chronological order of his most important services to his country. Certainly, the contribution that he made to the statesmanship of his day cannot be adequately measured by a recital of the positions of trust and honor which he held. He was a man of splendid character, of unquestioned integrity, and of outstanding ability. The author well remembers seeing him sitting at his desk in the Senate chamber during the winter of 1897, just a few weeks, in fact, before his resignation. He was then an old man, but he was erect and dignified. He was clad in a long frock-coat of ancient fashion with a high, open, white collar and a thin string tie of glossy black. His long hair was as white as snow, and his thin sallow face was criss-crossed with innumerable lines of thought and care. His eyes were perhaps his most notable feature; they were large, dark, and singularly expressive. Altogether he was a personage in any setting, and even the casual observer could not mistake his significance or fail to consider him the notable man that he unquestionably was.

Mr. Sherman's career as a member of the House and Senate was so long and active that naturally enough he espoused many causes, and was connected with most of the important political movements of his day. An ardent anti-slavery man, his first battles were in opposition to the Missouri Compromise and the Kansas-Nebraska Bill of 1854 which was substituted for it. It was not, however, until he became a member of the Senate, that his ability in matters financial began to be generally recognized. He served upon the Finance Committee of the Senate, and after 1867, became its chairman. In this capacity he had much to do with the enactment of all the important laws of the reconstruction period affecting finance, and the ability he displayed at this time influenced President Hayes to appoint him Secretary of the Treasury in his Cabinet.

Like many great men, Sherman was open to the charge of inconsistency. As he went along, he changed his mind on a number of important matters. Though never a victim of the greenback heresy, he was liberal in his currency views, and vigorously opposed Secretary McCulloch and his friends when, immediately after the war, they came out in favor of contraction. He had voted for the legal tenders, and he never considered them the instruments of evil which many other conservative leaders earnestly believed them to be. Sherman was never an extremist, but, though a conservative, and a

strict party man, he was nevertheless almost as great a compromiser as Henry Clay. Always he endeavored to bring
contesting factions together and achieve a result which, even
if not wholly satisfactory to either party, nevertheless contained elements acceptable to both and constituted real
progress. This line of thought and action controlled him
throughout his entire career. Thus in 1890, twenty-five years
after the Civil War was over, we find Mr. Sherman before
the public eye as the author of the famous Sherman Anti-
trust Law, a statute which was so completely a compromise
between those who did and those who did not believe in controlling corporations by a business code, that its provisions
proved ineffective for the purposes for which they were designed, until in the Standard Oil case of 1911, the Supreme
Court, by enunciating the famous "Rule of Reason," put teeth
into the law, which it had never previously had.

It is men like this, however, who rise to great heights in
political life. The dashing leader of a contentious faction who
is unable to sacrifice any considerable portion of his ideals to
attain a much-desired result, may flash across the political
sky like a meteor, but he will not join the constellation of the
wise, and his light, instead of shining steadily for years, will
be bright but evanescent, and will soon fade from view. Such
a man was Roscoe Conkling, the brilliant, erratic, masterful
Senator who represented New York during the eighties. Such
a man also was Lord Randolph Churchill who rose to fame
in English politics with startling rapidity a generation ago;
then, in a few brief years, after quarrelling with his most loyal
supporters as well as with his inveterate enemies, left what
was in reality a slender fame to be carried on and greatly
augmented by his equally brilliant but somewhat less erratic
son, Winston Spencer Churchill, who is still a power in British
public life.

John Sherman learned the trade of politics in the House of

Representatives. Almost from the moment he entered the Senate, he was respected and followed as a man of moderate and sane views and a wise leader who was willing to indulge in the give-and-take of political life, to compromise where necessary, and where some vital principle was not involved, and who, in the end, was likely to attain the greater part of his objective, more slowly perhaps than some other men would have done, but after all, more effectively. It is doubtless true that Sherman's policy of compromise and moderation seemed hesitant and uncertain to many of his contemporaries, and it is also true that when he changed his opinions as to various matters of policy, which he certainly did from time to time, he confused even his most ardent admirers. At the same time, he always knew where he was heading and he was much more interested in eventual results than in intervening situations.

Let us now consider the financial situation of the United States immediately after the Civil War, and the more important events which took place in connection with the national finances during the reconstruction era.

In 1865, there were two outstanding necessities. The debt of the nation had to be funded, and that with the utmost rapidity. It was in a shocking condition, so confused as to terms and maturities that even experts were doubtful as to what it really consisted of, and when the various loans were to come due. There was equal need to restore value to the currency, for that had been complicated not only by a flood of legal tender notes but also by the liberal issue of Government short-time paper and the mass of state bank-notes, and, after 1863, by the addition of notes issued under the National Banking Act of that year.

Everything in this world is relative—we do not need the Einstein theory to prove the point. Although the figures of over seventy years ago do not seem unduly large to us today, we must remember how much smaller and weaker our nation was at that time, and judge them by the standards of their period, and according to those standards they were high indeed. Thus on September 1, 1865, the public debt amounted to the net sum of $2,758,000,000. Less than one-third of this was funded, $433,160,000 was represented by legal tender notes, and the rest was in fractional currency and a multiplicity of other forms of short-term obligations. So little foresight had been used in negotiating the debt, that even when Senator Fessenden succeeded Chase before the war was ended, the frequent maturity of Government loans gave him the greatest concern. His successors in the Treasury were continually harassed by the situation, which grew worse and worse as time went on, and which was not effectively relieved until the passage of the refunding laws of 1870.

The funding operations of Secretary McCulloch, who succeeded Senator Fessenden, were hampered by the fact that he was the most prominent advocate of a policy of contraction, and from 1866 onward, was in constant disagreement with Congress on this account. We shall have occasion to examine his administration with relation to the early policy of resumption of specie payments, but at this time our principal consideration is to trace the funding of the national debt. This did not make much progress until George S. Boutwell of Massachusetts succeeded McCulloch as Secretary in 1869. Boutwell was not a contractionist, and, though no advocate of greenbackism, he was not the fanatic in this regard that McCulloch was. Hence he readily obtained congressional backing to carry out the policy which he had most at heart, namely, the funding of the national debt at a low rate of interest. Thus the important acts of July 14, 1870, and January 20, 1871, were framed largely as a result of his suggestions. These acts authorized the issue of $500,000,000 bonds at 5 per cent redeemable after ten years, $300,000,00 at 4½ per cent redeemable after fifteen years, and $1,000,000,000 at 4 per cent redeemable after thirty years. It was also provided that these bonds of the Government must be paid in coin, be exempt from national and local taxation, and that none of them should be sold at less than par in gold. Other acts with the same object in view were adopted on December 17, 1873, January 14, 1875, and March 3, 1875. The result of this legislation was to place the war debt of the country on a stable basis and to provide for its liquidation at regular intervals, with an intervening interest charge of such a size as not to imperil general prosperity.

When the funding acts were first proposed, it was generally believed that the interest rates were far too low, and that it would be impossible to convert the outstanding national debt at such figures. The trend of the times justified the experiment, however, and long before the funded debt was finally paid, the interest rates appeared as high as they had originally seemed to be low. Thus, largely through the ability and vision of Secretary Boutwell, one of the two great objectives of the reconstruction period was speedily obtained. It is regrettable that the other objective, namely, the support of the currency and resumption of specie payment, was not handled with the same ability and consequently did not meet with equal success in the same space of time.

In 1865 the war was just over, the armies of the North and South were disbanded and for the most part unemployed, prices were high, debts were many, and the country was in the throes of a post-war slump. It was at this time that Secretary McCulloch made up his mind to carry out a policy of currency contraction looking to a speedy resumption of specie payment. There is no doubt that the Secretary sincerely believed that the country needed a sound currency much more than it needed an extensive one. He thought that the thing to do was to get the Treasury on a basis of gold payment as soon as possible, with the idea that, when this standard was attained, the natural increase of business prosperity would soon result in an economic situation which would make it comparatively easy to readjust the currency on a broader basis. It should be remembered in connection with this theory, that Secretary McCulloch had been trained as a banker in the Middle West, had served as Comptroller of the Currency, and had been largely concerned in establishing the national banking system. He was thus by training as well as by natural tendency, a conservative financier, and his policy was directly in line with his turn of mind.

Secretary McCulloch presented his views to Congress in his report of December, 1865, strongly advocating the retirement of the legal tender notes at the earliest possible day. He considered them a war measure, and believed that, having served their original purpose, they should no longer be allowed to cumber the national currency. His bold advocacy of a policy of contraction met with an immediate and favorable response from Congress, the House passing a resolution concurring with the Secretary's views on December 18, 1865. It is a well-known fact, however, that Congress is a body of unstable opinion, and usually reflects the public sentiment of any particular time. Thus the resolution of 1865 was entirely out of date by 1866, owing to a change in the economic situation of the American people.

The United States recovered from the Civil War much more rapidly than anyone supposed possible. Within a year after Lee's surrender, a great resumpton of trade had already set in. The railroads of the country were expanding rapidly, and there had begun that tremendous tide of immigration from Continental Europe which was to people the middle western states, develop agriculture as well as manufacturing, and bring to the nation a condition of prosperity that was to continue until the panic of 1873.

This rapid development of post-war America had a direct

effect upon our financial policy. As has just been said, within a year after Congress had concurred with the plans of Secretary McCulloch to contract the currency and retire the legal tenders, the waves of increasing business had caused a demand for currency of almost any kind, which literally swept the politicians of that day off their feet. Thus when the Act of April 12, 1866, was passed it incorporated several purposes. It was the first attempt to accomplish at least a partial funding of the national debt; and it conferred power upon the Secretary to convert temporary and short-time interest-bearing securities into long-term bonds already previously authorized. This was undoubtedly its most useful feature, and McCulloch was quick to take advantage of it. Its legal tender provisions, however, must have been extremely galling to him, for here Congress showed an appreciation of his eagerness to effect contraction, grudgingly giving him authority to retire $10,000,-000 of legal tender notes within six months and providing that not more than $4,000,000 should be retired in any one month thereafter. Even this limited authority was revoked by the Act of February 4, 1868, which in clear-cut terms prohibited any further reduction of legal tenders. By this time, however, Secretary McCulloch had already redeemed $44,-000,000 legal tenders, leaving $356,000,000 still outstanding.

The legislation affecting legal tenders had by this time become confused; moreover, a speculative element was being connected with it, because of the fact that it was generally understood that the Secretary of the Treasury had the power to add to the number of legal tenders within certain limits by executive order. The uncertainty as to when the Secretary would exercise his authority in this regard, was an unsettling factor in general finance, and the cause of considerable speculation in Wall Street. It has already been said that Secretary Boutwell was not a confirmed contractionist like McCulloch, and on occasion he exercised the power of adding to the legal tender currency. Thus in October, 1871, he issued $1,500,000 legal tenders, and in 1872, $4,637,000. In due time Boutwell retired from the Treasury, and Secretary Richardson who succeeded him was even more liberal in his legal tender views than his predecessor. The result of his attitude was that in the panic year of 1873, undoubtedly under the greatest pressure, he issued $26,000,000 legal tender notes as an emergency measure, thus raising the amount of legal tenders outstanding to $382,000,000.

By this time the so-called greenback party had gained much power and prestige, and probably as a result of Secretary Richardson's large issue of legal tenders, the greenbackers propelled a bill through Congress in 1874 which inaugurated a new phase of legal tender policy. It should be remembered that up to this time the various issues of legal tender notes which had been made by Secretaries Boutwell and Richardson, had represented merely the reissue of legal tenders which had been authorized and originally put out in time of war, and had not amounted to the issue of legal tender notes as a new proposition in peace time. The Act of 1874, however, constituted a clean-cut change in policy, because it provided that in time of peace there should be a permanent increase of legal tender notes from $382,000,000 to $400,000,000. Fortunately, President Grant vetoed the bill on April 22, 1874, in a message which is one of the most creditable documents he ever penned. Therein he stated unequivocally his unwavering adherence to the doctrine of a sound currency, and his unwillingness to permit any emission of legal tenders in time of peace, a policy which in his judgment would tend to lower the value of the currency of the United States. It took courage at that time to write such a veto message, but although Ulysses S. Grant may have been guilty at various times of poor judgment, and although he did not shine in the White House as

he did on the field of battle, no one who knew him ever
doubted his bravery or his patriotic love of the United States.

We have thus traced very briefly the most important events
in the battle to expand the legal tender notes of the war
period into a national currency of indeterminate value. It
may be profitable, however, to examine the arguments which
were made for and against the retention of the legal tenders
as a basic portion of our national currency. In doing this we
should be broad enough to admit that there was a good deal
to be said on both sides, particularly at the time when the
debate occurred. The financial policies in vogue during the
Civil War were admittedly imperfect, and no one who has
read the part of this book devoted to Civil War finance, will
have failed to observe that these faulty policies inevitably resulted in a condition of general inflation in which the currency was by no means spared. Granted that the legal tenders
were a necessity of war-time, they nevertheless operated to
make the money of the country comparatively cheap. As life
flowed along in many of its accustomed channels despite the
smoke and powder of the Wilderness and Gettysburg, large
numbers of the people contracted debts in terms of cheap
money, and naturally, after the war was over, desired to repay
them in currency of no greater value. This was natural; indeed, entirely human. If the reader had mortgaged his house
for $5000 in 1863 and received legal tenders in exchange for
his obligation, it would hardly be reasonable not to expect him
to put up a good fight to repay the loan in legal tenders
when it came due five years later. This was one of the basic
causes of the opposition to McCulloch's policy of rapid contraction and speedy resumption of specie payment.

Many people had other reasons for advocating the retention
of the legal tenders. From 1866 onward, business increased by
leaps and bounds. All lines of trade finished the war with
depleted inventories, and the immediate result was such a

demand for goods of all kinds, that the country started manufacturing again at a tremendous rate of speed. Scores of contracts were made daily involving many thousands of dollars. Bookkeeping would not take care of the mutual interchange of goods and services. Money was needed to adjust accounts and more money was needed than was available at that time. Our very success in the resumption of trade led to a new era of development; and immediately we began to borrow huge sums from the nations of Continental Europe, while the balance of trade set steadily against us through the greater part of the reconstruction period. Hence we were not getting gold from abroad, but were steadily exporting the precious metal from our own dwindling stores. Furthermore, we had great difficulty in selling United States bonds abroad, for Europe was far more willing at that time to purchase the bonds of our private businesses than it was to take our Government obligations. The reasons for this attitude were complex and make little difference now, but the effect was distinctly disturbing. It is entirely true that in the late sixties and the early seventies, this country in a period of rapid expansion developed a great and increasing need of currency, and it is really a wonder that under the circumstances, we did not extend our legal tender policy and continue the issue of this convenient form of currency in peace time. Fortunately, as has been said, wiser counsels prevailed, but the point to be emphasized is that the need of almost any kind of currency was very great, and this constituted one of the most valid arguments against a policy of contraction.

On the other hand, the opponents of the legal tenders were those whose knowledge of economics rose superior to mere opportunism. Statesmen like Fessenden, McCulloch, and Boutwell realized that no nation could maintain an independent policy as to its currency, which was contrary to the usage of the civilized world. The world at large had at last realized the primacy of the gold standard, and the necessity of basing essential currency values upon that precious metal. It might be all very well to mobilize the nation's credit during time of war in the form of legal tender notes, but with the passing of such a crisis there must be an orderly return to the standard of other nations if, in the end, national prosperity was to be attained. At the same time, the method to be employed in the accomplishment of resumption was the subject of animated debate even among those whose financial ideas were thoroughly conservative. Thus John Sherman, though always a resumptionist, was nevertheless by no means a contractionist. He was not in favor of a rapid retirement of legal tender notes and a coincident accumulation of a relatively large gold reserve. He believed that such a policy would be entirely too drastic for the conditions of commerce and banking which then obtained. Nor did he believe with some extremists that resumption could be easily accomplished as the result of a mere executive order on the part of the Treasury. In spite of his national pride, he realized that such an order would be useless from an economic point of view, without long and arduous preparation to make it effective. His theory, and it still has much to recommend it, was that the thing to do was to take no precipitate action looking toward resumption, and without increasing the legal tenders, to let them stay about as they were.

Sherman believed that, as this prosperity increased and the great western country opened up to commerce, the balance of trade would gradually change in favor of the United States, the tide of gold would slowly turn in our direction, and in the course of a comparatively short term of years, the natural advance of prosperity in the United States would give to our currency a new value which would make eventual resumption of specie payment a matter of little difficulty when the right moment should arrive. That is, Sherman was willing to wait until the prosperity of America gave additional value to the national currency. Such a policy might be compared with that of the late Judge Gary who as president of the United States Steel Corporation suspended dividends on the common stock and plowed back the earnings of the corporation into the business over a period of years, until by such a method he had squeezed out the large amount of water which the original capitalization contained, and had given a new value to the capital stock of the company.

With the later doctrine of inflation which was represented by the greenback party, Sherman had no sympathy whatever. The greenback heresy, as it was called, was an elaboration of the arguments used by those favorable to legal tenders and was a frank championship of fiat money. The greenbackers believed that money had no value except as it represented the wealth and power of a nation, that it was merely a medium of exchange for goods and services, that it needed no arbitrary standard of value such as gold or gold and silver, but depended solely on the strength of the nation issuing it as expressed by a series of executive orders. Much the same idea is entertained today by no less a personage than Mr. Henry Ford, whose economic theories are, fortunately for him, less understandable than his automobile engine.

The general theory back of the greenback faction is not novel in any way, but has appeared at various times in the world's history and is based on ignorance and greed. It is neither logical nor persuasive to any educated person—but a theory does not need to be either one or the other in order to achieve political success, and for a time greenbackism was a real menace to the welfare of our country. The policy which was pursued by the United States Treasury under several secretaries approximated Senator Sherman's fundamental conception of what should be done. It is true that, particularly in 1873, there was a greater issue of legal tenders than Sherman would in all probability have desired personally, but on the whole, the resumption of specie payments was delayed long enough to enable the country to recover from the effects of the war and enter vigorously upon a new and highly prosperous period.

The most curious thing connected with the matter, however, is that it was not until after the panic of 1873, when the Republican Party, partly as a result of that financial cataclysm, had lost the control of a government which it had possessed unrestrained for more than two generations, that the majority party under the direction of Senator Sherman took the first overt action to bring about that resumption of specie payment which the Senator had personally desired for many years. It is doubtful if such action would have been taken at that time if the Republicans had not been well aware of the fact that in the next Congress they would be in the minority. It is a fair inference that they determined to get all the credit possible from the passage of a resumption law, and then to leave that law on the doorstep of the incoming Democratic majority— very much as a good billiard player who sees that he is about to finish his run always endeavors to leave the balls in as bad a position as possible, so that his opponent will have the greatest difficulty in making a successful shot when his turn comes.

There were other phases of the greenback heresy besides the constant urge to increase the number of legal tender notes outstanding. One question which grew out of the cheap money craze and remained unanswered for a long time was the question: What medium should be employed to pay off the bonds of the United States as they matured? Most of the acts under which these bonds had been issued during the war period stated unequivocally that they should be paid "in coin." Nevertheless, after the war was over and the fight for cheap money was under way, a large and constantly increasing portion of the population made every effort to abrogate this solemn promise made by their own Government and to substitute for it payment in Government notes.

At times even more dangerous suggestions were made, as for instance, when President Johnson suggested that instead of paying the interest on the Government bonds it should be applied to the reduction of the principal, a suggestion which if it had ever been adopted, would have amounted to partial repudiation of the debt. Fortunately this particular sub-issue did not last very long, for it was decided in the presidential campaign of 1868. The Democrats believed that it would have popular appeal to favor the use of paper to pay specie debts; the Republicans, however, with their usual canny appreciation of the attitude of big business, stuck manfully to the hard money argument and, as the result proved, more accurately sensed the feelings of the people and won the election. The successful candidate for the presidency, General Ulysses S. Grant, did not hesitate with respect to this matter, which he regarded of vital import. In his inaugural address, delivered March 4, 1869, he definitely affirmed the policy of his party, and gave full assurance that when Government bonds became due under his administration, they would be paid in gold.

To return now to the Resumption Act which was passed on January 14, 1875. This act was a curious example of ill-considered hodge-podge legislation. It had many provisions, most of which are of no special interest at the present time. It did, however, cover two subjects of outstanding importance. It provided, in the first place, that specie payment should be resumed by the Government on January 1, 1879; that this end might be accomplished the Secretary of the Treasury was authorized to use any surplus specie in the Treasury, and, if he deemed it necessary to do so, to sell bonds of the classes authorized under the Act of July 14, 1870, so that additional gold might be obtained. The second important provision was that the greenback circulation should be reduced to $300,-

000,000 by a method therein indicated, after which there was to be no further reduction of this form of currency.

Thus, just as they left office, the Republicans framed up a prodigious task for those who should be in control of the Congress between that time and January 1, 1879, a five-year period during at least two of which they were certain that the Democrats would be in control, and would have the greatest difficulty in preparing for resumption; whereas, if the Democrats should decide to repeal the Resumption Act, they would be certain to antagonize a large and important part of the nation, particularly the banking and corporate interests, and would give themselves an issue which it would be difficult for them to explain in the presidential election two years later.

From a political point of view the Resumption Act was one of the cleverest, indeed one of the most ingenious, measures which was ever adopted by the United States Congress, but the way in which it eventually worked out really amounted to an ironical jest so far as the Republican Party was concerned.

The Democrats fully realized that the Resumption Act was loaded with dynamite, and shortly after they became the majority party, they made strenuous efforts to have it repealed in the hope that if they got rid of it quickly, they would minimize the effect of its repeal upon the next presidential election. That election was probably the most bitterly contested and most unsatisfactory one ever held in the United States. It is still a problem as to who was actually elected President in 1876. There is no doubt that the vote was extremely close, and the final decision of the matter by the electoral commission was never satisfactory to the Democrats, nor indeed to many fair-minded Republicans. It will always be a regrettable fact that a man with as much ability as Rutherford B. Hayes should have been pursued, throughout his term of office, by such a cloud upon his title to it. However, we are not now discussing the result of the Hayes-Tilden contest except as it affected the resumption of specie payments.

One of the first appointments which President Hayes made was that of John Sherman as Secretary of the Treasury. Sherman accepted, and although it is uncertain whether or not he appreciated fully the humor of the situation, he was immediately compelled to undertake preparation for the resumption of specie payments in strict accordance with the provisions of the bill which a few years previously he had helped to prepare, with the principal object of embarrassing the Democratic Party and making political capital for himself and his associates.

We may now note that there existed a great difference between John Sherman as Senator and John Sherman as Secretary of the Treasury. Many men are poor legislators and good executives, and *vice versa*. Few men are so versatile that they can shine equally in every rôle. President Taft, for example, left much to be desired in his discharge of the duties of the presidential office, but completely rehabilitated his fame during the last decade of his career because of the manner in which he discharged the onerous obligations of Chief Justice of the Supreme Court. So it was with Sherman. As a legislator he showed qualities of leadership, but he was unstable of opinion, equivocating, and perpetually prone to compromise even at times at the expense of principle. On the other hand, as soon as he became Secretary of the Treasury in the Hayes Cabinet, he displayed a firmness, judgment, and energy which caused men to rub their eyes with astonishment, for they never had seen him exhibit such qualities before. Instantly he began to prepare for resumption—and no one knew how to do it better than he did, for he had been acquainted for twenty years with the difficulties involved.

He was convinced that, in order to resume specie payment with any certainty of being able to continue it, the United

States must have and must maintain a gold reserve amounting to approximately 40 per cent of the United States notes outstanding. The difficulty, of course, was to accumulate such a reserve in the brief time at his disposal. In order to attain the desired end, the Secretary initiated and carried out a policy of prudent economy. He exerted all the influence he possessed to restrain the always lavish expenditures of Congress; he consistently saved the funds received by the Treasury from payments of customs duties; and he also sold Government bonds when he could obtain a fair market for them. As a result of these accumulative efforts, he was able by January 1, 1879, to establish a gold reserve of $133,000,000 over and above all liabilities—an amount only $4,000,000 less than the 40 per cent which years before he had selected as his ultimate goal.

The Secretary took another step in the interest of resumption which evinced a touch of financial genius. It does not seem as astounding to us today as it did to Sherman's contemporaries, but when the Treasury suddenly applied for membership in the New York Clearing House, Wall Street was utterly taken aback. Even after the institution of the sub-treasury system and the operation of the National Banking Act, the United States Treasury had still continued to be regarded as a somewhat sacred institution to be administered wholly apart from the ordinary machinery of finance, so that, when Secretary Sherman applied for the admission of the Treasury to the Clearing House Association, he broke all precedents and amazed all beholders. There was, however, a very definite and excellent reason for admitting the Treasury to the Clearing House: it would enable the Government to avoid specie payment with the other members to a very large extent, as balances would be used to settle mutual obligations and the greater part of inter-member dealings would be handled by bookkeeping entries. This wise move was of the greatest assistance to the Treasury after specie payment was resumed.

Sherman, however, foresaw one difficulty which he knew it would be hard to surmount. This was the legal provision forbidding cancellation of United States notes redeemed in gold and compelling their reissue. In its inception this restriction was purely political and thoroughly bad from an economic point of view, but there seemed little hope of getting Congress to repeal it at that time. Secretary Sherman therefore met the issue squarely and when redemption was an accomplished fact, refused to reissue redeemed notes on the theory that it was illegal to reissue United States notes which had been paid out of the gold reserve. The strength of the authority on which the Secretary based his view of the situation has always been open to serious doubt, but the practical advisability of the policy he pursued in accordance with this theory has never been seriously questioned. Nevertheless, in spite of all the careful preparations which Sherman made, it is extremely doubtful if resumption would have been a success, indeed if it could even have been maintained, had it not been for a situation which developed almost at the last moment and which was of such great assistance to the Secretary in connection with his resumption policy, that it may even now be regarded almost in the light of a gift from above. At any rate, it was a clear illustration of the old saying that "it is an ill wind that blows nobody good."

The year 1879 was in many ways a peculiar one. In the early part, business in the United States was bad, and the rate of exchange was dangerously near the point of gold export. It looked as though it would take only a slight push to throw the balance of trade definitely against the United States, and if this should occur, it seemed impossible that resumption of specie payment could be initiated, let alone maintained. However, as the year progressed, the weather began to play a freakish and yet dominating part in influencing both agriculture and international trade.

In America, the spring and summer of 1879 were normal and even benign. It was a harvest of bumper crops, and in particular, wheat and other cereals showed unexpectedly fine results. In England and on the Continent of Europe, however, it was a season of almost continuous rain, sleet, and cold. It was remembered in England for a long time as "the year without a summer." Wheat and all other grains rotted in the ground, and by July everyone was praying for relief and making contracts to import grain from the United States. This was the final factor which worked wonders in favor of the resumption policy. The grain exports in 1879 from the United States to Europe were far in excess of any previous year. Immediately all danger of an adverse balance of trade was dissipated, and the gold, instead of being steadily drawn away from this country, started to pour in in a steady stream. The result was that on January 1, 1879, Secretary Sherman resumed specie payments in accordance with the provisions of the Act of 1875, and thanks to his careful foresight, strength of character, and wise preparations, together with the fortunate economic situation just alluded to, he was able to continue this vitally important policy with increasing success, so that by 1880 its permanency was assured.

There has probably never been a period of such political and economic chaos as that which began immediately after the Civil War and which terminated, officially at least, with the resumption of specie payment in 1879. It was one of those times of stress and darkness through which every great country must pass; and among those who bore its burdens and faced its problems and terrors with courage, ability, and resource, no name now stands out more clearly and with more honor than that of John Sherman of Ohio.

Chapter XIV

THE TARIFF AS AN ISSUE IN THE UNITED STATES

In any large country there are bound to be many issues which arise in each period and which divide the sentiment of the people into strongly contending camps. Nearly all the issues which arise are basically economic in character, but a few become so vividly important that they lose their economic significance and become political.

There have been four such issues in the United States since its foundation, the tariff, monetary standard of value, slavery, and prohibition.

Elsewhere we shall deal with the interesting history of "free silver." Slavery and prohibition we shall not touch. In this chapter, we shall endeavor to trace briefly the history of the tariff laws of the United States.

The difficulty about the tariff in the past, the present, and the future, has been and is that though essentially purely economic it has of necessity been raised as a battle standard by each one of the contending political parties in the country, and therefore has been surrounded with much more bitter contention than it should have aroused. It has been attacked and defended, not on a basis of scientific inquiry, but on grounds of self-interest and ambitious partisanship so intense that the truth regarding it was certain to be obscured and a wealth of misinformation concerning it was sure to be disseminated.

General Hancock was no economist, but a great-hearted, simple-minded soldier, and it is probable that no one has contributed a more thoroughly wise comment in connection with the tariff than he did when he remarked that "the tariff is a local issue." As a matter of fact, it has been always a local issue and is so today. The bitterness on both sides has been largely dictated by the geographical location of the contending factions. Had the Democratic Party been dominant in the northern and central tiers of states, it would probably have been as much in favor of a protective tariff policy as the Republican Party would have been in favor of free trade or tariff for revenue only, if it had been located as the majority political organization of the South and the Southwest.

In colonial days, and indeed for a generation after the Revolution, the tariff was an academic question. This was due to the absence of an important manufacturing interest in the country. New England was the shipping center and the seat of our fisheries; the middle states and the South were preponderantly agricultural. Then came the long period of the Napoleonic Wars with the conflicting decrees of England and France, prohibiting the United States from trading with either country. As the result of this international impasse, our youthful government adopted the Embargo and Non-Intercourse Acts which nearly amounted to commercial suicide, and left our ships rotting at their wharves, rather than precipitate a conflict with either of the two great nations who were locked in deadly conflict across the sea.

It was during this period of trade abstention, that the northern and middle states first made real progress in manufactures. Up to this time America had been importing all her luxuries and many of her necessities from abroad. Even the bricks of the fine old colonial mansions were imported from England as ballast, and such things as coffee, tea, silks, and furniture were brought over in large quantities and were readily disposed of to the well-to-do members of the community. From 1807 onward, however, this trade was seriously interrupted and often completely closed so that the American people were forced by law and circumstance to make their own goods or go without them entirely. This situation was intensified by the War of 1812, for during that time of strife it was impossible for us to buy goods from our best and most logical customer, England, and it was very difficult because of the activity of the British navy for us to purchase them elsewhere. Hence we can readily understand why manufacturing became in a comparatively short time an important feature of the economic life of the middle Atlantic states and from them gradually extended to New England and the West. One can also understand why the new interest in manufacturing did not arouse much interest in the South and Southwest. There were two reasons for this. Climatically the South was well adapted to agriculture and particularly to the growth of cotton. From the earliest colonial times, advantage had been taken of this fact by the settlers in that region, and slavery had been employed as an economic tool to foster agriculture under the direction of a supervising class of land holders and slave owners. There was no middle class in the South comparable with that in the North, and colored slaves did not possess the energy, the industry, or the mentality necessary to enable them to function successfully as factory hands. This situation was fundamental and was instantly recognized by the governing class in each part of the country, so that, from the beginning of the period when the manufacturing interest of the country began to develop vigorously, the tariff as an issue assumed the important place in American political life which it has maintained until the present day.

It is quite true that the tariff was discussed in theory by our leading statesmen long before it became a practical consideration. Alexander Hamilton in that one of his five great reports which was devoted to the subject of manufactures discussed the tariff problem from every angle available in his day, and declared himself in favor of a moderately protective policy, but it was not until after the war of 1812, that the tariff became a vital issue.

What do we mean by the tariff?

It is an inclusive term and indefinite. Speaking generally, a tariff law means an act imposing customs duties on imported goods. Thus, strictly speaking, any import duties, however slight, constitute a tariff system; but there is the greatest possible difference between the basic theories on which such a system may be founded.

The theory which has always appealed to the South and Southwest as represented by the Anti-Federalists, Republican-Democratic, and Democratic parties has been that import duties should be imposed only for the purpose of obtaining sufficient revenue to pay part of the cost of maintaining the Federal Government. The theory which has been stoutly advocated by the North and West as represented at various times by the Federalists, the Whig, and the Republican parties, has been that import duties should be levied not only to help defray the operating cost of the Federal Government, but for the further purpose of protecting various industries of the United States, which, largely because of a radical difference between the wage scale here and abroad, would be unable to compete with foreign industries of a similar character, without the assistance of equalizing import duties designed to prevent the citizens of this country from purchasing foreign goods in competition with those of domestic manufacture.

The actual development of the tariff laws of the United States may be divided into two principal parts, the first extending from 1789 to 1860 and the second from 1860 to the present day.

The first part covers a series of acts of a much more moderate character than those which were adopted during the second part. The best way to trace the evolution of our tariff policy is to discuss briefly the more important acts of each period. Thus we find that the Act of 1789, which was based on Alexander Hamilton's Report on Manufactures, though protective in theory was actually very moderate so far as its particular duties were concerned. The Act of 1816 was the first law which raised duties on imported goods to any material extent; this was followed by the Acts of 1824, 1828, and 1832, which progressively raised import duties to heights which though satisfactory to the manufacturing interests of the North, were increasingly unacceptable to the agricultural commonwealths of the South. During this period the Whig Party, which was directly descended politically from the Federalists, was in its lusty hey-day under the domination of Henry Clay, one of the most brilliant statesmen of the early republic. Clay and his most eminent associate, Daniel Webster, were the acknowledged leaders of the Whigs. Webster was primarily a great orator and a profound lawyer; Clay was not only an effective speaker, but he possessed infinite shrewdness and a sense of political values. These men and their associates represented in Congress the manufacturing states of the North, and at the behest of their constituents, they missed no opportunity to increase the duties on imports in order that the trade competition of continental Europe might be minimized in favor of domestic business.

On the other side, the Democratic Party, representing the planters of the South and led by such intellectual giants as John C. Calhoun of South Carolina and Thomas H. Benton of Missouri, fought vigorously every move of their opponents for tariff increase. They did their utmost to attain the ideal of free trade, which was cherished by their constituents for the reason that the South was not a manufacturing section and desired freedom to purchase its goods at the lowest prices. The South was further influenced by the fact that cotton was fast becoming the staple product of the southern plantations, and it was greatly feared that if the North succeeded in erecting a high tariff wall England would retaliate by placing a high duty on cotton which would result in great loss to the South. This situation developed slowly over a period of about fifteen years, and eventually resulted in a tense situation which almost precipitated civil war, namely the Nullification Proclamation of South Carolina in 1832.

It is unnecessary to do more than refer to this violent and unfortunate dispute, but, had it not been for the courage and patriotism of Andrew Jackson, then President of the United States, it is highly probable that the country would have been engulfed in the vortex of civil war at least two generations before such a conflict was actually experienced. Jackson, however, stood firmly as a rock for the preservation of the Union, and South Carolina being unable to obtain sufficient support from the rest of the South to start hostilities with any chance of success, submitted to the inevitable with very bad grace.

At this critical moment, however, Henry Clay with that ability which has entitled him to rank as one of our greatest statesmen in spite of the political chicanery to which he sometimes descended, realized a compromise on the tariff must be arrived at between the contending factions, if civil war was to be averted, so he set out to frame such a compromise law without delay. The result was a curious piece of legislation known as the "Compromise Tariff of 1833." It was thoroughly unscientific, with economic implications of an unfortunate and dangerous character, but unlike many laws of this country, it accomplished the purpose for which it was designed. It was an important factor in bringing about a truce between the contending factions which, if it did not amount to a permanent peace, at least gave both sides a breathing spell. In conjunction with Clay's other great measure, which dealt with the slavery question, and is still famous as the Missouri Compromise, it remanded the agony of civil war for a period of nearly thirty years.

In framing the tariff of 1833, a plan was employed which was calculated to secure a gradual reduction of duties over a period of nine years. The idea was to meet the wishes of the southern leaders, and at the end of that time, to have the tariff duties adjusted to a level of 20 per cent. In order to avoid undue hardship to northern business men, the reductions during the first part of the period were made relatively slight, but towards the end of the period they were greatly increased. In order to arrange for the contemplated reductions, the tariff of 1832 was taken as a basis. It was provided that all duties in that tariff which exceeded 20 per cent were to have one-tenth of the amount by which they exceeded 20 per cent taken off by January 1, 1834. Then there were to be similar reductions of additional tenths from the same basic rates on January 1, 1836, January 1, 1838, and January 1, 1840. Accordingly, on January 1, 1840, all duties in the act of 1832 exceeding 20 per cent would have been reduced by four-tenths of such excess. After 1840 the machinery of the act began to work much more rapidly, for the law provided that on January 1, 1842, one-half of the remaining excess was to be deducted and the other half was to be eliminated on July 1, 1842. Thus, on and after July 1, 1842, all tariff duties would be reduced to a horizontal level not exceeding 20 per cent.

There never was another tariff law like this one and there probably never will be another in any way resembling it. The reason for its peculiar system of reductions was essentially political, and in this sense alone it was successful. There was no economic purpose back of the act, and as a matter of fact sound economic policy was disregarded in drafting it, so that from such a standpoint it proved to be a failure. The worst thing about it was the sudden drop in tariff levels after January 1, 1842. It was impossible to prepare the business world for such an event, and when it came it considerably upset the trade and commerce of the time. Nothing was said in the act about what should be done about specific tariff duties, but the Treasury so interpreted the law that they were placed on an ad valorem basis. In the end the country had, instead of a well-constructed and naturally varying schedule of tariff duties, a general duty rate of 20 per cent which applied to all tariffs and was lacking in discrimination and common sense.

It is interesting to note that during the period when this law operated, the country experienced its first great panic and depression, in 1837, but luckily the law did not work out fully until after that panic was over and better times were beginning to arrive. It was obviously, however, without the elements of permanency which its sponsors believed it to possess, and it remained in full force and effect for a period of only two months.

In 1842 the Whigs were in power. Generally speaking, they were believers in a moderately high tariff, so on September 1, 1842, a new law was passed, which, though not a high tariff according to our present standards, was nevertheless so regarded by all parties at the time of its adoption. Taking the Act of 1842 as a whole, it may be fairly said that it practically did away with most of the reductions obtained under the Act of 1833 and brought the situation back almost to where it had been ten years before in 1832.

In 1846 the Act of 1842 was superseded by another bill of a very different character, because by this time the Democrats had once more come into power. The party was fortunate in having a Secretary of the Treasury who was blessed with an unusual amount of brains. Secretary Walker not only understood the Democratic theory of tariff duties, but he took an active part in framing the bill. The supporters of the measure claimed that it exemplified the principle of free trade, but it did not go nearly so far. It was really a measure enacted in accordance with the principles of modern protection. It was, however, far more carefully drawn than most of its prede-

cessors, and for the first time the plan of segregating related
tariff duties into separate schedules was initiated. In 1857
the Democratic Party, being still in power, adopted a new
act which once more materially lowered the rates, so much so
in fact that those applied to most protected commodities fell
as low as 24 per cent. This Act of 1857 remained in force until
the Civil War. The tariff laws of this pre-war period have been
much criticized and commented upon both by the adherents of
protection and free trade. Every effort has been made to blame
the depression of 1837 on the tariff of 1833, and the panic of
1857 on the tariff act of that year, while the free traders have
ascribed the period of prosperity which existed just prior to the
Civil War, to the low tariff acts of 1846 and 1857.

Again, it should be emphasized that in this country the
tariff, though properly related purely to economics, has been
in practice a political matter, and hence both sides of the question have been deeply affected by political partisanship. There
is little doubt that during the period we have been considering,
the tariff laws were more than slightly related to the various
national depressions, but on the other hand there are many
better ways of accounting for pre-war prosperity than through
the lowering of tariff duties.

The Civil War was an epoch-making event in the history
of our country. Like all great social disturbances, its effects
could not be predicted in advance. Even at the present time it
is difficult to trace fully the results of that national calamity.

In the field of the tariff duties, however, the war had some
definite and indeed extremely rapid effects. The South as a
whole had been opposed to high tariffs, indeed, opposed
even to moderate tariffs ever since the War of 1812. As soon
as the war began, the southern senators and representatives
deserted Congress and returned to their respective states. This
left the old Whigs and the new Republicans representing the
North in full control of the legislative branch of the Govern-

ment—which was the worst thing that ever happened to the Republican Party. It takes no argument to prove not only that a responsible opposition is of the greatest value to the maintenance of good government, but that in a two-party state, it is just as important from the standpoint of the opposing group. Men are very human, and unrestricted opportunity is bound to result in license and unbridled exercise of power. This was what happened in connection with the tariff legislation during the Civil War period and after. The Tariff Acts of 1862, 1864, and 1865 represented a steady increase in rates on dutiable articles, far in advance of anything which had ever been thought of previously. It is true that there was reason for a considerable advance in tariff at this time. From 1864 onward, internal revenue duties were much increased in order to provide money to win the war, and in order to equalize matters for the business men of the North who were compelled to pay heavy internal revenue taxes, the tariff duties were coincidentally raised as a matter of justice and relief. The trouble was not that the theory was wrong, but that in practice the steps taken in tariff legislation far exceeded the economic needs of the people. The men in charge of congressional affairs at this time were conspicuously intolerant of opinions adverse to their own. These were the days when Thaddeus Stevens of Pennsylvania ruled the House, with Justin Morrill as his principal aide and coadjutor. To their minds the great issue of the day was the preservation of the Union, and incidentally the firm establishment of the Republican Party as a national dominating force. In accomplishing their designs they considered that a high protective tariff would be of great value, and so they raised the rates without compunction, believing that in doing so they were conferring a distinct benefit upon the American people.

After the Civil War, throughout the violent and unhappy years of national reconstruction, a strong effort was made by the Republican leaders to keep the tariff up to the Civil War levels. Under the guidance of John Sherman, Blaine, Garfield, and others, the Republican Party definitely adopted a permanent system of high tariffs. Thus the Acts of 1870, 1872, and 1875 were all highly protective, maintaining the new levels of tariff duties which had been introduced into our economics during the Civil War period. The only attempted modification during these years was a general 10 per cent reduction in the Act of 1872, which, as the result of the panic and depression of 1873, was promptly repealed by the Act of 1875.

By 1883, however, a new generation had arrived. Most of its members had been born either during the war period or immediately afterwards, and as they had no recollection of the struggle, and only an academic appreciation of the violent feelings which brought it about, they naturally looked with considerable doubt upon the ultra-high tariffs to which the people of the United States had been forced to submit since the war. It was beginning to be increasingly difficult for Republican orators to convince their hearers that Meade's victory on the third day of the Battle of Gettysburg was an excellent reason for raising the tariff on hides. The Republican leaders began to perceive that their open season was approaching a close, and they consented to make a considerable number of alterations in the tariffs, which they embodied in the Act of 1883. Although the Republicans claimed they had made many reductions, their alterations in rates left the tariff still high, and the act in question may be said to have been more of a revision than a methodical reduction. Shortly thereafter, the Democratic Party elected its first presidential candidate since the Civil War, Grover Cleveland. Cleveland was a big man in every way. He was rough and crude, particularly in foreign relations, but he was honesty personified and a true patriot. In 1887, at the close of his first term, when he appeared to have a splendid chance of reelection, he considered it his duty to warn the

country of the dangers which lay in the unreasonably high
tariff policy which had existed for so many years. By his
famous tariff message of 1887, which destroyed his chances for
the presidency, he brought before his countrymen in a forceful
way the whole question of tariff revision. No doubt this satisfied his conscience; it certainly constituted a great public
service.

Of course when the Republican Party came into power they
considered that they held a mandate from the American people to revise the tariff upward, and the McKinley Act of 1890
was the result. This act was purely partisan, representing the
extreme views of the Republican Party along the line of high
protective tariff legislation. It was not so important in itself,
for it was no great departure one way or the other from the
acts which had preceded it, but it was important in that it
was a contributing factor to the defeat of the Republicans at
the next election. The Democrats came back to office feeling
as certain that they had a public duty to perform in connection
with the tariff as the Republicans had felt four years previously.

At this point, however, the curious series of alternating
tariff policies was decisively and violently broken. The so-
called Wilson Act of 1894 will long be remembered because
it registered the first serious break within the Democratic
ranks regarding the tariff. This break may be explained by the
changes which had been taking place in the economic condition
of the South since the Civil War. A new South was growing
up, for there had been a great deal of penetration by northern
manufacturing interests. North Carolina had entered on a
career of manufacturing which it has since pursued with great
profit. Georgia and Alabama were following in North Carolina's wake, and Atlanta and Birmingham were almost like
northern towns. Even in far-off Louisiana, the sugar industry
was growing rapidly, and the wealthy planters of that state

were calling upon their senators and representatives to see that the infant industry which meant so much to them was properly protected. They cared nothing whatever as to whether such protection should be construed as heresy to the Democratic Party.

Thus, when President Cleveland urged upon Congress the necessity of a genuine tariff reduction bill, he found that he was no longer supported by his party leaders as a unit. Some were loyal, many were sullen, and a few—unfortunately men of great ability—were openly defiant and rebellious. The act as it passed the House of Representatives was not so bad; it represented a sincere effort to accomplish tariff reduction. But when it got into the Senate, it was so amended that its original sponsors could hardly recognize it. Senator Arthur Pew Gorman of Maryland was the leader of the group of protective Democrats, a man of fine mentality, native shrewdness, and infinite resource. When the bill finally went to the President it was in effect a moderately protective measure, and so contrary to Mr. Cleveland's ideas and beliefs that he refused to sign it. He did not veto it, however, because bad as it was, he considered it a distinct improvement on the McKinley Act, but in grief and rage he allowed it to become a law without his signature.

The next election was not fought upon the tariff as an issue, but the contest was based on the currency question which had been coming to a head for years and had suddenly become so vital that it dominated American politics. This was the first Bryan campaign. When William McKinley was elected, he determined to return to the tariff and make that a leading feature of his administration, in order to avoid the currency issue. A good many able leaders in his own party believed in silver, notably Senator Teller and his western colleagues who composed the group which walked out of the Republican convention rather than support a man who was believed to be wedded to the gold standard. McKinley, therefore, thought that the safe thing to do was to keep away from the currency, and bring the tariff back because it was a good old Republican issue. Everybody knew where the Republican Party stood upon it, and even though it would make trouble, it was not loaded with dynamite as was the currency question.

Therefore, after much discussion in Congress and out, the Dingley tariff was adopted. This was another highly protective act, but it had the distinction of lasting longer than any other tariff law in our history. It was not replaced by other legislation until 1909. The reasons for this were two-fold: one was that the country was recovering from the panic of 1893 and just entering a period of great prosperity, and the other was that Theodore Roosevelt had become President after McKinley was assassinated. He was an exceedingly able politician, and believed that conditions were such that the revival of the tariff as an issue would bring about national uneasiness and much discussion accompanied by violent feeling which would probably embarrass and cripple his administration. By adroit maneuvering he was able to let it alone throughout his time as President.

In 1909, however, when William Howard Taft occupied the White House, it was found necessary to revise the tariff in response to a wide-spread demand for lower duties on the part of the public. The trouble was that, when Congress formulated its tariff policy, President Taft was found to be too weak a leader to control the situation, and the tariff was revised upward under the guidance of Senator Aldrich of Rhode Island and Senator Penrose of Pennsylvania. Both were men of great experience and outstanding ability, and both were thoroughly persuaded that the salvation of the United States depended upon the maintenance of the policy of high protection. The Payne Act of 1909 was undoubtedly one of the causes of Taft's failure to be reelected President.

It was regarded by many of his own party as a distinct breach of faith. Indeed, the moderate protectionist group among the Republicans was growing fast, and the strength of this body was first displayed in connection with the debates regarding the Payne Act. As a sop to the moderate protectionists, a Tariff Board was established in 1911, but it had very little effect upon the situation except to give some hope for the future.

Again there was a change in party control when Woodrow Wilson became President of the United States. Whatever may be said of Wilson in connection with his foreign policies, it is generally admitted today that much good domestic legislation was adopted during his administration. The tariff act of 1913 was of course a Democratic measure. At the time it was passed, Wilson had a working control of Congress and the act therefore represented his economic ideas in this field. It was a low tariff act, with some of its parts representing a policy of moderate protection. More important than the act itself was the establishment by the Wilson administration of a permanent Tariff Board with a considerable degree of power and ability to operate autonomously. This act was received by the American people with a considerable degree of general approval. It seemed to mark a distinct change in the attitude of the two great parties toward the tariff. In other words, a large body of the Republican voters was standing out vigorously for moderate protection as opposed to the old high tariff policy, while an equally important group in the Democratic Party was insisting on moderate protection instead of the old shibboleth of free trade.

Since 1913 both parties have to a certain extent come together on a theory of moderate protection, differing only in degree and in the ways in which they seek to apply the principle. It is quite true, however, that the tariff radicals in both parties sometimes get the upper hand. This was the case in connection with the tariff of June 17, 1930, the most recent statute, which started in to be moderately protective and limited to a definite number of schedules, but ended by being closer to the Payne Act than was generally anticipated.

The Act of 1913 lasted until 1922, the intervening period being notable for the establishment of a tariff commission with stronger powers in the year 1916. In 1922, during President Harding's administration, a tariff act was adopted which on the whole was moderately protective in theory and in practice. It was more of a non-partisan measure than the Republican Party had ever previously agreed to. Of course it had some rates which were indefensibly high, but it represented a distinct modification in Republican doctrine. This change of view, however, has not lasted very long, for by the act of 1930 the Republicans have shown that they intend to return to their historic policy of a high tariff.

The purpose of this brief review of the tariff acts of the United States, has been to call the reader's attention to one outstanding fact; namely, that the tariff, inherently a matter of economics, has been for more than a hundred years a political issue in this country and, regrettably, bids fair to continue so to be. It is to be hoped, however, that, as we progress, we will become nationally conscious of the serious error involved in making a purely economic matter a political football, and will place our tariff legislation of the future on a basis far more scientific and non-partisan than it is today.

Chapter XV

CORNELIUS VANDERBILT—MASTER OF
TRANSPORTATION

A LITTLE brick town over which the spire of old Trinity Church towered amazingly; no houses beyond Grand Street and waves of river water lapping the shore beyond the spot where Canal Street now is—such was New York in 1810 when a lanky, broad-shouldered lad with a face hard and serious beyond his years, ran a clumsy sailboat known as a *Periauger* between Staten Island and the Battery. The lad was Cornelius Vanderbilt, born May 27, 1794, on Staten Island, and destined all his life long to be connected in some way or other with various kinds of transportation.

Some men are bound to succeed and give evidence of a brilliant future at an early age. Cornelius Vanderbilt was a man of this type. On his father's side he had the stubborn Dutch character which gives one staying power; from his mother, Phebe Hand, a New Jersey lass, he inherited the sturdy traits of a long line of English yeomen. Life was hard for the boy. His father was shiftless and a failure at business, and the family was a large one, most of the other children being girls. Cornelius from his earliest years showed a tremendous capacity for work and an enduring love of it. He also showed the utmost determination in accomplishing whatever he set out to do. His life reveals very few unfinished chapters. Indeed, about the only thing he ever failed in was his ambition to acquire control of the Erie Railroad, and it is only fair to say that although he did not succeed in this, it is doubtful if any other man situated as he was, could have come as near as he did to the attainment of his objective.

An interesting story has been related on many occasions to the effect that young Vanderbilt bought his first boat, the famous *Periauger*, with one hundred dollars which he borrowed from his stout-hearted mother, and that as a condition precedent he was obliged to clear a rocky tract of land in a short space of time, plow it, and plant it with corn. Both his parents believed that he could never manage to perform this labor within the time set, but they did not know Cornelius. He grinned, accepted the challenge, and then induced nearly all the boys in the neighborhood to help him with the work by promising them that when he got his sailboat he would give them free rides for the rest of the summer. Needless to say, he finished the job on time, although he was nearly exhausted physically by his efforts. But as usual, the joke was on the other fellows, for whereas they supposed that his main idea in purchasing the boat was to use it as a pleasure craft, the fact was that this steely-eyed young giant really intended nothing of the kind. Rather, he wanted to use the boat as a regular ferry between Staten Island and the Battery Landing in New York. Although he kept his word to the letter, the free rides that his young companions received were confined to ferry trips when if they did not look out they were virtually compelled to act as deck hands for the ambitious young captain, who gathered in the shekels with the utmost care and gave strict attention to his business and very little to his playmates.

At the end of the first year, Cornelius not only paid back to his mother the sum he had borrowed but also gave her a thousand dollars in addition to help her in her efforts to maintain her numerous family. This may not sound so extraordinary today, but one hundred and twenty years ago it represented the most tireless and unremitting labor. Man and boy, Cornelius Vanderbilt was one of the hardest workers this country has ever known. At seventeen he had the stature and strength of a grown man and the serious mental attitude which seemed well calculated to bring him success. He had practically no education except in the school of experience and hard knocks. All his life his speech was rough, crude, and profane. Even when he was the wealthiest man in New York and the object of flattery and adulation on all sides, his grammar was so weird that it was shocking to anyone of refined sensibilities, and his stock of profane expletives was so vast that even sailors, stevedores, and newsboys looked up to him with unfeigned admiration. In brief, he was a masterful youth, stout-hearted, strong of arm, and at all times utterly determined to get what he wanted and to wring success out of life, however great the opposition might be. In his youth he was a fighter, not exactly a brawler but with a chip on his shoulder for the benefit of anyone who came along and sought to interfere with whatever he wanted to do. We can readily imagine him as the fistic champion of the Staten Island docks with a hard word and a ready blow for anyone who stood in his way.

This being true, it is remarkable that he did not enlist in the navy during the War of 1812. It is inconceivable that he had any fear of the dangers of such service, and it is likely that if he had consulted his own wishes merely he would have been a man-of-war's man during the conflict. In accounting for his abstention, however, we must never forget that the urge of self-interest was always superior in his mind to any feeling of patriotism. The War of 1812 was not generally popular, and Vanderbilt probably felt that no principle was involved which he cared much about.

On the other hand, he must have been quick to realize that for a sober and industrious youth who stayed at home and minded his own business, the contest would be sure to offer considerable opportunity for quick profit. In this he was not mistaken, for from 1813 to the close of the struggle, he served the Government under contract and ferried large quantities of supplies to the New York Harbor forts. His charge was fair and his services could always be relied upon. Indeed, then as always throughout his life reliability was one of his greatest assets as a business man. Slow to give his word, he would spend any amount of energy and money in order to make it good when he had once given it.

It was in this same year of 1813 that the young captain married his first cousin, Sophia Johnson. As a young girl she must have been pretty with a trim figure and considerable native charm. No truthful biographer, however, can feel that Cornelius Vanderbilt helped his career in the long run by his marriage. Indeed, Sophia seemed to bring out the worst qualities her husband possessed. She obviously had no idea how to handle him

His mother, Phebe Hand, he feared to the day of her death in her eighty-fifth year. She was as determined as he, as hard-handed and as violent in temper, and the result was that for over half a century a most curious relationship existed between mother and son. With Phebe Hand, the domineering Commodore was always a small boy. He relied on her judgment, he confided to her his troubles, and from her more than from any other human being he took advice.

With Sophia, however, he was entirely different. He bullied and browbeat her outrageously almost from their marriage night. He ordered her around as though she were a slave. He dragged her from one house to another without in the least considering her personal wishes and with no thought of her personal happiness except as an adjunct to his own. It is probable that she brought this course of treatment upon herself by her genuine sweetness of character and the adoration for her husband which she was always foolish enough to show. He was a god to her and she worshipped at his shrine; human nature being as it is, this was exactly the worst course of treatment which any woman could have pursued with such a man as Vanderbilt. Early in the game he learned to regard his Sophia with contempt, and during most of their life together he treated her with scant tolerance, exacting implicit obedience and in her youth much physical labor, and repaying her devotion with treatment which at the best amounted to scant courtesy and at the worst descended to sheer brutality. It is not a pretty picture, this view of Vanderbilt's married career, but it is necessary to understand this side of his character if one would appreciate the rest of it.

Even during the War of 1812 young Captain Vanderbilt began to branch out and increase his trading facilities at a rapid rate. Between 1814 and 1818 he was able to acquire several small but speedy ships with which he entered the coasting trade, thus accomplishing within five years what many men would have considered enough for a lifetime of success. By 1818 the youthful ferryman had passed out of the picture, and in his stead we find a sturdy, energetic young captain who was a ship-owner and already a power in the coast-wise trade.

Had Vanderbilt continued in this type of sea-going occupation he would, in all probability, with his various characteristics, have accumulated a tidy fortune by the time he was fifty years of age and would then have retired to some pleasant farm within sound of the sea where he would have led a retired and useful life among pleasant surroundings. In other words, his life would have been cheerful, successful, but undistinguished. The man, however, was made of sterner stuff, and just as his original purchase of the *Periauger* marked an epoch in his career, so at the end of December, 1817, he reached another fateful decision which influenced his entire future life. At that time he was twenty-three and he owned three ships and had $9000 in cash. The easy thing to do was just to keep on going, and that was doubtless what his good wife Sophia tearfully advised. Young Cornelius, however, possessed a virile, inquisitive, and far-seeing intellect. His mind was of the single-track variety in that he was always figuring what line of conduct would result most favorably for himself.

We shall not understand this man either in youth or age if we do not realize that his motives were always intensely selfish. He was probably one of the most selfish men in American history, yet curiously enough his name comes down to us unassociated with the cloud of hatred and ill-will which surrounds the memories of men like Drew, Fiske, and Gould, who in later years were his contemporaries and strove with him in Wall Street and elsewhere, using no worse ethics than he and being just as determined to sacrifice everything and everybody if necessary in order that they might individually benefit and prosper. There was a difference, however, between Vanderbilt and these other leaders of his time, and that difference was expressed in a number of ways. For instance, the people used to say, "Drew and his crowd are the bears of Wall Street but the Commodore is always a bull." Put in another way, Cornelius Vanderbilt, excessively selfish though he was, was nevertheless a constructive genius. He was a builder, not a wrecker. He bought ships and sold them not merely for the profit involved but that he might buy other and bigger ships. In his day he mastered almost every known form of transportation. He was ferryman and coast-trader, he owned steamboat lines and transatlantic liners, and finally he became the great railroad king of his time. Yet always he pushed onward, ever onward. He was a man of genius, of inexhaustible energy and power. He lived to be eighty-two, and the accumulating years never caused him to cease his gigantic labors or even to slow down to an appreciable extent.

We have not yet, however, examined the decision which Vanderbilt made in 1817. Briefly, he decided after mature thought that the end of sailing ships was well in sight and that the future lay with steam. Like Kipling's "Sir Anthony Gloucester" he determined to be among the first to exploit the new and wondrous method of transportation. To do this he had to learn about steam-boats and he determined to begin at the bottom. He had noticed with interest and intense curiosity the wood-burning craft which snorted up the Hudson, and he knew that these boats carried the inventions of Robert Fulton and were protected by a state monopoly secured for Fulton's benefit by his partner Chancellor Livingston.

Much as he admired the principle of steam, however, Vanderbilt felt certain that, as a practical shipping man, he could vastly improve the design of these river steamers if he could work on them and learn more about them. In order to do this, he made a sacrifice which only a man of innately strong character would have dared to make. He sold his three ships, left the sea, quit business indeed as an independent ship-owner and sea captain, and hired himself to a wealthy man named Gibbons who ran a ferry line between New York and New Brunswick in opposition to the Livingston-Fulton monopoly. In short, he became a hired man for the steam-boat owner, and as one of Gibbons' captains, he set out to learn all there was to learn about this new-fangled method of transportation. It took nerve to do anything so revolutionary—and more than that, it took vision. This was perhaps the most valuable characteristic that young Vanderbilt possessed. He had then and indeed throughout his life an uncanny ability to foretell the trend of future events; he was always thinking ahead and visualizing the possibilities of the future with distinct relation to his own personal profit and eventual benefit.

At the same time, he determined to do everything in his power to make up for the loss of income which he felt was inevitable during the period of apprenticeship which he had laid out for himself. Therefore, with his usual disregard of

Mrs. Vanderbilt's susceptibilities and personal inclinations, he took her out of her comfortable home on Staten Island and installed her as mistress of a wayside inn near New Brunswick owned by his patron Gibbons and known as Bellona Hall. For ten years this faithful woman ran the country hotel with vigor and success, certainly contributing her share to the success of the family enterprise.

The years that Vanderbilt spent as one of Gibbons' steamboat captains not only were profitable from the standpoint of the knowledge of steam-boating which he acquired, but they had an adventurous quality which probably made them one of the happiest periods of the young man's vigorous career. Lawyers and laymen alike are acquainted with the famous case of Gibbons *vs.* Ogden by which the Supreme Court of the United States decided that no state could constitute a monopoly of the use of waters flowing through its boundaries. John Marshall, the greatest of our chief justices, wrote the opinion, and the argument was a battle of giants. It was in this case that Daniel Webster made one of the greatest forensic efforts of his career.

Before the ruling was obtained, however, the situation on the Hudson and other waters adjacent to New York amounted almost to a state of war. The Livingston-Fulton crowd, backed by all the power of New York State, earnestly endeavored to maintain their monopoly and shut out all competitors. Young Vanderbilt, as a captain in the employ of Gibbons, a rank outsider, came in for a great deal of attention at their hands. Again and again his opponents sought to serve all kinds of writs and injunctions upon him, but he was as slippery as the traditional eel. Many a time he hid successfully when his boat touched the New York shore, and he was even known to carry over-eager constables away on his boat and threaten to take them to New Jersey and have them jailed there if they did not leave peaceably without trying to serve him with legal process. Once when arrested on the New York side he was able to prove that he had hired his boat for the day to a member of the monopolistic combine, and he was thus enabled to laugh at those who sought to prosecute him. It was a great time for Vanderbilt. He was in the first vigor of youth. He feared no man, and he had a lust for life and for battle. His was one of those strong independent souls which fatten on conflict and seem to enjoy constant trouble and excitement.

The day came, however, when, in spite of all the scrapping, the beating of constables, the speed trials with the enemy on the broad river, and the constant flow of various and interesting trade, this energetic young man felt that his student days were over and that it was time for another great decision. Again he must strike out for himself. It was 1829, he was thirty-five years old, and he had one of those curious impulses which came to him from time to time. Now he felt was the appointed hour. He would be a hired man no longer. The bell of fate had rung. Sink or swim, live or die, the time had come when the name of Vanderbilt must stand for something big in the history of American transportation.

It is improbable that he put these thoughts into words when he broke the news to his old employer Gibbons. All he probably said was, "Well, boss, I'm a-goin' to quit." It was a blow to his employer, just as he knew it would be. Gibbons was a wealthy man and he had courage, but he was getting along in years and he could not run the *Bellona* as Vanderbilt had run her. Also he had no other horny-handed young giant with an eye of fire, a hand of steel, and a cold hard glance to take over the dangerous but profitable job that Cornelius wished to lay down. He begged and pled with his young associate not to throw up a good connection but to stick to the job and share in the profits. He offered to double his salary and to give him a partnership interest. Indeed, he was willing practically to let the young man name his own terms if he would only stay. As usual, however, with his mind once made up, Cornelius was as stubborn as a mule. He was nice to Mr. Gibbons who had always been fair with him, but he told him plainly that he thought his days of big profits were about over and he intended to go in for bigger game.

Again with that mystic vision which was always his, Vanderbilt perceived the untold possibilities of the Hudson River as a commercial highway, and he was determined to be one of the first to exploit it. Much to her disgust, he routed Sophia out of the comfortable inn at New Brunswick where she had made the one great successful venture of her life, and brought her and his fast-growing family across the Bay to a modest house in New York City, where for a long time they were decidedly unhappy for they were all country bred. Little did Cornelius care, however, what his family thought about their living conditions. All his life he dumped them around, and ordered them to enjoy themselves where he put them. He was not a home-body, his real interest lay elsewhere. Nevertheless, he did not neglect his brood in any material way. They were always on his mind and he had the same attitude toward them that a lion has for its cubs. He bit them, mauled them, fed them, and was only pleased with them when on rare occasions they got up the nerve to scratch him in return.

But to return to the Hudson which for some years to come was to be Vanderbilt's favorite battleground. With the money which he and Sophia had saved as a result of his early successes and his frugal method of life during the preceding ten years, Cornelius started his first line of river boats. Almost immediately he found himself in bitter competition with other lines powerful and long established on the river. Thus he fought the Stevens line and began a running fight with Daniel Drew which was to continue for nearly forty years and was to embrace steam-boats, railroads, and the stock market.

The conditions on the river in those days were exciting. Rates were cut on every side. Speed was one of the chief objectives. The boats were long white side-wheelers with big black stacks from which when they got under way poured huge volumes of smoke and flame. They were wood burners one and all, and they were operated with the utmost dare-deviltry and disregard of public convenience. Boiler explosions were frequent. Rival captains would steam up the river with their safety valves tied down and every ounce of steam pressure that their boilers would bear, so that the vessels shivered from stem to stern and every human on them was in constant danger of sudden death. Until they were deterred by several fatal accidents, and some rare prohibitive legislation, they used to make what was known as "flying landings" in order to save time at the river towns where they were supposed to stop. Passengers would be placed in small row-boats and towed astern. Then the river steamer would nose in toward the wharf, not stopping but slowing up and giving the passengers a chance to catch the pilings and clamber out of the small boat as the big steamer shot by. It was a fine scheme for athletic young men, but poorly designed for women, children, and those who were sick or aged. It was, however, quite characteristic of the crude conditions of acute competition and near-warfare which ruled the river when young Vanderbilt began his battle with Drew and others for the domination of the stream.

Those were wild years indeed. "Live Oak" George Law, another competitor of Vanderbilt's, made things as difficult for him as possible. There was a famous race in 1845 between the steamer *Oregon* owned by Law and the *Traveller* belonging to Cornelius Vanderbilt, and in the next year an even greater contest was staged between the *Oregon* and Vanderbilt's new boat which with becoming modesty he christened the *Cornelius Vanderbilt*. It was a close race, but Vanderbilt lost it— one of the few contests in a long life in which he was ever

bested. Those were the days. Talk about combinations in restraint of trade. The authors of the Sherman Act would have
stood aghast if they had ever faced such conditions. Each
line had its own force of commercial boosters and loaded
freight and passengers amid a cloud of threats and profanity.
Innocent people were literally dragged on board steamers they
did not intend to go on and physically held there to keep them
from boarding the boat of a rival line. Freight was stolen
from the wharf and shipped on the wrong boat. There were
no such things as fixed rates. Passenger tariffs varied by the
hour. Yet in all this cloud of violence, deception, and dirty
dealing Vanderbilt continued to prosper. His boats made
money, and his reputation became great in the land. It must
have been at this time that by general consent he acquired
the title of "Commodore," which stayed with him until he
died. He was admittedly the cock of the river, and his success
was known and talked about from Battery Dock to the Albany
river front.

As was usual with him, when he got to a position of dominance on the river and had also added a coasting trade as an
adjunct, all of which occupied only some fifteen years, he
felt that life was beginning to be a little boring. It was getting too easy, in other words, to run the show, and so perhaps unconsciously he looked about for new worlds to conquer, which in his case meant something new in the world
of transportation. When in 1849 gold was discovered in the
California sands, there came that historic nation-wide rush to
the west coast which not only had a lasting effect upon the
economic prosperity of the United States but as an incident
gave another brilliant opportunity to this masterful captain of
men.

Almost as soon as the exodus to the west coast began, the
Pacific Mail Company, a line of financial resources and established reputation, made rapid preparations to handle the busi-

ness. There was, of course, no such thing in those days as a transcontinental ship canal, although it was even then a favorite topic of conversation among those whose interests would be served by its construction. At several places, however, in Central America the distance between the two oceans was very short, and the Pacific Mail located their ports and intervening line of transit across the Isthmus of Panama.

Vanderbilt was not the first in the field, but he very soon determined that there was a grand opportunity here for successful competition and that the route across Nicaragua could be so utilized as to save considerable time in the completed journey. He therefore by herculean efforts organized his own company, the American Atlantic and Pacific Ship Canal Company, and got it into operation in a remarkably short space of time.

In the beginning the Commodore seriously considered the advisability of digging a canal, but fortunately for his success, he was really too canny to venture on such an expensive and problematical experiment without a great deal of money back of him, and he found out in a short time that the English bankers on whom he relied for financial support, were loath to put the first money into such an enterprise although they were quite willing that he should personally assume the risk of such a venture, and unquestionably would come in and help him at such time as they believed that he was likely to be successful in the tremendous undertaking. Wisely unwilling to take the initial risk, Vanderbilt gave up the canal idea, and perfected his own line of steam-ship and land transport. As was usual with him, the proposition as he put it together was colorful and soon attracted popular support.

Many stories are told of his personal experiences in starting up his company. As was to be expected, he went down himself to boss the job. Naturally, he wanted to utilize the water route as much as possible. To do this he had to get his boats well up the San Juan River, but his engineers reported that the river was full of rapids and for most of its length impassable. Such a report failed to convince the old steam-boat captain. Indeed, it merely infuriated him. With a flood of outlandish profanity, he took command of a boat himself and started upstream. How he did it no one has yet clearly explained, but by taking every conceivable chance he forced his craft, creaking and trembling in every timber, over sand bars and through rapids, twice as far up the river as any engineer believed to be possible. He bumped the boat along at full speed and finally stopped only when he hit such a collection of rocks as could have been surmounted only by a bird. Of course this record trip was never repeated, but the engineers took heart, and under the old man's stimulating direction they blasted enough rocks out of the river to greatly improve the course of the transit company. It was then only a short haul from the end of the Atlantic boat line to the port on the Pacific, and this haul was accomplished in gaily painted wagons which were an encouragement to the passengers and a source of pride to the Commodore. The trip, indeed, was interesting, shorter than that by the Pacific Mail, and though lacking in Government support it was well patronized by the continually increasing mob of people who wanted to get to California in a hurry.

Vanderbilt, however, made one capital mistake. He underestimated the nuisance value of the native government. He had agreed to pay the Nicaraguans $10,000 a year for his concession, but according to the best testimony he soon forgot to do it. Therefore, when an adventurous young southerner by the name of Walker, a true soldier of fortune, suddenly appeared on the scene, he was able to make all kinds of trouble for the Vanderbilt Company. Meanwhile, however, the Commodore had been engaging in a merry rate war with the Panama Lines, and in a short time he managed to upset completely the entire transportation situation between the two oceans. It is probable that, as usual, he enjoyed this kind of a row to the utmost, but he did not enjoy the trouble which Walker caused him. Walker ran a revolution in Panama and in Vanderbilt's absence, had his concession abrogated on the correct ground that the company's contract had not been kept. For a time the Commodore's business was seriously interrupted, indeed practically suspended, but those who thought that the old man was defeated did not know him. Opposition of this kind merely aroused his interest and whetted his love of battle. The Commodore, finding himself at a disadvantage in South America, made a successful effort to obtain aid from Washington. He managed to have the United States Navy sent South, so that after a number of years of varying success and much fighting, not only as to rates but with actual gunpowder, he finally had the satisfaction of seeing Walker's adventurous filibusters defeated and expelled from Nicaragua by the United States forces. Then he resumed operations stronger than ever.

Probably he would not have had as much trouble as he did in the Nicaragua venture if his vanity had not begun to get the better of him. It was very seldom in that long, active, and contentious career that he ever left his guns, but for one momentous period in his life he did for a while forget business, and made what almost amounted to a royal progress, in a private yacht which he had specially built and which he called the *North Star*. It was the latest word in those days— really as big as any passenger steamship of the time, and magnificently fitted up. With the Commodore, his family, and a party of his closest friends on board, a cruise of almost world-wide proportions was undertaken in 1854. Commodore Vanderbilt never believed in doing anything by halves, so he went abroad in style. He took with him the long-suffering Sophia, fortified by a large assortment of unaccustomed and uncomfortable gowns, and the rest of the family were stowed away in the luxurious staterooms of the yacht, together with the family doctor and a pallid and subservient clergyman who acted as chaplain and historian of the trip.

It was on his return from this cruise that Vanderbilt found that the men he had left in charge of the Transit Company and the Nicaragua business had played him false, and that not only was there danger of revolution, which afterwards materialized, but that the business had been managed in such a way that his own interest was very adversely affected. It was then that he penned his most historic letter. He wrote to his former associates as follows:

Gentlemen:
     You have undertaken to cheat me. I will not sue you be-
cause the law takes too long. I will ruin you.
                                    Sincerely yours,
                                    CORNELIUS VANDERBILT[1]

No communication could have more accurately reflected the character of its author than this one which condensed a man's soul and energy in two lines of print.

However, the Commodore's desire to exhibit himself and his progeny in a suitable and expensive setting before the crowned heads and merchant princes of the earth, probably had one result which was wholly to the business advantage of the principal actor in the show. It drew Vanderbilt's attention for the first time to the possibilities of steamship business on the north Atlantic. Again he performed one of those curious right-about-face movements for which he was more noted than any other industrial leader of his time. It was getting on to the late fifties, and he was about through with Nicaragua. Besides, he had had a lot of trouble down there, and although he had conquered his enemies and made, as well as spent, a lot of money, he was getting a little tired of the South American fracas and as usual yearned for something new.

Again he was not by any means the first on the field. Just

_____
[1] A. D. Howden Smith, "Commodore Vanderbilt," p. 202.

as in Nicaragua he had been obliged to compete with the
Pacific Mail from a standing start, so when he decided to go
into the north Atlantic business in a big way he found the
Collins Line not only well established but apparently securely
buttressed by Government support and congressional sub-
sidies. It was a good line, too, composed of the *Arctic*, the
Atlantic, and the *Pacific*, 3000-ton ships—the best of their day.
Their only close rival was the Cunard Line, also operating
under subsidy from the British Government. On the surface
it looked as though the Commodore would have a hard time
to break into such a well-protected situation. Said situation,
however, was merely a challenge to Vanderbilt's sporting
blood, and at it he went full tilt. With his usual rapidity of action, he soon launched and put into operation three fine ships,
the *Ariel*, the *Harvest Queen*, and the *Vanderbilt*—the last
named being a large steamer of 5000 tons.

Meanwhile fate took a hand in the situation in Vanderbilt's
interest. The Collins Line had a series of misfortunes, wholly
unexpected and shattering in effect. The *Arctic* was sunk in
a collision. The *Vesta* went down a short time later; and then
to make a bad matter worse, a violent political attack was
made on the subsidy system in Congress, and it was finally
wiped out by a close vote.

At this distance of time, it is difficult to determine just how
successful Commodore Vanderbilt was in his steamship traffic
just before the Civil War, but we have reason to believe that
he met with a considerable degree of success. The basic reason
for this was that he had had years of experience in shipping
and ran his vessels with the sole purpose of making them pay.
He never depended on a Government subsidy as Collins
did, and by his knowledge, energy, and ingenuity he seems
to have been able to do very well without it. He finally conquered the Collins Line by having the nerve to carry the
United States mails free, and the Crimean War, occurring in

the late fifties, put out of commission the Cunard boats, his only other rivals, and enabled him to emerge triumphantly from a situation which a few years previously had appeared certain to result in his defeat. Indeed, this uneducated, loud-mouthed, bullying steam-boat captain seemed to bear a charmed life in the business world. Everything he touched apparently turned to gold, and the most impossible situations yielded to the magic of his energy and to the accuracy of his business foresight.

Then came the Civil War, and with it the *Alabama* and the other swift privateers of the Confederacy. Once more the Commodore took account of stock and decided that he was through with ocean shipping. By that time he was worth more than $15,000,000, and was feared and respected from New York to San Francisco. The panic of 1857 had injured him only on paper. Although he was well over sixty years of age, the years had passed over him lightly, so that physically he was in the full power and vigor of his manhood. He must have had an iron constitution, for when he was over seventy, he had the surpassing energy of boyhood and led a life of ceaseless activity and unremitting labor.

As usual, he abandoned one form of transportation only in order to engage in another, and that is one element of his character which we should never forget. That is why this chapter has been entitled "Cornelius Vanderbilt—Master of Transportation." He was not always engaged in the same kind of transportation, but, in one way or another, for almost seventy years, he was the transportation genius of the American continent. In accordance with his general custom, when war conditions had rendered the ocean-carrying game less interesting and profitable than it ought to be, he turned his attention to railway transport, which, with his old and practiced eyes, he could see more plainly than his contemporaries was destined to become the greatest single factor in the business development of the United States.

But that was not all that he did. First among the men of his time he realized fully the inefficiency of the American railroad structure. In the sixties, the United States was literally cursed with small railroads. For more than twenty years, waves of railroad promotion had been sweeping the country, and the dire need of the people had caused them to be betrayed by the greatest crooks and scalawags with which any industrial movement was ever afflicted. There were no large railroad systems, but all kinds of small lines, often much less than one hundred miles in length, with rails of different gauges, heavy mortgage debts, inexperienced officers and directors, and almost every other disadvantage. Vanderbilt saw that the most effective economic and technical method which could be employed to cure this situation was that of merger and consolidation, and with his usual energy and his great financial power he started to put it into effect. He sold his ships and mobilized his money.

In 1857 he became a director, and in 1863 president of the New York and Harlem Railway Company, a small road which ran between New York and Chatham Four Corners in Columbia County. With the acquisition of the control of this railway, Vanderbilt again came into collision with his old acquaintance and former competitor, Daniel Drew. If he was to develop the New York and Harlem he must extend this line into the center of the city, and this he thought he could do without much trouble for he believed that he had matters arranged with the city council. How he had fixed the city fathers, it would not be profitable to inquire too closely. So when in April, 1863, he obtained an ordinance to build a street railway from the end of his road down to the Battery he was well content. However, "Uncle Daniel Drew" was watching and waiting like a crocodile on an African river-bank, and when things got to this stage, Drew formed an alliance with Tweed, who was then boss of Tammany, and between them these two worthies had the ordinance revoked. There was a resultant flurry in the market with heavy short selling by the political group, and then something happened which Tweed and Drew had not counted on.

The Commodore had far more ready money than they suspected, and when they came to cover their short sales, they found him sitting on top of a corner. When the corner was ended, Messrs. Drew and Tweed were several million dollars out of pocket. It was the Commodore's first stock-market victory in the railroad field, and after it was over he must have felt a warm glow of satisfaction.

Also, it taught him something about his friend Drew. But the curious thing about that is that, although Vanderbilt must have known that Daniel Drew was an arrant scoundrel, nevertheless, all through his life he had a weak spot in his heart for the old rascal, and time and again when he had him crushed to earth and begging for mercy, he relented and gave him a fresh start, and every time he did so, Drew repaid his kindness by double-crossing him at the next opportunity and doing him the maximum amount of injury. It was a curious human situation between the two men which has never been adequately explained. The author's guess is that Vanderbilt had something of the disposition of the lion-tamer. He knew that Drew was as dangerous and as treacherous as a wild beast and that made him rather fascinating to the Commodore who therefore did not wish to kill him because if he did so he would never have the fun of playing with him again. One cannot guarantee this explanation, though it seems quite plausible.

It was not, however, the aim of Commodore Vanderbilt merely to buy up a railroad here and there and indulge in stock-market contests as a result of his promotions. To regard him as this type of operator is to do him a great injustice. It seems quite clear that early in the game the old man had a big vision. He certainly saw the valley of the Hudson from the Great Lakes to the sea as the roadbed of an integrated and powerful system to be put together through the exercise of his genius from a number of weak and physically ill-constructed subsidiary lines. Who shall say at what stage of the adventure his old eyes gazed even farther to the west and visioned the final consummation of his great life plan, which was to bring the Middle West from Chicago on the Michigan lake-shore in close and coherent touch with New York, the great metropolis of our eastern coast. To most men, however able, such a vision would have been merely a dream. But to this wonderful human dynamo, old in years but young in spirit and resourceful and strong beyond the thought of lesser men, such a dream was merely an incentive to concrete accomplishment, and he was to live to see that dream translated into fact.

His next step after the New York and Harlem corner was to acquire a controlling interest in the Hudson River Railway; he became president of this road in 1865. Then came the big struggle to acquire the New York Central, a far more important line than either of the others, which then stretched between the key cities of Albany and Buffalo. He already had had trouble enough in working out his previous plans. At every hand the politicians tried to hold him up. It was an age of corruption, of venality, and of the basest kind of ethics, and the old leader must have spent money like water to accomplish his designs. The wonder is that he still remained the cheerful optimist that he always was. His opinion of politicians must have been quite as low as that of Jay Gould. But though it is likely that he bought them by the pound, their weakness and corruption never seemed to affect seriously his fundamental belief in the honesty and the conquering energy of the American race. They were merely obnoxious animals to be used and cast aside, but the great body of the people were, in his judgment, always to be relied upon, and he never failed them nor they him. His struggle to acquire the New York Central was extremely bitter, but he finally secured a stock control and started to reorganize the road with his usual energy and dispatch. His final step in the accomplishment of his dream was taken in 1873, in which year he secured control of the Lake Shore and Michigan Southern Railway, and when this was done, his coordinated railroad system between New York and Chicago was complete.

The only thing which he set out to do that he failed to accomplish was to get control of the Erie Railroad. Just as E. H. Harriman never succeeded in acquiring the Northern Pacific on another memorable occasion, so Commodore Vanderbilt was unable to bring the Erie into camp, and the principal reason for this was Daniel Drew.

It was in 1868 that this famous contest took place. The Erie Railroad had for years been in an unfortunate position. Though neither well built nor well operated, strategically it commanded an important position because of its right of entry into New York City. It was therefore of great interest speculatively, and it early attracted the attention of the worthy Mr. Drew who had invested a considerable amount of money in its securities and had gradually attained a position of dominance in its councils which caused him to be known as the "Speculative Director of the Erie Road." To Commodore Vanderbilt it was particularly alluring because if he could get possession of it he would practically dominate the entire railroad situation in and about New York City.

In the fall of 1867 Daniel Drew was instrumental in getting two young men who were friends of his on the board of directors. These gentlemen were Jay Gould and Jim Fiske, just then rising above mediocrity as brokers and stock-market manipulators. Drew's combination with these young men constituted a trinity of evil which was to be long remembered in the annals of American finance. Early in the situation, Drew, seeming to have sensed the fact that the Commodore was watching the Erie with greedy eyes, took a shrewd step looking toward that gentleman's eventual discomfiture. Briefly, he got the directors of the road to authorize the issue of $10,000,000 of convertible bonds, presumably for the purpose of replacing worn-out rails and standardizing the gauge of the road. How much of the money derived from these bonds was ever used for this estimable purpose it is now impossible to determine, but in all probability it was no very great amount.

The real idea back of this bond issue was to put in the hands of Drew a potentiality which he could use market-wise to accomplish the destruction of any opponent. As long as he held this enormous number of convertible bonds he would have the power of flooding the market with additional stock whenever it pleased him to do so. Therefore, when a short time later, Commodore Vanderbilt began a serious effort to buy a stock control of the Erie road, he was really playing against a stacked deck, although he did not know it. Thousands of shares the old man purchased through his frightened brokers without being able to exhaust the market.

The contest degenerated into a series of legal moves too complicated for brief repetition. Both sides had judges who were bought and paid for and batteries of lawyers to carry out their designs. Drew, Gould, and Fiske as a last move unloosed a veritable flood of stock upon the Commodore regardless of injunctions and regardless of the dictates of common honesty. They then fled over night to Jersey City and started to run the Erie Railroad from the parlor of the Taylor House, a local hotel. This move was followed by a shameless effort on the part of Gould to buy legislation at Albany which would regularize the bogus stock with which they had defeated the

Commodore. Then almost over night the four gentlemen most deeply concerned got together in a small room and a settlement between them was made which is famous or infamous, as you may choose to view it, even to the present day. Vanderbilt, because of his great power, forced them to buy back most of his stock at a price which did not save him from loss but minimized that loss very considerably. Drew got a good deal of money but had to get off the Erie board and stay off. Jay Gould and Jim Fiske, being the youngsters in the combination, got very little cash but were given the Erie Railroad by the two old men in order that they might see if they could squeeze some more money out of that unfortunate line, which they promptly proceeded most effectively to do.

This Erie deal is mentioned not because it inspires any admiration of Commodore Vanderbilt, but because no sketch of his career is complete without some description of one of the most important events which characterized it. In this miserable affair Vanderbilt was, of course, greatly to blame. He was brutal and unscrupulous, and he bought judges and injunctions with a free hand. But he shines by comparison with the three other men who were concerned in it with him. Fundamentally, Vanderbilt all through this Erie deal was trying to do a big thing in a big way. He was endeavoring to unify the transportation system of New York City and New York State, and he considered the Erie road a necessary link in the chain he was trying to forge. On the other hand, Drew, Gould, and Fiske had no such worthy motive, but were simply endeavoring to fleece the Commodore and line their own pockets with ill-gotten wealth. In the end it was a drawn battle, with the net result in favor of Drew and his associates, and it was about the only time in a career that spanned nearly a century when the Commodore failed to accomplish a primary objective.

However, it had very little effect on his fame or his general plan of railroad consolidation. He lived for another decade, consolidating his railroad system and increasing his fortune, and finally on January 4, 1877, he passed away. In his later years he suffered from a variety of physical ailments and experienced the grief of an active and energetic spirit which, hating physical dissolution, is nevertheless aware of the steady and relentless approach of death. The faithful Sophia died in 1868. Although he was more than seventy years old the Commodore soon elected her successor. In doing so he fared far better than he deserved, for he married a fine woman much younger than himself who exercised an excellent influence over his later years.

It is amazing to view this remarkable life in its entirety. Vanderbilt was undoubtedly one of the greatest and ablest financial and business leaders of his generation. He was uneducated but naturally intelligent. He was a great egotist but blessed with saving common sense. He was honest according to the rules of the game as it was played in his day, yet he did not hesitate to do outrageous things to gain his point and he continued along this line to the end. He was never servile to the strong, but he was brutal to the weak. He respected only those who fought him and apparently could not understand an attitude of kindness and generosity. He treated the wife of his youth with cruelty and an almost complete lack of consideration. He disliked many of his own children and distrusted most of them, and yet he showed a consideration and fondness for Daniel Drew, his malevolent enemy, which seems utterly inconsistent with his known character.

In spite of all these inconsistencies, faults, and really bad characteristics, Commodore Vanderbilt will for generations be remembered as the great constructive genius of American transportation. It was his energy and foresight that placed the first big steam-boats on the Hudson River. It was his daring and energy which carried hordes of adventurers to California in 1849. It was his courage and competitive ability which showed the way toward the successful operation of mighty steamers on the north Atlantic without Government aid. And, finally, it was his almost supernatural vision and the resistless power of his nature despite the handicap of advancing years which succeeded in making one of the greatest and earliest of the outstanding railroad consolidations of the United States. These are the things for which he will be remembered by generations yet unborn long after the malodorous circumstances of the contest over the Erie road have faded into oblivion. He will for ages to come be a stimulating example for the youth of America, and he will be looked up to as an historic figure, a grand old fighter, and the first master of transportation in the United States.

JAY GOULD

CHAPTER XVI

JAY GOULD AND THE AGE OF INNOCENCE

In 1920, at the close of the Great War when our civilization was still rocking under a shock such as it had never previously known, a reactionary writer, probably a cultured and rather high-minded gentleman of Mr. Gould's own era, published in the *Atlantic Monthly* over the nom de plume of Mr. Grundy an interesting article most unfavorably dealing with the sins and vices of modern youth and comparing the morals and behavior of our young people with those of his own playmates and school friends.

This article aroused more than ephemeral interest, and he was quickly answered by that brilliant essayist Katherine Fullerton Gerould, and a little later by a young man named Carter who contributed to the *Atlantic Monthly* of September, 1920, a most thrilling though somewhat crudely defiant essay under the much-quoted title, "These Wild Young People," in the course of which he said, referring of course to the preceding generation:

Life for them was bright and pleasant. Like all normal youngsters, they had their little tin-pot ideals, their sweet little visions, their naïve enthusiasms, their nice little sets of beliefs. Christianity had emerged from the blow dealt by Darwin, emerged rather in the shape of social dogma. Man was a noble and perfectible creature. Women were angels (whom they smugly sweated in their industries and prostituted in their slums). Right was downing might. The nobility and the divine mission of the race were factors that led our fathers to work wholeheartedly for a millennium, which they caught a glimpse of just around the turn of the century.

Why, there were Hague Tribunals! International peace was at last assured, and according to current reports, never officially denied, the American delegates held out for the use of poison gas in warfare, just as the men of that generation were later to ruin Wilson's great ideal of a league of nations, on the ground that such a scheme was an invasion of American rights. But still, everything, masked by ingrained hypocrisy and prudishness, seemed simple, beautiful, inevitable.

Mr. Carter then went on to speak of the debacle caused by the World War and the sudden toppling of the smug ideals and institutions of the 1880's and 1890's, dwelling with force upon the necessary result, namely, the cynical disillusionment of the younger generation with the taboos and fetishes of their fathers, and the resultant era of straight thinking and plain speaking and perhaps coarse acting which has ensued. He then proceeded with his argument as follows:

It is the older generation who forced us to see all this—which has left us with social and political institutions staggering blind in the fierce white light that, for us, should beat only about the enthroned ideal. And now, through the soft-headed folly of these painfully shocked Grundys, we have that devastating wisdom which is safe only for the burned-out embers of grizzled, cautious old men. We may be fire, but it was they who made us play with gunpowder. And now they are surprised that a great many of us, because they have taken away our apple-cheeked ideals, are seriously considering whether or no *their* game be worth *our* candle. . . . Oh, I suppose that it's too bad that we aren't humble, starry-eyed, shy, respectful innocents, standing reverently at their side for instructions, playing pretty little games, in which they no longer believe, except for us. But we aren't, and the best thing the oldsters can do about it is to go into their respective backyards and dig for worms, great big pink ones—for the Grundy tribe are now just about as important as they are, and they will doubtless make company more congenial and docile than "these wild young people"—the men and women of my generation.

Strong words, these, and arresting ones.

Those of us who have any connection with the Grundy tribe are forced by such a brave denial and such an enthusiastic bit of special pleading to take account of ourselves and our beliefs in an endeavor to see what justification "these wild young people" may really have for the slight estimation in which they hold the things that counted in the age of their fathers. In order to solve this problem, it will be profitable to examine the life and times of a great captain of finance, who, whatever his shortcomings may have been, was never in his own estimation a hypocrite.

Close your eyes then, and return in fancy a short distance along the road to yesterday. Go back some forty years to a cold December night in 1892 and take post with a little group of shivering newspapermen outside a great brownstone palace on Fifth Avenue in New York, in the plainest room of which Jay Gould lay dying.

It was the same small room in which his beautiful wife had passed away some years before, and it opened upon his study where the stock-ticker, the inevitable pendulum of his life, beat out its fateful items until a few hours before his passing. In that room were gathered his immediate family, his sons, George, Howard, and Frank, trained to succeed him and build up another great dynasty of money comparable to that erected by Astor and his old antagonist Vanderbilt, which should go on and on through the ages until it became a veritable Juggernaut of power to trample upon the rights of countless millions yet unborn.

Dr. Munn and Dr. Janeway were in close attendance, and Mr. Russell Sage, fittingly one of the dying man's closest friends, kept in touch with the situation from hour to hour.

Outside, the whole city watched and waited with interest and varying feelings the outcome of the bitter struggle which the great captain was making for his life. Even the raising of a window by one of the Gould family was reported in the papers next day, so close was the watch, so intense the interest.

With the very dew of death upon that pallid bearded face, America could scarce believe that the man who had amassed a fortune of $80,000,000 in the brief period of fifty-six years must succumb to the laws of nature as humbly and respectfully as the poorest of his fellow men.

It was characteristic of Jay Gould that, although he had known for two years that he was a doomed man and that both of his lungs were tubercular, he had confided the information to no one except his two oldest sons, and had spent his last twenty-four months of life in arranging his great fortune to meet the shock of his going so that there would be no panic among the ship's company when the captain went down the side.

Silent, inscrutable, reticent, careful of his millions and greedy of his power, he faced his end with coolness and courage, just as during the terrible closing hours of Black Friday he had faced the howling raging mob of ruined brokers who went in search of him with murder in their hearts when driven by his cold-blooded and triumphant operations out of the New York Stock Exchange, crazed and broken men.

But Gould did not die that night. Too much vitality was still left in that frail body, too much of the iron will still remained in the feeble flesh that was his, and it was not until a quarter of nine on December 2, 1892, that this strange, silent man was overtaken by the great mystery of life and passed onward and outward from the city of his triumph and his shame to appear before the great Judge of all men and plead his cause before the Bar of Divine Justice.

He died—and instantly the industrial and financial world of America paused to do him honor. The street cars of New York were draped in black, and the wheels of a thousand locomotives paused at the hour of his funeral. His old friends and his old enemies gave forth interviews of praise and blame. The press notices collected by his family would, it is estimated, have made, if pieced together, a paper link covering ten miles of ground.

And then, after a short flurry, the stock market rebounded and apparently financial confidence went to a higher plane. The securities of the very properties in which Mr. Gould was most largely interested at his death, namely, Missouri Pacific and Western Union Telegraph Company, advanced smartly in response to his decease. And although it is true that Wall Street had discounted his death, that during the last decade of his career he had ceased to stage his mad speculative dramas, nevertheless, in spite of all this, the action of the market and the action of mankind showed that a new era of confidence had come, just as many a head rested easier in the Republic of Mexico when it was known that General Villa, peaceful and retired though he was supposed to be, had at last met death.

And then Gould was forgotten, at least as the world counts forgetting, so that now when one desires to speak of him with authority it is necessary to delve deeply into the contemporary history of the past and research beyond the limits necessary in the case of lesser men.

There is actually no authoritative life of Gould, only some partial accounts of his career, a few scattered articles in contemporary periodicals, and the great mass of newspaper comment and carefully prepared obituaries which appeared at the time of his death. And of all the group of men who knew him so well and so intimately, few survive today. Time, however, is history's best servant, so today we are able to arrive, even with the scanty information at our command, at an estimation of Jay Gould, his comrades, and his times far more accurate, more kind, and more just than would have been possible a quarter of a century ago.

Shakespeare says: "The evil that men do lives after them, the good is oft interrèd with their bones." Like many other sayings of the great Elizabethan, this statement is so true that it has become trite. Let us then trace Jay Gould's remarkable career, observe what effect it had upon the times in which he lived, and see if we can discern any connection between his story and his influence and these controversial articles of Messrs. Grundy and Carter in the *Atlantic Monthly* of the year 1920.

Jay Gould was a farmer's son, born on May 27, 1836, at Roxbury in Delaware County, New York. Life was hard in those days for plain people, and the Gould family were certainly poor and plain. In spite of young Gould's tireless industry and will to conquer, it will never cease to be a mystery how he acquired the education which was certainly his. He was tutored by an older sister, and left home when a little over twelve years old to make his own way in the world. For a year he kept the books of a blacksmith in order to study at Hobart Academy, and after that, while engaged with a tinsmith, he used to rise at three or four o'clock in the morning in order to study mathematics and surveying. When he was twenty years of age, he wrote a book entitled "History of Delaware County, New York" which is now very rare. The writer has read this book with a great deal of interest. The first half of it shows industry, research, and real ability in the use of the English language, although the style is somewhat over-colored and has the flamboyancy of early youth. The last half is largely composed of labored arguments connected with the anti-rent war which went on in northern New York in Gould's youth and is therefore of no interest at the present day.

It is curious how men change as they go onward along the great road of life, and few who knew Jay Gould in the days when he dominated the financial world of America with

HISTORY

OF

DELAWARE COUNTY,

AND

Border Wars of New York.

CONTAINING

A SKETCH OF THE EARLY SETTLEMENTS IN THE COUNTY,

AND

A HISTORY OF THE

LATE ANTI-RENT DIFFICULTIES IN DELAWARE,

WITH

Other Historical and Miscellaneous Matter,

NEVER BEFORE PUBLISHED.

BY JAY GOULD.

ROXBURY:
KEENY & GOULD, PUBLISHERS.
1856.

TITLE PAGE, "HISTORY OF DELAWARE COUNTY," BY JAY GOULD

shining ability and almost impersonal cruelty would ever believe that the following words were penned by him at any age. In his book above referred to, dealing somewhat abstractly with the subject of history, Mr. Gould said:

It is the saying of an eminent historian that "liberty and history go hand in hand, the health and vigor of the one dependent upon and co-existent with the other" and it is certain that the more enlightened and free a people become the more the government devolves upon themselves; and hence the necessity of a careful study of history which by showing the height to which man as an intellectual being is capable of lifting himself in the scale of usefulness and moral worth teaches that the virtues of the good man are held in sacred emulation by his countrymen for ages succeeding, long after the scythe of time has gathered the earthly remains of the actor to the silent grave. Such thoughts, or rather such reflections as these, inspire within the human bosom an ardent desire to attain that which is good and shun that which is evil, an honest and laudable ambition to become both great and good; or as another has beautifully written, "great only as we are good."

In subsequent years the story goes that these brave words of youth were quoted with bitter sarcasm against their writer and received by him in stony silence. He is never known to have referred to his one and only excursion into authorship.

Gould first came to New York in 1853 when he was seventeen years old, and characteristically got a job without much difficulty. In a little while he was discharged because of a certain performance of his in connection with a piece of property which his employer asked him to negotiate for in his interest. This property was to be sold by executors, and the price was $2500. Gould's boss offered $2000, which was declined. Gould knew the value of the property and was sure it would appreciate. Before his employer could reconsider and raise his bid, Gould had borrowed $2500 from his father and bought the property for himself. He was promptly fired for breach of trust, but in a short time he resold his purchase for $4000, which gave him a clear gain of $1500. This little transaction occurred before he was twenty-one.

There is not space to deal with his life as a surveyor, but it is known that he made several careful and accurate maps of Delaware and Ulster Counties; nor shall we do more than touch upon his excursion into the leather business except to note that he was credited, through his speculative performances in leather, with the suicide of his rich partner Leupp, and that after Leupp's death he engaged in a pitched battle with Leupp's other partner Lee over the possession of the tannery which both claimed.

Gould's own account of his method of capturing the tannery was as follows:

I quietly selected fifty men, commanding the reserve to keep behind. I divided them into two companies, one of which I despatched to the upper end of the building, directing them to take off the boards, while I headed the other to open a large front door. I burst open the door and sprang in. I was immediately saluted with a shower of bullets, forcing my men to retire. Then I brought them up a second and third time and pressed them into the building. By this time the company at the upper end of the tannery had succeeded in effecting an entrance, and the firing now became general on all sides and the bullets were whistling in all directions. After a hard contested struggle on both sides, we became the victors and our opponents went flying from the tannery, some of them making fearful leaps from the second story.

The account given by his enemies was much more picturesque. As soon as he arrived Gould took active charge of the campaign. Finding that he was faced by an army of more than a hundred cut-throats under the leadership of Lee, and firmly entrenched in the tannery, Gould looked about for the nucleus of an invading army. Being well known to the people of the town, he painted for them a vivid picture of Lee and his cohorts as a band of robbers who were seeking to despoil an upright and innocent citizen of his property. After an oyster supper at the local hostelry, where whiskey probably flowed more freely than oysters, and an eloquent soap-box oration on the part of Gould, the mob moved on the tannery. Hearing that Lee had a loaded musket reserved especially for him, Gould, like a good general, discreetly remained in the rear to direct operations.

Whiskey and oysters did their work, and in the ensuing attack one of Lee's men was shot through the chest. Warrants were issued for everyone concerned and many fled never again to return to the town. Those arrested, later were released on bail when once the furor had subsided.

Gould remained, master of the scene; but his victory was an empty one. Lee immediately began a series of legal actions, and since Gould had not yet risen to the affluence of maintaining his own retinue of judges, he was blocked by the courts. The result of the whole matter was that the business was completely ruined.

After this fiasco Gould again tackled New York and soon made what was for him a most fortunate marriage. He married Miss Helen Miller, and his father-in-law, a man of considerable standing in the business world, soon secured him the position of manager of the Rensselaer and Saratoga Railroad connecting Troy and Saratoga. This road was under a cloud and its securities were selling for a few cents on the dollar. Here was Gould's opportunity. He managed the road well, made valuable and paying connections, and brought it up to positive value. Meanwhile, little by little, Gould obtained possession of it all. He paid about five cents on the dollar for the stock to all but Vanderbilt, who made him pay fifteen cents, and the consequence was that after selling out again he returned to New York with a clear profit of $750,000. This was Gould's start in the railway world. Thereafter he never faltered but pursued the career for which his unusual talents had so well prepared him.

There is no doubt that Jay Gould was the greatest speculator financial America has ever seen. In his later years he used every method, many of them dubious, first to depress the stock of one great road after another, and then, when such stock was acquired, by the application of his genius, he time after time "bulled" the market and sold out his holdings with profits running into millions of dollars.

Nevertheless, to regard Gould as a speculator pure and simple would be to acknowledge but half the truth. From the early days when he personally managed the little Rensselaer and Troy road he turned his great mind to the acquisition of railroad knowledge of any and every kind. Like E. H. Harriman, his great successor, he actually knew the railroad business as few men have ever known it before or since.

It would be idle to say that any spirit of altruism guided his labors. It is doubtful if he ever beheld the America of today in all the glory of material success girt by bands of gleaming steel, the result of his labors and the labors of his associates, with factories and mines tributary to the roads of the present, and developed by the same geniuses which made those roads powerful and great. His was not a sympathetic nature, nor, as far as is known, was it a nature that comprised any particular love of his country or of his fellow men. But the point is that although he speculated enormously, he did not only speculate; and although it is true that from one angle he may be regarded as a remorseless railroad wrecker, and his conscienceless inflation of the capital stock of the much-battered Erie Road confirms such a statement, nevertheless history must record that he wrecked roads only at odd times and for definite purposes, and that, generally speaking, he was not a wrecker but a builder, so that the great systems of America today, especially those of our wonderful Southwest,

owe their start and in many instances their completion to
his genius and industry.

Wise he was in the selection of his battleground; never did
he willingly choose a part of the country for railroad development in which he would have to meet the competition of great
established systems, but he went down into the Southwest
when he was able to choose, and there he built up great
roads—monuments to his daring and to his almost uncanny
foresight and prophetic knowledge of the future.

From out of the welter of deals and counterdeals, of schemes
and subterfuges, of lies and half-truths, of temporary defeats
and lasting victories, two principal incidents arise in the
life of this great manipulator, railroad builder, and financier.
The first incident is his connection with what has come to
be known as the Erie War—and war indeed it was, bitter,
cruel, remorseless warfare. The second incident, serious and
scandalous, was his connection with the famous gold corner
which resulted in that most terrible of financial crises, Black
Friday of September, 1869. No man has been more harshly
criticized for both of the above events than was Jay Gould,
and no sketch of his variegated career can be complete without
definite reference to them; but in making such reference it
is well to insist at the outset that, no matter what Gould's
sins may have been in connection with Erie and with gold,
they were sins made possible by the conditions of the time in
which he lived, did business, and prospered.

Let us consider then for a brief space the mighty struggle
for control of the Erie. The contest came to a head in 1868.
Gould was then in the early thirties, in the prime of life, and
regarded as one of the shrewdest and most daring of the young
men of Wall Street. In the Erie War he became allied with
a curious, illiterate, shrewd, unscrupulous man, Daniel Drew,
the "speculative director" of the Erie Road. Also, for the first
time, he operated in close partnership with the infamous Jim

Fiske, one of the most picturesque and colorful blackguards of American finance.

This motley crew was opposed to the great Commodore Vanderbilt, the president and almost proprietor of the New York Central and allied lines. It was Vanderbilt's imperious desire to acquire the Erie and thereby obtain for himself a railroad monopoly of New York which initiated this gigantic struggle between opposing forces of such strength, ability, and resource as this country had never before seen.

Though part of this story has been recounted in a previous chapter, it may be well to enlarge upon it here, since it was more important to Gould than to Vanderbilt. As has already been stated, Vanderbilt tried to buy all the Erie stock that he could in order to capture control of that road, and Drew, Gould, and Fiske allowed him to suppose that he was getting it all and that they were beaten men, when suddenly, by the unscrupulous use of convertible Erie bonds which they suddenly transformed into common stock, they let loose upon him a flood of new shares which he was compelled to absorb to avoid his own ruin. Then Drew, Gould, Fiske and Company suddenly and dramatically decamped in a single night to avoid the processes of the law which the infuriated Commodore had speedily invoked against them, and set up business across the ferry in the Taylor House of Jersey City, where, guarded by thugs and black-legs, and sitting, so to speak, on millions of Vanderbilt's money, they openly defied the Courts of New York and the power of the Commodore.

Such a situation was unprecedented in American railroad annals, but this was not all. With a touch of mingled effrontery and genius, Jay Gould suddenly appeared once more within the boundaries of New York State. He was promptly arrested and held to bail, but risking his fate, he proceeded to Albany and at once entered into the closest relationship with one of the most venal and corrupt legislatures the state had ever seen. What he did, what sums he paid, for what purposes they were given we shall never know, although he admitted before a congressional committee that he had paid large sums for legal services of the details of which he was not aware. The result, however, is interesting in the extreme. In a short time the Legislature of New York passed a bill legalizing the enormous issues of stock which Gould and his associates had made, and shortly thereafter Commodore Vanderbilt withdrew from the contest, for once in his life a thoroughly defeated man.

But this is not all that can be said of the Erie War. It was distinguished by the most outrageous misuse of legal writs and processes, the most shameful influence of the judiciary, the most contradictory injunctions, decrees, and orders which the courts of New York or any other state in the Union had ever seen. The names of some of those judges have come down to us today surrounded by an atmosphere of legal chicanery and influence of the money power which is a stench in the nostrils of honest men.

At the conclusion of this battle of giants, Vanderbilt sent for his old crony, Daniel Drew, and arranged a treaty of peace by the terms of which the conspirators repurchased the greater part of the stock which they had compelled Vanderbilt to buy and Drew was eliminated as a director but with a well-lined purse. Thus in the end the fight may be considered a "standoff."

When it was all over, Gould and Fiske, though they got very little cash money from the settlement with Vanderbilt, were left in control of the Erie Road, and proceeded immediately to make that road pay them and pay them well. Within a short period, by frequent stock issues which Mr. Gould explained were largely for the purchase of steel rails, the stock of the Erie was inflated from approximately $34,000,000 to $57,000,000.

Meanwhile these financial bandits entered upon a course of action unparallelled in the history of this land. They purchased the Grand Opera House in New York and into that building moved the offices of the Erie Railroad. In the lobby of the Opera House were oil paintings of Messrs. Gould and Fiske, and in the decorations upon the proscentium boxes their monograms were beautifully intertwined.

During their brief régime, the friends and customers of the Erie Road were entertained gratis by expensive productions of the most risqué and tuneful French light operas. With the railroad offices in one part of the building, and the Opera House going full tilt in another part, there was still a third portion of this remarkable railroad office, namely, the private suite of Mr. Fiske, where amid surroundings of garish splendor he entertained with great frequency and much noise the good-looking young opera singers who worked in one part of the building, and the long-bearded old gentlemen who sent freight over the road and had their business dealings in an entirely different part.

Mr. Fiske was usually costumed in his uniform as a member of a well-known yacht club, and in brass buttons, blue coat, and white cap, it was his custom to drive down into the business section of New York in a red coach driven by four white horses with at least one young lady of the opera seated on either side of his imperial person.

It is but fair to say, however, that Mr. Fiske's partner led a very different existence. Mr. Gould was a family man; he was also always connected with a religious organization. He was good and kind to his wife and children. He never smoked and only drank a little claret at dinner. He was small and slight of build, black-coated, eagle-eyed, with an Hebraic nose and dome-like head with a high white forehead. If he did not love strongly, he did not hate deeply. He was no roué, no libertine. He did not approve of Mr. Fiske, nor did he like Mr. Fiske's goings on, but he was Mr. Fiske's partner and together they ran the Erie Road.

He sometimes went to the opera and watched Fiske's young lady friends cavort upon the stage, and on such occasions he would usually sit in a box with Boss Tweed, the political dictator of New York, whom he had taken in and given a big interest in the Erie Road. Later, when Boss Tweed was arrested and in danger of jail and when a great mass of New York citizens arose in their wrath to blot this infamous corrupt man out of existence once and for all, who went his bail? Why, strangely enough, Mr. Gould, the good Mr. Gould, the religious Mr. Gould, he went Mr. Tweed's bail. That bail, by the way, was set by an irate judge, in the hope that it never could be secured, at the unusual figure of $1,000,000. Yes, for once in his life, Mr. Gould was thoughtful of others, Mr. Gould was unselfish, Mr. Gould was very generous, and he went Mr. Tweed's bail.

All this orgy of sin and shame and financial crime and hypocrisy, all this dirty mixture of corrupt politics and inflated frenzied finance came to an end on that day in 1872 when Jim Fiske, ascending a staircase, shameless, proud, and defiant, was met by the bullet of a jealous rival and tumbled mortally wounded to the foot of the stairs.

They closed in on the Erie then, and Gould sought other fields to conquer. Incidentally, he made a settlement with the aroused and wrathful security holders and handed back to them about $9,000,000 which they said he had abstracted as loot, but which he always claimed he had merely held aside as a trustee.

What is the truth of it all? Who can tell? It is a generation and more ago, but it affected our whole social system and made possible the remarks of Mr. Carter in his essay on

"These Wild Young People" who are now so much condemned.

Now a few words about Black Friday and the corner in gold. It was in 1869 that Gould first conceived the bold idea of cornering the gold market. It was a bad time to attempt such a thing. The country was prosperous and it would take enormous resources and unparallelled nerve, but this magician of finance hesitated at nothing. He was willing to risk all, dare all, for the great gain he saw before him. His method was simplicity itself, but its execution was complicated in the extreme. He and a few friends controlled about fourteen millions of gold. The banks had some fifteen millions on deposit and about twenty millions were loose in the country besides more than eighty millions held in the United States Treasury.

Gould's plan was to corner the market in gold in the hope that, with the advance in gold prices, wheat would advance to such an extent that western farmers would sell and there would be a consequent tremendous movement of breadstuffs from west to east with resulting increase of freight business for the Erie Road. His first move was to tie up the gold in the banks by getting the various banks to certify his checks and those of his associates so that over fourteen millions could not be released, and then he used these certified checks to borrow enormous sums of greenbacks and thereby withdrew these greenbacks from circulation and caused an artificial money stringency throughout the country. He then went in upon his credit and started to buy gold in large quantities, intending to force it up to the unprecedented figure of 200.

Gould well knew that there was one weak link in his chain. He could not possibly control the eighty millions of the yellow metal securely held in the Treasury vaults, and if, at any time during the construction and operation of his corner, the United States should come into the market and sell gold, the bottom would fall out of his entire scheme. To prevent this, he got into close and intimate relations with Corbin, President Grant's brother-in-law, and secure in his influence, endeavored to obtain the President's good will and to influence the highest official in the land to prevent his Secretary of the Treasury from selling gold until he, Gould, gave the word.

There never was in the author's judgment a more honorable, upright, simple-minded gentleman than Ulysses Simpson Grant. He was one of the greatest generals of all time, but as President of the United States his very simplicity and innate honesty, his very belief in all men, almost proved his undoing. In this instance he very nearly had to bear the entire burden of blame for the most terrible "corner" the United States ever had seen. Only in the nick of time, when separated by many miles from New York City, did he realize at the last moment the position into which Jay Gould was forcing him, and not too late he ordered his Secretary of the Treasury to release the flood of federal coin which saved the country from the panic which Gould had so ingeniously prepared for it.

But here comes one of the most curious incidents of the whole miserable affair; Gould learned a few hours before the end that his calculations had miscarried, that Corbin could not deliver the President of the United States, that the Treasury was going to sell its gold upon the exchange and relieve the stringency, and then, what did he do? Why, we must remember that Mr. Gould was a quiet man, a good man, and he acted accordingly. He is said to have concluded that if anybody had to be ruined it ought not to be an estimable citizen like himself, but that he should deliver to the lions his partner, the bad Mr. Fiske, the immoral Mr. Fiske. And so on that last great day, Mr. Gould is said to have sent for Mr. Fiske and to have told Mr. Fiske that only a few hours remained before victory, that he was at the end of his resources, and that Mr. Fiske must come forward into the breach, that he relied on Mr. Fiske to support the market, and that Mr. Fiske must buy, buy, buy gold until it hurt him. Mr. Fiske did it, and through other brokers whose names Mr. Fiske did not even guess, good Mr. Gould proceeded in that last fatal twenty-four hours to sell, sell, sell gold to Mr. Fiske. When on that frenzied frightful afternoon a dishevelled man without collar or coat pushed madly into the hell of seething brokers on the floor of the Exchange and cried in stentorian tones: "Any part or all of ten millions, the Government is selling," and when the price of gold dropped with startling rapidity from 162½ to 132, it was Mr. Fiske who faced ruin, disaster, financial annihilation, and it was good Mr. Gould, upright Mr. Gould, Mr. Gould of the age of innocence, of church-going and church-giving, who in the vulgar language of the street had "saved his bacon."

It is but fair to state that Mr. Gould always denied that he had treated his friend Mr. Fiske in any such a way. He said he had instructed his brokers not to sell to Mr. Fiske's brokers, and if they had disobeyed his orders he could not help it. But the judgment of history will always be one at least of doubt, and although it cannot be said dogmatically that Mr. Gould intended to ruin Mr. Fiske, nor can we tell how much he deceived him, and although it must be admitted that he turned around afterward and gave Mr. Fiske much-needed relief (he is said to have invented the scheme of having Fiske repudiate his brokers' stock purchases for lack of written confirmations), yet it seems highly credible that Mr. Gould believed that it was a mighty tight corner, that both he and Mr. Fiske were in the tiger's den, and that if the tiger had to eat one of them he had better sup on Mr. Fiske.

Now let us return in fancy to the night of Gould's passing. Once more we are back on that December evening in 1892 gazing at the dimly lit windows of the great Fifth Avenue

house in company with the young reporters of a by-gone day
and the weary private detectives who never left Gould's side
in his later years. The death watch is on; the Mighty Reaper
is hovering above the house of Midas; the money bags at last
are powerless, and this great captain of industry is summoned
to his last account.

What shall we say of this man and his times? As a gleaming diamond reflects twenty different shafts of light at twenty
different angles, so the life of Gould reflects twenty different
characteristics, some good and many evil. We know that
he was brave, we know that he was kindly when his own self-
interest was not disturbed. His old friend, Thurlow Weed,
has left imperishable testimony to the silent deeds of charity
for which his friend, he avers, was known. We do know positively that at the time of the great Memphis disaster he tele-
graphed the mayor of that city to draw upon him without
limit for all money needed to help the people of the stricken
town. We know that he was abstemious, faithful to his wife,
and a kind and loving father to his children, and we know
that more than once he stepped into the breach with his power
and his money to aid old friends. For all this he will doubtless receive his reward.

On the other hand, we know that he regarded business as a
great remorseless conscienceless game. We know that he would
crush weaker men without regret and without pity. We know
that he had no conception of the duty he owed to the stockholders of the mighty railroads with which he played as
an expert chess player moves pawns upon the board. We
know that though he wrecked some roads he built up others
with rare skill, industry, and ingenuity, but we must believe
that he rescued and rebuilt them for his own selfish purposes.
We know that he regarded with the utmost contempt the
law-makers, the lawyers, and the judges of his day. We know
that he believed most sincerely and thoroughly that every man

had his price, and we know that he justified his actions to himself, believing that smaller men had always been his enemies, had always regarded him with envy and distrust, had always been anxious and willing to ruin him, and that therefore he was justified in taking any means to annihilate and ruin them.

Such a life evokes pity more than censure. Think of the good which this man might have accomplished had he devoted his talents to higher ideals. Think of the loss mankind sustained because of the path he chose to follow. He loved flowers, so did Robespierre. He had a gentle side to his nature, so had Cromwell. Yet he must go down in history as an unscrupulous financial captain, and a man who left the world worse because he had lived in it for the brief space of fifty-six years.

Now let us draw the analogy which all the time has been in the background. It is perhaps natural for each age to look back to that immediately preceding it as a time of higher ideals, better standards, more inspired living; to look back upon its fathers and its mothers as superior people and to regard the sins and vices of its own time with less charity and more condemnation; but let us not be led into any such error. The young people of today have the same human virtues and the same human faults that our fathers and mothers had.

The Age of Innocence as wonderfully reflected by Edith Wharton in her famous novel was not an age of innocence at all. It was an age when politics was more corrupt than it is today, when business was on a distinctly lower level and ideals were much worse than at the present, when there was no such thing, for instance, as the regulation of railroads by the Interstate Commerce Commission, or of public service corporations by utility commissions of the various states; it was a time of greed, of avarice, of chicanery; and above all, it was a time of hypocrisy. Today we may be more crude than our fathers, more frank in our vices, but at the same time we are more sincere and we have a distinctly better atmosphere and higher ideals. The world, the author believes, is getting steadily better than it ever was before.

Jay Gould could not live again at this time and repeat the performances which made him famous between 1856 and 1892 —that much is clear gain.

CHAPTER XVII

GEORGE WESTINGHOUSE—ENGINEER, INVENTOR AND BUSINESS LEADER

MANY men still in the prime of life remember well the insurance investigation of 1905. Probably there was no greater shock to public confidence in established institutions than the discovery made in that year, thanks to the ability and pertinacity of Charles Evans Hughes, that the officers and directors of many of the great insurance corporations of the United States were misusing their position as trustees of the savings of hundreds of thousands of their fellow citizens, and employing the funds of the poor for their own selfish benefit at the expense of the best interest of those whom they represented.

After the smoke had cleared away, it was found urgently necessary to reorganize several of the biggest insurance companies in the country, and none stood in greater need of drastic reorganization than the Equitable Life Assurance Society. At this point Mr. Thomas Fortune Ryan of New York, a millionaire many times over, stepped forward and offered to supply the funds necessary to reorganize the company for the benefit of its policy-holders. Mr. Ryan realized even before he made his offer that, human nature being as it is, his action would not receive popular support nor would his motives escape criticism if he did not take steps which would convince the entire world that for once in his successful and somewhat stormy career he was doing an altruistic thing in a big way. He therefore obtained the consent of three outstanding men to act as trustees of the Equitable, elect its board of directors, and supervise its policies. These men had to be of such stature that their mere nomination would inspire public confidence, and it is needless to say that men of this type were the only ones considered. After a series of thoughtful and careful eliminations, only three remained, and after-events proved that the entire country was benefited by their unselfish willingness to serve. These trustees were Grover Cleveland, one-time President of the United States; Morgan F. O'Brien, Justice of the Court of Appeals of the State of New York; and George Westinghouse, engineer and business man. Probably during long and honorable careers no one of the three ever received a more genuine certificate of character and public faith than that furnished by selection to serve upon this memorable trustees committee.

We are not interested at this time with either ex-President Cleveland or Judge O'Brien, but we are greatly interested in George Westinghouse. He was one of those unusual men who seem to be born in a country at infrequent intervals and who are bound to leave a marked impress upon the times and generation in which they live. Young Westinghouse was a product of the farm. He was born at Central Bridge, New York, on October 6, 1846. He was fortunate in his parentage. His people were of sturdy stock; his mother had a German strain which may have contributed to the thoroughness which later developed in the character of her great son.

It is by no means an invariable rule that boyish traits foretell the permanent characteristics of a man, though certain trends in boyhood are apt to continue during later years. In the case of George Westinghouse, however, certain fundamental traits of character were early observable which continued until the end. George was a younger son in one of those families which in the forties were not unusual but which would be considered large today. There were several boys ahead of him, and as they were all highly individualistic he had to fight his own battles and struggle considerably to impress himself upon his family, his friends, and neighbors.

From infancy he displayed two dominant characteristics. He was tremendously self-willed and utterly determined to get what he wanted, and in addition he showed a mechanical ability which was little short of marvellous. There is no doubt that he inherited this ability from his father, who had left farming in middle life and established himself first at Central Bridge and later at Schenectady, New York, as a small manufacturer of farming implements and machinery. The boy's talents, however, were far superior to those possessed by his father, even during his youth, and sad to say, it is extremely doubtful if the elder Westinghouse ever appreciated the character and ability of his distinguished son. It has often been said that it does a boy good to be brought up in a hard school, but that is one of those generalizations which experience proves is subject to many exceptions. The school may be exceedingly hard without harming any lad, but if the man or men who are doing the schooling are lacking in sympathy with the pupil it is difficult to understand how the pupil may profit from the schooling he obtains. Mr. Westinghouse, from all we can learn, was utterly out of sympathy with George. The father had been compelled to fight hard for everything he got. He was not exactly a pioneer but he lived his life in times when American citizens of moderate means were obliged to live frugally and work faithfully with little expectation, even so, of obtaining more than a bare living and a decent burial. Thus the older man seemed unable to understand anything outside of the doctrine of continuous labor and useful occupation. It never occurred to him that a twelve-year-old boy might like to play occasionally, and it certainly never entered his mind that a lad might spend hours in inventing a machine, the object of which was to save himself personal labor, with any good result.

In this connection a story is told of George Westinghouse which is worth repeating. The youngster, being obliged to look out for himself from his cradle, soon conceived the idea that if he worked for his father out of school hours he ought to be paid for it. With some difficulty he forced his father to accept his theory of compensation, though on a very modest basis. The senior Westinghouse, however, countered by insisting that George should work in his shop every Saturday afternoon, rain, hail, or shine, and this did not conform with the boy's ideas of occasional holidays. Hence upon one occasion when he wanted to get off early, probably in order to go swimming, he invented a most ingenious power line from a machine in his father's shop to a courtyard where there was a large pile of pipe which he was expected to cut by hand. Having hitched up the power by a new and complicated system of transmission, young Westinghouse cut the pipe in two hours and was off to the old swimming hole.

One would suppose that such an exhibition of inventive genius would have greatly pleased the older Westinghouse and impressed him with his son's remarkable ability. As a matter of fact, however, it seems to have irritated him greatly and to have added further force to the conviction he already possessed that his son George was incapable of steady and useful work and would in all probability become an erratic ne'er-do-well. Fortunately for the boy, however, there was an old foreman in his father's shop who thought differently, and by the aid of his kindly efforts, George was supplied with a little shop of his own in a nearby attic where he exercised his natural inventiveness safely shielded from the dubious parental eye.

Like most men of his type, George Westinghouse had an uneven mentality. He was brilliant in any mathematical work, which came easily to him, but he was no linguist and seemed incapable of applying himself to such studies as English and history.

When the Civil War broke out, the lad was fourteen years old, and from the time the first gun was fired on Fort Sumpter he was eager to enlist in the service of his country. His father, however, managed to keep him at home until he was sixteen, when he overcame all objections and joined the army. He was first in the infantry, then changed to the cavalry because he thought it was less tiresome than marching in the dust. Finding, however, that in spite of an easier mode of locomotion he was compelled to act as valet to his horse every night, he soon wearied of this branch of the service, and eventually—and not without considerable difficulty,—managed to change over to the navy, and served during the balance of the conflict in a very junior capacity but nevertheless as an officer, in a mechanical department. He was, in fact, Acting Third Assistant Engineer on a federal gun-boat, and it appears that in this capacity he gave entire satisfaction, having at last enlisted in a branch of the service where his abilities had considerable scope.

At the close of the war, George Westinghouse, though still a minor, had really become a man both physically and mentally. When he returned to Schenectady and his father urged him to go to college and complete his education, he displayed anything but enthusiasm. Finally he was prevailed upon to enter Union College, but he soon found that it was impossible for him to apply himself to the courses of study which then comprised the curriculum of that institution. He stayed only a few months, and before leaving, when the president of the college catechised him severely in an effort to account for his lack of even performance, he told that dignitary very frankly that he believed he could do better work at Union if the studies there did not interfere so much with the things in which he was more interested. Quite naturally this surprised the president and he asked the lad what he meant. This gave Westinghouse a splendid opportunity to produce a number of drawings and blue prints and display his most recent inventions to his astonished questioner. It may be said to the credit of that long-departed and worthy gentleman that he seemed to comprehend without difficulty the peculiar situation of the young student, and advised him to leave college immediately and engage in work more suited to his mentality and ultimate desires.

Accordingly, George went back to his father's shop and again took his place at the work-bench. There is no doubt that Westinghouse senior was bitterly disappointed at his son's failure to complete the course at Union, and looked forward to a dull future for the young man with little hope of eventual success. Such a point of view merely shows how thoroughly an older man can misunderstand a younger one. It is one of the tragic situations in life which is repeated in every generation and never gets any more bearable because of repetition.

If Mr. Westinghouse believed, however, that George was going to be content to work in his shop indefinitely for a small wage, he was deluding himself. Such an idea never entered the young fellow's mind. From his infancy he was constantly inventing things, only after his return from the war his inventions did not have to be veiled in a cloud of secrecy as they had been when he occupied the little shop in the attic of the old factory. It was upon these inventions past, present, and future that the young man based his determination to succeed.

He had not been working for his father very long when he made two inventions which were to be the foundation of his later success. He invented a reversible steel frog for railroads and a device known as a car-replacer, the purpose of which was to reinstate cars upon the rails after a wreck. This might seem an unprofitable invention at the present time, but sixty cr seventy years ago wrecks were much more numerous than they are today and it filled a real want.

George Westinghouse, however, had no money, and although on a number of occasions he tried to enlist Westinghouse senior's financial support, he found his father obdurate and had to seek his backers elsewhere. Also, about this time he gave hostages to fortune by getting married. In many ways it was one of the best things he ever did. His bride was Marguerite Erskine Walker, a beautiful girl slightly older than himself who gave him the most loyal support and the best of advice during the rest of his career. Marriage also acted as a tremendous incentive and spurred Westinghouse on to supreme effort.

His early inventions proved unprofitable and his partners unmanageable (as a matter of fact they tried, though unsuccessfully, to take his patents away from him). Westinghouse left Schenectady, and settled in Pittsburgh. George Westinghouse went to Pittsburgh primarily to get his car-replacer and reversible frog manufactured there. He had broken with his former partners and had to make such an arrangement in order to live. It was his purpose to travel about the country and sell these inventions to the railroads.

At the same time he had another invention by which he set great store. Indeed, throughout his career he always had one or more inventions in a state of incubation and was always thinking and planning ahead. It happened that this invention which he took with him to Pittsburgh in an experimental state, was one of the great basic inventions of his life, and one which will ever be associated with his name. It was the first rough, crude plan of what later developed into the famous Westinghouse air-brake. In those days and for years thereafter, one of the curses of railroading was the inability of the engineer and the train crew to stop the train within a short space of time and distance. Westinghouse, realizing this, determined to supply one of the greatest needs of railroad transportation. It was, however, a most difficult thing to accomplish. For months he concentrated on the solution of the problem.

Then by chance the solution was suggested to him in an entirely accidental way. A young woman from whom, out of sympathy, he had purchased a subscription to the magazine *Living Age* was the unconscious instrument of his success. In looking over the copy of the magazine which she had left with him, he stumbled upon a description of the Mount Cenis tunnel between France and Switzerland which was then in course of construction, and he noticed, with that sixth sense which every great inventor seems to have at his command, that the tunnel under the Alps was being bored by the use of compressed air. When Westinghouse read this statement he gave a yell of delight and tossed the magazine up to the ceiling. He had found the answer to the problem which, up to that time, had baffled him. Surely if compressed air could bore a hole under the Alps, it could be used to stop a train if properly applied to the axles of the cars.

The principle was there, and this to his mind removed 75 per cent of the difficulty. The application, however, was not easy, nor did he arrive at it immediately. Indeed, before he perfected this important invention he met with all kinds of disparagement and discouragement at the hands of eminent railroad men and other inventors. Nevertheless he persisted, and with the aid of a few loyal friends in Pittsburgh, he finally obtained a hearing from the officials in charge of motive power of the Pennsylvania Railroad. Once more the problem of ready money became an almost insurmountable obstacle. The Pennsylvania people were interested, deeply interested it seemed, but they were not sufficiently impressed to pay for the installation on one of their trains which, of course, was necessary in order to demonstrate the new invention.

Finally, after many unsuccessful attempts to get the necessary cash, George Westinghouse raised enough money to pay for the apparatus necessary to equip a four-car train, and the Panhandle Railroad agreed to give the new idea a thorough trial on its Stuebenville branch. The invention at that time was embryonic, and the application of the compressed air to the brakes was not automatic as it is today. The engineer in the cab controlled the air and threw it on as one throws on a hand-brake. Reservoirs were provided underneath the cars, and the compressed air was distributed along the train in such a way that, when the impulse was given by the engineer's hand, the air was applied rapidly and uniformly to all the brakes, and the train was brought to what was then considered a most abrupt stop.

An interesting story is told of the trial trip during which the air-brake was first tested. The train was running on a special schedule and approached a grade crossing at a time when no train was expected there. A truck was caught on the tracks and, the horses balking, the driver was thrown directly across the right-of-way in imminent danger of death under the wheels of the locomotive. It was a most unexpected opportunity to show what the brake could do, and the engineer was equal to the occasion. Instead of applying the compressed air gradually as Westinghouse had instructed him to do, he threw on all the power at once, with the result that the train came to a grinding stop in record time, only four feet from the terrified truck-driver who lay across the rails. The railroad officials who were riding in the rear car to observe the test were thrown all around by the force of the stoppage. Some went over seats and some on the floor. Indeed, so thoroughly did the invention work that, if it had not been ascertained that a stop at this point was made to save human life and was not the usual way in which the Westinghouse air-brake performed, there is little doubt that the officials present would have voted unanimously against the adoption of the device. As a matter of fact, however, after they had picked themselves up and anointed their bruises, these gentlemen were so thoroughly converted to the principle of the Westinghouse air-brake that a number of them became directors in the new company which was soon formed to promote it and put their own money and that of their friends into the proposition.

We have now reached a distinct milestone in the career of George Westinghouse. In July, 1869, he organized the Westinghouse Air-Brake Company under the laws of Pennsylvania, and from that time on, he became increasingly important not only as an inventor but as a manufacturer and a producer of goods vital to American success. The company was capitalized for a half million dollars, which was a modest sum even in those days, but on the board there were names to conjure with. A. J. Cassatt, Robert Pitcairn, and W. W. Carr, all important and rising men in the Pennsylvania Railroad Company, were members. Westinghouse, of course, was president. From this time on the business success of Westinghouse was rapid and assured. He could not have invented anything which was more necessary to the progress of transportation at that time than the air-brake, and its adoption by the leading railroads of the United States was not only sure but speedy.

Not content, however, with the daily harvest of success he was reaping in his own country, Westinghouse displayed at this time that ambition for world conquest in his own line which was to be one of the leading characteristics of his later life. Soon after he had his air-brake factory well started in America, the young man went to England and stormed the ultra-conservative railroad interest of that country. For more than a decade he spent a great deal of his time abroad, and after many setbacks and much experience with the objection that some of our British cousins have to adopting new ideas, he eventually succeeded in getting his air-brake installed by the leading railroads of the United Kingdom and also by the leading roads of many countries on the Continent of Europe, including France and Sweden.

Thus from 1869 until the late eighties, we find that a great deal of Mr. Westinghouse's time and attention was devoted to promoting his air-brake and getting it generally adopted. He found time, however, in 1884 to strike out on a side line which in the end was to bring important results. It is not generally known that George Westinghouse was the first man to develop natural gas in the Pittsburgh district and make it a commercial proposition. He had a beautiful estate on the outskirts of Pittsburgh known as "Solitude," where in 1884, after he had become convinced by his wide reading that natural gas should be in the vicinity, he drilled the first well and opened up what was to prove a veritable mine of wealth, and one of the greatest assets the city of Pittsburgh has ever known.

The original well was dug in spite of the sneers and laughter of all the neighbors. In the end when gas was reached, there was a tremendous explosion, and for some time it seemed almost impossible to control the great subterranean giant which one man's genius had loosed upon the world. However, the well was soon capped, and then the problem arose as to what to do with it. Again the talent which George Westinghouse had for business promotion displayed itself in a marked way. It was clear that natural gas could be used for a great variety of useful purposes, but the new corporation law of Pennsylvania forbade the incorporation of any company for more than one principal purpose. Obviously what Mr. Westinghouse needed was an old special charter so broad in its terms that it would permit almost any kind of business activity. His attorney at that time was Honorable John Dalzell, long a distinguished member of Congress from the State of Pennsylvania. Mr. Dalzell at Mr. Westinghouse's request started on a hunt for a charter of the desired type. In a short time he discovered one, and though he had to pay roundly for it, secured it for his employer. This was the start of the great Philadelphia Company which today supplies the Pittsburgh district with almost every kind of public service it requires, including electricity, natural gas, and transit facilities.

One might suppose that such a success as Westinghouse had obtained in connection with his air-brake and the introduction and development of natural gas supply in the Pittsburgh district, would have been sufficient reward for even a man brilliant beyond ordinary standards, but with Westinghouse these early victories were merely stepping-stones in the scheme of life. In order to make natural gas commercial, Westinghouse and his engineers had been obliged to study and solve the problem of controlling and restraining its flow. In other words, before it could be successfully employed either for manufacturing or domestic purposes, the force of its transmission had to be so reduced as to render its use both practical and profitable. After many experiments, this result was finally obtained, and success in this field led the mind of the inventor by a natural progression to a neighboring territory in which was to be found the then virgin industry of electric power.

In those days the only kind of current generally employed was the direct current. Edison, the master mind of the electric industry, had become convinced that future progress lay in the perfection of the direct current rather than in the developing and adoption of another system. Edison's fame was great in the land. He was then as he was until his death the principal human exponent of the electric industry, and to many his word was law. That Westinghouse, although admittedly a successful inventor, should have the temerity to contest with Edison on a matter of theory in Edison's own field was a matter of universal astonishment. Westinghouse, however, convinced by his experience in natural gas transmission that he was fundamentally right in his ideas, and possessing perfect self-confidence, was not in the least afraid to combat the theories of Edison and to attempt to better them in practice. The trouble with the direct current was that its cost of distribution was excessive, whereas the so-called alternating current, although distributed at a much higher voltage and therefore requiring to be reduced before it was used, could nevertheless be transmitted at much less expense and over lighter wire.

Mr. Westinghouse became interested in this problem at the same time he was engaged in his development of natural gas, and in a way he worked out the problems of the two forms of energy simultaneously. He never claimed to be and in fact was not the inventor of a system of alternating-current distribution, although he and his associates did much to perfect the basic idea after they acquired the American rights of the fundamental patents. These patents covered the inventions of two young engineers who had perfected them in France. They were known as the Gaulard-Gibbs patents and were purchased by Westinghouse in 1886.

The adoption of these patents and their perfection and promotion by the Westinghouse Electric Company marked an epoch in the electrical industry in the United States. By 1888, in spite of much popular prejudice which had to be overcome, the Westinghouse Electric Company was booking more orders for the new type of equipment than it could conveniently fill. It was curious that there should have been so much popular feeling against the use of the alternating current when it first became a feature in the electric world, and yet looking back we can see that the reason for this sincere though ignorant opposition was that the new type of current was admittedly much more powerful than the old and had to be transformed before it could be used. Hence the general public believed that it was fraught with great additional danger to human life. Such was not the case, but it took a good many years of educational work to prove the fact to the satisfaction of the American people.

Meanwhile the Westinghouse Electric Company was experiencing its first flood-tide of success, and Westinghouse himself was evidencing the contradictory traits of character which in a sense were to both make him and break him. He was a big man. Both physically and intellectually he towered above his contemporaries. He was a tireless worker; he had a naturally brilliant mechanical brain which ran like some well-oiled piece of his own machinery, but he was a great egotist and a lonely worker in the sense that he preferred to accomplish his ends with little advice from other men. He had vision, illimitable self-confidence, and until he died he was a complete optimist. He believed in his country with a faith that moveth mountains. He always regarded his own success as assured, and what other men would have understood as a defeat, he considered merely in the light of a temporary setback. He was absolutely sure that the United States as a whole needed his inventions so that the alternating current might be generally employed, and feeling sure of this need, he believed that it should be supplied by his company, and bent himself to the task with what amounted to missionary fervor.

It never occurred to him that a man must walk before he can leap. He never bothered his head with the problem of where his working capital was to come from. He was sure that the people of the country wanted to use his inventions, and believing this he was equally certain that the banks which held the savings of the people should and would supply him with the funds he needed to carry out his great work. His egotism was so complete that he never seems to have realized that he might be incapable of directing the finances of his corporations as well as supervising their mechanical operations. In this lay one of the greatest faults of his character, and it proved to be his undoing on more than one occasion. It should be stated now with definiteness, because it is impossible to comprehend the curious history of the Westinghouse Electric and Manufacturing Company unless one understands fully the character of the man who dominated the corporation during most of his active life and ruled it with a rod of iron. He was indeed a despot in his own business, though a benevolent one.

Thus we approach the critical year of 1890, which was to witness the first great business storm in the career of this unusual man. In that year the total sales of the company amounted to over $4,000,000, which represented a tremendous growth, because the company was only five years old, and in its first full year of operation, 1887, the total sales had amounted to approximately $800,000.

On the face of the record, the company had attained phenomenal success, but as a matter of fact the credit structure which had been erected by those in charge was decidedly shaky. The business was new in character, its fame was local; even the banks of Pittsburgh were unconvinced as to its permanency and unwilling to lend too much money, and naturally the bankers carefully watched the loans they did make. Westinghouse met the situation by doubling the stock issue, increasing it from $5,000,000 to $10,000,000 in July, 1890, and at the same time changing the name of the corporation from the Westinghouse Electric Company to the Westinghouse Electric and Manufacturing Company. In spite of the enthusiasm of its founder and his willingness to subscribe heavily to the new stock, the issue was not successfully marketed, and the burden of debt, which then amounted to over $2,000,000 and was owing not only to bankers but to merchandise creditors, was frozen, although the interest was paid. Throughout the year Westinghouse and his associates made desperate efforts to sell enough of the new stock to relieve the company's drastic need for ready money. In spite of their efforts, rumors started that the company was in serious difficulties.

In the early part of 1891, only about one-half the new stock had been sold. The company had obtained from this source about $1,400,000, which was less than one-half of the floating indebtedness. New capital must be obtained and quickly, so Mr. Westinghouse presented a plan of reorganization which involved the surrender on the part of the stockholders of 40 per cent of their stock, the 60 per cent retained to be known as "assenting stock." On this assenting stock it was provided that a 7 per cent dividend should be paid regularly. At the time this scheme was proposed, the company had outstanding stock amounting to $7,250,000; and by virtue of this surrender of 40 per cent of stock $2,700,000 of the common stock was returned to the treasury, thus greatly lightening the load which the company had to carry.

In spite of these efforts to put the company into a condition in which it might go on successfully, the grave question of providing new capital remained unsolved. This problem was taken up by a reorganization committee in which August Belmont and Company played a leading part. Under the new set-up $3,000,000 of preferred stock had to be subscribed for, and the bankers agreed to take $2,000,000 of it but were unwilling to take it all. At this point a most unusual thing occurred which showed very clearly the extent of the popular confidence in the integrity and ability of George Westinghouse. The merchandise creditors to whom money was owing for goods sold came forward and agreed to take a considerable portion of their claims in preferred stock. Under these conditions, the stock issue was brought before the public during October, 1891, and with a great deal of earnest work was eventually put over. When the reorganization was completed there was outstanding $3,642,200 in preferred stock and $5,201,514 in assenting stock. Thanks to the cooperation of practically everyone connected with the company, particularly the stockholders and the merchandise creditors, this first reorganization was a success, and by February 29, 1892, the bills payable account of the company had been reduced to $600,000 while accounts receivable had risen to twice that amount.

Dr. Arthur S. Dewing, from whose work "Corporate Promotions and Reorganizations" the foregoing statistics have been taken, clearly sums up the facts of the plan as follows:

The good results of the reorganization were clearly manifest. The company had over $3,000,000 in floating debt and nearly $7,000,000 of common stock outstanding giving a total outstanding liability of over $10,000,000 at the end of March, 1891, or just before the reorganization. This involved current interest charged of over $180,000. After the reorganization there were no corresponding floating debts or interest charges, and the total liabilities amounted to less than $9,000,000 of any stock. The large floating debt had been funded into a permanent capital liability. The company thus passed successfully through this first reorganization, and emerged even stronger than it was in the years immediately before. This first reorganization of the Westinghouse Company was a remarkable instance of a corporation with a fairly wide distribution of its stock and known to be on the verge of bankruptcy which accomplished a drastic reorganization without the aid of a receivership. The trouble was brought on by an optimistic business policy, combined with too rapid investment in fixed capital, and by failure to keep the fluid assets sufficiently large. It was relieved through the voluntary sacrifice by the stockholders of a portion of their shares and the willingness of the bankers and creditors to take preferred stock in an enterprise of unknown future. In brief, the floating debt was transferred into a stock liability. The company's truly remarkable success in consummating the reorganization was due largely to the personality of Mr. Westinghouse—his hopefulness, his resourcefulness, and his strong personal hold on the stockholders.[1]

[1] See "Corporate Promotions and Reorganizations," by A. S. Dewing (1914), Chapter VII.

It is difficult to estimate the effect that this serious financial situation had upon the mind of George Westinghouse. Most men would have been sobered and saddened by such a narrow escape from bankruptcy, but it is greatly to be feared that Mr. Westinghouse viewed the matter in an entirely different light. He must have realized that the ship of his fortunes had been very near the breakers, but to a man of his temperament, the fact that he had escaped the rocks and found safety in the open sea, was the only thing that he permanently remembered, and it is to be feared that from that time on he lost all apprehension of serious danger on the theory that having gotten out of one financial imbroglio he could always rely upon himself to get out of another.

Then came one of the greatest triumphs of this remarkable career. The Westinghouse Electric and Manufacturing Company put in a low bid for the contract of lighting the World's Fair at Chicago, and upon obtaining the contract started out to fulfill it in such a way as to make a lasting national and even international impression. No one who ever saw the Chicago Exposition at night with its massive buildings of shimmering white illuminated by hundreds of thousands of gleaming globes will ever forget the spectacle of beauty which it presented to the eyes of all beholders.

As is usually the case, most of the exhibits were missing when the World's Fair opened its gates on May 1, 1893, but the lighting plant of the Westinghouse Company had been fully installed and began to function at once. There were 12 enormous dynamos weighing 75 tons apiece and a switchboard of marble 1000 feet square. There were 250,000 incandescent lamps so placed that only 180,000 were used at one time while 70,000 were held in reserve. The entire installation was so ingeniously arranged that it was under the complete control of one man at the master switchboard. Probably there has never been a single advertisement which paid such big dividends to the advertiser as the Westinghouse installation at the Chicago World's Fair. It was a brilliant example of the evolutionary development of electric lighting, and it put the Westinghouse Company on the map not only in this country but as an industry whose influence was soon to be world-wide.

Westinghouse, however, had the restless ambition of an early pioneer. He went on from one prodigious triumph to another. It was his energy and resource which had much to do with installing the gigantic machinery which first turned the power of Niagara Falls to commercial use, and shortly thereafter he devoted his attention to the electrification of railroads—something which strongly attracted his fertile intellect and with which he busied himself until the end of his career. Throughout the nineties, Westinghouse was consolidating his commercial gains and speeding up his inventive mind to solve problem after problem connected with the group of companies with which he had identified himself. Undoubtedly during these years his principal interest was in the electrical field, but he did not forget his first love, the air-brake, nor did he cease to be continuously interested in the development of the steam railroads.

After the Chicago World's Fair, the general public, the colleges and universities of the country, and many learned societies both at home and abroad signally honored him. One of the greatest honors which he received was the Gold Medal of the Franklin Institute, which was awarded to him for his inventions in air-brake construction. By the turn of the century he was recognized as one of the two biggest figures in the American electrical industry—Edison being the other.

Meanwhile the business of his companies, particularly the Westinghouse Electric and Manufacturing Company, rapidly increased, and from a material point of view he was riding the crest of the waves. Once more, however, the same personal characteristics which had betrayed him in 1891 were insidiously at work to compass his later downfall. The tremendous period of expansion and business progress which began shortly before 1900 and terminated with the violent panic of 1907, undoubtedly had a great effect upon the mentality and plans of George Westinghouse. Always an optimist, he was loath to admit an inflated condition of business and eager to believe that the United States, in which he had such a deep and unfaltering faith, was simply proceeding in an orderly way from one prosperous level to another with no limit in sight, and that material welfare for everyone was not merely the order of the day but of the generation.

Thus he steadily increased his plants, his equipment, and the gross amount of business performed. He did more than this. He was so certain of the future that it was a basic principle of his to be extremely easy with his creditors when it came to the question of paying cash for goods. He carried innumerable dealers in electric equipment, and later on he carried electric railroads for indefinite periods. His main idea seemed to be to get out the supplies needed to electrify the country, and he depended with child-like faith upon his banking resources and upon his customers, who he felt sure would pay for what they bought as soon as they could arrange to do so. This policy unfortunately went well enough during a rather long period of increasing national prosperity, but when that prosperity degenerated into inflation, and when the credit structure of the country became topheavy and insecure, the eventual defeat of such a generous method of operation became inevitable.

During the period above referred to, the Westinghouse Company had steadily increased its regular dividends on both preferred and common stock, and in the year 1907, while there was a fund applicable to dividends of about $2,800,000, the dividends themselves were so large that only about $300,000 or less was left after they had been paid—very little to go on for a company as large as his. The only answer was to increase the bank loans, and this was done as long as it could be accomplished. The current floating debt, however, went steadily upward, and again Westinghouse tried his old scheme of issuing more stock, but once again this simple expedient failed to work, and instead of $7,500,000 as a result of the stock sales, only about one-third of that amount was received, and much less would have come in had it not been that Mr. Westinghouse and a few of his associates subscribed for all they could possibly carry. At that time the floating debt amounted to more than $14,000,000, and the capital structure was so extended that nothing more could be done in that direction. The old story was repeating itself. The banks were suspicious, and the merchandise creditors were clamoring for cash. Of course the company had progressed so rapidly in the intervening years that the figures in 1907 were far ahead of those which had prevailed in 1891, so that the crisis was much more serious and affected thousands of people whereas the first reorganization had affected hundreds.

On October 22 the national panic began with the failure of the Knickerbocker Trust Company in New York, and all hopes of averting the crash in Westinghouse were immediately given up. On the twenty-third the Westinghouse Electric and Manufacturing Company went into court and asked for a receivership, a petition which was immediately granted. Once more the court, the bankers, and the world at large were shocked and puzzled by the situation which the Westinghouse Company presented. It resembled the case of a man starving in the midst of plenty. The company itself was obviously successful, its basic patents were sound, it had been splendidly operated and had accumulated in a short space of time an enormous and paying business, but financially it was a hollow shell. It had an enormous burden of debt, and its own debtors were heavily in arrears to it. Almost every canon of conservative finance had been either forgotten or disobeyed by Mr. Westinghouse and his associates, and they were now paying the piper. The condition was disastrous, and the feeling displayed on the part of the bankers and many of the creditors was bitter and highly critical.

There was much greater difficulty in getting the situation in hand than had been experienced sixteen years before. Out of many schemes of resuscitation, however, one was finally adopted which was commonly known as the merchandise creditors plan. Once more the central feature of this proposition was that the merchandise creditors should sacrifice themselves on the altar of the common good, and take $4,000,000 of new stock in payment of their claims. It was estimated that $10,000,000 would be needed to put the company on its feet and get rid of the receivership, and the plan further provided that the additional $6,000,000 of stock should be sold to existing stockholders. The banks were asked to take one-half of their claims in 5 per cent convertible bonds and the other half either in stock or in fifteen-year notes, with the option that the second half might be divided, 60 per cent going into 5 per cent notes, maturing in four, five, and six years, and the remaining 40 per cent in stock at par. None of the various groups most intimately concerned in the reorganization were pleased with the plan as a whole, which perhaps was the most complimentary thing that could be said about it, for it proved that it did not favor any one faction at the expense of the others. It was finally put over, however, because everyone concerned feared that if it was not adopted the bond holders who otherwise had no great place in the picture, would take a hand in the situation and through foreclosure proceedings wipe out the rights of the stockholders and the merchandise creditors altogether. Finally on December 5, 1908, the receivership was dissolved and the company returned to its owners. It came back pale and anemic, but considerably purged of debt, which had been reduced, as a matter of fact, from

$44,000,000 to $31,000,000. Of course the capital stock had been relatively increased from $29,000,000 to $41,000,000, but this was a much better thing than appeared on the surface, for the new capital stock really included the greatest part of the floating debt.

There was one result, however, which might readily have been foreseen by anyone who was close to the picture. Bankers are just men as a general rule, but they are hard men, and they have to be severe in view of their position as trustees for other people's money. George Westinghouse was such a wonderful man with such a brilliant mentality and so much personal magnetism and persuasiveness that his flagrant mistakes in connection with the first failure of his company had been forgiven even by the close-fisted bankers who were most deeply concerned. However, no man is big enough to make mistakes of this character twice; hence a basic condition of the second reorganization was that thereafter Mr. Westinghouse should step out of his position of dominant control, and allow the company to be carried on by other men more expert than he in the field of business. It must have been a bitter pill for the old man to swallow, and it is doubtful if he realized for a long time exactly the part which he had to perform, but gradually it was borne upon him that his favorite company, the pride of his soul and the crown of his life's labors, was no longer his, and with resignation, even though one fears without humility, he gave up the position which he had held so long and so proudly, and turned his ever-active and fertile mind to other things.

After his retirement from the management of the Westinghouse Electric and Manufacturing Company, George Westinghouse turned his attention to the development of the Westinghouse Machine Company, which had not been affected by the debacle in the electric end of the business and was in fact in excellent shape. There was no such danger here

in connection with over-rapid and unwise development as
he had found to be a controlling temptation in the case of
the Electric Company. He was getting well along in years,
but his intellect was just as fertile as formerly; he was just
as energetic and possessed as much initiative as in his youthful days. It is a splendid tribute to his unwillingness to accept
defeat that, under his personal guidance, the Machine Company became more successful than ever; it really seemed as
though a youthful executive had taken charge of its forces,
when as a matter of fact it was merely the effect of the old
chief returning to his first love.

It is pleasant to think that in spite of the blow to his pride
which would have shattered other men, particularly at his
age, Westinghouse was able to survive the shock and the
humiliation and not only to begin a new career in a different
industry, but also to take the time to become more generally
known to the American people. He was in great demand for
addresses before technical societies and large public gatherings, and although he had always feared public speaking and
felt much hesitancy in facing his audiences, he seems to have
determined to overcome this trepidation of spirit, for in his last
years he signally improved as a public speaker. He had a
straightforward, downright method of statement and a clear-
cut and sincere delivery which carried conviction and exhibited
the personal charm of the man who spoke. It was an excellent
thing, so far as his eventual reputation was concerned, that he
was granted a few more years after 1911 in which to prove
the intrepidity of his spirit and the sterling qualities of character that he possessed before he was called away from the
scene of his labors.

To the end he was venerated by all who had ever worked
for him, and thousands of laborers in the Pittsburgh district
still speak of him affectionately as "the old man." He had

been fair and understanding to labor, absolutely democratic with his men, and protective to the multitude of people who worked in his behalf. This was repaid by an affectionate respect which few employers have known.

The years, however, were creeping on. Undoubtedly, in his inmost soul, Westinghouse felt deeply the one great defeat of his career. Yet he never complained of his physical or his mental sufferings. He was always trying something new. His inventive brain never ceased to fashion new ideas into concrete form. Even in his last illness he occupied himself by designing a new type of invalid chair which was a great improvement on the standard equipment then in use. In the summer of 1913 he fell out of a flat-bottom skiff in the pond on his Lenox estate, and contracted a severe cold as a result of his wetting which brought on a complication of diseases that finally proved too much for his stalwart constitution. He was taken from Lenox to Pittsburgh, then to New York, where he lingered for several months, and finally died quite peacefully on March 12, 1914.

It is an interesting fact that toward the end, he seems to have appraised his life in a peculiar way. It is probable that he was so familiar with his mechanical achievements and his many inventions that they had ceased to mean nearly as much to him as they did to his countrymen. It is no uncommon thing for men to return in spirit to the days of youth when the veil is partly drawn and the great mystery of death is near. Thus in those last days this prince of industry and invention seems to have put aside his titles and his glory and to have dwelt on his early experiences when he was an unknown junior officer in the service of his country. His enlistment in service in the Civil War appeared to him to have been the great altruistic adventure of his long and useful life, and so at his request he was buried at Arlington with his comrades of the

Navy and there he lies with the following simple inscription above his grave:

1846—GEORGE WESTINGHOUSE—1914

Acting Third Assistant Engineer, U. S. Navy, 1864-1865.

Here we may leave him like Sir John Moore "alone in his glory." He was a big man in the post-war period of American industry, a great inventor, a mighty organizer, and a successful operator. The electrical development of modern America owes him an incalculable debt, and yet perhaps we may learn as much from the weakness of his life as from its strength. His egotism was colossal, his self-confidence superb, and although these characteristics were undoubted assets they were also great liabilities. His fellow citizens may well remember that he met his Waterloo because he failed to realize his own limitations, and attempted to achieve success in the field of finance when he should have restricted his efforts to the mechanical arts. This flaw in the idol, however, merely endears his figure to us. His name is great in the land today, and his splendid life will for many years constitute a shining example to aspiring youth. He served his country long and well; he led a good life and died a good death. His fame is secure.

CHAPTER XVIII

GROVER CLEVELAND AND THE SILVER PROBLEM

THE silver issue was one of those sporadic affairs which crop up from time to time in the politics of every nation and which, like rank weeds, have a rapid growth, give an infinite amount of trouble, and are then disposed of. It was never a moral issue like slavery or prohibition but resembled the tariff because, although actually economic in character, it soon became a football of politics and thereafter was handled with a minimum of logic and a maximum of oratory.

There was never any real trouble about the maintenance of the gold standard in the United States until two factors running along parallel lines became united shortly after the Civil War. The demand for cheap money, the first expression of which was the greenback heresy, was combined during the seventies with an economic urge for a great silver market in this country resulting from the discovery about that time of unexpected amounts of silver in Colorado and other parts of the West. In a short time the silver-mining industry became a big factor in the life of several western states, and naturally enough the mine owners, and indeed all the inhabitants of the territory affected, were soon insistent upon the purchase of their annual output by a Government which they thought, to that extent at least, ought to be paternal. Of course, as is usually the case, the real motives of the silver party were camouflaged by a great deal of economic theory and a demand for the free and unlimited coinage of silver in order to give the poor man a chance and defeat the selfish interests of the capitalistic group.

It was not long before a strong silver delegation was formed in Congress, and when they joined forces they found, much to their disgust, that in 1873, as the result of the report of a monetary commission, a law had been passed in the nature of a mint bill by the terms of which the coinage of silver dollars had been discontinued and the gold dollar made the standard unit of the country. The only exception to the rule was a trade dollar to contain 420 grains of silver which was adopted as a side issue in order to facilitate trade with such countries as Mexico and India where it was of considerable practical service.

So bitterly did the silver crowd view this demonetization of the silver dollar, which at the time it was effected caused little comment and no serious opposition, that they always referred to it as the "crime of 1873," which it assuredly was not. Such a reference, however, showed the lack of logic and partisan feeling which were displayed from the beginning by the advocates of free silver. The leader of this organized faction was Honorable Richard P. Bland of Missouri, a man of great persistence, some ability, with a single-track mind and a rough-and-ready talent for oratory and debate.

It is doubtful, however, if the agitation in favor of the free and unlimited coinage of silver would have been as successful as it was had it not been for the panic of 1873 which, it will be remembered, caused the Secretary of the Treasury to increase the legal tender notes and made even conservative citizens anxious for additional money with which to carry on the failing business of the country. From 1876 until the act was finally passed in 1878, Mr. Bland and his friends conducted a vigorous campaign for legislation which would provide for the free and unlimited coinage of silver. In the end they did not get what they wanted, but they did get a good deal more than under ordinary conditions they would have had any right to expect.

The Act of 1878 made the silver dollar legal tender and
gave the Secretary of the Treasury authority to purchase silver
in bulk at the market price in amounts of not less than
$2,000,000 nor more than $4,000,000 per month, and the law
further directed that this bullion should be coined into dollars. It also provided for the issue of certificates backed by
the deposit of silver dollars in denominations of not less than
$10. In vain did President Hayes veto the measure. Congress
was determined to enact such a law and passed the bill over
his veto. The result was that for the next twelve years the
Treasury was compelled to spend at least $24,000,000 a year in
the purchase of silver, and although for a period the burden
was sustained with unexpected ease, it proved in the end to
be intolerable. The reason why the Treasury was able to get
along somehow under this compulsory purchase act was
that, with the exception of a setback in 1884-85, the times
were as a whole prosperous. It was the middle period between the panic of 1873 and that of 1893. Our railroads
were expanding rapidly, hundreds of thousands of immigrants
were coming in from Europe every year and settling in the
West, production was increasing, the demand for goods in the
domestic field was going up by leaps and bounds, and it took
more than an unwise law of this kind to shake seriously the
structure of national success. The act, however, did cause that
structure to crack badly, and any economist could see that,
when another national earthquake took place, the building
was apt to fall.

Of course, the Bland-Allison Act, as it was called, gave the
greatest help and comfort to the silver party, and although in
the beginning the group was largely composed of Democrats,
it enlarged and spread to such an extent that before very long
both political parties were much affected. The situation indeed
with regard to the silver issue was comparable to that which
exists today in connection with prohibition. There were silver

men in both parties in large numbers, so that the political leaders felt that their wishes must be considered, and as usual the leaders began to talk in terms of compromise.

This situation came to a head in 1890 shortly after Benjamin Harrison had been elected President of the United States. His Secretary of the Treasury, Mr. Windom, combined in an extraordinary degree the attributes of a student and a politician. He had an unusual grasp of the entire silver question, and he was shrewd and plausible in his exposition of it, but he was by no means a doctrinaire with regard to the matter. He was eminently practical. He realized more fully than his associates did that, in the newly admitted states in the western part of the country, there were a number of senatorial votes which he felt would be sure to increase greatly the power of the silver party in the highest legislative body of the United States. He therefore looked about him for some method of getting a compromise law adopted which, without actually saying so, would be in effect a free silver act, and would sufficiently pacify the western senators to enable the Republican Party to put through its tariff program without serious opposition, which, after all, was their main objective.

Beyond question, he must have been aware of the bad effects of the Bland-Allison law. The figures were beyond contravention. In the period between 1878 and 1890, the Government had coined 378,166,000 silver dollars at a purchase price of $308,279,000 for the necessary bullion, the difference of nearly $70,000,000 representing a variation between what the silver was worth and what the Government proclaimed it was worth. It was also evident that, no matter how much the people of the United States might like the theory of silver coinage, they disliked to use silver money. During this twelve-year period, the Government made every effort to compel the general use of silver coins, but without avail. Whenever possible, our citizens deposited the coins with the banks and the banks passed them back to the Treasury. They were clumsy, heavy, and a nuisance to handle, and as a practical matter the Treasury simply could not make them circulate in amounts proportionate to the mass of bullion which was being coined every year for distribution to the people. However, these were practical considerations which, though they may have caused the Secretary of the Treasury to hesitate, did not divert him from his main purpose.

Even the Act of 1886 which had authorized the issue of silver certificates in smaller denominations than $10, viz., $1, $2, and $5, had not proved effective in increasing the practical use of silver and its representative certificates. And yet the Secretary was unimpressed with the plain facts which were staring him in the face. He was undoubtedly more impressed by the general unrest which had been a feature of the late eighties. This unrest encouraged the masses of people in the West, most of whom were new settlers, to continue their appeals for more money and cheaper money as a necessary factor in the development of the great territory in which they were the pioneers.

Mr. Windom's report of December, 1889, was an able state paper. It was a compendium of most of the arguments in favor of the free use of silver as currency. It dealt with a number of alternative policies. The only one which now seems to have had great possibilities was the suggestion of an international agreement by means of which a ratio between gold and silver might be definitely fixed and thereafter maintained by general agreement of the great powers. This, indeed, went to the vital point of the entire situation, which was the inadvisability of the United States adopting any ratio in connection with the precious metals independently of the other leading nations of the earth. It is not surprising that the politicians of the country, particularly those from the interior and far western states, failed to realize that, though isolated and powerful, the United States was not in any position to play a lone hand on the currency issue. Mr. Windom also discussed the advisability of continuing the policy of the Bland-Allison Act, and he took up the free coinage of silver with considerable boldness, finally suggesting a number of compromise plans, none of which, however, was adopted by the Congress.

The report, however, was symptomatic of a vast change of heart on the part of the Republican Party leaders, and it did result in legislation of definite benefit to the silver group. As usual, John Sherman, of Ohio, was the senator who fathered the bill. He was undoubtedly the greatest compromiser of the period, besides which he had been Secretary of the Treasury and had performed a wonderful task in the resumption of specie payment. He was much respected and had a great following. On July 14, 1890, the so-called Sherman Act was finally passed, by terms of which the Secretary of the Treasury was authorized to purchase 4,500,000 ounces of silver bullion each month and to issue in payment thereof Treasury notes of full legal tender. Dr. Davis R. Dewey well sums up the effect of this act as follows:[1]

The essential differences between this act and that of 1878 were: increase in the monthly purchase of silver; treasury notes to be full instead of partial legal tender, as in the case of the silver certificates; redemption of treasury notes either in gold or silver coin at the discretion of the secretary. After July 1, 1891, standard silver dollars were to be coined only when necessary for the redemption of the notes.

On the whole, the measure provided for the purchase of all the American product of silver, but did not admit unlimited coinage. In order to reassure those who feared that such large purchases would result in depreciation of the standard, the act declared that it was the established policy of the United States to maintain the

[1] See "Financial History of the United States" by Davis R. Dewey, Chapter XIX, pp. 437-438. Reprinted by permission of Longmans, Green & Co., Publishers.

two metals on a parity with each other. This was afterwards interpreted by the treasury as "a virtual promise that the notes shall always be redeemed in gold or its exact equivalent." Although an increase of silver purchases is apparently required by the Sherman Act as compared with the Bland Act, this would not necessarily follow; for by the act of 1890 the annual additions to the currency would grow less if the price of silver fell, while by the Bland Act the annual additions grew larger as the price of silver fell. For substituting the measurement of purchases by ounces instead of by dollars, Senator Sherman has the credit, and its importance becomes obvious in view of the subsequent fall in the value of silver.

The Act of 1890 was in effect for about two and a half years before the next change of administration.

Grover Cleveland was elected President of the United States for the second time in November, 1892, and assumed office on March 4, 1893. When he came into office he found a dangerous and discouraging situation so far as the currency was concerned. The Act of 1890 had operated very much in the same way as do leeches when applied to the human body, and had caused a steady and practically automatic drain upon the national gold reserve. This strain on the Treasury was bad enough during the prosperous period which was just closing, but in the early summer of 1893 there occurred one of the most frightful financial panics and depressions in the history of our country. So far-reaching and devastating were its effects, that the President called Congress together in special session on August 7, and his first demand was that the compulsory silver purchase law should be repealed. In spite of the obvious need of such legislation because of the panic then existing, the silver party in Congress was strong enough to delay if it could not defeat the repeal bill which the President had requested. It was not passed until October 30, 1893, and then it was within an ace of being too late. A great part of the damage had already been accomplished.

There were outstanding at that time approximately $450,-000,000 of United States notes and greenbacks, and on demand these had to be redeemed in gold. Not only that, but under the unwise provisions of the law such notes had to be reissued and were then immediately available for re-presentation. This situation came to be known as the "endless chain," and it was quite clear to all informed people that unless drastic steps were taken, it was only a question of a short time before the gold reserve of the country would be exhausted and the Secretary of the Treasury would be forced to refuse payment in gold and to make payment in silver. Such a situation was probably exactly what the partisans of silver desired to bring about, but had it ever occurred, as it very nearly did, it would have automatically injured the credit standing of the United States with all the powerful nations of the earth, and would have been the beginning of a new era of Government finance which, as far as we can see today, would have resulted in placing the currency of the country upon a new and lower level comparable with the currency of such countries as Mexico, China, and some of the South American republics. That this most unfortunate result was avoided we can never be sufficiently grateful, and our gratitude is due largely to President Cleveland.

Grover Cleveland was a rare character, and he stands out today as one of the really great Presidents of the United States. He was a man of proven bravery, large of body and of mind, sometimes crude and untactful in his speech, but the soul of honesty and with a patriotic devotion to duty and a respect for his oath of office which has never been exceeded even in the case of such men as George Washington and Abraham Lincoln. At this juncture he clearly perceived that immediate action was necessary if the gold standard was to be preserved and the credit of the United States protected. There is little doubt that he hated the thought of increasing the national debt by the sale of a large amount of bonds in time of peace, but nevertheless he considered that the danger made such action not only defensible but necessary. The Government was much restricted in issuing bonds even for the high purpose of defending the national honor. The only act under which they could be put out was that of January 14, 1875, under the terms of which the bonds so issued were not made payable in gold but in "coin," which, though it had always been interpreted to mean gold, bore no such assurance as to the future, particularly in view of the power and success which the silver group could boast of at that time.

After the repeal of the silver purchase act, Mr. Cleveland struggled along through the fall, but at the turn of the year he realized that something must be done very quickly. By general agreement, $100,000,000 was considered the lowest point at which the national gold reserve ought to stand, and on January 17, 1894, the reserve was $70,000,000. Therefore the Secretary of the Treasury gave notice of an issue of Government bonds in the amount of $50,000,000 bearing interest at 5 per cent redeemable in ten years and of course to be paid in "coin." As was expected, however, the public showed no degree of enthusiasm to take up the issue, and it was necessary for the administration to appeal to the eastern bankers. This was done with success. The issue netted the Government $58,660,917.63, so that the reserve was raised temporarily to $107,440,802—which was not much above the danger line.

Having won a breathing spell, Mr. Cleveland appealed to Congress for better legislation in order to protect the gold reserve, asking for a clear-cut declaration that bonds issued for this purpose should be redeemable in gold. Unfortunately, however, before this request could be either accepted or rejected by Congress, a vicious bill was passed by both houses and sent to the President. It was known as the Seigniorage Bill and provided for the coining of approxi-

mately $50,000,000 out of the excess silver in the Treasury
which represented the difference between the actual cost of
the bullion bought under the compulsory purchase act and the
silver dollars actually coined from it in accordance with the
provisions of the law.

To a man of less courage and of a more equivocating temperament, this would probably have constituted an unconquerable temptation. Mr. Cleveland knew that to veto this
act would prevent the passage of any law designed to aid him
in the issue of Government bonds, but though he hesitated
briefly he never wavered in his determination to do the right
thing as he saw it regardless of the consequences. He vetoed the
bill in such language that his motive could not be misunderstood. In the course of this famous veto message the President
said:

My strong desire to avoid disagreement with those in both Houses
of Congress who have supported this bill would lead me to approve
it if I could believe that the public good would not be thereby
endangered and that such action on my part would be a proper
discharge of official duty. Inasmuch, however, as I am unable to
satisfy myself that the proposed legislation is either wise or oppor-
tune, my conception of the obligations and responsibilities attached
to the great office I hold forbids the indulgence of my personal
desire and inexorably confines me to that course which is dictated
by my reason and judgment, and pointed out by a sincere purpose
to protect and promote the general interests of our people.

After this veto it was clear that Congress and the administration had arrived at a hopeless deadlock over the currency,
and there was nothing for the President to do but to go ahead
independently of Congress. The endless chain was working as
silently and as efficiently as a well-oiled machine, and the
Government's store of gold was dwindling with alarming
rapidity. Hence on November 14, 1894, the Treasury brought
out a second bond issue of $50,000,000 of 5 per cent bonds, and

again there was increasing difficulty in marketing them. Eventually a group of banks and individuals formed a syndicate which made a bid for "all or none," and the Government realized $58,538,500 from the sale of the issue. Once more for a short time the gold reserve was safe; yet in a sense these bond issues were but temporary in character, and it was almost like trying to dry up Niagara with a mop. Both sides of the silver issue realized fully the terrible difficulty which Cleveland faced in trying to preserve the gold standard, and public opinion was sharply divided over that as well as other political questions.

Never since the days of Abraham Lincoln had any President stood so alone as Mr. Cleveland. Never since the days of Lincoln had any President been endowed with such courage and adherence to principle. It was indeed fortunate for our country that Grover Cleveland was the man of the hour. The President fully realized that something further must be done, and he looked about at last for expert help in his time of need. He did this reluctantly, for he was a man of the people, a Democrat born and bred, and though eminently fair, he unquestionably viewed Wall Street and its exponents with suspicion and distrust. At this juncture, however, he called into council a mind as rugged and able as his own, and on February 7, 1895, a momentous interview took place at the White House between Grover Cleveland and J. P. Morgan.[2]

The old lion of Wall Street came at once and gave Cleveland his advice as to this vital financial problem which was extremely hard to solve. Mr. Olney, the Attorney-General, and

[2] See "Grover Cleveland, The Man and the Statesman," by Robert McElroy, Harpers, 1923, Vol. II, Chapter 3, p. 85 *et seq.*, for an account of this interview attributed to Cleveland himself. McElroy, who quotes Cleveland, places the interview at night but Winkler and Lynch speak of it as having taken place in the morning. (See "Morgan the Magnificent" by J. K. Winkler, chap. 9, p. 153, and "Grover Cleveland" by Denis Tilden Lynch, chap. LXXIII, p. 457.) Personally the author prefers to follow McElroy, although the point involved does not seem of great importance.

Mr. Carlisle, Secretary of the Treasury, were also present at
the conference, which lasted well into the night. After a
lengthy interchange of views, Mr. Morgan expressed doubt
that further bond issues could be sold by popular subscription
except at a discount which would cause the Government great
loss. He suggested, however, that there might be another way
and called the attention of the President to Section 3700 of the
Revised Statutes of the United States which reads as follows:

> *Section 3700.* The Secretary of the Treasury may purchase coin
> with any of the bonds or notes of the United States, authorized by
> law, at such rates and upon such terms as he may deem most ad-
> vantageous to the public interest.

Curiously enough, this section of the law had been overlooked by all present except Mr. Morgan because it was designed for a different purpose and no one had thought of it
as available in the present crisis. The Attorney-General and
Mr. Cleveland, both of whom were leading members of the
American bar, made a quick decision in favor of the appli-
cability of this section of the statutes to the case in hand, and
it was immediately decided to proceed under its provisions.
It was also agreed that if a large amount of gold was purchased by the Government from Mr. Morgan and his associates in a syndicate to be formed, the syndicate members
would exert every effort to protect the Government from
losing the gold thus acquired. In other words, some of the
most powerful financiers of the United States would be bound
to do their best to slow up if they could not altogether stop
the operation of the "endless chain."

It was agreed, therefore, toward the end of this memorable
night, that J. P. Morgan and Company of New York, acting for
themselves and for J. S. Morgan and Company of London,
together with August Belmont and Company of New York,
acting for themselves and for N. M. Rothschild and Sons of

London, should sell and deliver to the United States Government 3,500,000 ounces of standard gold coin of the United States, to be paid for in bonds bearing annual interest at the rate of 4 per cent per annum, payable in coin at the discretion of the Government after thirty years, the bonds to be issued and delivered from time to time as the gold coin to be furnished was deposited by the contracting bankers in the sub-treasuries or other depositories of the United States. It was also agreed that at least one-half of the gold so delivered was to be obtained in Europe, but this provision was later somewhat departed from. The amount of gold thus contracted for totalled roughly $60,000,000, and again raised the gold reserve to the level of approximately $100,000,000.

It is difficult after the lapse of nearly forty years to appreciate the storm of criticism, mud-slinging and vilification which greeted the President of the United States and his Cabinet when this gold contract was frankly announced to Congress, which of course was immediately done. The President's motives were violently assailed by a partisan press. His friendship with Commodore Benedict was immediately called to mind, and it was insinuated that he must be getting some direct pecuniary advantage from what his opponents openly declared was the most damnable conspiracy between the powers of Wall Street and a President of the United States that had ever occurred. Despite the whirlwind of opposition and detraction, Grover Cleveland went calmly on, fortified by a clear conscience, and the knowledge that he was saving his country's financial honor in accordance with his adherence to his oath of office.

Then too, human nature asserted itself at this point in a rather amusing way. Undoubtedly, if those bonds had been issued directly to the general public instead of being employed under Section 3700 of the Revised Statute to purchase gold bullion from a crowd of prominent bankers, they could not have been sold except at a discount, and a drastic one at that. As it was, the mere knowledge that they had been purchased by J. P. Morgan and Company, Belmont and Company, and the Rothschilds, so affected the public mind that, in spite of the criticism they were showering on the administration, the investors of the country fairly stormed the offices of the bankers where the bonds were to be sold. On February 20 the bonds were disposed of in a few minutes by the bankers concerned, and generally speaking they sold bonds for which they had paid 104½ to the Government for approximately 118½ on the public resale. Furthermore, people were delighted to get them at that price, although they cursed the bankers and the administration for making it possible for them to do so.

However, we are not through with the story. The purchase of gold from the banking syndicate under Section 3700 was a brilliant coup and temporarily useful, but after all it only raised the gold reserve to an amount slightly above the danger level and it soon became clear that another purchase of gold in exchange for bonds was imperative. The first purchase of gold for bonds had taken place in February, 1895, and the funds so obtained, by careful husbanding, were made to last out the year, but again by January, 1896, the gold reserve was so badly decreased that another effort was made in its defense. Accordingly, on January 6, 1896, the United States Treasury brought out a thirty-year 4 per cent issue of bonds in the sum of $100,000,000. This time, however, the administration was not so frightfully pressed for time as on the first occasion, so that the bonds were thrown open to the public, and a month's time was allowed within which bids could be made. Finally the bonds were distributed among several bidders, but again J. P. Morgan and Company, having made a favorable offer, obtained $62,321,150 of the bonds. Again the failing gold reserve was replenished, and from the dangerous low level of $50,000,000 in January, 1896, it was raised during

February by means of the gold obtained through the new loan to $124,000,000.

This was the last loan negotiated by the Cleveland administration, and it preserved the gold standard until the next presidential election. It did more than this. It served to concentrate public opinion upon the entire situation in a way which less drastic action would have failed utterly to accomplish. There is no doubt that the silver issue by this time had become the paramount subject of conflict between the two great political parties of the United States, and this would probably have happened even if Grover Cleveland had failed in his duty. However, there is no doubt that the unswerving rectitude of this great Democrat and his adherence to principle in spite of the clamors within his own party, had much to do with the triumph of the gold standard in the succeeding election when William Jennings Bryan, running on a silver platform, was decisively defeated by William McKinley, who represented those who were determined to establish the gold standard once and for all in the polity of the American people.

When the election was over, McKinley and his Cabinet faced a delicate situation. The Republicans had returned to office with an undoubted mandate from the people to confirm the gold standard by necessary legislation. On the other hand, the party had been divided on the silver issue, and many of its ablest legislative representatives both in the House and Senate were sore distressed at the defeat of silver. These men were in an ugly frame of mind, and the Republican leaders believed that it was the part of wisdom not to act hastily in establishing the gold standard.

They therefore turned their attention first to the tariff which, as always, stood in the forefront of Republican issues, and thus allowed the wounds of the late contest to heal before attempting to place a gold standard act on the statute book. Then, rather fortuitously from a political viewpoint, the war

with Spain intervened and gave a further breathing spell before this troublesome problem had to be finally solved. At
last, however, after several years had elapsed, the Republican
majority mobilized its strength, and the Act of March 14,
1900, was adopted by Congress and approved by the President.
This act marked the end of the silver issue, for it provided
in unequivocal terms that gold should thereafter be the
standard of currency in the United States, and it directed the
Secretary of the Treasury to maintain all other money at parity
with gold. The machinery provided for putting the act into
effect was by no means perfect, but it has proved adequate,
and the great advantage of the law has been that since its
adoption there has been no question of the existence and maintenance of the gold standard in the United States. It is also
true that the subsequent establishment of the Federal Reserve
System has served as a further bulwark and greatly facilitated
the efforts of the Treasury both as to the maintenance of an
adequate gold reserve and the protection of the currency in
times of stress and depression.

As we look back upon the troubled period of more than a
quarter of a century during which the silver issue was a vital
point of conflict in American politics, we should rejoice that
the vexing problem it presented was solved in such a way as to
preserve our national credit and prepare us to assume that
primacy in finance which has been ours since the Great War.
Yet, after the passage of so many years, we should also feel
considerable sympathy with those sincere advocates of silver
coinage who were actuated by a really difficult economic condition of affairs, and who with earnestness strove to obtain an
enlarged supply of the circulating medium for the benefit of
thousands of people who, as they believed, were actually being
oppressed by the selfish actions of Wall Street financiers. That
they were fundamentally wrong now seems apparent to all,
but, with the exception of those who were motivated by a

purely selfish interest in the silver mines of the West, they were the representatives of a real cause and they strove to accomplish what they believed to be right.

Fortunately as time progressed and wiser counsels prevailed, the currency of the country was improved, enlarged, and fortified in perfect accordance with the gold standard, and without the necessity of placing the United States in an indefensible position among the nations of the earth. It is fortunate that such a result was at last obtained, and it is even more fortunate that through the patriotism of many courageous men it was attained in a conservative and proper way. Grover Cleveland rendered many services to his country, but he never rendered a greater than when almost single-handed he maintained her financial honor during the dark days of his second administration.

Chapter XIX

THE RISE OF THE PACKING INDUSTRY

PROBABLY no business affects the daily life of the people of this country more than what is known as the meat-packing industry. It is not merely a national matter but is of international importance as well. Man is a meat-eating animal, and with the exception of a few vegetarians, most men eat meat. In the United States they eat a great deal of it. Prior to the Civil War, meat supply was a local matter, but since that time a great change has taken place. Today very little of the meat that we eat is raised and killed locally. Nearly all of it comes from the West, and particularly from Chicago, which is the seat of the packing industry.

The word "packing" is sometimes misunderstood. Packing connotes slaughtering, the preparation of the slaughtered meat for the market, and then packing, shipment, and eventual distribution. The business has grown up very rapidly in this country; indeed, it has developed on a large scale only since the Civil War. The meat trade is one of our great businesses, ranking with the production of oil in its appeal to the American people because it is an intimate factor in the daily life of all. It may properly be viewed from two widely separate angles. Undoubtedly its pioneers displayed initiative, courage, and ability to overcome obstacles, and as a result they attained in a comparatively short time a success which was world-wide. As it stands today, our great packing companies feed not only America but a considerable part of Europe as well.

At the same time, the business has from its early days tended to become a monopoly, and has displayed the advantages and disadvantages of a monopolistic system. There are five big packing companies, and the control and operation of these great corporations have been closely held. At the present time at least four of these companies are directly descended from small organizations put together two generations ago by a number of able men, all of whom were born at about the same time, and who, after years of competition in their field, eventually got together on a basis of business understanding which constituted a monopoly of the meat trade in the United States. Undoubtedly in many ways the country has benefited by the combination. The people, however, from time to time have been the victims of the meat monopoly.

There are two sides to the story. Even though the prices for meat are not nearly as high proportionately as prices for many other national necessities, many of the practices which the big packers have followed in order to consolidate their power and make it effective throughout the land, cannot easily be defended. But we owe a great deal to the inventive genius of the packers which has produced the refrigerator car and the refrigerator steamship. If it were not for these remarkable inventions we should be paying two or three times as much for meat as we are paying, and the meat that we got would not be nearly as good.

The purpose of this chapter is not to examine the record of the packers with regard to monopoly and unfair methods of competition, but rather to trace the romantic history of the packing industry through the lives and accomplishments of a few of its leaders. At the same time a brief explanation of the darker side of the picture may be in order so that the reader will not suppose that this account is intended merely as the panegyric or a eulogy of the dead leaders of the industry.

At this point let us quote the summary of findings of the Federal Trade Commission, which examined the packing industry and filed its report on July 3, 1918. As preface to the quotation, it is interesting to note that the only panacea which the commission suggested for the violations of the law which it claimed to have discovered, was that the Government should acquire from the railroad administration all rolling stock used for the transportation of meat animals, and that such ownership be declared a Government monopoly. It further advised that the Government should likewise acquire the principal stockyards and control and operate them in the same way, and it even carried the theory of Government ownership to the extent of advising the acquisition of all privately owned refrigerator cars, branch houses, cold-storage plants, and warehouses. In fact, the Commission advised general Government ownership of the entire industry. Congress, however, did not see fit to accept the suggestion of the Federal Trade Commission, and instead of adopting Government ownership as applied to the packing trade, a suit was brought in one of the United States courts which ended in what is known as a "consent decree" (by which is meant a decree to which both sides assented) providing that the packers should be prohibited from continuing to distribute their products along certain side lines into which they had entered with considerable success, namely, the grocery and the canned meat products business, and should also be prohibited from doing business as retailers of meat. This "consent decree" has now been reopened and is before the Supreme Court of the United States on appeal for decision.

The report of the Federal Trade Commission in 1918 was very valuable in one particular. It represented a thorough study of a great mass of testimony, and as a fact-finding report it was on the whole a good one. It is therefore interesting to review a part of the summary of findings contained in the report, viz.:

Five corporations—Armour & Co., Swift & Co., Morris & Co., Wilson & Co., Inc., and the Cudahy Packing Co.—hereafter referred to as the "Big Five" or "The Packers," together with their subsidiaries and affiliated companies, not only have a monopolistic control over the American meat industry, but have secured control, similar in purpose if not yet in extent, over the principal substitutes for meat, such as eggs, cheese, and vegetable-oil products, and are rapidly extending their power to cover fish and nearly every kind of foodstuff.

In addition to these immense properties in the United States, the Armour, Swift, Morris and Wilson interests, either separately or jointly, own or control more than half of the export-meat production of Argentina, Brazil, and Uruguay, and have large investments in other surplus meat-producing countries, including Australia. Under present shipping conditions the big American packers control more than half of the meat upon which the allies are dependent.

The monopolistic position of the Big Five is based not only upon the large proportion of the meat business which they handle, ranging from 61 to 86 per cent in the principal lines, but primarily upon their ownership, separately or jointly, of stockyards, car lines, cold-storage plants, branch houses, and the other essential facilities for the distribution of perishable foods.

The control of these five great corporations, furthermore, rests in the hands of a small group of individuals, namely, J. Ogden Armour, the Swift brothers, the Morris brothers, Thomas E. Wilson (acting under the veto of a small group of bankers), and the Cudahys.

A new and important aspect was added to the situation when the control of Sulzberger & Sons Co. (now known as Wilson & Co., Inc.) was secured in 1916, by a group of New York banks—Chase National Bank; Guaranty Trust Co.; Kuhn, Loeb & Co.; William Salomon Co.; and Hallgarten & Co. The report of the committee appointed by the House of Representatives to "Investigate the concentration of control of money and credit" (the Pujo committee) states (p. 59): "Morgan & Co. controls absolutely the Guaranty Trust Co." The Chase National Bank, a majority of its stock being owned by George F. Baker, is closely affiliated with the First National Bank. William Saloman & Co. and Hallgarten & Co.

are closely affiliated with Kuhn, Loeb & Co. Thus we have three of the most powerful banking groups in the country, which the Pujo committee classed among the six "most active agents in forwarding and bringing about the concentration of control of money and credit," now participating in the rapidly maturing food monopoly above described. The entrance of the bankers into the packing business, it should also be noted, was not at all displeasing to the big packers. J. Ogden Armour and Louis F. Swift were frequently consulted during the negotiations, and Paul D. Cravath is quoted by Henry Veeder as giving assurance that the final arrangements would be "more than satisfactory" to Armour and Swift.

The menace of this concentrated control of the nation's food is increased by the fact that these five corporations and their five hundred and odd subsidiary, controlled, and affiliated companies are bound together by joint ownership, agreements, understandings, communities of interest, and family relationships.

The combination among the Big Five is not a casual agreement brought about by indirect and obscure methods, but a definite and positive conspiracy for the purpose of regulating purchases of live stock and controlling the price of meat, the terms of the conspiracy being found in certain documents which are in our possession.

There are undoubtedly rivalries in certain lines among the five corporations. Their agreements do not cover every phase of their manifold activities, nor is each of the five corporations a party to all agreements and understandings which exist. Each of the companies is free to secure advantages and profits for itself so long as it does not disturb the basic compact. Elaborate steps have been taken to disguise their real relations by maintaining a show of intense competition at the most conspicuous points of contact.

The Armour, Swift, Morris, and Wilson interests have entered into a combination with certain foreign corporations by which export shipments of beef, mutton, and other meats from the principal South American meat-producing countries are apportioned among the several companies on the basis of agreed percentages. In conjunction with this conspiracy, meetings are held for the pur-

pose of securing the maintenance of the agreement and making
such readjustments as from time to time may be desirable. The
agreements restrict South American shipments to European countries and to the United States.

Since the meat supplies of North and South America constitute
practically the only sources from which the United States and her
allies can satisfy their needs for their armies, navies, and civil popu-
lations, these two agreements constitute a conspiracy on the part
of the Big Five, in conjunction with certain foreign corporations,
to monopolize an essential of the food of the United States, England, France, and Italy.

It will readily be seen from the foregoing findings of the
Federal Trade Commission that no matter how interesting
and romantic the rise of the packing industry may be, no
matter how vital its continued economical operation may
prove to the welfare of our people, there always has been
and is today a big element of monopoly in the actual transaction of the meat business as a whole, and it is believed that
it will finally come down to a point closely resembling the
United States Steel investigation where the Government will
have to concede, as in a sense it has already done, the monopolistic character of the packing industry and decide its future
on the ground of its usefulness to the American people. In
other words, we again have the question before us as to
whether or not the meat trust is a good or a bad trust. Under
any circumstances the future of the packing business is one
of the most interesting present-day problems of American
economics.[1]

[1] To show how big the industry is, Swift and Company's Consolidated Balance
Sheet as of November 1, 1930, was as follows:

ASSETS

Cash .... $ 18,639,884.30
Accounts Receivable 57,701,784.28
Inventories 101,764,920.95
Stocks and Bonds 33,546,887.60

Let us now go back and trace the romantic and interesting development of the industry through the lives of some of the great men who were responsible for its development.

The first name which stands out is that of Philip D. Armour. He was a world character long before he died. He

Land, Buildings, Machinery and Equipment, including Refrigerator Cars, etc. $189,464,988.50
Less: Depreciation to date 80,357,644.10

109,107,344.40
Discount and Expense on Ten Year Gold Notes—Being Amortized..   979,803.69

$321,740,625.22

LIABILITIES AND CAPITAL

Accounts Payable ....$ 19,424,144.16
Notes Payable 9,105,765.70
Ten Year 5% Gold Notes, Due Sept. 1, 1940 .... 30,000,000.00
5% First Mortgage Sinking Fund Gold Bonds, Due July 1, 1944.... 22,916,000.00
Reserves 12,586,827.22
Capital Stock—$25 Par Value:
  Authorized and Issued $150,000,000.00
Surplus 77,707,888.14

Total Stockholders' Investment 227,707,888.14

$321,740,625.22

INCOME AND SURPLUS

Net Earnings, before Depreciation, Interest, and Federal Income Tax.$ 27,938,283.38
Provisions for Depreciation 8,627,952.12

$ 19,310,331.26
Interest Paid on First Mortgage Bonds, Gold Notes, Notes Payable,
  etc., including Amortization of Debt Discount and Expense......   5,221,341.55

$ 14,088,989.71
Reserved for Federal Income Tax 1,597,800.73

Net Earnings for Year ....$ 12,491,188.98
Dividends, 8% 12,000,000.00

Surplus for Year ....$ 491,188.98
Surplus, Previous Year 77,216,699.16

Surplus, November 1, 1930 ....$ 77,707,888.14

was the greatest citizen of Chicago, diversified in his interests
and broad in his civic efforts. He was born at Stockbridge,
New York, on May 16, 1832. It is interesting to note some of
the characteristics that most of these great packers had in
common. Practically none of these men had any great amount
of early education. Armour had very little; what he had, he
got through the public schools. When he was about nineteen years old, in 1851, two years after the great rush to the
gold fields took place, Armour started out for California with
three older boys. One of them died on the way, two others
quit, but Armour got there. There in California, when twenty
years of age, he showed one of the traits which distinguished
him throughout life. He did not start in to search for gold and
stake a claim. He had been a farmer's son and he knew something about digging. He decided that he would let the other
fellows get the gold and he would dig their trenches. He
hired two or three other men to help him and started in to
work. Soon he was bossing many other men in digging
trenches and in a short time made $8000 from it.

Pleased with his success, Armour started home on a visit
and stopped off at Milwaukee, then the leading city of the
Middle West. He decided that Milwaukee had a great future
and that he would come back to it after he returned from
New York, which he did. Just before the Civil War he entered into partnership with an older man named Plankinton
who was engaged in the food-supply business. They started in
to pack hogs. Finally they instituted a Chicago branch, and
their business grew and prospered very rapidly.

Long before almost any other man Armour realized the importance of Chicago, and finally he left Milwaukee, settling
permanently in the former city. Most of the people believed
that Milwaukee would be the great city of the Middle West,
but Armour felt that the position of Chicago made it the
dominating lake city, so he went there and started to work.

Soon Armour & Company was organized; he brought his brothers on to join him, and the new company began to grow rapidly.

At the same time, a great many other men were coming to Chicago and starting in the packing business. There was Nelson Morris, who started Nelson Morris & Company. He was a hard-working, able boy who landed from Germany in Philadelphia, walked to New York, drifted to Buffalo, and beat his way to Chicago on a lake vessel. Many of these men seemed to arrive in Chicago like tramps, except Armour who already had achieved some reputation. We should not forget Michael Cudahy, who began to attract notice when he was a foreman in one of the big plants. How he arrived in Chicago must be conjectured.

In 1865 a very important step was taken in the Chicago packing trade, for in that year the big union stockyards were instituted. These stockyards had an interesting and curious career. They were started at the request of the packers by the railroad companies. As the railroads got most of the profit from moving the live stock, the packers said they should be willing to keep up the stockyards. The packers induced nine railroads to put up the money to do this, and the railroads let the packers run them until a time, some thirty-five years later, when it became evident that they had become enormously valuable and profitable. Then the packers, by a series of intricate steps, forced the railroads to give them the stockyards. It was in 1890 that the packers decided they had made a mistake in not establishing the stockyards themselves. So they bought a piece of land in Indiana and said to the railroads: "Listen, you either sell the stockyards to our holding company at an agreed price and make a reasonable contract with us, or we are going to pull all the steers out of Chicago and we are going to move the yards to Indiana. We are going to take the whole packing industry to Indiana." The railroads thought they were bluffing. However, they were not quite sure what the packers were going to do, so they invoked the assistance of Chauncey M. Depew. In the end they made an adjustment and settlement, but by the time they got through, the railroads had lost a great deal of power and property and the packers had matters about as they wanted them.

Let us now take up the career of Mr. G. F. Swift. He was born on Cape Cod on June 24, 1839. He died in 1903. He was a butcher by trade, and during his early life he gave good evidence of the ability he was going to display in later years. One of the interesting childhood stories of Gus Swift recounts how once he went to his grandmother and said to the old lady: "Grandma, I want to buy that old white hen for forty cents." His grandmother was astonished for she did not know where he had obtained forty cents; but he had it, and after making the purchase he went out and sold the hen for sixty cents. He was very good at that sort of thing. When he was eighteen years old he borrowed $400 and went off to a place called Brighton, where he bought 400 hogs. He knew he could not sell them in Brighton so he drove them home and peddled them along the route; when he got back he had $550 and no hogs. He had what might be called a natural talent for business.

It was not that the boy was avaricious. He was neither greedy nor crooked. He played the game straight as he understood it. He learned the butcher trade right at home. His brothers were butchers, and except for Gus they always would have remained butchers.

Swift was not satisfied. He conceived the idea that he knew a great deal about cattle. He decided he would leave the butchering business and get into the commission business. He did, and made a success of that. He became associated with a man named Hathaway, and the firm of Hathaway and Swift was formed with headquarters in Boston. Soon extending his field of operations, he started to do business in Albany and Buffalo, and began shipping western cattle to New England. He was not yet satisfied, however, and in the early seventies went to Chicago, still in partnership with Hathaway. He determined that he would start a commission business with the buying headquarters in Chicago to serve the eastern markets.

Now comes one of the most interesting points in his career. If there is one thing that is always rewarded it is practical business vision. If there is one thing that is disastrous it is impractical business vision of any kind. Swift had a practical conception of what he wished to accomplish, and real business vision; he could see far ahead, could think in terms of the future and not forget the present. As soon as he located in Chicago he began to think of the future of the food-producing industry all over the country, and he was the first big man to realize that the system then in existence of shipping food animals alive across the continent was bound to go into the discard, that it must soon disappear. He was the first man to realize that the whole industry could and would be revolutionized if the refrigerator car could be perfected, and he set about to perfect it.

Do not believe, however, that he had only the difficulty of refrigeration to fight. He had all the railroads of the country against him for a very obvious reason. If a steer is killed, cut up and packed in a refrigerator car, it occupies less than half the space that it did when alive; moreover, it does not have to be fed nor does it need any water. The railroads were making a lot of money out of shipping these animals alive, and furthermore, they had a large number of live stock cars which would have to be junked if this new idea came in, so they exercised their influence against the use of western dressed beef in the East.

Swift went at the problem in two ways. He bought the pat-

ents of two inventors who had been working on the refrigerator
car and set his own experts to working on them in an effort to
perfect it. Next he found a railroad, the Grank Trunk Railway, that did not have any live stock transportation because
it had too long a route—too long for shipping steers. He
went to this railroad, which happened to be situated independently with regard to the other roads, and asked the management if they would like to have an enormous amount of
freight traffic. He said all they had to do was to build these
refrigerator cars. The railroad officials were interested but
said he must build the cars and furnish the freight, so it was
done on that basis. That was the beginning of the privately
owned refrigerator cars which more than any other single
factor has enabled the "Big Five" among the packers to dominate the meat industry of the United States.

Having got that far, he still had to overcome an enormous
public prejudice against the use of western dressed meat which
prevailed in the East. Mr. Swift never let up for one moment.
He kept on fighting prejudice and ignorance until in the end
he overcame them. He was never content with any success,
no matter how great. It merely served to lead him on to something bigger. It was not long before the other packers took
up this system and shortly after that they dominated the American trade.

Mr. Swift then conceived the idea of refrigerator steamships.
He went to London, where for six weeks he got up at three
or four o'clock in the morning in order that he might go to
the biggest meat markets in London, to see that the American
beef was being properly sold and distributed.

His was a single-track mind. He did not take much part in
civic work in Chicago, but his cash contributions to it were
generous and liberal. Swift was in the beef-packing industry
for only twenty-five years, yet as a result of that short business life of absolute concentration, tremendous industry, and

complete devotion to a single idea, joined with business vision and great mental capacity, he left a monumental concern which now has capital assets in excess of $337,000,000. But we cannot estimate the life of such a man in terms of mere money. He was a dreamer, a visionary, a devoted soul of the stuff of which the old champions were made, and it was only just a matter of coincidence that instead of being a character like Savonarola with a great ideal of spiritual reform, he devoted his ability, his dreams, and his visions to pigs and sheep and cattle.

CHAPTER XX

ANDREW CARNEGIE—THE KINGDOM OF STEEL

THE city of Pittsburgh in 1850 was a raw, crude place, but it suggested power. An interior city, it could not rely on its shipping and must succeed, if at all, as a center of production. True, it was a natural railroad terminus and freight depot, but it had to be far more than that to fulfill the amibtion of its settlers.

In those days a casual visitor might never have noticed a bright-eyed little fellow about twelve years old who brushed by him on the street intent on carrying messages for the Telegraph Company, and holding his job as messenger boy at the princely salary of three dollars a week. The lad was bright-eyed, sandy-haired, and extremely active in spite of his small size and lack of physical strength. When he spoke he showed at once that he was a Scotchman, born and bred. This little fellow was Andrew Carnegie, destined to be the most prominent citizen of the town and at his death to be justly known as the greatest master of steel the world had ever seen.

Young Carnegie belonged to a great generation. He was born in the old Abbey town of Dunfermline on November 25, 1835. His people were Scotch Chartists. They were stiff-necked Covenanters who lived hard, worked hard, and did their own thinking. It was probably because of their unusual independence of thought that they emigrated to America in order to be free from the trammels of caste and prejudice. So it was that at eleven years of age the boy Carnegie began to work for his living, first in a cotton factory and later as a telegraph messenger. From the beginning he was not content with his

ANDREW CARNEGIE

job. Indeed, for many years he never was. He came early to the office and studied telegraphy before his work began. He soon became an expert operator and was promptly given a better job in this capacity. Still under twenty, he attracted the attention of Thomas A. Scott, one of the great presidents of the Pennsylvania Railroad, and was taken by him into the employ of the road first as a telegrapher and later as Scott's private secretary.

There is no better account of these early years than that contained in Mr. Carnegie's own autobiography. This remarkable book, written with the sure touch of a man who has passed through the fire of life, attained success, and gained his knowledge, may be thought by some to be an egotistical account of a great career; to a considerable extent it is, but it charms the reader by its utter naturalness and by the evident desire of the author to state the facts of his life sincerely and without affectation for the benefit of generations yet to come. Mr. Carnegie tells us of the bitter struggles of those early days and the honest pride which every small success gave him. He speaks with love and respect of his mother and of her help and encouragement in those critical days. He tells us how his first investment in the stock of the Adams Express Company was made possible by her determination to raise the money and her willingness to mortgage their little home in order to do it. She grasped the fact that the offer of the stock coming from Mr. Scott himself afforded her son an opportunity to enroll himself in the investing class at an early age, thereby winning the respect of his employer, and she went to the limit of her strength and ability in order to accomplish the end in view.

If there was one characteristic which Andrew Carnegie possessed in youth it was that of self-confidence. He was willing to accept responsibility, and in the great game of life such willingness is the thing which differentiates the man with a

career from his mediocre associates. The world is full of men
and women who are capable of doing good work under the
direction of other people, who are honest, industrious, and
upright, but who when faced with the necessity of assuming
definite responsibility, exhibit fear and thereby prove themselves incapable of undertaking the more difficult and worth-
while tasks of life.

Little Andrew, however, was not of this breed. He was almost too willing to seize authority and exercise it. While he
was assistant to Mr. Scott, that gentleman failed to appear at
the office one day, being absent on an inspection trip.
Word came over the wires that there was a wreck on the road
and that traffic was in a very confused condition. An express
train was proceeding completely off schedule going very
slowly with a flag man ahead at every curve, and a number of
freight trains were tied up on various sidings along the line,
which in those days was a one-track affair. Under a very
definite rule of the service, the situation could be cleared only
by telegraphic orders sent out by the division superintendent.
In his absence no one dared to give such an order, that is to say,
no one except Carnegie, who by that time was known famil-
iarly as "Tom Scott's Andy." He looked over the situation and
felt sure he could clear it. He knew he would be held responsible for any failure and would be severely punished if not
discharged if anything went wrong. This knowledge, however,
did not even make him hesitate. He wrote a pile of train orders
readjusting the time of the express and the various freight
trains and sent them all out signed "T. A. Scott, Superintendent." Later in the day Mr. Scott came bustling in considerably worried because he had heard that traffic was all tied
up. He asked Andy what the situation was. The lad replied:
"It was bad, but now it is all right."

"Who moved the traffic?" Scott inquired.

"I did," said Andrew. "Here are the orders," and he handed

Mr. Scott a sheaf of train dispatches all signed with his superior's name.

Mr. Carnegie in his autobiography describes the trepidation with which he faced the superintendent on this occasion,
and says that much to his surprise Mr. Scott, after looking over
the orders, handed them back in silence. He said no word of
praise or blame, but Carnegie knew that his very silence was
commendation, and he learned later that Scott had boasted
about him the same day to other officials of the road.

Throughout the decade which preceded the Civil War,
Andrew Carnegie continued to work in close association with
Scott, a man of ability and great personal magnetism, who
became the boy's ideal. Then much earlier than in most cases
Carnegie reaped a definite reward. When his friend and
patron became vice-president of the Pennsylvania Railroad in
1859, Andrew, then only twenty-two years old, succeeded him
as superintendent of the western division, a most responsible
and important position. As usual he made good, and although
just entering manhood and in charge of a large number of
men, most of whom were old enough to be his father, there
was no question whatever as to who was boss of the division.

In two years the great national crisis arrived, and Scott
was called to Washington as Assistant Secretary of War
in charge of the transportation of troops. At once he called
to his side the sandy-haired youth who had been so dependable
in the old Pittsburgh days and together they worked night
and day for two years in the service of the country. Then,
having been of material assistance in organizing the vitally
important transportation system of the war period, Carnegie
received an honorable dismissal and returned to the city of
his adoption.

It was at just about this time that he began to display that
shrewd appreciation of investment opportunity which distinguished him throughout the balance of his career. He had

managed to save a little money, and after a lucky speculation
in sleeping-car stock, he and several associates bought the old
Storey farm on Oil Creek near Pittsburgh, and joined the increasing crowd who at that time were seeking to wring fortunes from the bosom of the earth. Oil was a new idea in those
days, and the Pennsylvania field was unproved, risky, but fascinating to adventurous spirits like Carnegie. He was not to go
on and become a competitor of his contemporary, John D.
Rockefeller, in the oil game, but he was to be blessed with a
great streak of luck, and he was to derive from his first flyer in
oil a comfortable fortune with which to build fame and success
in another field.

The oil on the Storey farm exceeded all expectations. Carnegie and his friends paid $40,000 for the original oil land
they acquired, and found to their astonishment that the
meager output of 100 barrels a day, which was the amount
flowing at the time of the purchase, rapidly increased until
the new reservoirs they constructed were full to overflowing
and the return on the investment seemed well-nigh fabulous.
It was not long in fact before the purchasers were dividing a
profit in excess of a million dollars a year from the oil they
found on the Storey farm. It was an indication of the canny
foresight of the young man that he declined to continue in
the oil game, realizing as he did that it was a business of
uncertainty, essentially speculative in character, and if he kept
on he would be likely to lose much of his profit and perhaps
in the end be just where he started.

Doubtless Carnegie's business inclinations had been greatly
affected by his early training on the railroad. He was convinced that the United States had an almost limitless future
and that its vast extent must be supplied with adequate means
of transportation. This meant not only locomotives, rolling
stock, and skilled railroad operators, but it meant bands of
gleaming steel which should bind the Atlantic coast to the

Pacific and cover the entire continent with a great network over which the products of the factory and the farm should be carried to many markets and to the great ports of the land. Early in this young man's career he learned to think in terms of steel. Naturally at the beginning he was willing to work in iron, for the Bessemer process had not been invented in those days, and iron was the best material the men of that day knew.

Toward the close of the Civil War, Andrew Carnegie became definitely interested in the iron business. He joined forces with his brother Tom. He became acquainted with Phipps, afterwards to become one of his most famous partners, and he began to work up a series of consolidations and alliances including the Kloman-Phipps interests and others as well. The result of these various corporate experiments was the Union Mills, in which both the Carnegies and Phipps were concerned. A little later Andrew Carnegie in conjunction with the firm of Piper and Shiffler formed the Keystone Bridge Company, and about 1866 began a career of successful bridge building which was greatly aided by the post-war boom that set in about then.

In 1872 Andrew Carnegie went to Europe to sell some bonds for the Pennsylvania Railroad, and while there he took advantage of the opportunity to study the new Bessemer process at first hand. He found that steel made under the Bessemer process was already much used abroad, and it took little time to convince him of its great superiority to the old iron rails which were still generally employed on American roads. It happened that he had made more than $200,000 as a commission for selling bonds for his old railroad friends, and he was therefore in funds to extend his already considerable interests in the Pittsburgh district. With his usual Scotch caution he made no attempt to swing the deal alone, for he realized that much money would be required and working capital must be secured in sufficient quantity to assure success. He therefore called to his aid the men who were gradually solidifying into a Carnegie group—Kloman, Phipps, McCandless, Scott, Stewart, Tom Carnegie and a number of others—to join with him to form a corporation which was to become one of the most famous steel-producing units of the United States.

Mr. Thompson, president of the Pennsylvania Railroad, became interested in a modest way, and partly as a compliment for his participation in an unproved scheme, and partly because of the prestige likely to accrue, Carnegie named his new company the J. Edgar Thompson Steel Works. From the beginning the new company seemed blessed with unusual luck. Although scarcely organized when the panic of 1873 swept the land, it survived the financial whirlwind, perhaps because it was a very young company and was not cursed with past indebtedness. Steadily the business grew, and with the resumption of prosperity in the late seventies the Thompson Company became a leader in the steel trade.

During the eighties Carnegie not only enlarged his enterprises, but by mergers and consolidations he greatly strengthened his position in the steel business, while through judicious stock purchases he acquired a constantly increasing control over the vast aggregation of capital which he had been instrumental in forming. Probably his wisest step in the direction of expansion was his purchase in 1883 of the Homestead Steel Works across the river from the Thompson plant. This company had been a vigorous business competitor, but its owners had engaged in unprofitable labor disputes, and the price of steel turning downward at a critical moment, they lost heart and sold out to Carnegie, who with his usual self-confidence and belief in the recuperative powers of the United States, was only too willing to take them over at a price.

It was during the middle eighties also that Carnegie teamed

up with a man who is considered by many people to have
been his intellectual equal if not his superior—H. C. Frick,
whose name will always be associated with that of the old
iron master. Carnegie and Frick were utterly different types
of men. Carnegie was shrewd, personable, attractive in manner, and on occasion talkative. He had a flair for publicity and
loved the limelight. He was a big man and he knew it.
Whether as king of steel or practical philanthropist he naturally sought the center of the stage. Frick, on the other hand,
was equally cold-blooded but quiet, unobtrusive, calculating,
and a born business negotiator. He was never the international
figure that Carnegie was, nor did he seek to be, but our generation realizes his ability and his steadfast devotion to the
interests of the Carnegie firm.

Mr. Frick first became associated with Carnegie through his
coal and coke business which was a natural adjunct to the
manufacture of steel. Before very long, however, he ceased to
be a mere business acquaintance, and in a short time was in
the very center of the group of men which surrounded the
little chief. He was instrumental in bringing the Duquesne
Steel Company into the combination. This occurred in 1890,
and as a result the Carnegie Companies profited greatly by
means of improved methods of steel manufacture which the
Duquesne Company controlled and employed. It was not
enough, however, that Carnegie and his partners should combine a series of operating companies into a single great organization for the manufacture of steel, but it was necessary in
order to attain that primacy which they so desperately desired,
that they should make their gigantic organization into an
economic unit with a strength hitherto unknown in the annals
of American business. It is a matter of dispute who first conceived the great idea from which this unheard of strength
was to be derived. Mr. Carnegie's friends loyally gave him

credit for it, but many men who were close to Henry C. Frick insisted that the conception originated in his fertile brain.

In a word the thought was this: In order to be absolutely independent of its competitors and other business enemies, the Carnegie Steel Company must control the manufacture of steel from the mine where the ore was wrested from the earth, across the miles of water and rail necessary to bring that ore to the plant, through the various stages of manufacture to the marketable product, and out of the plant at last to the market-place where it should eventually be sold.

It has been well said that there is nothing new under the sun, and probably the same idea was exemplified in bygone days by some group of bearded merchants in Ur of the Chaldees. Yet each generation must think its own thoughts and be responsible for its own deeds, and in our time Carnegie and his partners were the first group of men who conceived the purpose of making a mighty corporation into a great independent economic unit. More than that, they not only conceived the idea but over a period of time they translated it into an accomplished fact. It was indeed a slow process and one fraught with much difficulty and in constant danger of failure. Of necessity, it must be done largely in secret, and this multiplied the difficulties an hundredfold.

It was at the beginning of the nineties that H. C. Frick assumed the heaviest burden in carrying out the great scheme of unification. He managed to acquire from a rich Pittsburgher named Oliver a half interest in certain important mines on the farther side of the lakes, and in 1896 he leased additional mines from the Rockefellers; at the same time his agents were busy buying up all available options covering likely claims in the surrounding country. Gradually the Carnegie firm acquired a fleet of lake steamers to transport their ore to a rail head of their own selection, and then about 1897 they got control of the Pittsburgh, Shenango

ANDREW CARNEGIE

415

and Lake Erie Railroad, which was in serious financial difficulties, put it on its feet, and used it as another link in the
chain which they were steadily perfecting. Meanwhile they
had built a local railroad connecting all their plants and
mills within the Pittsburgh district so that when their plan
was complete just before the turn of the century they were
in a position of unexampled strength and power. They had
their own mines, their own steamers, their own railroad,
and a complete and physically connected system of mills
and manufacturing plants. Mr. Carnegie could indeed say to
the world as he very soon did that the Carnegie Company feared
no one and would pursue its own destiny in accordance with a
policy which was conceived and executed without relation to
others and consequently without their consent.

It was at this time that Carnegie came to grips with J. Pierpont Morgan.

The panic of 1893 had left the country strewn with the
wreckage of many different kinds of corporations. Most of
the important railroads were in the hands of receivers, and
the great industrials were scarcely better off. About the time
of the Spanish War, when business began to recover from the
terrible blows it had received, the dominant financial leader
was Mr. Morgan. This was the beginning of that era of
trust formation which formed such a colorful and important epoch in the business history of the United States. J. P.
Morgan's first love and most important interest was the
field of railroad reorganization, but he was so much esteemed
by all the leaders in the commercial world that he was constantly importuned to devote his talents to the consummation
of industrial consolidations. In this way after a while he became interested in the steel business, and particularly in that
class of steel companies whose business it was to take the
raw ingots and turn them out into manufactured form: for
example, such corporations as the National Tube Works Com-

pany and other companies engaged in the manufacture of structural steel and completed rails. The Carnegie Steel Company had never engaged in this kind of business, but through their open-hearth furnaces had produced increasing quantities of steel ingots which in turn were transformed into the finished product by these other corporations.

In effect, in the years just preceding 1900, the steel business was in a condition of delicate balance somewhat resembling the modern situation in one of our great metropolitan areas where two gangs of bootleggers divide the territory by imaginary lines for the sake of mutual profit. As long as the gentlemen's agreement is observed, peace prevails, but with the first breach of the unwritten contract the machine guns begin to bark and chaos reigns supreme. So it was in the steel business when the century began, and it is only fair to Mr. Carnegie to say that it seems to be true that the first breaches of the unexecuted contract were made by the other side. The American Steel and Wire Company and other corporations which hitherto had been content with the final processes of steel production began to build plants and buy equipment looking toward an entry into the production of steel ingots from the crude ore. It all came from the pinch of the panic and the natural desire of ambitious men to profit from the first real resumption of better business.

These avaricious steel masters had failed to count the cost of their acts of trespass. They had reckoned without a due appreciation of the determination, cool courage, and shrewd humor of the little Scotchman who blocked their way to ultimate success. Carnegie was small, neat, dapper, grey-bearded, and courteous, but he was the embodiment of determination. When he realized, as he soon did, what his competitors were trying to do, he made known the fact that he and his partners contemplated retaliatory measures. He said he thought they would build some big new plants and engage in the manufacture of finished steel products. The result of this simple announcement was startling and important. In effect it was a declaration of war, and everybody in the steel trade knew it. With one accord the steel men flocked to Broad and Wall Streets and besought Pierpont Morgan to come to their assistance. He and he alone, they asserted, could deal with Andrew Carnegie and put an end to the threat of war which if allowed to become a fact would disorganize the entire steel business in the United States.

Mr. Morgan listened to their pleas with more than usual attention. From a selfish point of view he could not afford a series of battles in the kingdom of steel. Already the era of trust formation was well advanced, and the country was in a state of expansion in which the success of many businesses was so interwoven that none of them could afford to allow any of the others to experience serious trouble if there happened to be any possible way of avoiding it. Obviously the thing to do was to induce Mr. Carnegie to agree to a huge consolidation which should take in his own organization and the leading independent companies. Through the mediation of Charles M. Schwab, whom Carnegie had made president of his company after the Frick quarrel, the two opposing camps were brought together and an offer was made.[1] Carnegie was polite but apparently not deeply interested. He had previously refused a number of exceedingly flattering offers for his splendid company. He was in a very

[1] It is difficult indeed to determine exactly how the negotiations began. According to Ida M. Tarbell in "The Life of Elbert H. Gary" (p. 110), Schwab seems to have been sent as a semi-official emissary to the Morgan interests, and to Judge Gary in particular. John Moody in "The Masters of Capital" (p. 82) relates that Schwab and John W. Gates approached Morgan, rather than Schwab and Gary. However, he states that "whether Schwab's overtures were directed by Carnegie or not may never be known." Winkler in "Morgan the Magnificent" (p. 208) claims that Carnegie deliberately planned to use Schwab as his emissary, but that the meeting between Morgan and the latter took place at a dinner in New York. And thus it goes. At least, if coy at first, the maid was willing.

strong position and he knew it. He also had the satisfaction of realizing that J. P. Morgan knew it just as well as he did.

The negotiations were necessarily somewhat protracted. There was a good deal of dealing and counter-dealing on both sides. It was a huge consolidation, and it was arranged by giants. Into this new concern were herded 213 steel manufacturing plants and transportation companies, 41 mills, more than 100 miles of railroad, and 112 lake steamers. The machinery of consolidation when the terms were agreed upon was fairly simple, being based upon an exchange of the stock of subsidiaries for that of the new holding company. The real trouble in the situation, however, arose from the hard terms which Carnegie imposed. He had a good thing to sell, he was not particularly anxious to part with it, and he intended to extract the last million from the Morgan crowd. The final terms were as follows:

Carnegie and his associates received as the purchase price for the Carnegie Steel Company $303,450,000 in bonds, and stock in the new United States Steel Corporation having a par value of approximately $200,000,000. Carnegie and several other members of his family were paid on the basis of $1500 per share for the 96,000 shares which they owned, the total payment of $144,000,000 being made in bonds of the United States Steel Company. Of these shares, Carnegie himself owned 86,382 and received for them the sum of $129,573,000. Carnegie also owned $88,147,000 of bonds of the Carnegie Steel Company which were taken over by the new corporation at their face value and which brought Carnegie's proceeds from the sale of his interests to $217,720,000.

The balance of the United States Steel Corporation bond issue was used to retire $160,000,000 bonds of the Carnegie Company. Stockholders other than the Carnegies, holding 64,000 shares of stock, received $98,277,120 in preferred stock and $90,279,040 in common stock of the United States Steel

Corporation. At the time when the sale was consummated the bonds and preferred stock were at par and the common stock sold at 50, which made a total paid to the Carnegie Company at the then market value of the securities involved amounting to approximately $447,416,640.[2] This was probably the largest transaction of the kind that had ever been carried through in the United States up to that date, and there is no doubt that it represented a top price for the Carnegie assets and would never have been paid except under the peculiar circumstances which then existed. J. P. Morgan and his friends greatly feared the effect of a war in the steel industry upon the general security market of that day, for it was at the height of the trust movement and the country was full of undigested securities representing many other huge consolidations of capital in almost every field of industry. These securities were newly fledged, and unassimilated by the public, and Morgan felt that it would never do to have strife in the business world at that time. It was better in his judgment to pay an outrageous price for the Carnegie Steel Company rather than run the risk of precipitating a national panic which would affect investments of every type.

The result of the Carnegie purchase is well known. Morgan and his associates used it as the keystone of the United States Steel Corporation which was immediately formed. The other leading unit of the new company was the Federal Steel, and to these two great corporations were added in the new consolidation American Bridge, American Sheet Steel, American Steel Hoop, American Steel and Wire, American Tin Plate, Lake Superior Consolidated Iron Mines, National Steel, and the National Tube. This huge amalgamation of the steel trade represented about 65 per cent of the steel business of the United States. The new corporation started life with an

[2] "History of the Carnegie Steel Company" by James Howard Bridge, pp. 356, 363-364.

authorized capital of $550,000,000 each of preferred and common stocks and $304,000,000 of bonds, the total of $1,404,-000,000 being the largest aggregation of corporate capital in the history of American industry.

When it was all over Andrew Carnegie found himself one of the richest men in the world. He was worth more than $150,000,000 in cash and in the bonds of the United States Steel Corporation. The rest of his career does not deal intimately with American finance but is of intense human interest. It is reasonable to say that Carnegie was never popular with the American people. There were several reasons for this and they are not difficult to comprehend. To begin with, he was always very Scotch and extremely proud of his origin. He believed in the greatness of America and he had confidence in the ingenuity and energy of the American people, but it is doubtful if he ever considered himself an American.

As soon as he acquired a fortune he was quick to renew his touch with the land of his birth, and during the later years of his business career he spent a great part of his time at Skibo Castle in Scotland which he had purchased and which he made his most prominent residence. Pittsburgh saw him only from time to time. Of course he never took his hand from the throttle of his business machine even when he was in residence at his Scottish home; the ocean cables were kept hot with messages backward and forward between Carnegie and his Pittsburgh lieutenants, of whom H. C. Frick and Henry Phipps were for many years the most important. Nevertheless, he gradually assumed in the mind of the American public the rôle of an absentee landlord, and it is not to be questioned that his frequent absences irritated and hampered his partners considerably. His principal biographer, J. H. Bridge, is of the opinion that, because of his absence, he misunderstood much that was going on and often blocked the progress of his great corporation by his unwillingness to allow Frick and Phipps to pursue policies which were justified and most advantageous to the business. However that may be (Bridge very probably was prejudiced against Mr. Carnegie and therefore biased in his account), the public got to know him as the "Laird of Skibo," and his unpopularity grew apace.

Then in 1892 came the great Homestead strike which brought all the Carnegie partners into national disfavor. When the strike occurred, Mr. Carnegie, as usual, was away from home, and in his autobiography he attempts to evade a full measure of responsibility for what took place by the following characteristic statement:[3]

While upon the subject of our manufacturing interests, I may record that on July 1, 1892, during my absence in the Highlands of Scotland, there occurred the one really serious quarrel with our workmen in our whole history. For twenty-six years I had been actively in charge of the relations between ourselves and our men, and it was the pride of my life to think how delightfully satisfactory these had been and were. I hope I fully deserved what my chief partner, Mr. Phipps, said in his letter to the *New York Herald*, January 30, 1904, in reply to one who had declared I had remained abroad during the Homestead strike, instead of flying back to support my partners. It was to the effect that "I was always disposed to yield to the demands of the men, however unreasonable"; hence one or two of my partners did not wish me to return. Taking no account of the reward that comes from feeling that you and your employees are friends and judging only from economical results, I believe that higher wages to men who respect their employers and are happy and contented are a good investment, yielding, indeed, big dividends.

However true it may have been that Mr. Phipps feared Mr. Carnegie's kindness of heart, the fact remains that the captain was away when the trouble occurred, and it was serious trouble indeed. Frick handled the situation with a strong hand but with some unfortunate results. The striking workmen

[3] Reprinted by permission from "The Autobiography of Andrew Carnegie." Published by Houghton, Mifflin Co., Publishers.

turned on Frick's detectives and there was fierce fighting, bloodshed, and death. Without going into the rights of the case, and at this length of time it seems as though the company was more sane and reasonable than the strikers. The final result, however, was disastrous from the standpoint of the company's public relations; the memory of it continued to harass the Carnegie partners for many years, nor is it entirely forgotten today.

Thus, after he had been bought out by the Morgan group and stood before the world as one of its most powerful multimillionaires, it is probable that Andrew Carnegie looked about him to determine just what he should do with the rest of his life. The choice he made was notable and important, not only to him but to the world at large. He did not know it, of course, but he had eighteen more years of life before him. He was still in his prime, and his entire career had represented thrift, industry, and constant occupation. Hence it was clear to him that he could not retire from active life and he certainly had no desire to do so. It must have been at this time that he conceived the important theory that it was a sin for a man to die leaving a huge fortune. He became impressed with the thought that the money he had received was in the nature of a public trust and that it belonged to him only as the representative of society in general. Such a mental concept is surprising in view of the selfishness which he had shown throughout his entire past career and the hardness he had displayed in using every legitimate means to acquire the millions which now were his. Life, however, is full of contradictions, and this particular contradiction was of the greatest use to humanity.

Carnegie, then, just after the beginning of the century, started his remarkable race against death, and it was his consistent effort during nearly a score of years to re-allocate his store of gold where it would do the most good to the world and its people. That he was always successful in carrying out this design is not contended here, but his motive is above suspicion and much that he builded did inestimable good, although some of his gifts were open to question. He was a great believer in educating the masses, and with this in mind he started to endow a series of libraries all over the United States and to some extent abroad. He set aside a huge sum of money which has assisted in the erection of almost three thousand libraries, showing, as usual, his Scotch caution by insisting that maintenance should be provided by those in the locality which was to be benefited by the gift. One of the first charities he established was the Andrew Carnegie Relief Fund which he set up for the benefit of the steel workers in Pittsburgh and for which purpose he donated between $4,000,000 and $5,000,000.

In 1902 he founded the Carnegie Institution at Washington with a gift of $10,000,000 in steel bonds, to which subsequent additions were made, raising the amount to $25,000,000. This particular beneficence constituted one of his wisest gifts. The purpose as set forth in the Congressional Enabling Act of April 28, 1904, is as follows:

To encourage in the broadest and most liberal manner investigations, research, and discovery, and the application of knowledge to the improvement of mankind; and, in particular, to conduct, endow and assist investigation in any department of science, literature or art, and to this end to cooperate with governments, universities, colleges, technical schools, learned societies, and individuals.

If Mr. Carnegie had done nothing else than establish this great corporation to aid research and scientific investigation, he would have done enough to earn the eternal gratitude of his fellow-citizens. As a matter of fact, however, he did much more. He established a Hero Fund which, although it has caused a certain amount of mirth among those whose sense of humor is over-developed, has nevertheless performed a real service in rewarding acts of unselfishness and courage. Carnegie also established a pension fund for aged university professors and contributed $15,000,000 toward its maintenance. It is regrettable to relate that this particular fund has fallen on evil days, not because of any lack of foresight on Mr. Carnegie's part, but because of the lack of skill with which it seems to have been administered.

In addition to this outstanding gift, Mr. Carnegie established the Carnegie Trust for the Universities of Scotland in 1902, and as a side issue gave away more than six hundred church organs, a curious kind of donation, the wisdom of which is directly related to the ability of local organists. Also from time to time he made contributions for the benefit of his native town of Dunfermline in Scotland. His foreign gifts were rewarded in various ways. He was presented with the freedom of his native city and in 1902 was elected Lord Rector of St. Andrew's University.

He also gave $600,000 to Tuskegee Institute to forward the education of the colored race, and finally as a crowning benefaction he contributed the funds necessary to build the Peace Palace at The Hague. Indeed, during his later years he was obsessed with a deep-seated desire to promote the peace of the world. It is the height of irony that this shrewd, simpleminded Scotch business man should have been overcome with admiration for the German Kaiser and should have regarded him as an Apostle of Peace. In the closing pages of his autobiography he wrote as follows:[4]

I have for some time been haunted with the feeling that the Emperor was indeed a Man of Destiny. My interviews with him have strengthened that feeling. I have great hopes of him in the future doing something really great and good. He may yet have a part to play that will give him a place among the immortals.

[4] Reprinted by permission from "The Autobiography of Andrew Carnegie." Published by Houghton, Mifflin Co., Publishers.

He has ruled Germany in peace for twenty-seven years, but something beyond even this record is due from one who has the power to establish peace among civilized nations through positive action. Maintaining peace in his own land is not sufficient from one whose invitation to other leading civilized nations to combine and establish arbitration of all international disputes would be gladly responded to. Whether he is to pass into history as only the preserver of internal peace at home or is to rise to his appointed mission as the Apostle of Peace among leading civilized nations, the future has still to reveal.

The year before last [1912] I stood before him in the grand palace in Berlin and presented the American address of congratulation upon his peaceful reign of twenty-five years, his hand unstained by human blood. As I approached to hand him the casket containing the address, he recognized me and with outstretched arms, exclaimed:

"Carnegie, twenty-five years of peace, and we hope for many more."

I could not help responding:

"And in this noblest of all missions you are our chief ally."

* * * *

As I read this today [1914] what a change! The world convulsed by war as never before! Men slaying each other like wild beasts! I dare not relinquish all hope. In recent days I see another ruler coming forward upon the world stage, who may prove himself the immortal one. The man who vindicated his country's honor in the Panama Canal toll dispute is now President. He has the indomitable will of genius, and true hope which we are told,

"Kings it makes gods, and meaner creatures kings."

Nothing is impossible to genius! Watch President Wilson! He has Scotch blood in his veins.

These are the closing words in the great Scotchman's autobiography. After them comes the pathetic note:

Here the manuscript ends abruptly.

Could anything be more tragic than the disillusionment of a man of such mental and physical energy? Carnegie had devoted the best years of his life to constructive effort and to the execution of a charitable program which for variety and comprehensiveness has never been equaled in the history of mankind. Then at the end of life came the cataclysm of the World War, a shock which was too great for him to sustain. He died on the eleventh day of August, 1919, and may in a sense be regarded as a war casualty. He succumbed to a shock which to his mind seemed to shatter a considerable part of his life's work.

Looking back upon Carnegie's full and interesting life we must admit many virtues and a considerable number of faults. Like all big men, he was a curious combination of contrasting and even contradictory characteristics. He had a hard youth and he was brought up to work and not to play. He was a born leader of men, and he had more than a touch of constructive genius. He was not only a business builder, he was a business getter. He was an alien who made his money in America and spent it both here and abroad, yet he was not a cosmopolitan type such as J. P. Morgan, but he was always distinctively a Scotchman. He was simple and sincere in his charities and toward his personal friends. His family life was beyond criticism, yet he was not above playing his partners one against another, and in a business deal he was as brilliant and as hard as a bright piece of platinum. In his relation to American finance he will long be remembered because, whether by his own original conception or through his ability to adapt the thoughts of others to his own purposes, he first visioned and put into concrete form the development of a great business corporation as a self-sustaining economic unit— an idea which has been perfected and carried to completion in our own generation through the remarkable ability of Henry Ford. If it had not been for Carnegie's successful establishment of the Carnegie Steel Company as an entirely independent entity in the world of steel, he would never have forced the Morgan group to purchase his corporation for a huge consideration, and consequently he would never have spent the nearly twenty years that remained to him on earth in building up a series of charitable institutions which for generations to come will preserve his fame, not only as a great man but as a distinguished altruist.

It is true that during his active business career he was unpopular and perhaps deservedly so, but in the last years of his life he achieved a reputation which was worth much more in the last analysis than personal popularity could ever have been to a man with his spiritual endowments. Of all the financial leaders who have passed across the pages of this book he is in many ways the most complex, both as to mentality and performance. It is difficult today to appraise Andrew Carnegie adequately. It may be equally difficult to do so after another century has rolled away.

Chapter XXI

JAMES J. HILL—BUILDER OF THE NORTHWEST

Until a time well within the memory of men still living, our northern tier of states was an undeveloped territory, rich in mineral wealth and natural resources, sparsely settled, and waiting a magic touch which should cause the long stretches of bleak and dreary land to change into fields of waving grain and people the country with a sturdy race of industrious and successful men. This magic touch was railroad communication. In a sense, these northern states were our last frontier. They must be conquered in order to complete the wonderful development of the United States, which in less than a century and a half had been extended to cover the major portion of one of the greatest and richest continents in the world.

The ways of Providence are peculiar, and there seemed little relation between the conquest of the last frontier and the birth of a male child in the home of a farmer near Guelph, Canada, on September 16, 1838. Yet the two events were closely connected. James J. Hill, the farmer's son who was to be the principal factor in the building of the American Northwest, grew up as a lad in a comfortable but unpretentious home on the Canadian side of the line. While he was still in his teens his father died, and after that the boy had to work hard to complete his education and get a start in life. It is true that he had obtained a solid grounding in the rudiments of English and mathematics at Rookwood Academy, but higher education was not for him, although perhaps his naturally studious trend of mind and his ability to learn many things from other men supplied the omission of more formal training.

We can only guess why Hill did not stay in Canada. Certainly, one would suppose that he had a better chance of a career there than in the United States. It is probable, however, that the Celtic strain in his nature made him long to see the world and try his fortune in unknown places. He probably felt some of the wanderlust which Kipling refers to when he says:

> For to admire an' for to see,
>   For to be'old this world so wide—
> It never done no good to me,
>   But I can't drop it if I tried!

At any rate, in 1856 when he was eighteen years old, we find him at St. Paul, Minnesota, then a frontier town on the upper reaches of the Mississippi. It is said that his first job at St. Paul was that of a stevedore. However, he was unquestionably a clerk about this time, in the employ of a firm of agents for Mississippi River steamers, and he was known as a tall, big-boned, good-natured lad, something of a dreamer, and quite willing to swap stories and experiences with all the varied types who used the great river as a highway.

From the beginning, Jim Hill, as everyone called him, was something of a character in the sprawling river town where he had come in extreme youth, and with which he was to be identified all his life. He had personality. He was industrious and gave evidence of having a better intellectual equipment than the average lad; yet many people laughed at his suggestions for the improvement of the town and the reconstruction of the waterfront. Some thought he was showing the bumptiousness of youth, and others that he was becoming a visionary and talkative young man. He was doing nothing of the kind, however. He was indulging in a vocation in which a man is always somewhat lonely. He was using his mind to think.

One thing he evidently determined, and that was that he would not remain a hired man for other people any longer than was absolutely necessary. So gradually during the next ten or twelve years we find him rising above the ruck and finally starting in business on his own account, first as a river agent and later as the owner and operator of his own river transport line. He was always a booster for the northwest country. His imagination was captured by the vast stretches of prairie that opened up from the banks of the Red River of the north and lost themselves in blue haze in the direction of the Canadian boundary line. Then, too, he visioned the miles of unconquered plains and valleys that stretched westward toward the headwaters of the distant Columbia, and it seemed to him that here was an empire ready for a taker. He talked and talked, and tried to convince those about him that there was at least one more great adventure left to American explorers and the railroad gangs who must inevitably follow in their trail—one more expanse to be conquered, one more barren section of the country to be peopled, planted, and exploited. He was never down-hearted because people did not see with his eyes or dream his dreams. His was an optimistic soul and a courageous one. He desired that all his friends should share in the bounteous opportunity which he perceived, but if some were too stupid to take advantage of the greatest chance they would ever experience, he was still even more determined to take advantage of it himself.

The land, however, was not absolutely devoid of rail communication. Far to the north the Canadian Pacific was building, and to the south the Northern Pacific was, to a considerable extent, an accomplished fact. Yet there was a wonderful opportunity in the debatable land between these two great traffic highways to push another and perhaps a more efficient line to the Pacific coast. One thing about Hill was that even though he always had the big vision he was willing to begin things in a small way. Yet he differed from other men in that, when he started what looked like a small operation, he had in the back of his head a matured plan of which his immediate effort was apt to be but a minor part. Thus it is probable that when he organized his own river transport line he had already planned his transcontinental road, and when he made an early traffic agreement about 1870 with the St. Paul and Pacific Railway Company it was what we should now call a first step in a well-conceived program of railway building.

Do not forget that this young man started his business career with no capital except his own strong hands. There is no question that for years before he succeeded in establishing his first link of railroad he was looking constantly and longingly for such an opening, and it is also probable that he had long considered that the St. Paul and Pacific Railroad, small though it was, would eventually afford him his first chance to begin the prosecution of his big plan. At this time the St. Paul and Pacific was one of those small and to a great extent useless roads which had wandered into the north country, for a distance of some 380 miles, without any strong reason for doing so. Its roadbed was rough, its equipment insufficient and poor in quality, the country it traversed had failed to respond with the expected amount of business, and naturally enough, when one analyzed the situation, one discovered that it had been built by foreign capital, doubtless because of flowery representations which had never been justified. Its bonds were largely held by Dutch business men; the key to its ownership was in Holland.

In a period of prosperity it struggled along, just about making both ends meet, but it was in no condition to withstand the drastic effect of a nation-wide depression. All of this Jim Hill doubtless knew, and he was content to bide his time.

Then came the panic and depression of 1873, and in that period when banks and corporations crashed daily in ever-increasing numbers, the St. Paul and Pacific went the way of the majority. It failed for about $27,000,000, and Hill's eyes became bright with interest and ambition. At last the appointed hour had arrived.

During the years of work on the river, Hill had not been content to sit quietly at a desk in St. Paul. He never ran business in that way. He was always a wanderer in spirit and in body. He was big and strong and husky, and he loved to get out into the field. Thus he had chugged along all the navigable streams in that part of the country. He had traversed the badly constructed railroads, and in the great spaces where there was neither steam-boat nor train, he had tramped and ridden and explored to his heart's content.

There is an interesting tale that once during a bitter winter Hill was travelling behind a dog team up near the Canadian line when he saw a stranger approaching him behind another team of huskies. The men passed with a wave of the hand and then, curiously, they stopped, turned, and came back to one another. In some inexplicable way an electric current seemed to have passed between these two pioneers, and there in the dark twilight of a northern winter on a great snow plain and in zero weather was begun an historic friendship which was to be potent in its effect upon the transportation of the northern states. The traveller who thus met Hill was none other than Donald Smith, one of the two great enterprisers whose names will forever be connected with the early development of Canada. Later on, as Sir Donald A. Smith and finally as Lord Strathcona, this chance traveller was to become a railroad king in his own land, and with him was to be joined another named George Stephen, who was also to be ennobled by a grateful Sovereign and to die Lord Mount Stephen.

JAMES J. HILL

These two men, as great in their way as Hill was in his, and in essentials very much like him, formed with Hill a splendid triumvirate, and it was due to their energy, foresight, and ability to command capital that Hill's original scheme of rail dominion was translated from theory into an accomplished fact. Therefore, when the St. Paul and Pacific Road failed in 1873, Hill sought out his Canadian friends without delay and the three of them conferred to see how they might acquire a controlling interest in the road and reorganize it on a new and better basis. George Stephen was sent to Holland where he was soon successful in buying up a controlling interest in the bonds held there. By 1878 these men had the old St. Paul and Pacific reorganized, and under the new name of St. Paul, Minneapolis and Manitoba Railroad they began extensions which soon increased the road's mileage from 250 to 600 miles. This was the genesis of the Great Northern system which exists at the present time under the name of the Great Northern Railroad.

Unquestionably the most romantic period in Hill's adventurous life was between 1878 and 1893, for it was during these vital years that he pushed his rails to the Pacific coast and at the same time gradually overcame the competition of his greatest rival, the older and financially stronger Northern Pacific road. The first ten years of Hill's ownership and operation of the St. Paul, Minneapolis and Manitoba amounted to a constant contest with the Northern Pacific. In this contest Hill was always victorious, principally because of certain innate characteristics. Hill was a curious combination. He was a Celt on his emotional side and a man of warm human sympathy, a good mixer, by no means reticent, a man's man who lived a full life with all kinds of people and exchanged experiences with men of every condition and station. He had strong likes and dislikes, a warm heart, and in many ways a nature as sensitive as a child. These traits, however, are possessed by many men and are by no means inconsistent with mediocrity. Hill differed from other men of such qualities in that he had another side which many people failed to appreciate. In matters of business he was cold-blooded, mathematical, and cautious, although from the first he was able to see visions and dream dreams. Yet unlike most visionaries and dreamers, he was eminently practical, and hence, when his complex character is summed up, it will readily be seen that in a sense he was not one man but many men. His was a combination of mental and spiritual qualities of such diversity that only once in a generation is anyone found possessing them all at the same time.

Thus when we view Hill's contest with the Northern Pacific during his early days we must devote our attention to his foresight and his cold, calculating genius. He was opposed at this juncture by a remarkable man who resembled him to some extent. Henry Villard had been elected president of the Northern Pacific upon its reorganization subsequent to its failure during the panic of 1873, when Jay Cooke & Company failed because of their inability to complete the financing of the road. Villard had the support of the foreign capitalists who had invested money in the Northern Pacific, among whom the Deutsche Bank of Berlin was the most prominent. He was a brilliant man, and like Hill had a good deal of vision; but unlike Hill, he was unwilling to master details and often went ahead without figuring out exactly where he was going.

Villard was obsessed by an ambitious desire to extend the Northern Pacific to the coast before any other road. He had another reason for haste in the matter. He had obtained control of the Columbia River traffic through purchase and reorganization of the Oregon Railway and Navigation Company, and he wanted to join that company and the Northern Pacific into a single operating system at the earliest possible day. When he took hold of the Northern Pacific as president in 1881, he found about $34,000,000 in the treasury, which represented the proceeds of bond sales which had taken place after its reorganization. These were capital funds which he should have husbanded and used with frugality; instead of which, as has been said before, he let his ambition run away with him and strained every nerve and used the road's credit as well as its cash to the utmost in order to get through to the coast in record time.

He finally managed to do this in 1883, and the driving of the last spike in the line of the Northern Pacific was made the occasion by Villard of a great celebration, which was attended by all the leading characters of the Northwest and many important men from the East. It must have been a big day. Jim Hill was there along with the others, and it is recorded that he showed the best of temper and heartily congratulated Mr. Villard upon his great accomplishment.

As usual, however, Jim Hill did not tell all that was in his mind. He did not reveal that he had been content to push his road more slowly, and, while doing so, to build it more economically with easier grades and better facilities for cheap transportation. Then, as later, Jim Hill knew his facts. His figures were right. Long before the day of the cost accountant, Hill was using the same system to squeeze out fancy and reduce his problem to incontestable fact. He could and did tell his intimate friends just what it would cost his road to haul freight in comparison with what it would cost the Northern Pacific. He frequently said that figures did not lie, and his figures, which he had checked and rechecked, showed that in the long run—and not a very long run at that—the St. Paul, Minneapolis and Manitoba was bound to outdistance the Northern Pacific in competitive transportation. The business was there, but as yet it was hardly enough for both roads. The best-operated road and the road which could do the work cheapest would get the business. Hill was not worried, he knew the facts were with him, and therefore he attended Villard's party with a light heart.

It was to be many years, however, before the Northern Pacific was to drop into Hill's lap like a rich ripe apple, and meanwhile the months and years were crowded with constructive work. Some day the story of the genesis of the Great Northern Railway system will be told from original sources— as thrilling and romantic a tale as any account in the annals of American industry. It will also be a distinctly personal story. For years Hill, to employ an expressive modern phrase, "lived in a suitcase." He had married in his early days a charming girl named Mary Mahegan, who was as poor as he was, and at the time of their marriage worked in a hotel at St. Paul. This union was a singularly happy one and was blessed with a number of children, both boys and girls. It is doubtful, however, if the children saw very much of their famous father during their infancy and adolescence, and their mother must have been a woman of unselfish character and deep understanding to have sustained without complaint the frequent absences of her husband.

Hill duplicated Harriman's behavior in reconstructing the Union Pacific. He had hundreds of men working for him, and for years his construction gangs were busy at widely separated points throughout the northwestern states. Hill himself wandered from one gang to another, examining everything with an eye for details, stimulating the morale of his men, firing them with an ambition to give him their best efforts and complete their labors within the appointed time. Thus gradually his great system grew. It pushed through northern Minnesota, connecting with Lake Superior at the city of Duluth. It passed through the Dakotas, spanned Montana, traversed Idaho, and in due time completed the last lap to the Pacific coast. Seattle was the Pacific port selected by Hill as his far western terminus; a glance at the map will show the strategic position it occupied, with Portland to the south and the whole northern country immediately south of the Canadian line in a tributary position, awaiting the natural increase in trade which Hill and his associates felt certain was sure to come. In a few years the Hill system had grown from the original insignificant mileage of less than 400 into a great national road of more than 6000 miles.

Another strong resemblance between James J. Hill and his great rival, E. H. Harriman, was the ability of each man to attend to a multiplicity of details without obscuring the distant objective of the big plan. Some of Hill's note-books have come down to us, and it is marvellous to observe how on his numberless trips over his roads he noted all kinds of little things which should be corrected, his idea being that no chain is stronger than its weakest link, and his able mind concentrated itself constantly upon one fundamental point. He was always determined to discover and follow the line of most economical and profitable operation.

Unlike Villard, he did not have constantly before his eyes the necessity of paying dividends to his stockholders. Such a tendency belonged properly in his judgment to the speculative railroad man or perhaps to an investment banker who felt a responsibility toward those who had ventured their funds at his suggestion. With Hill the entire problem was on a different basis. He was not constructing a road for the benefit of a limited number of men who had lent money through him for its construction and must at various intervals be given their pounds of flesh. No indeed! He was doing something much more worth while. Although he never neglected the interest of his stockholders as he saw it, he believed, and frequently said, that in the long run their interest was to construct and develop a great railroad system, and along with that system to people a virgin land with industrious citizens, so that the road might transport the new inhabitants and their goods at a fair fee. This attitude of mind was one of the reasons why in the end the Great Northern acquired control of the Northern Pacific. Villard was building for time; Hill, for eternity.

Let us therefore visualize Hill in middle life, energetically intent upon constructing a great system of railroads which should efficiently serve the northern states of the country, and at the same time equally intent upon developing those very northern states in a complementary way. He succeeded in this great ambition as well as he succeeded in erecting the Great Northern road. Thus we may readily account for the interest in agriculture, which as the years advanced became a dominating interest of his life. He knew that the Great Northern passed through a country which was ideal for farming, and it was his pleasure to assist the incoming hordes with the most scientific and helpful information that he could obtain, so that the Dakotas, Montana, Wyoming, Idaho, Washington, and Oregon might become, as they are today, great states with tremendous agricultural resources.

By 1887, Hill had practically completed his early construction work, and the Great Northern system was an accomplished fact. There was still much to be done, and Hill kept at it in a feverish manner. Meanwhile the northern country was fast becoming a wheat-growing area, and in this transformation Hill as usual played a leading part. Also important stock farms were being started, and in a tentative way modern appliances were coming in. Telephone poles were beginning to dot the prairie, and plows and reapers were being sent on from Chicago to aid the farmers of this fast-developing land.

All this time the silent contest between the two great competing roads was going on, but, year by year, as the Great Northern system continued to extend, the Northern Pacific, under the management of Villard and his associates, became gradually relegated into a more and more unfavorable position. Then the panic of 1893 broke over the country, and after the débris had been cleared away, Mr. Hill saw that at last his great opportunity seemed to have arrived. The Northern Pacific was in another one of its financial slumps and had been handed over to J. P. Morgan for reorganization. Hill, who admired Morgan greatly, got in touch with him and a protracted series of negotiations began which were consummated at Morgan's London home in 1895, when Hill and his associates secured a controlling interest in the Northern Pacific in return for their financial support, for it was their money and their credit that were employed to put the reorganized road upon its feet. Thereafter the two roads were operated under a policy of common interest which made them in fact a great united transportation system.

Then it was, just as the new century was dawning, that a series of events took place which progressively brought Messrs. Hill and Morgan into conflict with E. H. Harriman and his allies, Kuhn, Loeb and Company and the magnates of the Standard Oil. It will be related in another chapter how Harriman did his best to obtain from Hill and Morgan a participation in the purchase of the Chicago, Burlington and Quincy Railroad, which occupied a position that made it useful to both the Great Northern and the Illinois Central as a "feeder line." Defeated in this effort, Harriman then conceived the Napoleonic plan of buying a controlling interest in the Northern Pacific itself. He had all the advantage which a great general always reaps from a surprise move, for the Northern Pacific was a $155,000,000 corporation and the Morgan crowd never dreamed that Harriman would attempt to buy control of it in the open market. However, they seriously under-estimated the courage, ingenuity, and resources of the little leader. Harriman did try it, and nearly succeeded. This story has also been told in detail elsewhere. When the fight was over and a devastating panic in Wall Street had been barely averted, Hill, Harriman, and Morgan sat about a table and unscrambled the situation in a manner which was far more satisfactory to the Morgan-Hill interests than to the Harriman group. Harriman never had another chance to control the Northern Pacific road, but he was able to sell the stock he got back from the Northern Securities Company at such a profit that, in the few years which still remained to him, he was a constant menace to the peace of the American railroad world—so far-reaching was his ambition and so great were the resources at his command.

James J. Hill, on the other hand, entertained no such consuming desire to dominate the transportation industry throughout the world. He retired in good order, having really profited far more than his opponent from the entire affair. He returned to the north country where, man and boy, he had lived the life of the people and been the great dynamic force that had caused the northern states to become populous and prosperous years before they otherwise would have done so. Hill had more than a decade of life still before him after the fierce battles which raged around the Northern Pacific were at an end, and during those years he made his headquarters in the city which he loved more than any spot on earth—the fast-growing northern metropolis of St. Paul, Minnesota. It is true that his big work was done. Had he died at any moment after 1905 his reputation would have been essentially the same as it is today, and yet so energetic was this man, so devoted was he to the interests of those whom he regarded as his people, that in his latter years he performed prodigies in their behalf. He was now withdrawing from the active operation of his roads and training his sons to succeed him. He resigned as president of the Great Northern Railroad in 1907 and became chairman of the board, and he resigned as chairman in 1912. Those who did not know him may have supposed that he was about to retire from active business life and seek the rest and relaxation in which, despite his wealth, he had never had time to indulge. However, a man with the mentality of Hill never retires until death.

In 1913 he devoted himself to an utterly new line of work. For years he had felt that the citizens of St. Paul needed greater banking facilities in order to enable them to finance the growing needs of the community, so in 1913 he conceived and carried through a program of merger and consolidation which brought together into one corporation the First and Second National Banks of St. Paul, the two leading commercial banks of the city. This valuable piece of work in a field to which he was by no means accustomed was accomplished at the age of seventy-five. Truly such men are timeless, for the spirit within them never grows old.

During the last thirty years of his life Hill became a well-known collector of pictures, Oriental rugs, and objects of art, and he achieved real distinction as an expert judge of art objects. In this he was unlike Morgan, who never acquired any deep knowledge of the things he bought but relied almost entirely upon the judgment of experts. Hill was also an acknowledged judge of precious stones. He did not care to collect things he did not know about, and he brought to the study of his hobbies the same general plan of accumulating knowledge which he had employed so successfully in the railroad business. He found the best sources of information; he studied them with that ability of complete concentration which was the wonder of all his contemporaries, and when he had finished his study, he knew how to select a valuable emerald from a collection of good and bad stones with the same accuracy which he had displayed many years before when engaged in figuring what it would cost the St. Paul, Minneapolis and Manitoba to haul a ton of freight for a mile in comparison with a similar cost in the case of the Northern Pacific road.

Men like Hill do not just happen in this world. They are unusual because essentially they combine the qualities of many different types of men, and when they do occur they are usually acknowledged leaders, and are remembered long after the close of their earthly careers. Of all the railroad builders of the last generation no one was more worthy and forceful than Hill and no one did more for the United States as a whole. For generations to come the inhabitants of the great Northwest may justly regard James J. Hill as their patron saint.

CHAPTER XXII

THE CAREER OF EDWARD H. HARRIMAN AND ITS EFFECT ON AMERICAN RAILWAY FINANCE

WALL STREET was a hectic place during the Civil War period. It seethed with excitement for different reasons but in much the same manner that it does today. The Stock Exchange, however, operated without many of the advantages in rapid communication which it now possesses. There were no stock-tickers in those days and no telephones. Typewriters had not been invented, and a modern broker placed in the surroundings of seventy-five years ago would feel almost as though he had been put back in the time of Queen Elizabeth.

In those days it was the custom of the brokers to obtain long slips of paper from the officials of the Exchange showing stock sales at intervals of fifteen minutes throughout the business day. These slips were then entrusted to boys and young men who acted as runners, delivering them at top speed to the various offices. It was a crude and clumsy method of disseminating stock-market prices, but it was the best that could be done at that time.

Among the numerous urchins who carried the slips around New York was a small, bright-eyed, square-shouldered youngster called Ed Harriman, the son of a retired clergyman who earned a precarious living as a bookkeeper and lived on Long Island. Indeed, it was in the little Episcopal Rectory at Hempstead that Edward H. Harriman was born on February 20, 1848. He was the third son of the family, and as there was little money for any of the brood, his education was very limited. At fourteen he had to leave Trinity School, where he

443

had been an unusually bright student, and go to work. His first job was that of a messenger for the brokerage house of D. C. Hayes.

Even as a boy he made an impression upon his associates and the older men for whom he worked. In the matter of spreading the news of stock sales, he attempted an innovation with success. Time was the essence of this particular job. Usually when a messenger arrived at a brokerage office with a list of the most recent sales, he was surrounded by an eager crowd all of whom wanted to read the slip at once—something which was obviously impossible. Harriman soon cultivated his naturally retentive memory to such an extent that, between the Stock Exchange and his home office, he was able to memorize the long list of stock prices; as soon as he came through the door he began to call out the names of the stocks and the prices at which they had just sold. This not only amused his auditors but impressed them with the fact that here was a boy with initiative, who was several steps ahead of his competitors.

The result was that he soon became managing clerk for the Hayes firm. In 1870, when he was twenty-two years old, he obtained a loan of $3,000 from his wealthy uncle, Oliver Harriman, with which he bought a seat on the New York Stock Exchange, and immediately started in on his own behalf. Harriman in his youth made friends easily; he had already attracted a number of men who had money and who liked him, and were willing to back him in his new venture. He soon became known as a progressive, active, and brilliant young broker who was quite able to take care of himself and his friends in the hurlyburly of the Street. For several years he did a steadily increasing business of a straight brokerage character, making several fortunate turns in the market, and also at times heavy losses, but he was never seriously embarrassed and he was steadily making new friends.

We should remember that Harriman, although he had no money to begin with, did have an influential family connection and a social position in the aristocratic New York of those days, which was calculated to be of the greatest service to him provided he knew how to make use of it, and this, as the event proved, he did. Then, too, he was a young man of attractive personality, and he indulged in many of the social and athletic activities of his day and age. He joined the Union Club, and he enlisted in the Seventh Regiment which then was a well-known National Guard organization patronized by many young men of the best families in New York. He was an excellent boxer and a crack shot. He was a judge of horse flesh and he loved to drive. He also became interested in social service work. In 1876 he founded the Boys Club, which, from a gathering of three East-side youngsters who met him in a back room to discuss the possibility of organizing a recreational association for the tough lads of the neighborhood, grew into one of the greatest charities of New York. All through his career Mr. Harriman never wavered in his benevolent interest in this splendid work which he had personally started, and after he died, Mrs. Harriman at his request cancelled the mortgage on the club and continued the support which he had given it. It is interesting in reflecting upon the career of this great railroad builder to contrast his many fierce battles in the world of business with his unchanging kindness and continual support of the Boys Club whose founder he was. Even in the shadow of death he never forgot the poor boys of the city.

We are not, however, apt to think of Mr. Harriman for any great length of time in the light of a philanthropist. Certainly such a rôle was not the motivating principle of his career. He was ambitious, and like most men of his type, largely controlled by self-interest, but with all, his was a constructive genius. He was a builder just as Commodore Vanderbilt was.

His labors were titanic, and he left the railroad map of the United States far more complete than he had found it.

Harriman's career between 1870, when he was elected to membership in the Stock Exchange, and 1881 was not distinguished by any remarkable events in business enterprise. He was a successful young broker of good family who was making steady progress in the Street and accumulating a body of powerful and socially important friends. However, in 1879, something occurred of the greatest possible importance to Harriman. In a word, he was married. His bride was Mary Williamson Averell, a daughter of William J. Averell, the leading banker of Ogdensburg, New York. Mr. Averell was interested in some of the small railway lines of northern New York, and naturally his son-in-law was soon attracted to them as well. His first feat in the field of railroad finance was the reorganization and rehabilitation of the Lake Ontario and Southern Railway, in which he became interested in 1881. After three years of effort, he managed to sell it to the Pennsylvania at a considerable profit.

Meanwhile in 1883, Harriman made a much more important connection in the railroad world. As a young man, he had become the close friend of a wealthy young New Yorker, Stuyvesant Fish, whose father had been Secretary of State under President Grant. Fish was a protégé of William H. Osborne, who years before had invested a large fortune in the stock of the Illinois Central Road and had induced many of his friends to follow his lead, so that in the eighties, many of the best people in New York had large holdings of Illinois Central stock. It was considered the thing to do and regarded in much the same light as holding a pew in Trinity Church. Osborne was getting old, and he recognized that the road needed young blood. He therefore took Fish into the directorate and also made him an officer of the road.

Shortly thereafter Harriman as Fish's friend, began to invest a considerable amount in Illinois Central stock, and in 1883 his interest was recognized by his election to the board of directors. From that time on, Harriman inspired Fish to aid him in a policy of expansion and enlargement of business opportunities. It did not take long for this budding railroad czar to realize that his real future lay in the world of rails. The ordinary business of a stock broker no longer held much attraction for him. He retired from the firm of E. H. Harriman and Company, and devoted nearly all his time and attention to his railroad interests.

E. H. Harriman was truly a remarkable man and his greatness was reflected by his actions at this time. He was one of those rare combinations of financier and operator which is seldom found. James J. Hill was just as able a railroad manager as was Harriman, and J. Pierpont Morgan was his equal if not his superior in the field of finance. Hill, however, was no financier, and Morgan could not operate a railroad but had to hire men to do it for him, whereas Harriman could not only manage the finances of his roads with skill and adroitness, but could skilfully direct their operation.

A natural question is: how did he acquire such great and diverse abilities? And the answer is: by the hardest kind of hard work. Before he became associated with the direction of the Illinois Central Road he knew very little about practical railroading. Furthermore, the Illinois Central was not a main line running east and west but a north and south road running through the Middle West, for a long time principally employed to carry grain to the port of Chicago. According to our standards today, it was a poor enough affair. Nevertheless it had many experienced men in its employ, and from such men, particularly the old foremen, Harriman learned the fundamentals of railroading. In a sense, Harriman greatly resembled his antagonist of later years, Theodore Roosevelt, because he learned far more from men than from books. Just as Roosevelt was accustomed to gather together at his famous breakfasts and luncheons the most opposite personalities, including sometimes a western sheriff, a bishop, a banker, and a champion prize-fighter, so Harriman signallized his entrance into the railroad field by going out on the road and hobnobbing with all the old hands he could find—engineers, firemen, shop-foremen, auditors, station-masters and signal-tower operators—and he learned something from them all.

At one time he procured an old freight car of the open variety and fastened several cane-seated chairs by cleats to its floor. He then sat down in one of the chairs and, smoking innumerable long black cigars, was drawn over the right-of-way at a rate of about five miles an hour, observing every stick and stone as he went, stopping at every station of any size, and asking every worker and official he chanced to meet all the questions he could think of. It was this thoroughness and patient, determined attention to detail which gave Harriman the background he possessed in the railroad business, and enabled him on many occasions to exercise an irresistible power in the directors' room. He did not theorize regarding the needs of a road; he actually knew what they were, and he went into conference with a depth of knowledge of his subject which made him unconquerable in debate. Considerable stress is put on this custom of Harriman's at this point, because it was first displayed during his early days as a director and official of the Illinois Central Road, and it continued until he died.

We are now approaching an important event in Mr. Harriman's career which took place in 1887. It arose through his connection with the Illinois Central, but it had to do with the Dubuque and Sioux City Railroad. This was a subsidiary line which the Illinois Central had leased for some time, but which the directors felt the road ought to acquire by stock purchase, as the leasing situation had proved unsatisfactory. A dispute, however, arose over the terms of purchase, and a

EDWARD H. HARRIMAN

group of stockholders of the Dubuque and Sioux City went to J. P. Morgan and asked him to represent them as trustee in an endeavor to better the terms which they were trying to get from the Illinois Central for the sale of their stock. A very stiff fight developed between the opposing interests. When the annual meeting was held in February, 1887, Harriman attended in person with several members of his legal staff, while Mr. Morgan, who probably did not consider the situation either troublesome or important, stayed in New York.

At the meeting, Mr. Harriman showed that daring and disrespect of persons which characterized his actions throughout his career. He was not awed by the fact that Mr. Morgan was against him, and he had the temerity to question the validity of Morgan's proxy for a large number of shares, by making the point that Mr. Morgan had signed the proxy as an individual and not in his capacity as trustee for the stockholders. The result was a complete disagreement between the two factions represented, and the selection of two sets of directors which, of course, threw the whole matter into court. It was finally settled by a compromise, under the terms of which the Harriman faction bought out the Morgan stockholders not at par as they desired but at a price of $80 a share.

The results of this contest were very far-reaching. Up to this time, J. Pierpont Morgan had paid little attention to Edward H. Harriman, and in fact probably regarded him in the light of a pushing young broker with some ability and more impudence. After the contest over the Dubuque and Sioux City, however, J. P. Morgan conceived an intense personal dislike for Harriman which remained with him all his life and had a positive effect upon the development of railroads in the United States.

The author has been unsuccessful in representing Mr. Harriman's character and tendencies if he has failed already to indicate that, even as a young man, he was bold, resourceful, with a knowledge of what he wanted and an unshakable determination to get it. As a youth he was genial, but as age crept upon him and his responsibilities increased, he became brusque and sometimes brutal to his competitors, and even on occasion to his friends and associates. He must have known from the very beginning that J. Pierpont Morgan was a man of giant intellectual stature and a master of railroad finance, but unfortunately from 1887 onward, these two great minds were in constant and violent opposition in the railroad field. As far as can be determined, neither one of them made any real effort to heal the breach. Morgan was always gruff and contemptuous when speaking of Harriman, and Harriman had an even more irritating method of dealing with Mr. Morgan. As has been said, Harriman went about a great deal socially, particularly in his younger days. He belonged to most of the important clubs in New York, and was a frequenter of the opera and many other places where men and women meet. If need be he could be extremely reticent, but when he thought it would serve his purposes he talked freely, frequently, and well. After the Dubuque and Sioux City affair, he adopted a line of conversation about Morgan which was a pose, but it was a well-thought-out pose and thoroughly calculated to infuriate the older man. Harriman's attitude, as he expressed it, was that he supposed J. P. Morgan must be a great man and an able financier as everyone seemed to be agreed upon it. So far as he was concerned, he couldn't see it. He really could not, and he would then begin to give a long list of his reasons which included every piece of bad luck and every mistake which J. P. Morgan had ever had or made. Naturally this kind of conversation got back to the old lion at Broad and Wall Streets, and greatly increased his dislike for young Mr. Harriman.

To return to Harriman's operation of the Illinois Central. In 1889 E. H. Harriman had become vice-president of the

Illinois Central Road, and having served a practical apprenticeship in the field, he soon decided to be a good deal more
than a figure-head in the operation of the property. There was
one stumbling-block in his way, however—a man named
Jeffrey, who was then general manager of the road, and who
was nationally known as one of the most expert railroad managers in the United States. He had for many years enjoyed
the confidence of Mr. Fish, the president, and it is probable
that he did not particularly relish the appearance on the scene
of an operating vice-president.

At this juncture two events of importance occurred. The
Interstate Commerce Commission which had been recently
instituted, started a campaign against discriminating rates, and,
in line with the attitude of the Commission, the Illinois
Central board adopted resolutions which required all rate
changes to be approved by the board. Formerly the question
of rates had been handled almost autocratically by the general manager, and both Mr. Fish and Mr. Jeffrey interpreted
the resolution of the board in a Pickwickian sense. In other
words, Mr. Jeffrey continued to fix the rates and Mr. Fish
allowed him to do it. Then Fish went to Europe and Harriman sent for Jeffrey and told him that in Mr. Fish's absence,
he expected him to obey the resolution of the board of directors and submit his rates for approval. Jeffrey, who certainly
seems to have over-estimated his own importance, said that
if Mr. Harriman felt that way about it he would resign
immediately, to take effect at five o'clock that afternoon. Mr.
Harriman said he was very sorry but if that was Mr. Jeffrey's
decision, he had better stick to it.

The result was that Mr. Jeffrey walked out that night, and
the entire railroad world believed that Harriman would be up
against an impossible situation and would probably have to
ask him to return. Nothing of the kind happened. Harriman
went to work with vigor and soon displayed an intimate

knowledge of railroad operation which most of his friends had no idea he possessed. Until he could train a successor to Mr. Jeffrey, he ran the road personally, and he ran it extremely well. When Mr. Fish got back from Europe he was astonished, but he had the good sense to back Harriman up. This incident really showed for the first time Harriman's character and courage.

Harriman, however, had much more than character and courage. He had an uncanny ability to foresee the financial future of the United States. He also had great influence in every board of which he was a member. This influence was felt even when he was absent and sometimes resulted in curious situations. Thus in the year 1890, at a time when Mr. Harriman was ill in New York, the Illinois Central board, thinking that they were working in line with his policies, voted to expend a large sum of money on extensions and improvements to the road. They were ignorant, however, of the workings of Harriman's remarkable mind. He had already sensed the inflated condition of American industry and the near-approach of a great business depression. When he heard of the extravagant program of the Illinois Central board, he sent a red-hot message from his sick bed in which he stated his unalterable opposition to any such policy of free expenditure. Doubtless his fellow members were much surprised when they learned his point of view, but his influence was so great that they executed a right-about-face and entered upon a policy of such economy and retrenchment that the Illinois Central Road was one of the very few which emerged from the panic of 1893 in a sound financial condition.

There is not time in this brief review of Mr. Harriman's career to deal with more than the most outstanding epochs of his life, so we must pass hurriedly over most of the nineties, and come down to the critical period beginning about 1898, during which he became engaged in one of his greatest and

most successful efforts—the purchase and reorganization of
the Union Pacific Road.

In 1897 Harriman's attention was first attracted by the
possibilities of the Union Pacific. It was one of the great transcontinental lines built largely out of federal appropriations in
the period following the Civil War, and its career for more
than twenty years had been one of steadily accumulating ill
fortune. It had been badly financed, poorly built, and ineffi-
ciently operated. It was commonly referred to as "two streaks
of rust across the prairies." It seemed to have little future, and
its stock was on the market a prey to speculation, and apparently offering little promise.

In this situation, Mr. Harriman started to acquire a considerable interest in Union Pacific stock. It was a big issue, however,
and he was not the only man who thought that it might prove
to be a good buy. The strong firm of Kuhn, Loeb and Company entered the field at the same time to get control of the
road. The most important member of this famous house in
those days was Jacob Schiff, an honest, shrewd, and brilliant
man. Mr. Schiff soon became aware that someone was in the
field against him, someone strong enough apparently to prevent his getting a working control of the road. Genuinely
puzzled and unable definitely to locate his opponent, he determined on a bold stroke. Putting on his hat he went to J. P.
Morgan and asked him if he was responsible for his difficulty
in getting control of the Union Pacific. Mr. Morgan said no
and assured Mr. Schiff that he was not personally interested.
He added, however, that he thought he could find out in
twenty-four hours who was blocking Mr. Schiff and he would
be glad to do so. He sent for Mr. Schiff the next day and said
to him: "That little fellow Harriman is blocking you and
you want to keep your eyes on him," a remark which Mr.
Morgan must have been greatly pleased to make because he

disliked Mr. Harriman so intensely that he doubtless got a lot of satisfaction out of putting Mr. Schiff on his trail.

Mr. Schiff then conferred with Harriman and told him exactly what Mr. Morgan had said. Mr. Harriman with equal frankness admitted that he was the man who was responsible for Mr. Schiff's difficulties. Mr. Schiff then quietly asked Mr. Harriman what he wanted, and Mr. Harriman did not hesitate to tell him that in the first place he wanted a large stock interest in the Union Pacific, election to the board of directors, and finally he wanted to be made chairman of the executive committee. He made these various requests his conditions for cooperation with Kuhn, Loeb and Company in obtaining control of and reorganizing the road. Mr. Schiff was torn between an admiration for Mr. Harriman's astuteness and ability and dislike for his egotism and excessive demands. He was, however, an inscrutable person and always quiet in his manner and methods. After thinking the situation over, he spoke to Mr. Harriman substantially as follows: "I will make you a proposition because I think you are a good sport. I will put you on the board and give you a large interest as you suggest. Then in two years if you are not chairman of the executive committee, that will be your fault."

This suggestion on the part of Mr. Schiff did not take place at the first interview between the two men. Indeed, when they first met they were unable to come to any agreement whatever, but it was finally made after Harriman had demonstrated not only that he was able to block the plans of Kuhn, Loeb and Company regarding the Union Pacific reorganization, but that by the use of the credit and funds of the Illinois Central he could handle the reorganization quite as effectively and at a lower money cost than his opponents. Hence eventually Mr. Harriman accepted Mr. Schiff's suggestion, and from that time on the two became firm friends. They cooperated effectively, reorganized the Union Pacific together, and in two years, as

Schiff had predicted, Edward H. Harriman was chairman of
the executive committee.

It was one thing, however, to reorganize the Union Pacific
on paper and give it a new and more hopeful financial set-up.
It was an entirely different matter to rebuild it and turn it
into a modern and paying railroad. The traffic and engineer-
ing problems which had to be solved were many and various.
The Union Pacific ran from Omaha, Nebraska, to Ogden,
Utah, covering the worst portion of the transcontinental journey. In short, it was like a giant straddling the Rocky Mountains, and it depended for its eventual success upon the effec-
tiveness of both its eastern and western connecting lines.
Already the east was in pretty good shape, but at Ogden
where the Central Pacific connected with the Union Pacific
and negotiated the last part of the journey to San Francisco,
all kinds of trouble arose. The Central Pacific was another
decrepit railroad; it was controlled by the Southern Pacific
which in turn was practically the personal property of Collis
P. Huntingdon, the pioneer railroad builder of the Pacific
coast.

In the beginning, however, Harriman did not worry much
about the Central Pacific. He had enough to do to reconstruct
and reform the Union Pacific Road. He found it badly constructed, with light rails, poor locomotives and rolling stock,
and, as was to be expected in a mountainous country, a great
number of dangerous curves and stiff grades, so steep as to be
prohibitive when it came to handling any large amount of
through-freight.

Harriman, with his remarkable business foresight, had already visioned a rapid recovery from the depression of 1893,
and he foresaw that within a short time, there would be a
tremendous demand for transportation which he determined
that the Union Pacific should be ready to meet when it came.
He therefore attacked the problem before him with his usual

energy, giving to it the inspiration of his personal leadership. It has been for years a matter of wonder how this stocky little sharp-eyed man was capable of inspiring his subordinates with a kind of religious fervor, so that they would devote themselves to the most herculean tasks, working night and day even without food or sleep, in order to accomplish the objective which by means of his surpassing personal magnetism he managed to hold before their eyes as something sacred and beautiful which they must be ready to lay down their lives in order to attain.

He first persuaded the board of directors that it was absolutely necessary to spend a large sum of money in rebuilding and reconstructing the road. Having obtained authority to engage in a program of construction calling for an expenditure of $25,000,000, he rushed into the field at the head of a specially recruited force of engineers and workmen, and proceeded to do the job in the shortest space of time and in so effective a manner that the entire railroad world was astounded at the quick accomplishment of Harriman's program. He knew what he wanted to do, he was well aware of the difficulties ahead, and he stayed on the job until the work was done. All the contractors were his friends, and even the common laborers well-nigh worshiped his energy and ability. In a short space of time he completely made over the road, eliminating a majority of the most dangerous curves and greatly reducing grades. In the end the Union Pacific was practically a new road. The Harriman ideal had been attained in record time. Prosperity was at hand, and the Union Pacific was ready to handle the great increase in freight and traffic which Harriman had known was sure to come.

One difficulty, however, Harriman had been aware of for a long time, but had been unable to overcome. This was the poor condition of the Central Pacific Railroad from Ogden, Utah, to the coast. On a number of occasions, Harriman had tried to buy this road from Collis P. Huntingdon, who controlled it through his ownership of the Southern Pacific, but Huntingdon was proud of his system and unwilling to deplete it for the benefit of an eastern rival.

About this time, however, Mr. Huntingdon died, and Mr. Harriman was quick to take advantage of the changed situation. Even then he was unable to buy the Central Pacific alone, but this did not deter him, and he bought a controlling interest in the Southern Pacific so that he got both roads at the same time. This gave him a new system extending from Omaha to San Francisco plus the long lines parallelling the Pacific coast which were the Southern Pacific Railroad. As soon as this system was complete, Harriman by means of the same methods he had employed in reconstructing the Union Pacific, so improved the Central Pacific that he eliminated freight and passenger congestion, and gave the country the benefit of a transcontinental service which it had never known before.

These triumphs, however, could not have been accomplished if it had not been for the powerful financial backing which Harriman by this time had been able to acquire. He not only had the support of Kuhn, Loeb and Company, which next to J. P. Morgan and Company, was the biggest house in Wall Street, but through the alliances of that firm he drew into his supporting group such men as H. H. Rogers, the Rockefellers, and the rest of what was known as the Standard Oil crowd. This meant almost unlimited funds, and Mr. Harriman was quite confident that he could ably direct the expenditure of any amount of money in the transportation field.

It must be remembered that, in addition to his new transcontinental and Pacific coast system, Harriman also at this time controlled the Illinois Central and its subsidiary roads. By the end of the century, he occupied such a dominant position in the railroad world that he compelled the respect of even his most powerful competitors. The years from 1901 to 1905 were the most vital and important of Harriman's career. They covered the great adventure of the Northern Pacific and included that vision of world-wide domination which was responsible for the incorporation of the ill-fated Northern Securities Company.

The story of these crowded years reads like a fairy tale. Its interest is compelling.

At the beginning of the twentieth century the railroad situation in the United States was beginning to alter into something like its present form. Just as after a kaleidoscope is shaken, the many pieces of varicolored glass assemble themselves into a geometric pattern, so, after the speculative fever of the seventies and the receiverships and reorganizations that followed the panic of 1893, a new era began in the railroad world, and the great systems of the present day commenced slowly to evolve. Naturally these systems did not form themselves. They resulted from the genius and energy of a number of great railroad builders. Vanderbilt and Depew, Tom Scott and Cassatt, Hill, Villard and Harriman, and finally J. Pierpont Morgan towered above their fellows in the work of constructing railroad systems, each of which was intended to dominate the transportation field in a large portion of the United States.

After completing his transcontinental system it is not surprising that Harriman should have turned his attention to the Chicago, Burlington and Quincy road which occupied a strategic position in the Middle West, and would function excellently as a feeder to the Illinois Central which his group also controlled.

Unfortunately the same thought had occurred to one of Harriman's ablest competitors about the same time. James J. Hill cast longing eyes upon the Chicago, Burlington and Quincy because it would unquestionably prove a splendid feeder to his Great Northern road.

It is interesting to note that at that time the Chicago, Burlington and Quincy was one of the few roads at loose ends. Morgan and Hill controlled the Northwest which was served by the Northern Pacific and the Great Northern. The Pennsylvania Railroad and the New York Central divided the East, although the Baltimore and Ohio and the Reading occupied subordinate positions of considerable importance. Harriman, through the Union Pacific and his other roads, was in the saddle in the Central West; the Goulds controlled the southwestern railroad situation. The Chicago, Burlington and Quincy was therefore a real gage of battle.

Harriman, however, preferred peace if it could be obtained. He and his associates, Kuhn, Loeb and Company and the Standard Oil crowd, did their best to get Hill to let them have an interest in the Chicago, Burlington and Quincy purchase, recognizing that Hill and Morgan by quick action had assumed a controlling position in the affairs of the road. Jim Hill, however, was one of the last of the old pioneer types. He was a strong man, rough, uncouth in many ways, and yet determined, calculating, and cold-blooded in business. It is believed that in spite of his genuine dislike for Harriman, Morgan would have agreed to a division of ownership in the Chicago, Burlington and Quincy; but Hill was adamant and refused most positively even to consider the suggestion. In effect this meant that Harriman was beaten, and everyone thought the matter was at an end. The world, however, had not yet arrived at a correct estimate of the daring and ability of the little man with the bright cold glance and the big bushy mustache. Harriman was the kind of man who could not be defeated because he was never conscious of such a possibility.

He did not believe in post-mortems. He recognized that, as

far as the immediate purchase of an interest in the Chicago,
Burlington and Quincy was concerned he was defeated. He
did not recognize, however, that his main objective was in any
way unattainable. He could not buy into the Chicago, Burlington and Quincy. Very well, he would try again and this time
for much bigger game. He knew that Hill and Morgan had
acquired the road for the benefit of the Northern Pacific, and
he also knew that the last thing in the world they would consider possible, would be that he would attempt to obtain a
stock control of the Northern Pacific Railroad. He therefore
had the advantage of surprise on his side, in case he decided to
make such an attempt. Like a talented general he got out his
maps and his statistics and devoted himself to an intensive
analysis of all the factors in the case, and at the end of his
study came to a great decision. He determined with the aid of
his powerful associates and the resources and credit of the
Union Pacific, to endeavor to wrest the control of the Northern
Pacific from Morgan and Hill before they realized what he
was about.

He knew that he had a certain amount of time to bring off
such a coup because his two principal opponents were far
away from the field of battle. At the conclusion of the Chicago, Burlington and Quincy purchase, Hill had departed for
the Pacific coast on an inspection tour, and Morgan had sailed
for Italy to take a needed vacation and add to his collection
of rare objects of art. Harriman, however, stayed right on
the job and quietly began, with the utmost secrecy, to acquire
as much Northern Pacific as he could purchase without disturbing the market so as to indicate that a great buying campaign was on. The task he had set before himself was stupendous. The Northern Pacific was a $155,000,000 company.
In order to control the common stock he would have to
acquire approximately 400,000 shares. He would need between $80,000,000 and $85,000,000 to swing the deal. Yet these

considerations did not deter him from the effort. Indeed, it is probable that they merely stimulated and inspired him.

The situation he created also favored him in his effort. As the price of the stock rose under the increasing demand, a good many conservative members of the Morgan clique began to diminish their holdings in order to take profits on a rising market. The Morgan firm itself walked into the trap without realizing what was going on. It is probable that such an unusual misstep would never have been taken if the senior partner had been at home, but Morgan was in Rome buying pictures, and Robert Bacon, one of his favorite younger partners, was in charge. Bacon was an able man but he was no Morgan, and he further suffered from the handicap of comparative youth. As a matter of fact, it was Hill himself who first became suspicious when he noted the performances of Northern Pacific in the market.

During April, 1901, Harriman secretly bought a huge amount of Northern Pacific stock. About the first of May he was convinced that he held a majority, and was in shape to control the road. However, a peculiar situation existed in Northern Pacific. Unlike most corporations of that time, both the preferred and the common stock had voting power, and Harriman's control was based upon his ownership of a majority of both preferred and common shares taken together. The charter of the road, however, provided that the directors might call in the preferred stock and retire it, and the board of directors at that time represented the Hill-Morgan interests. Such being the situation in the early days of May, Fate began to take a hand in the game. The events of a certain Saturday morning, curiously enough, were decisive of the future of several of the greatest railroads in the United States, and also intimately affected the careers of a number of the most prominent leaders in the financial and railroad worlds.

For years E. H. Harriman had been a sick man. He was so

energetic, so self-contained, so supremely confident, that no one thought of him in connection with illness. Nevertheless, at several critical points of his life illness interfered with the workings of his dynamic mind. On this occasion he was lying ill in bed in his house on 55th Street, and of course mulling over the big deal which meant so much to him and his friends. As he lay there cogitating, he became more and more convinced that it was unsafe to depend upon a control based upon the preferred and common stocks in combination, so, being unable to go himself, he communicated with the office of Kuhn, Loeb and Company and ordered that firm to buy 40,000 more shares of Northern Pacific common that morning at market.

Ordinarily his order would have been instantly executed, but this time Fate was taking a hand. It was Saturday morning, and Schiff was an Orthodox Jew. He was in the synagogue, and had left word that he was on no account to be disturbed there. Young Mr. Hinsheimer, a junior partner, was in charge, and when he got the order to buy 40,000 shares of Northern Pacific at market, which meant the expenditure of more than a million dollars in cash, he was frightened. He refused to execute the order without Mr. Schiff's approval, probably thinking that Mr. Harriman's illness had affected his mind. They finally reached Schiff at the synagogue and he instructed Hinsheimer not to execute the order assuming full responsibility for the cancellation. Soon thereafter the twelve o'clock bell rang upon the Exchange and trading was over for the day.[1]

Meanwhile a special train was breaking all records across the continent. In that train sat a man, old, shrewd, successful, and wise, with a great domed head fringed with snow-white

[1] See Harriman's own account of the incident in "E. H. Harriman, A Biography," by George Kennan, Houghton, Mifflin & Co., 1922, Vol. I, Chapter XI, pp. 305 et seq.

hair. Far out on the Pacific coast he had noticed the curious quotations of Northern Pacific on the New York Exchange. He was well aware of the ability of the little giant who was pitted against him, and he was equally well aware of the fact that his great ally Morgan was in Rome buying pictures. He first became annoyed, then nervous, then really frightened, and using his power over the transportation systems of the country, he started a wild trip across the continent to take command of the battle in person. There were no taxis in those days, but we can readily imagine Jim Hill jumping from the front platform of his special, dashing into a four-wheeler, and shortly thereafter appearing before Mr. Bacon at Broad and Wall Streets with fire in his eye, determined to stop the Harriman raid at all costs.

As a matter of fact, the game was up as far as Harriman was concerned, and a great adventure was spoiled by the illness of one man, the piety of another, and the hesitation of a third. A frantic cable was sent to Morgan in Rome. It was immediately answered, and the men at home were given permission to buy 150,000 shares of Northern Pacific at market. Afraid to trust to their own efforts in such a crisis, the Morgan firm employed James R. Keene, one of the greatest speculative geniuses of his day, to buy the stock for them. Between May 3 and May 7 the Morgan group bought more than $15,000,000 of Northern Pacific stock.

We now come to the most sordid part of the story, the shame of which belongs by no means to the principal participants. It should rather be placed upon the great mass of camp followers who had dashed into the market, and, without realizing just what the tremendous conflict meant, had attempted to anticipate the break they thought was sure to come, by an extensive short-selling campaign. The trouble was that in this particular instance far more was involved than ordinary speculation. The buying was real, and hence it had

been most effectively performed. When Morgan had secured
his control of the common, and Harriman had obtained an
enormous minority interest in both common and preferred, the
stock continued to be held; the break did not come, and the
short sellers were caught and ground between the upper and
nether mill-stones.

Then dawned the ninth of May, 1901, a day which will be
remembered on the Street for many generations. The sudden realization that there was a corner in Northern Pacific
swept financial New York like a prairie fire. The short sellers
made frantic efforts to cover. The price mounted rapidly,
finally touching $1,000 a share, with hardly any stock in sight
at that enormous price. Had the two great factions stood pat,
it would have meant real tragedy for the bankers and brokers
of the country and enormous loss to individual speculators as
well. Fortunately the factions were headed by great financiers
who did not desire to bring about general ruin as the result of
their private fight. In order to save the situation, they got
together and permitted the short sellers to settle on the basis of
$150 a share. This relieved the situation immediately, and Wall
Street staggered gasping out of the arena. Unquestionably the
contest had been highly unfortunate for American finance. It
gave the farmers of the West and the clerks of the East another
cause for complaint against the stock market and its devotees.

The immediate outcome of the encounter was the effort to
establish the Northern Securities Company, conceived by the
interested parties as an efficient method of uniting both factions in the ownership of a great transportation system. It
is not our purpose to go into the story of the Northern
Securities Company in detail in this chapter. Suffice it to say
that the country as a whole was alarmed at the monopolistic
possibilities of the new corporation, and after a legal battle
in which the most acute minds of the American bar appeared
on both sides, the Supreme Court in 1905 decreed that the

Northern Securities Company must be dissolved as it was contrary to the Sherman Anti-Trust Law. Necessarily a general unscrambling of the stock situation followed. There was no one who possessed as much ability in such a crisis as J. P. Morgan. Mr. Harriman always maintained that in the unscrambling of the Northern Securities Company he and his friends were the losers. They probably were. Mr. Morgan was an adept when it came to readjusting financial set-ups.

However, although his dream of national control and eventual world domination was shattered, Mr. Harriman was still one of the great powers in the American railroad world. He still controlled the Illinois Central, the Union Pacific, the Central Pacific, and the Southern Pacific, and on every hand he was hailed as a railroad genius with a great constructive mind. Morgan even named Harriman for election to the Northern Pacific board. It is not too much to say, however, that 1905 represents the high-water mark of Harriman's success. It is true that he bided his time and disposed of his new holdings acquired from the unscrambling of the Northern Securities Corporation at a very large profit. With the proceeds of these stock sales he began the construction of a great railroad empire which, had he lived, might have made him the controlling influence in a vast international transportation monopoly. However, after 1905 he was never quite able to attain a peak of power as high as that which for a brief time he occupied when he and Morgan were acknowledged to be the controlling factors in the far-flung and unprecedentedly powerful corporation which they had jointly created.

We may now close this exciting tale and turn to other conflicts.

In 1906 Mr. Harriman came into bitter opposition to the most picturesque, colorful, and courageous character of the time—Theodore Roosevelt, President of the United States. It would be unprofitable to trace this pitiable quarrel from its inception to its close. It never should have occurred. Both men did much for their common country, and it is a matter of regret that they should have quarrelled so bitterly. Apparently Mr. Harriman was misquoted to President Roosevelt, and the impression was given that he had severely criticized his old friend, the President, and spoken in a contemptuous manner of Roosevelt, the Republican Party, the Judiciary, and even the law itself. The accuracy of such a series of remarks seems to rest entirely upon the testimony of one man, James S. Sherman, and was vigorously denied not only by Mr. Harriman but by others present at the time the conversation took place. No amount of testimony, however, could convince Roosevelt that Harriman had not expressed the views he was reported to have held, and he wrote Mr. Sherman a letter in which he accused Harriman of "cynicism" and "deep-seated corruption," and said that in his opinion he was "at least as undesirable a citizen as Debs, or Moyer, or Heywood." After this letter of October 8, 1906, was made public, there was no hope that two such strong men would ever heal the breach between them.[2]

This quarrel, however, would have been unimportant in the lives of either one of its principals had it not been for its results. During the same year the Interstate Commerce Commission started what purported to be a general inquiry into the consolidation and combination of carriers. As a matter of fact, it was not a general inquiry but an investigation of several roads in the reorganization of which E. H. Harriman had played a leading part. The outstanding road so examined was the Chicago and Alton which Harriman and a group of associates, including Schiff, James Stillman, and George Gould, had reorganized in 1899. This reorganization of the Chicago

[2] See "E. H. Harriman, A Biography," by George Kennan, Vol. II, Chapter XXV, pp. 174 *et seq.*, where the famous Sherman letter is quoted in full and the entire incident carefully dealt with although evidently with a decided bias in Mr. Harriman's favor.

and Alton already has caused a great deal of discussion, and probably for generations to come will constitute one of the mooted points of American railroad finance.

Apparently the Harriman crowd did some things in connection with the Chicago and Alton reorganization, which were unwise and indefensible. For instance, the addition of $12,444,000 to the surplus account on the theory that it represented expenditures made by the previous management for betterments and repairs, which expenditures should have been taken from capital funds but as a matter of fact were taken from current income, was a proceeding which was technically legal and could be plausibly defended. The inherent vice in the situation was that this huge sum of approximately twelve and one-half million dollars was not represented in the road itself as it stood in 1899. Undoubtedly the money had been spent and spent on the road, but in spite of that fact the road was not in good physical shape when Harriman took hold, hence, even though it was good bookkeeping perhaps to add such an amount to the corporate surplus, it did not represent a real surplus then in existence.

In the light of this fundamental fact, the further actions of the Harriman syndicate seem to be even more indefensible. They obtained this $12,444,000 by the sale of a new bond issue of $31,988,000 three per cent bonds. These bonds they sold to themselves at 65 and then resold to the public at 80 or better, and it was from the proceeds of this bond issue, that they got the $12,444,000 which they put into surplus. They then declared a cash dividend of 30 per cent from the surplus for the benefit of themselves and their associates as stockholders, and thus distributed the surplus which in effect was not there.

The entire transaction of which the above represents but a very small part was a feat of financial legerdemain which reflected considerable credit upon the ingenuity of those who conceived it, but at the same time constituted a distinct reflec-

tion upon their ethical ideals and business concepts. It is difficult, however, to agree with Dr. William Z. Ripley of Harvard
University in his sweeping and unmeasured condemnation of
the actions of Harriman and his associates in connection with
the Chicago and Alton reorganization. We must, to be fair,
judge Mr. Harriman and his friends not by the ethical standards of 1931 but by the rules under which the great game of
business was played in 1898, and there is a vast difference
between the standards of the two periods. Harriman and his
friends probably did not do anything in connection with the
Chicago and Alton which they considered in the least wrong or
improper. It may be conceded that Harriman, in recapitalizing
the road, put out his bonds at unusually low rates even for that
period, borrowing the money at 3½ per cent. It may also be
felt that a further injustice was done to Mr. Harriman in placing on his shoulders the blame for the eventual downfall of
the Chicago and Alton. He was not connected with the road
after 1903; when he left it, it was meeting its obligations, and
though heavily over-capitalized, was far from being in desperate straits. Furthermore, the Interstate Commerce investigation, though not instigated by President Roosevelt, nevertheless seemed to be in thorough accord with the bias which he
and his friends had by that time conceived against Mr. Harriman, and it certainly appears that, from 1906 onward, E. H.
Harriman was definitely selected as the scapegoat of American railroad finance. With these facts in mind, although we
should recognize the mistakes that Mr. Harriman made in
connection with the Chicago and Alton affair, we should be
slow to award him any more censure than we would award to
any of his contemporaries in connection with similar reorganizations which they carried through in accordance with the
accepted methods and moral standards of more than thirty
years ago.

The tide was running very fast against Harriman when

the investigation closed. He was still active in the railroad world, and he was always planning for the future and doing his tremendous work with the utmost efficiency. It was during these later years that he did yeoman's service for the stricken city of San Francisco after the great earthquake, and conducted an adventurous fight against the Colorado River for the preservation of the Imperial Valley. As late as 1908, he probably saved the Erie Railroad Company from bankruptcy by taking $5,500,000 of its notes. But not much time was left to this fervid soul. He knew already that he was close to the end of his earthly sojourn. He was a victim of cancer, and he was in constant pain. In the early summer of 1909, he went to Europe in the hope that a long rest and expert medical advice might alleviate his sufferings and extend his life, if indeed they could not result in a cure. It was useless, however, and he soon realized that this was so. In August he returned to America and went immediately to his beautiful estate at Arden, and there on September 9, 1909, he died.

His passing brought to an end one of the most interesting, adventurous, and constructive careers in the annals of our country. It is difficult to estimate such a character or to summarize such a life. Today Harriman's greatness is generally admitted, and his kindlier side is beginning to be appreciated. He was so dominating, so direct, and so brutal in his dealings with lesser men, that while he lived he was misunderstood by a majority of his fellow citizens, yet there is much testimony of his kindness to his employees and his loyalty to everyone, great or small, who belonged to his organization. He was a benevolent despot as far as his co-workers were concerned. His irritability must be largely accounted for by the fact that for years he was never free from pain. His devotion to his wife and family was simple, undeviating, and truly beautiful. He had the virtues and faults of a big man.

However, in our final summation of E. H. Harriman we

must remember above everything else that it was his genius and his dynamic energy which transformed many of the scattered and broken roads that afflicted our country after the Civil War into coordinated systems containing some of the most conservative and profitable roads of the present day. He knew railroading as well as finance. He was a practical builder and he did not wreck. He never used his roads merely for purposes of speculation. He built them up. He built them well. He did not build them to help him sell bonds or stock, but he constructed them with affectionate care to give the best service possible to the people of the United States. For that his memory should be held in genuine esteem.

J. PIERPONT MORGAN

CHAPTER XXIII

J. PIERPONT MORGAN

IN 1913 a committee of the House of Representatives of the
United States Congress, which had been appointed to investigate the concentration of control of money and credit, and
which was commonly known as the "Pujo Committee," made
a voluminous report of its investigations, and submitted a great
deal of testimony which had been obtained from a large number of the most important financial leaders of the country. One
of the transactions which this report dealt with in considerable detail was the purchase from Thomas Fortune Ryan and
from the estate of Edward H. Harriman, of $51,000 par value
of the stock of the Equitable Life Assurance Society. This
purchase had been made by J. Pierpont Morgan; George
Baker, president of the First National Bank; and James Stillman, president of the National City Bank. The consideration for this stock was approximately $3,000,000, and the
yield on the investment less than ⅛ per cent. It seemed entirely clear to the investigators and the public in general
that such a huge sum would never have been paid for such
a small amount of stock if it had not carried with it the control of the assets of the Life Insurance Company which at
that time amounted to some $504,000,000. It was impossible,
however, to get the purchasers to admit any such purpose
in connection with the acquisition of the Equitable's stock
control. It is, indeed, interesting to read a portion of Mr.
J. P. Morgan's testimony with regard to this purchase. The
testimony was as follows:

Q. You may explain, if you care to, Mr. Morgan, why you bought from Messrs. Ryan and Harriman $51,000 par value of stock that paid only $3,710 a year, for approximately $3,000,000, that could yield you only 1/8 or 1/9 of 1 per cent.

A. Because I thought it was a desirable thing for the situation to do that.

Q. That is very general, Mr. Morgan, when you speak of the situation. Was not that stock safe enough in Mr. Ryan's hands?

A. I suppose it was. I thought it was greatly improved by being in the hands of myself and these two gentlemen, provided I asked them to do so.

Q. How would that improve the situation over the situation that existed when Mr. Ryan and Mr. Harriman held the stock?

A. Mr. Ryan did not have it alone.

Q. Yes; but do you not know that Mr. Ryan originally bought it alone and Mr. Harriman insisted on having him give him a half?

A. I thought if he could pay for it that price I could. I thought that was a fair price.

Q. You thought it was good business, did you?

A. Yes.

Q. You thought it was good business to buy a stock that paid only 1/9 or 1/10 of 1 per cent a year?

A. I thought so.

Q. The normal rate of interest that you can earn on money is 5 per cent, is it not?

A. Not always; no.

Q. I say, ordinarily.

A. *I am not talking about it as a question of money.*

Q. The normal rate of interest would be from 4 to 5 per cent ordinarily, would it not?

A. Well?

Q. Where is the good business, then, in buying a security that only pays 1/9th of 1 per cent?

A. *Because I thought it was better there than it was where it was. That is all.*

Q. Was anything the matter with it in the hands of Mr. Ryan?

A. Nothing.

Q. In what respect would it be better where it is than with him?
A. That is the way it struck me.
Q. Is that all you have to say about it?
A. That is all I have to say about it.
Q. You care to make no further explanation about it?
A. No.[1]

Thus in terse and characteristic words did the master of the financial world decline to state his reasons with full knowledge that his unwillingness to do so would be generally misunderstood, and that an avid press would put the worst possible construction upon his stubborn silence. Yet as we examine this brief bit of testimony nearly a score of years after it was given, we perhaps may deduce from it another meaning than that which was accepted by almost everybody at the time the Pujo report was filed. That Morgan and his associates were intent upon a concentration of power in their own hands is unquestionably true, but that they were motivated merely by personal greed is, we may believe, absolutely untrue. With the single exception of Edward H. Harriman, Morgan's great contemporary, probably no man yearned for financial empire or did more to obtain it than J. Pierpont Morgan, but we may now perceive that his purpose in becoming the master of finance was by no means purely selfish.

From early manhood he had considered himself to be the accredited, and one might almost say divinely appointed agent of thousands of investors both at home and abroad. He represented not merely his own millions but the money-bags of the world, and just as Grover Cleveland once said that "a public office is a public trust," so Morgan believed that he stood in a position of unequalled responsibility because through faith in him many millions had been invested in the railroads, the utilities, and the great industrial corporations of

---

[1] U. S. Congress, House of Representatives, Banking and Currency Committee, Money Trust Investigation, Vol. 2, pp. 1068-1069. Investigation of Financial and Monetary Conditions in the United States under House Resolutions 429 and 504 before a subcommittee on banking and currency.

the United States. It was his creed that he must do all within his power to protect those who had placed their money in his keeping, and who had relied with implicit confidence upon his integrity, his brain power, and his dominating ability to control the field of American investments. Thus, when he said under oath that he had paid what was patently a huge sum for a ridiculously inadequate return in order to eliminate the man in the saddle of the great Equitable Insurance Company, he significantly added that he thought it was good business to buy the stock in order to get Mr. Ryan out of his controlling position, because he thought that the "situation" was "greatly improved" by shifting the control from Ryan to himself and his associates.

Undoubtedly his motives were mixed, and it would be foolish to deny that the vast resources of the Equitable did not appeal strongly to his sense of power. At the same time, it would be equally wrong to fail to credit him with the fundamental feeling that the shift in this control of such a vast stake, was worth all it cost because it would take these great resources from the hands of a man whose past had been daring but speculative, and place them in his own self-confident charge. He felt that, throughout his long years of service, he had acted not only for himself but for those who trusted him. This characteristic, more than any other, may be relied upon to serve as a key to his career, and that is why it should be emphasized at the beginning of this brief sketch of his fascinating life.

Men of genius are few and far between. Only once or twice in a generation does a transcendentally superior intellect occur in the great mass of humanity which is constantly being born upon this planet. It is pathetically easy to name the most exceptional men of the past—Julius Caesar, Alexander the Great, the Emperor Napoleon stand out among the millions of their contemporaries like beacon lights upon a long and dark coast. The Great War was notable as an historical period because not a single truly great man was connected with it. Marshall Foch and President Wilson probably came nearer to greatness than any of their contemporaries, but it was left to the post-war period to produce the real personalities of the era in the persons of Lenin the Russian and Benito Mussolini the Italian. It has often been said that great events produce great men, but there is grave doubt whether this is correct. On the contrary, great men often produce great events.

It is undoubtedly true that the battlefield is the most spectacular frame for the tremendous intellect, and even though Caesar or Napoleon would probably have been as successful in finance as they proved to be in war, their fame is more imperishable because it was based upon the pomp and circumstance of conflict, and the blood and agony of national sacrifice. However, a great man is great amid any surroundings, and a financier of the first rank will be long remembered, providing his accomplishments are so notable that they leave a deep impress upon the history of his time. Thus, no man can review the period in the United States which stretches from the year 1873 to 1913 without having his imagination captured by the over-shadowing intellect and the gigantic deeds of J. Pierpont Morgan in his chosen field of international finance.

Morgan was born on April 17, 1837, at Hartford, Conn. He came of good, plain, wholesome stock. On his father's side he was descended from a line of New England farmers; from his maternal grandfather, John Pierpont, a preacher, poet, and flaming controversialist, he inherited an emotional streak which as time went on was to become one of the strongest elements of his nature. Unlike E. H. Harriman, James J. Hill, or Gustavus Swift, he was not a poor boy. His father, Junius Spencer Morgan, started life well-to-do, and after a successful business career in Hartford and Boston, was taken into

partnership by one of the most interesting men of the day, a
canny merchant named George Peabody, who in 1837 had
established himself in London with the purpose of importing
American products to sell in the English market, exporting
English goods for sale in the United States, and subsequently
as a banker who should extend facilities to his American
shippers thus assisting their foreign trade.

It was in 1854 that Peabody took young Morgan's father
into partnership, and the family moved from Boston to London. Undoubtedly, this important change had much to do
with Pierpont Morgan's education. He left the English High
School in Boston and entered the University of Göttingen,
where he displayed an almost uncanny facility in the science
of mathematics. Indeed, he became so proficient as a mathe-
matician that he seriously considered remaining at Göttingen
and obtaining in due time a professorship. Fortunately for him
and for his country, his father dissuaded him from pursuing so
limited an ambition, and in 1856 we find him in London serving his apprenticeship with his father's firm. A year later he
was in New York, working as a clerk with the firm of Duncan, Sherman and Company, the American representatives
of Peabody and Company of London.

It will be noted that young Morgan arrived in his home
land at the age of twenty just as a great financial storm was
about to break. Indeed, few men had the same panic record
that he had. He could claim to have been an active partici-
pant in the major panics of 1857, 1873, 1893, and 1907. Few
captains of finance have ever had such an inclusive experience.

J. P. Morgan's financial life covered almost sixty years, and
during the greater part of that period, it is impossible to think
of American finance without thinking of him as well. What
changes he saw in that vitally important half century! When
he first came to Wall Street the stock ticker was unknown, and
the Stock Exchange was carried on in a small room around

tables by leisurely gentlemen who would have been utterly astounded had they visioned the howling pandemonium which now occurs daily upon the floor. As a young man he must have seen the black smoke pouring from the funnels of the big steam-boats owned by Commodore Vanderbilt and Daniel Drew as they swept madly up the Hudson with the safety valves tied down. He was a banker long before the national banking system came into existence. In his youth he witnessed the super-salesmanship of Jay Cooke, small and bright-eyed, as he marketed the huge issues of Government bonds during the Civil War. Later he was to cross swords with the dark and secretive evil genius of the Street, Jay Gould, and he was to look with cynical disapproval at the antics of big blond Jim Fiske, the play-boy of a crooked world gone mad. In his time he was to see John D. Rockefeller, the cold, stern, bloodless protagonist of acquisitive competition, collect into a mighty barony the wide-spread and disunited oil companies which were to be controlled and centralized into the greatest organization the business world had ever known. It was to be his fate to take part in the reorganization of the shattered remnants of many important railroads after the great panic of 1893, and his genius and dogged will in this time of strife and terror, were to bring order out of chaos, and lay the groundwork for the mighty systems of the present day. Mainly to J. P. Morgan the industrial barons of the nation turned for skillful aid in forming the huge trusts and holding companies, which from 1898 to 1903 became the leading feature of American finance. It was his fortune to form the greatest corporation that this country—indeed the world—had ever known, and he was to leave the United States Steel Corporation as a monument to his vision and ability, and to the equally important qualities of his famous coadjutor, Judge Elbert Gary.

All these crowded experiences, these triumphs, conflicts, and defeats, were to be crowded into a span of life of seventy-six years. It is a wonderful career, and in the space permitted to this work no more can be done than summarize it and point out its most important and interesting achievements.

To return, however, to Morgan in his youth. He did not stay long with Duncan, Sherman and Company, but three years after he went with that firm he formed a connection with his friend, Charles H. Dabney. The new firm was known as Dabney, Morgan and Company, and specialized in foreign exchange. Business also came to them because of their known connection with Peabody and Company, whose American representatives they were. Morgan, however, was still in school, and beyond a few fortunate speculations and clever strokes of business, he did nothing particularly striking until in 1871 he made a connection which was to mark an important epoch in his career. At that time Anthony J. Drexel, of Philadelphia, the senior partner of a conservative and thriving banking house, made overtures to young Morgan to go with him and take charge of a New York branch for his firm.

Undoubtedly, Mr. Drexel was actuated by a thorough knowledge of Morgan's powerful foreign connection, but at the same time he probably knew quite well that the young man had already displayed independent ability, and would undoubtedly prove an able and worthy member of his firm. It is quite clear that he did not associate Mr. Morgan with himself merely because of his father's reputation and financial power. At that time Morgan was thirty-four years old, and had already begun to display some of the traits of character which were to have great influence in shaping his future career. Like many other great men he was completely self-confident. His egotism was not vain-glorious nor offensive. It was far deeper than that. He had a brilliant mathematical mind which worked like a well-oiled piece of machinery, and he was intimately conscious of the fact. Also he had absorbed from his partner Dabney a thorough knowledge of accounting, and he could read a complicated financial statement as readily as an Indian could find a trail through the underbrush of a gloomy forest. He had much more actual knowledge and mental ability than his contemporaries, and this he also felt with calm and deep assurance.

Mr. Morgan was never a good mixer like Harriman, nor was he a bluff voluble companion like James J. Hill. He was always an aristocrat. He did not believe in democracy, and he said it. He believed that the world was composed of two kinds of men: those who could do big things and those who could help them do them. Yet this man was curious in his mental and spiritual contradictions. Beside him, Jay Gould, Harriman, and George Westinghouse are simple characters. During his lifetime many superficial observers of his career, noting with aversion that he was the rector's warden of St. George's Episcopal Church in New York City, believed that his occupancy of such a post was proof certain of innate hypocrisy. Nothing could be farther from the truth than such an idea. Again we must consider his emotional inheritance from his preacher grandfather, and a certain sentimental streak which ran through his hard nature like a thread of gold.

Morgan was no hypocrite. According to his lights he was a sincere and earnest Christian. For years he not only supported St. George's Church in great measure, but he submitted to frequent verbal castigations from its intrepid rector, the Reverend W. S. Rainsford, with whom he breakfasted every Monday morning. He was an authority on the history, customs, and ritual of the Protestant Episcopal Church. He delighted in her clergy, he loved her services, and he was never so happy as when he was standing up in his pew and singing the old hymns of his fathers in a great voice which to the last he considered tuneful.

He loved beautiful things. He was the greatest collector of

art objects of his time. His gifts formed the backbone of the famous collections of the Metropolitan Museum of Art, and his marble Library and Art Gallery at 37th Street and Madison Avenue still stands a perfect architectural gem. Of a moonlight night when its lines are softened and it is bathed in silvery splendor, it is a veritable dream of beauty, and even the most casual passerby is glad and grateful that Morgan left such a perfect gift to the city of his adoption.

We are, however, outrunning ourselves in point of time, for much of what we have been discussing represents the Morgan of the later years, and we are now intent upon Morgan in his youth. The young firm of Drexel, Morgan and Company came into being just at the time when the United States Government was conducting the refunding operations in connection with the huge Civil War debt. Jay Cooke had been the man of the hour in Civil War finance. Without his aid, Secretary Chase would have probably retired from the Treasury a discredited official. Undoubtedly, Cooke saved the day for Chase and for his country as well. Thus it was only natural that after the smoke of battle cleared away, he should consider himself as entitled to the utmost consideration at the hands of the Government and that he should believe that he should be entrusted with the underwriting and disposition of the refunding bonds.

Young Pierpont Morgan, however, was no respecter of persons. He was representing a substantial interest, and had behind him a big Philadelphia house and his father's London firm. He decided that his crowd ought to get in on the refunding operation, and he went after it with ability and determination. The first round was won by Cooke, who had behind him not only his own group, but many wealthy German Jewish bankers. Morgan, however, was not to be denied, and after losing the participation he desired in the first flotation, he came back harder than ever, and was successful eventually in securing a half interest in the refunding operation of 1873 which represented the sale of $300,000,000 of Government bonds. This was a big feather in the young man's cap; by putting it over he definitely made good with the Drexel firm.

Then Lady Luck took a hand and in the great panic of that year did him a good turn by putting his chief rival, Jay Cooke and Company, out of action because Cooke had grossly over-extended himself in an effort to rehabilitate the Northern Pacific Railroad. The panic of 1873 was unquestionably of great educational value to the young financier. He was already thoroughly versed in the intricacies of foreign exchange, and although a mere youth when he went through the panic of 1857, he had learned what it was to see a country's credit structure totter and tumble like a house of cards. In 1873 he was a mature man in the middle thirties, with over fifteen years of practical banking experience behind him; therefore he went through this panic not in the rôle of a freshman but as a graduate student.

It is probable that for the first time he realized fully that a national panic is a splendid illustration of the old saying that "It is an ill wind that blows nobody good." As long as corporations are in health they are usually difficult to control, hard to acquire, and oftentimes impossible to manage, but in days of sickness and affliction they become an easier prey to a determined and skillful mind. Thus, while Pierpont Morgan took little active part in the cataclysm of the seventies, he filled the rôle of an interested observer and continued to learn his job in the best of all schools—the school of experience.

In due time the panic passed away, and shortly afterwards the most picturesque figure of the time also faded into the shadows. Cornelius Vanderbilt, the bluff, profane genius of transportation, died in 1877, and his able but much less personable son, William H. Vanderbilt, reigned in his stead. It was an era of early muckraking and popular ill-will toward men of wealth. The dark days of 1873 had focussed the public mind upon the multimillionaires of Wall Street, and like the Roman mob, people were filled with unreasoning cruelty. At the slightest excuse they were inclined to turn their thumbs down when any captain of finance was brought before them for judgment. Thus in 1879 the younger Vanderbilt found himself in great difficulty and embarrassment. He personally owned 87 per cent of the capital stock of the powerful New York Central Railroad. He was the object not only of a storm of popular criticism because of his controlling ownership of a great factor in national transportation, but he was constantly threatened with legal prosecution by the state officials of New York and with adverse legislation at Albany.

In this dilemma, after much thought, he sought out Mr. Morgan and explained the situation to him. He was quite willing, he said, to part with his control of the New York Central and to dispose of a considerable portion of his holdings—250,000 shares in all—but the problem was how could he do it without breaking the market, suffering great loss, and perhaps starting another panic. Frankly, he did not know. Had Mr. Morgan any suggestion? Mr. Morgan had. Indeed, Mr. Morgan was probably the only man in a position to make a suggestion which would effectively solve Mr. Vanderbilt's problem. Morgan offered to sell the huge amount of stock which Vanderbilt wanted to get rid of in England, and he stated that he could do so secretly and without disturbing the American market. He insisted, however, that Mr. Vanderbilt should guarantee that an 8 per cent dividend would be maintained on the Central stock for a five-year period, and that Mr. Morgan or his nominee should be elected to the board of directors. He also demanded a large commission. Vanderbilt assented without argument. Indeed he was delighted to see a little light where all had been so dark before.

It is hardly necessary to say that the job was well done. The stock was disposed of to English investors. There was no leak, and when the negotiation was over Morgan's firm had pocketed $3,000,000 clear profit. It had accomplished far more, however, than the big commission represented. Morgan had done a big thing and an unusual thing in an unprecedented way, and had further established his reputation as a brilliant young leader in the world of finance. He had also at this early day evinced his consciousness of a fiduciary relation toward those who invested their money on his advice; in 1879 he had done precisely the same sort of thing as he did in 1913 when he bought the control of the Equitable Insurance Company, only in 1879 his performance was greeted with general approbation whereas in 1913 it was generally reprobated. Well may the ancient author of the book of Ecclesiastes say that "all is vanity." The ways of men are inscrutable and subject to violent change without reason.

The ten years between 1880 and 1890 formed an important era in Pierpont Morgan's career. They were as picturesque as the years which were to follow, and it was during this time that the firm of Drexel, Morgan and Company rose to a dominant position and consolidated its power. It should always be remembered that the firm was international in scope and had a particularly strong English connection. British investors entrusted their funds to the house of Morgan with entire confidence that the bankers would not merely treat them honestly but fight for their rights and give them a protection in the field of American finance which they could obtain in no other way. Morgan always felt that this attitude on the part of foreign investors placed him in the position of a trustee, and many of his actions were evidently dictated by this belief.

It was during the eighties that the American railroads indulged in unrestricted and destructive competition, the bitterest fight being that waged in the East between the New York Central and Pennsylvania Railroads. Regardless of the economic waste involved, parallel railroads were built in competition with the established roads of the country, greatly to the detriment of their outstanding securities. The West Shore road which was built on the opposite side of the Hudson for the clear purpose of forcing the New York Central to buy it up at a high price, was an excellent example of this sort of thing, but there were other situations equally bad though not as important. No Interstate Commerce Commission existed or any other regulative body and no legislation existed to prevent this sort of financial blackmail. But Pierpont Morgan soon became a powerful factor in the situation, exerting his great influence to eliminate useless competing lines and to reassemble the great systems on a basis which would enable them to pay their regular dividends, accumulate proper reserves, and protect their thousands of investors. It was a difficult rôle to play; no other man could have even attempted it. It cannot be said that Morgan was uniformly successful, but it is averred that in a time of low standards and destructive business philosophy he constantly endeavored to drive the speculators out of the railroad world, to place the roads themselves upon a firm economic basis, and having so placed them, to keep them there.

In working out such a policy Morgan met with much opposition. Throughout the period, indeed, he was in constant conflict with stubborn and brilliant men actuated by selfish interests and imbued with the false ideals of the time. George H. Roberts, president of the Pennsylvania, Charles Francis Adams of the Union Pacific, Vanderbilt of the New York Central, Jay Gould of the Erie, and many others were constantly finding the dour stocky man with the dome-like head and bull-dog manner, the one stumbling-block in the way of their schemes and machinations. Railroad presidents in those times regarded the roads almost in the sense of private property, and often pursued a policy of rule or ruin with callous indifference to those who had invested their funds in the securities of the corporations they headed. Pierpont Morgan, on the other hand, though no altruist, had an utterly different viewpoint; he believed that the roads were not the property of scheming officials but belonged in fact to those who had put their money into them. He also believed with considerable reason that he was the protector of many thousands of investors, and he was ready to function not merely as a financial adviser but as a policeman, censor, and if necessary an avenger. It was Morgan who engineered the purchase of the West Shore by the New York Central and arranged for the absorption of the South Pennsylvania by the Pennsylvania Railroad. It was Morgan who curbed the limitless ambition of the Reading under McLeod and began a series of reorganizations of that road which in the end were to put it on its feet.

It is a fact, however, that the years preceding the panic of 1893 were filled with difficulty for the comparatively few men who had the vision to perceive that the future of American transportation depended, not upon unrestricted competition, but upon a recognition by the leading railroad executives that eventual success and prosperity were bound up with the consolidation of many weak roads into a few important systems, and with the adoption of fair rate schedules and honest principles of business mutually maintained, so that the game might be played according to definite rules and severe penalties be imposed upon the weaklings and rascals who failed to obey them.

In due time came the panic of 1893, and with it the greatest opportunity of Morgan's career. He was then a man on the shady side of fifty, at the very height of his mental and physical powers. He was one of the senior partners in a strong international banking firm. He long had been recognized as a man of unusual ability in finance, and he had the confidence not only of American investors but of European investors as well. For more than twenty years, he had striven to impose his will upon the great corporations whose securities he helped to originate and, subsequently, on the basis of his reputation and world-wide connections, disposed of to the investing public. He had, however, been unable to control according to his desires because obviously he could not command the wealth necessary to purchase a majority interest in the stocks of the companies with whose affairs he was so vitally connected, and no one knew better than he that, in matters of business, persuasion is often impotent, reason futile, sensible advice wasted, and the only thing which wins respect is absolute power. Such power over American corporations Mr. Morgan did not possess prior to 1893. After that the picture changed; in a short space of time he became a virtual dictator where formerly he had often filled the rôle of a suppliant.

How was such a fundamental change brought about?

The answer is fascinating and really quite simple. To understand it fully, however, we must examine some of the immediate results of 1893. The panic itself was essentially similar to the panics of 1837, 1857, and 1873, in the sense that prosperous times had encouraged speculative mania on the part of the people, with the inevitable crash as the result. Yet every panic period differs from those which have preceded it in some particular factor or manifestation, and so we find that in 1893 the disturbance in the public mind regarding the currency undoubtedly had an important bearing upon the general situation. Ever since the Civil War, a considerable and influential group had been arguing and fighting for cheap money. The greenback heresy in turn had been succeeded by the free silver craze, and the equivocal position of legal tender notes and the erratic way in which they had been handled by a long succession of Treasury chiefs had all contributed to an unstable situation which, although it did not actually cause the panic of 1893, was nevertheless an important factor in bringing it about.

Another undoubted factor in the attainment of the panic stage was the policy pursued in the development and extension of American railroads after the Civil War. As has been mentioned previously, there was no regulative system and there was urgent need of increased transportation facilities. A series of unwise and improperly financed promotions and a great number of bitter and expensive railroad wars were the natural result. There was also a confused and complicated condition of affairs in connection with passenger and freight rates. Many of the leading roads in the United States were heavily over-bonded and carried additional burdens in the shape of enormous stock issues which were nothing more than mortgages on future prospects. In a time of prosperity and optimism such roads could stagger along, and by some kind of financial legerdemain appear to make both ends meet, but when a real crisis arrived, they were soon helpless and passed into the hands of receivers so rapidly as to remind one of a game of ten-pins. Receivers, however, as a rule could do nothing more than preserve the physical property of the roads, lighten their burdens, and start them off again with a chance of future success. Indeed, in that time of supreme anxiety and universal pessimism there was only one man to whom the harried bondholders turned for advice and skilled assistance, and that man was J. Pierpont Morgan.

In 1893 the firm of Drexel, Morgan and Company did not occupy the important position in the world of business which it subsequently attained; also it was not widely known for its work among the railroads of the country. However, J. P. Morgan had been engaged in a number of successful affairs which, without focussing public attention upon his acumen and ability as a reorganizer of railroad companies, had nevertheless gradually yet surely laid the basis for his sudden rise at this time to an exalted position in the world of rails. It will be remembered that he had won the gratitude of William H. Vanderbilt by his clever sale of New York Central stock abroad, and the part that he took in the first reorganization of the Philadelphia and Reading Railroad Company, and in rehabilitating the Chesapeake and Ohio Railroad gradually augmented his growing reputation. He had only one outstanding failure to his credit, namely, his effort to reorganize the Baltimore and Ohio, where he was defeated because the old speculative management was able to muster a heavy stock vote at a vital moment and thus overthrow his admirably conceived and thoroughly conservative plan. It is believed that Morgan never forgot the lesson he learned in connection with his attempt to control the Baltimore and Ohio for its own good, and undoubtedly he bided his time until a change in circumstances throughout the nation should make it possible for him to initiate a new system of control which would give permanency to the reorganizing management for a considerable period of time.

The first sick railroad which was brought to Morgan for medical attention was the Richmond and West Point Terminal Railway and Warehouse Company. This road was fairly representative of a large group of railway companies which had been conceived by promoters for immediate profit. Its financial structure resembled an old-fashioned patch-work quilt. Merely to analyze its situation required a man of financial genius. To rehabilitate it and simplify its complex mortgage system, required even greater ability. When it was first suggested to Mr. Morgan that he should attempt to reorganize the Richmond and West Point Terminal, he waved the proposition from him in disgust. A little later he admitted the possibility of devoting himself to the gigantic task, but made drastic conditions which, if submitted to by the management and security-holders of the Richmond, would mean a virtual dictatorship on his part. As those chiefly interested in the road's recovery were unwilling to submit themselves to Morgan in every particular, he abruptly declined to go on with the proposition. The depression, however, grew steadily worse, panic conditions obtained on every side, and the Richmond management soon found that apparently there was no other Moses who could or would attempt to lead them out of the wilderness. Accordingly, they made a final appeal to the Morgan firm and placed their affairs unreservedly in Mr. Morgan's hands.

It would take far too much space to attempt to describe the various steps by which Mr. Morgan proceeded to reduce the thoroughly complicated Richmond and West Point Terminal financial structure to a relatively simple form which had in it the possibility of future success. He accomplished the reorganization, however, by the end of 1894, and from the bankrupt maze which had been the Richmond and West Point Terminal there emerged a new company, the Southern Railway, which, though newly born and weak, possessed the vital element of future health.

It was in connection with this first great reorganization of his that Morgan brought forward the device which had been maturing in his mind for a number of years—a device which would have saved him at the time of the Baltimore and Ohio reorganization. It was that piece of financial machinery known as the voting trust, by means of which a voting control of the stock of a reorganized company was lodged in the hands of trustees for a period of years, thus insuring continuity of both financial and operating policies so that the plan of financial rejuvenation might not be disturbed, perhaps almost immediately, by the loss of a corporate election.

The rapid success which attended the reorganization of the Southern Railway by Mr. Morgan made him a national figure in the railroad world and drew to him, as iron filings to a magnet, the distracted men who were in charge of many other roads either bankrupt or hovering on the verge. Thus it was that Morgan came to take a leading part in the reorganization of the Philadelphia and Reading, one of the great coal-carrying roads, after it became bankrupt in 1893. Again he invoked the voting trust to obtain his objective, and again it worked efficiently. One of his most difficult reorganizations was that of the Erie Railroad, which had been left prostrate after the speculative manipulations of Drew and Jay Gould, and the operative insanity of Jim Fiske had well-nigh wrecked it forever. Mr. Morgan also at a somewhat later date reorganized the Hocking Valley and the Lehigh Valley Railroads, and, as usual, success attended his efforts. Perhaps, however, the most advantageous reorganization from his own point of view in which Morgan was engaged at this time was that of the Northern Pacific, because it was through this situation that he became first a friend and then a lifelong ally of James J. Hill, president of the Great Northern Road, and, at the time of the Northern Pacific reorganization, a large stockholder in that corporation as well.

Obviously it would have been impossible for Morgan, able as he was, to handle these gigantic reorganizations in such close succession had it not been for the valuable help he received from his partners. Morgan had great ability in picking men to assist him in his work; indeed, many interesting stories are told of his snap-shot decisions in this regard. He selected George W. Perkins as a partner during the second interview he had with him, and announced his decision by casually pointing to a desk in a corner of his office and asking the astonished Perkins if he would like to sit there permanently. He was, however, quite ruthless with his assistants after they once joined the firm. Possessing an iron constitution and inexhaustible energy himself, he assumed that all his men were equally blessed, and he drove them with unrelenting vigor. Indeed, many of them died while still quite young as the result of their unremitting labors in his behalf. Among this galaxy of brains, several stand out in bold relief. Restricting ourselves to those who were prominent at this particular period we may well quote from John Moody's interesting chapter entitled "Morgan and the Railroads" in his well-known book "The Masters of Capital":[2]

Credit must of course be given to other men for a substantial share in this great work. Aside from the Drexels, Morgan had been fortunate for years in securing the aid of partners of no mean ability. Perhaps he trained them; perhaps their qualities developed as a result of the environment in which he placed them. In any event, in these earlier years, several names stand out prominently. One of these is Egisto P. Fabbri, a native of Italy, who became Morgan's partner in 1876 and continued until 1884. Other conspicuous names in these and later days were J. Hood Wright, Charles H. Godfrey, George S. Bowdoin, and Charles H. Coster. All these men either retired rich in middle life or died in harness. Coster was a notable example of a man who worked himself to death. He was a great master of detail, besides being a genius at working out plans of reorganization. It is asserted that all the successful Morgan reorganization plans up to the time of Coster's death were his work. Perhaps this is true; at any rate during these trying years Coster was Morgan's right arm. He was a familiar figure in Wall Street—a white-faced, nervous man, hurrying from meeting to meeting and at evening carrying home his portfolios. He traveled across the country, studying railroad systems, watching roadbeds from the back platforms of trains, evidently never getting a chance for rest or leisure. When he died suddenly in the spring of 1900, the newspapers pointed out that he had been a director in fifty-nine corporations.

It is the general view that, in assuming the titanic task of reorganizing within a short period some of the greatest railroads of the country, Mr. Morgan was primarily motivated by the desire to make huge sums of money. It would be idle

[2] Vol. 41, "The Chronicles of America." (c) Yale University Press, Publishers.

to assert that the thought of gain was not always present in his mind, but he had another motive which has been previously referred to in connection with the events of his earlier life and which from now on became a dominating factor in his career. He and his father had been the great salesmen of American securities in England and on the continent of Europe, and thousands of innocent investors, separated from the land where their money was hazarded, by the broad stretch of the Atlantic Ocean, looked to Mr. Morgan to protect them as far as possible because he was the man who had sold them the goods. More than most financiers, Pierpont Morgan felt the great moral responsibility which resulted from such a situation, and to his last hour on earth he was inordinately proud that, without sparing himself either mentally or physically, he had kept the faith with those who had purchased securities offered by him, and who on the whole trusted him implicitly, and at all times displayed a confidence in his energy and ability which was really one of the great crowns of his career.

We may therefore observe that when the panic and depression of 1893 was over, just before 1900, the firm of Morgan and Company, and the senior partner himself, had measurably changed in the general estimation of the American public and indeed of the world at large. The power of the firm alone had been tremendously augmented from the steady use of the voting trust, and the employment of his partners upon the boards of the roads he had rehabilitated. Morgan had assumed a dictatorial position in the railroad world which he was to continue to hold for many years, a position, indeed, which was never seriously challenged except by Morgan's most brilliant competitor, Edward H. Harriman.

After 1893 there was never any serious question as to the primacy of J. Pierpont Morgan in the world of money. In another chapter of this book devoted to a discussion of the silver issue, the story has been told of Pierpont Morgan's successful effort during 1895 to preserve the gold reserve of the national Government and aid Grover Cleveland in his patriotic attempt to maintain the gold standard and the national honor. Repetition is unnecessary at this point. It will suffice to say that no man with less power could have stepped in at such a juncture and by the interposition of his own personality, disposed of Government bonds at a price approximately twelve points higher than the price he and his associates paid for them. Such a sale proved that at that particular moment the credit of J. P. Morgan occupied a stronger position in the world at large than that of the United States Treasury. Morgan, however, did not pass through this experience unscathed. He and the strong man in the White House were both subjected to a whirlwind of popular criticism in which the yellow journals of the time, headed by the *New York World*, played a leading part. Corrupt and improper motives were widely imputed to the men whose courage and obstinate adherence to principle had saved the country.

It would be ridiculous to say that criticism of this kind had no effect upon Morgan, and it would show a lack of appreciation of his unusual and many-sided character to believe anything of the kind. J. P. Morgan was an intensely personal man —and in this respect unlike many cold-blooded financial types of his own and our times. He was a man of strong likes and dislikes, and to a great extent his actions were controlled by his personal feeling. He lent large sums of money to men in whose integrity he thoroughly believed without demanding collateral security, and he refused to extend aid to others whom he distrusted even when gilt-edged collateral was offered him in return for the accommodation. His pet aversions among men seem to have been E. H. Harriman, Theodore Roosevelt, J. W. Gates, and Andrew Carnegie, and he was unswerving in his opinions about them up to the day of his death. Hence we may easily understand that, no matter how careless he might appear to public criticism, in reality it affected him considerably. It is probable that he never understood any of the attacks which during the last twenty years of his life were constantly hurled against him, and the great money power for which he stood.

If he were living today he would almost certainly fail to comprehend the socialistic trend of world thought. We may imagine him in fancy returning to Broad and Wall Streets some sunny morning on a brief vacation from the Land of Shadows. The first thing he would do would be to call for the *New York Times* and run his piercing glance up and down the financial columns seeking the familiar names. First he would look to see how United States Steel was getting along, then he would search for the old friends one by one—Northern Pacific, Union Pacific, Illinois Central, Pennsylvania, Reading, Baltimore and Ohio—one and all they would come before him in a rapid but comprehensive survey. Then he would call for his son and Lamont, two of the surviving partners upon whose judgment he could surely rely, and from them in quick staccato sentences he would demand a hasty but accurate summary of all that had happened in the world of politics and finance since March 31, 1913. Undoubtedly he would express his wonder and disgust at the futility and economic waste of the World War. He would probably be pleased at the working out of the Federal Reserve System, though one doubts if he would approve of the erratic policies of the Federal Reserve Board. As to prohibition, his comments may be left to the reader's imagination. The thing, however, that probably would touch him most nearly and cause the greatest explosion of all would be the history of Soviet Russia. He would be temperamentally unable to comprehend the just revolt of the down-trodden millions and would perceive only the mistaken policies of inexperienced and idealistic leaders. He would regard the Russian experiment as more

menacing to the institutions in which he believed than anything that had happened in the world since time began.

Such a man can be understood only if we realize the strength
of his intellect, the force of his will, the great physical power
that was his, and also the curious streak of sentiment which
complicated his mental processes, made him sensitive to the
opinions of others, and oftentimes affected his judgment and
clouded his view of other men.

We are passing, however, from the middle period of Morgan's life to the last but most important chapters of his great
career. Between 1898 and 1913, a stretch of sixteen years, J. P.
Morgan accomplished his greatest triumphs and experienced
his most humiliating failures. These were the years in which
his great trust formations were constructed. These were the
years when the titanic struggle for the control of the Northern Pacific occurred and when the formation of the Northern
Securities Company brought upon the scene a super-corpora-
tion calculated to insure a nation-wide monopoly of railroad
transportation. These were the years when the land was once
more shaken to its base by the panic of 1907, during which
unprecedented time Morgan played a supreme and useful part.
It is these years, filled to the brim with daring and romance,
that we shall now proceed to examine in some detail with
the purpose of using them as a background upon which to
throw in bold relief the life story of a strong and courageous
man.

Chronologically, one of the first events we should examine
would be the daring attempt of E. H. Harriman to capture control of the Northern Pacific from Morgan and J. J. Hill. This
tale, however, has been told at length in the chapter devoted
to Harriman's career. We may skip it here with a clear
conscience, and turn our attention to the situation which existed when the smoke of the fight had cleared away.

The battle between these financial giants had been a drawn

one. Harriman had a control of the Northern Pacific if his preferred and common stock could be considered as a voting entity. Morgan and Hill had control if the voting power of the common was to decide the matter. Harriman, however, was faced by the provision in the preferred stock that it might be retired at any time by the board of directors, and the existing board was adverse to him. Unquestionably it would require many millions to retire the Northern Pacific preferred, and it would strain the financial power of even so great a man as J. P. Morgan to bring this about; but it could be done, and those who knew Morgan and his hatred of Harriman believed that there was no doubt whatever that, if necessary, it would be done.

However, there were men in both camps who advocated peace. Jacob Schiff, the suave and smooth negotiator, probably did more than any other one man to bring the warring factions together. They met, they conferred, they argued, and in the end they agreed. There was, however, much danger in the agreement which they reached. It was along the line of partnership in power and consolidation of interests, and from their consultations arose the Northern Securities Company. This was a holding corporation constructed to comprise all the railroads then dominated by Morgan, Harriman, and Hill. In the railroad world it constituted a super state. It was capitalized at $400,000,000, and the plan was to exchange its stock for the stock of the Northern Pacific, a majority of the Great Northern, and numerous Harriman properties, including the Union Pacific and the Southern Pacific as the principal roads contributed by this group. It was brilliantly conceived, and the whole thing was actually put together in a comparatively brief space of time and in a highly workmanlike way.

The possibilities of nation-wide railroad consolidation implied in the Northern Securities Company were never to be realized. This, more than any trust formation in that great era of company consolidation, attracted the attention and aroused the animosity of the masses. It was regarded, and justly so, as the most open attempt to monopolize a vital national need— namely, transportation facilities—that had ever occurred in the history of the land. Fortunately for the public welfare Theodore Roosevelt was President at that time, and aroused by the menacing situation, he devoted his superb energy and active mind towards the important task of curbing this wild foray of capitalism.

The institution of a suit by the Government demanding the dissolution of the Northern Securities Company which was filed in the early winter of 1902 came as a distinct shock to the Wall Street community. Although Roosevelt had been regarded with some distrust and suspicion by the moneyed men of America, his statement that he would endeavor to carry out the McKinley policies and would proceed with caution in dealing with corporations had lulled the captains of finance into a sense of false security.

Suit was brought in the United States Circuit Court for the district of Minnesota, the basis of the Government's case being the contention that the essential character of the Northern Securities Company represented a consolidation of two competing transcontinental lines resulting in a monopoly, and that the corporation, therefore, had been formed contrary to the provisions of the Sherman Anti-Trust Law and should be dissolved. The lower court decided in favor of the Government in April, 1903, holding that the combination was well calculated to "suppress competition between two or more parallel and competing lines of railroad engaged in interstate commerce." About a year later the United States Supreme Court decided the case on appeal, and the Government won by the close vote of 5 to 4, the court deciding in effect that the Northern Securities Company represented a conspiracy to restrain trade and to create a gigantic transportation monopoly in the United States.

This decision was a severe blow to Morgan's power and prestige; it is doubtful if he ever recovered from the humiliation which it caused him. From his point of view it constituted a wholly unnecessary backward step in the field of railroad economics, and an unwarrantable interference on the part of the Government with the progressive development of American railways. The old leader was particularly bitter against President Roosevelt because he regarded him as a traitor to his class. Morgan thereafter always considered Roosevelt as one who had been born a gentleman, and who had sold his birthright for a mess of pottage. He thought of him as a bumptious politician who was willing to interfere with the orderly development of business consolidation in the country in order to curry favor with the masses. While we may consider Morgan's opinion as unjust to Roosevelt he firmly held it, and as this is his story and not Roosevelt's it is important that we should comprehend his viewpoint.

When the fight was over, a situation immediately arose which had not been previously anticipated and yet nevertheless was to be of primary importance in deciding the future of American commerce and transportation. In a word, the Northern Securities Company, having been dissolved by court order, necessarily had to be unscrambled, and the men who had traded in their stock for the securities of the big holding company had to get it back again in some form. At this point Morgan emerged from the crowd and as usual dominated the transaction. In vain Harriman held to the position that, as he had contributed a big block of Northern Pacific stock acquired as a result of his futile effort to obtain control he ought to get back exactly what he put in. Such a theory did not coincide with J. P. Morgan's ideas of what was either equitable or wise. The final arrangement made was that each owner of one share of Northern Securities should receive $39.27 in Northern Pacific stock and $30.17 in Great Northern stock.

Although Harriman was gravely dissatisfied, he was nevertheless immediately placed in a strong cash position of which he proceeded to take full advantage. In a short time he was able to sell his returned securities for a profit of some $58,000,-000, and with this ready money, which represented a considerable advance over the actual cost of the original securities to him, he began a new campaign to extend his power in the railroad world. As always he had behind him the credit and resources of his great key roads, the Union Pacific and the Illinois Central, and in the short time which still remained to him on earth he began a brilliant campaign, the objective of which was world empire in the field of transportation. This is well set forth by John Moody in "The Masters of Capital" as follows:[8]

Yet there was still rivalry between Harriman and Morgan. In the fall of 1908 Harriman induced the Mutual Life Insurance Company to sell him a half of the working control of the great Guaranty Trust Company with its $100,000,000 of assets. In the early part of the following year Harriman obtained an option on a half interest in the control of the Equitable Life Assurance Society. Harriman evidently proposed to form a banking power greater even than that of the National City Bank or of the Morgans, as a part of a colossal scheme which he was developing. The control of the Union Pacific system, the greatest railroad system on the American continent—for the Union Pacific at that time controlled two lines to the Atlantic seaboard—did not satisfy this man's ambition. He was working for a world railroad empire. Before the panic year Harriman had made his control of the Baltimore and Ohio practically secure. During the dark days of the panic he had taken over from Charles W. Morse the stock of the Central of Georgia and had made this railroad a subsidiary of the Illinois Central. Now he was planning a railroad system in Asia which would connect with the Siberian Railway in Russia and finally work through to the

[8] Vol. 41, "The Chronicles of America." (c) Yale University Press, Publishers.

capitals of Europe. He had already secured an option on the South
Manchurian Railway in China and was endeavoring to obtain the
cooperation and backing of the Japanese Government to further his
plans.

Had Harriman lived, no one knows what might have occurred in
railroad history during the following few years. But he was playing
a very difficult game and the strain was beginning to tell on him.
In the summer of 1909 he was taken seriously ill and died in the
early fall. The death of Harriman caused an almost immediate
change in the banking situation in New York. Within three months
Morgan and his associates had bought Harriman's stock in the
Guaranty Trust Company and with it the holdings of the Mutual
Life Insurance Company. Later Morgan acquired from Thomas
F. Ryan control of the Equitable Life Assurance Society which
had fallen into Ryan's hands in 1905. Thus we find Morgan in
practical control of the "Big Three" in life insurance in New York,
for he had already dominated the New York Life for many years.

The foregoing quotation has taken us rather ahead of our
story, because it gives the end of Harriman's campaign and
does not deal with the beginning of it, for he had acquired
the $58,000,000 from the Northern Securities unscrambling
some three years before Moody's account begins. In those
years, however, he laid the basis of his subsequent operations
by acquiring large stock interests in a number of important
railroads and consolidating his power with the purpose of
further expansion. The whole account, however, is deeply
interesting because it shows how impossible it was to subdue
J. P. Morgan's chief rival in the railroad world, and it also
leads us to the consideration of a brief space when Morgan's
star was unquestionably shining more faintly than at any
other period in his career.

The great leader was growing old. Younger men were
springing up, and although no one except Harriman approached him in ability, he was beginning to feel the strain
and for the first time in his turbulent life to long for green

pastures and quiet fields. Public criticism was harsh and constant. His original partners were dead or retired. New generations were growing up about him who viewed private property somewhat differently, and even the men of Wall Street no longer saw the game in the same way that he had regarded it in the days of his youth. These were the days when he began to make his trips abroad of longer duration. This was the period when he devoted himself to the accumulation of those wonderful collections of pictures and of objects of art which will serve to perpetuate his taste and generosity in the days of future generations.

Men were wont to say that Morgan was slipping, and many eager hands were outstretched to grasp his scepter. Such, however, was not the case. Pierpont Morgan was in such a position as the result of a lifetime of enormously constructive effort that he could not abdicate, he could not put aside his crown. For one thing, he had assumed a huge responsibility in 1901 which was to rest with increasing weight upon his shoulders until the day of his death. This was his connection with the United States Steel Corporation. The story of this billion dollar trust has been told from at least one important point of view in the chapter dealing with the life of Andrew Carnegie, so that only certain portions of it which are particularly applicable to Pierpont Morgan's career need be emphasized here. Also, in writing the life of this man, it is necessary from time to time to go back and forth across the period, for it seems more reasonable to follow such a life by its various trends rather than to attempt a mere chronological review according to the best standards of the Encyclopædia Britannica. Let us then, in order to understand why Morgan could not peacefully retire, project ourselves backward to the turn of the century and refresh our minds as to the circumstances under which he took on the burden of the trust in steel.

The trust movement constituted a distinct feature of the economic life of America; after an abortive start prior to the panic of 1893, it had its real growth between 1898 and 1903. During this era industrial consolidation was the slogan of the hour. In almost every trade, combinations of subsidiary companies were being made on a scale hitherto undreamed of. J. P. Morgan was not the only financial leader who was engaged in this nation-wide effort. Others less conservative went at it hammer and tongs. The Moore brothers were two famous promoters in the trust field, and John W. Gates, a gambler by nature, acquired a great reputation for the brilliant way in which he put together combinations of capital and traded in and out among them.

Every part of the field of business was subject to this movement, and the steel trade was no exception to the rule. Mr. Morgan got into the picture primarily through his interest in a number of important steel corporations, among which one of the most notable was the Illinois Steel Company. This corporation was merged with the Minnesota Iron Company in 1898 under Morgan's direction, and for the first time he then became associated with a man who was very different from himself but whose fame was to be intertwined with his until the day of his death. This was Judge Elbert J. Gary, one of the best executives in the history of corporate development and one of the most honorable and broadminded of men. It is a tribute to Morgan's power of vision that he was able from the beginning to estimate Gary's value correctly, and it is to be doubted if he would ever have consented to attempt to form the gigantic steel trust if he had not had Gary at his side to operate it.

Not only was Mr. Morgan interested in the Federal Steel Company which was the result of the above consolidation, but he had formed the National Tube Company and was interested in the American Steel Hoop Company, the American Sheet

Steel Company, the American Bridge Company, and a number of other important corporations. He thus was in the position which he frequently occupied, namely, that of trustee for thousands of investors who had placed their money in the steel business on the basis of his reputation and in full belief that he would protect their funds. One of the finest things about Morgan's character is the fact that regardless of personal strain and worry which such a position caused him he never wavered; even under the weight of advancing years and increasing lassitude, he always stuck to his guns with rugged determination. It may well have been that the power of money was his real god, but if so he was willing to make great sacrifices before its altar.

With Morgan in this situation, and the steel trade rapidly consolidating into a comparatively few units, it soon became apparent that it was necessary to deal with Andrew Carnegie. As has been previously described, Carnegie and his partners, particularly Messrs. Frick and Phipps, had succeeded in achieving a position of economic independence which no corporation had occupied before. The Carnegie Steel Corporation was an economic unit. It controlled its product from the ore mines beyond Lake Superior to the point of production of the finished steel. As a matter of fact, the company did not actually finish steel in a technical sense, and that was just where the rub eventually came. The Carnegie people were the biggest manufacturers of steel ingots, but the Morgan corporations took the raw steel and turned it into finished products, as for instance, in the case of the National Tube Company and other corporations of a similar character. Now the canny little Scot understood the situation just as well as the biggest man in Wall Street and had a clear appreciation of the impregnable position in which he stood. He was not in the market to sell his company. Indeed, he was always very careful never to assume such a position, but he realized that the other companies must buy him out or prepare to compete with him, and when it came to competition he felt that he could stand it much better than they could.

Remember it was a period of prosperity, a period of inflated security values owing to the great trust consolidations of the immediate past. It was a time when men like Morgan regarded a big battle in steel as the most unfortunate thing they could imagine because of its effect not only on the stock market but also on prices and economic conditions generally. In this situation Carnegie brought out his threat to erect mills and manufacturing plants which would compete with the Morgan corporations in the field of finished steel production. It was enough. Morgan hated Carnegie and Carnegie knew it. Again the clever little leader, acting with rare foresight, picked a suitable ambassador and sent to Morgan the man of his crowd whom Morgan liked best—Charles M. Schwab. The deal itself was the result of the most complicated and intense negotiation that the American business world had ever known; what actually happened is perhaps best described by Alexander Dana Noyes in his fascinating book entitled "Forty Years of American Finance"[4] as follows:

It was then that Mr. Morgan, during March, 1901, formed his "billion-dollar steel trust."

The idea of such a combination had been thrown out, in a tentative way, by the promoters of 1899, and had been discussed as the dream of excited brains. During 1900, however, as we have seen, the price of iron and steel had fallen, and the status of the numerous over-capitalized steel-making corporations which had come into the field began to be tested. Some of them had to cut their dividends, and on top of this, the most powerful steel-manufacturer in the field, Mr. Andrew Carnegie, announced his purpose of building new competitive mills and starting production of kinds of material which the new trusts of 1899 had thus far mainly monop-

[4] Pages 297-300. Reprinted by permission of G. P. Putnam's Sons, Publishers.

olized. Consternation followed among the financial magnates who had been building up the enormously capitalized steel trade combinations, and who had other plans in view, whose success was bound up with resumption of the "boom" on the Stock Exchange. Mr. J. P. Morgan, the acknowledged leader of the Wall Street consolidation movement, then opened negotiations with Carnegie.

Andrew Carnegie was a different proposition from the small manufacturers who had been bought out in the consolidations of 1899. He had, it is true, himself proposed, as early as 1889, to sell out to an English syndicate, and as late as 1899 had considered a proposition of American promoters to pay $250,000,000 for the steel property of himself and his associates; but the negotiations came to nothing. Between 1889 and 1897, moreover, the net annual profits of the Carnegie properties rose from $3,540,000 to $7,000,000, and from the latter figure they had risen by 1900 to no less than $40,000,000. Of the 160,000 shares of stock in the company, Carnegie himself owned 86,382; of the $160,000,000 bonds, he personally held $88,147,000. He was the key to the steel trade problem and he knew it. Mr. Morgan obtained conditional assent from the eight other most powerful steel trade combinations to be merged into one huge "holding company" through exchange of stock; Mr. Carnegie laid down, as his individual terms, the purchase of Carnegie Company stock at $1500 per share, paid in 5 per cent bonds secured by the stocks of all the amalgamated corporations, and the exchange of Carnegie Company bonds at par for the same security. This meant the payment of $217,720,000 to Carnegie himself. The extraordinary price was granted; his partners were bought out on somewhat less favorable terms; and to buy up his company and its competitors, the United States Steel Corporation was organized in February, 1901, with a capital stock of $1,018,000,000 and bonds of $301,000,000. The other combinations in the trade, whose individual capitalizations ranged from the $33,000,000 of the Steel Hoop company to the $99,000,000 of the Federal Steel, received the new shares on a basis running from equal exchange to 125 per cent of their old outstanding capital, and the "deal" was closed.

It remained to see how the new stock could be floated; for although in form the operation was nothing but substitution of new securities for old, in fact it was something very different. Displacement of capital on an enormous scale was certain to result. The beneficiaries of this remarkable operation could be counted on to turn a part of their new stock into cash, and a very substantial portion of the Steel Corporation's stock was to be used for procuring working capital. The promoters took no chances which they could avoid. A bankers' syndicate was formed to guarantee, up to $200,-000,000, the successful floating of the stock; it actually put up $25,-000,000 cash. Brokers, large and small, were engaged to urge the new stock upon investors throughout the United States. On the Stock Exchange, a celebrated manipulator of speculative values was employed, when the shares were listed, to create a semblance of great investment activity, and to sustain the price. The project met with remarkable success. Starting on the curb at a price of 38 for "Steel common" and 82¾ for the 7 per cent "Steel preferred," the Stock Exchange price advanced in a month to 55 and 101⅞ respectively. Half a million of the shares were dealt in during the first two days of their appearance on the Stock Exchange; the next week's record was a million. The greater part of this was doubtless merely "matching of orders" by the syndicate's agent, through the medium of other brokers; but the public did not know this. It caught the speculative fever; even in thrifty Western towns and New England country villages, the gossip of an evening was apt to concern itself with "Steel." So successful was the operation that, a year or two later, the $25,000,000 "underwriting syndicate" received back in cash its whole subscription, plus 200 per cent in dividends.

We may therefore see from the foregoing description of the biggest deal of the century why it was that Pierpont Morgan could not leave the field of battle for any length of time, even when he was entering upon his last decade.

We now come to consider what was perhaps the greatest service that Pierpont Morgan ever rendered to his country. Reference is made to his leadership during the great national panic of 1907. The panic of 1907 was a peculiar affair, and many efforts have been made to place the blame. It is probable, however, that, as is usually the case with panic eras, no one factor was sufficiently strong to produce it, but it resulted from the occurrence of a number of events at approximately the same time. Essentially it was caused by the things which cause all panics—false prosperity, over-production, and over-speculation. It was unquestionably out of place in the business cycle. According to the accepted rules of those days and to a certain extent even of the present, it should not have occurred until 1913. It therefore had a surprise feature which intensified its effects and increased the suffering it caused.

Throughout the latter part of 1906, speculation grew rapidly, and this was evidenced by the steady increase in demand loans and a great drain on bank reserves. Much speculative promotion was in the air. Harriman was pushing his buying campaign in railroad securities. Charles W. Morse was acquiring a chain of banks by pledging the securities of one bank in order to purchase those of another, and so on and on in a vicious circle. Heintze was plunging in mining, and many others of lesser rank were joining in the scramble for untold millions just ahead. There were signs, however, in the winter of 1906 that the situation was approaching a climax. Several big flotations were unexpectedly interfered with. Money became hard to obtain. Apparently someone was pulling in the reins. Plenty of enthusiasm was left, however, and as usual the brokers and the men in the street refused to believe that anything was seriously wrong. Then, all of a sudden, general business began to lag. Steel orders waned. Car-loadings went down, and finally a number of early failures threw securities into the market which were not readily absorbed. Then in October, 1907, Heintze failed and the Morse banks went down. Finally the Knickerbocker Trust Company closed its doors, and in doing

so, started one of the greatest runs of history, involving many
other banks and trust companies, particularly the Trust Company of North America and the Lincoln Trust Company.
Then, too, in October, the $34,000,000 Westinghouse Electric
and Manufacturing Company crashed for the second time
in its history—and the panic was on.

No Federal Reserve System was in operation at that time
and it was much more difficult to control panic conditions and
lend aid than it is today—and it is certainly far from easy to
do so at the present time. At this juncture, all eyes turned to
J. Pierpont Morgan. His was a name to conjure with. In spite
of his reputation as the chosen representative of America's
money power and his unpopularity with the great mass of
the people, no one else could by any possibility command
the desperate situation, and for at least a week Pierpont Morgan sat in his office at Broad and Wall Streets and exercised a
supreme dictatorship over the financial world of the United
States. Even the Secretary of the Treasury from his post across
the Street in the Sub-Treasury Building waited patiently to
learn Morgan's orders so that he might help to carry them
out.

In such a time of mutual danger, all factional differences
were forgotten. The strong men of every group met with Morgan and hung upon his words. James Stillman, president of
the National City Bank, the great repository of Standard
Oil funds, was there. George Baker was there. H. H. Rogers
was there. H. C. Frick was there. Even Edward H. Harriman, Morgan's pet aversion, sat quietly by and meekly did
as he was told. Never in all the long years of stress and
struggle did the supreme ability of Pierpont Morgan shine as
it did in those fall days of 1907. Seated at his desk, his thick
body and great head commanding the quiet room, with a
constant roar without, representing the frenzied fear and tan-
gled emotions of the seething Street, with his wonderful mind

working with the celerity and accuracy of a well-oiled machine, this magician of finance surveyed the field of battle, accumulated his reserves and directed his shock troops to the points where he knew they could succeed.

He handled millions of dollars as though they were so many cents. It was a tremendous task but one which he and he alone was qualified to perform. He directed the sale of bills of exchange in great quantities in order to force the shipment of gold from Europe to America, and he directed the Secretary of the Treasury just where to deposit the funds of the Government so that they would be most effective in bringing the situation back to normalcy. Finally he sent emissaries to the President of the United States to ask him a flat question and demand an immediate answer. Would Roosevelt permit the United States Steel Corporation to buy the Tennessee Coal and Iron Company at a cost of $30,000,000 in order to prevent the failure of the investment banking house of Moore & Schley which threatened to fall unless the purchase was made? It was long on Tennessee Coal and Iron stock, and this stock pledged in many banks was considered insufficient collateral as it stood but would be deemed highly acceptable if it really represented the steel trust as its ultimate owner.

In this critical hour Roosevelt again demonstrated his preference for direct action. Had he been disposed to be technical or narrow he would probably have refused a straight answer to a straight question, but that was not his way, and he decided that Morgan was right. The purchase should be made and he said all he could say, which amounted to this, "I will not advise it, but if it is made I see no reason to interfere with it." For years afterwards Roosevelt was bitterly criticized for taking such action, but though the wisdom of his policy is arguable the straightforward quality of it is attractive and unusual.

This was the last important act of Mr. Morgan in stem-
ming the panic of 1907. The rest of his work, though important, was largely a matter of detail in executing the policies
he had conceived to bring about a return of normal conditions.
No man in our history has rendered a more peculiar, unusual, and important service than J. P. Morgan did at this
particular time.

Now we come to the closing years, and it is pleasing to
think that they represented a happier era for the great leader
than the period which had succeeded the Northern Securities
dissolution. He was still an object of constant criticism. He
was called before the Pujo Committee and interrogated in
connection with his financial operations, particularly those
which resulted in the purchase of a controlling interest in
some of the greatest insurance companies of the United States;
yet, although he still remained to the western farmer as the
representative of all that was evil and greedy in the great
money power of the East, nevertheless thousands of people
understood and appreciated what he had done for the country
in the dark days of 1907, and on the whole a better and kindlier
estimate of the great man was prevalent during the five or six
years which immediately preceded his demise.

Gradually he began to draw out of the financial fray. In
those days he leaned heavily upon the judgment and efficient efforts of Thomas W. Lamont, Henry P. Davison, and
the son of whom he was so proud, John Pierpont Morgan,
Jr. As he drew nearer to the end of all worldly things he
seemed to soften and become reflective. Always a silent and
inscrutable man, he became even more reticent, and would
sit for hours with a look of intense absorption in his wise
old eyes. More and more as the years passed on he became attracted by the mystic charm of Egypt and the glorious and
eternal quality of Rome. He was regarded almost as a citizen
of that great and ancient capital, and there on the thirty-first

of March, 1913, he passed away. He died without great suffering in the city he loved. He was far from home, but in a
sense, although his active life had been spent within the confines of New York, he was essentially cosmopolitan and a
citizen of the world. When he died there was a feeling of ir-
reparable loss in the tumultuous world which he had fre-
quented with such distinction and which he had ruled for so
long with unexampled force and matchless ability.

His will is an indication of the emotional and sentimental
trend which has been previously noted. It began with a curious and interesting prayer to Almighty God, the utter sincerity of which, even in the eyes of his enemies, was beyond
question, and with this prayer I think it is well to leave him,
the captain, the lonely soul, the man of mind and yet unquestionably the man of heart. In beginning his now famous
testament, J. P. Morgan used these memorable words:

I commit my soul into the hands of my Saviour, in full confidence that having redeemed it and washed it in His most precious
blood, He will present it faultless before the throne of my Heavenly
Father; and I entreat my children to maintain and defend, at all
hazards and at any cost of personal sacrifice, the blessed doctrine of
the complete atonement for sin through the blood of Jesus Christ,
once offered, and through that alone.

Verily at the end the great man was humble and bared his
soul. His was a wonderful life and at the end a wonderful
passing, and thus we shall bid him farewell.

CHAPTER XXIV

ELBERT H. GARY—THE PHILOSOPHY OF MODERN BUSINESS

IT WAS in 1898 that J. Pierpont Morgan merged and consolidated several corporations into the Federal Steel Company. The largest unit in the consolidation was the Illinois Steel Company, and its counsel, Elbert H. Gary, a Chicago lawyer and a former county judge of Wheaton, Illinois, necessarily was in close contact with Mr. Morgan for several months while the new corporation was in process of formation.

Pierpont Morgan was a shrewd judge of men—the selective ability he displayed in choosing his partners proved that —and all through these protracted negotiations he must have been watching carefully the quiet, serious, self-controlled lawyer from the Middle West who not only displayed legal acumen of a high order, but added to that a most unusual business ability, a quality rarely found in professional men. Therefore, when the consolidation drew to a close, Mr. Morgan greatly surprised his new-found friend by stating to him with his accustomed bluntness that one of his demands on behalf of the capital invested through him in the new combination, was that Mr. Gary should leave Chicago forthwith, sacrifice a law practice believed to be worth $75,000 a year, remove to New York and become the president and executive head of Federal Steel.

Naturally enough, Mr. Gary hesitated. But Morgan was accustomed to having his way and he waved aside all objections and told Gary that salary was a secondary consideration; what he needed was a man of character and ability to

512

head the new combine, that in his judgment Gary was the man, and it was his duty to accept the job. He gave him twenty-four hours to make up his mind. At the end of that time Gary gave his consent, and an association began between two notable men which was to last without interruption for fifteen years, or until Morgan died.

Morgan and Gary were dissimilar in many ways and yet they had a number of important characteristics in common. Both were born leaders of men and both had an innate and well-developed sense of responsibility. Morgan always felt that he acted as a trustee for all those who invested their money through him, and Gary regarded the welfare of his stockholders as a personal trust. Their differences were as clearly marked. Morgan, in spite of a deep interest in the Episcopal Church, was essentially a devotee in the House of Mammon. To him the doctrine of private property was a thing to be reverenced and fought for. Gary, however, was a curious exception to the usual type of big business executive. He had been born on a farm near Wheaton, Illinois, on October 8, 1846, and his early life was that of the pioneer farm lad. His parents were simple folk and took life seriously, as most people in their circumstances were obliged to take it in those early days of struggle on the rough lands of the Middle West. Their son was brought up to believe that piety, truth, and straight dealing were the most fundamental and important qualities. Many men with such an up-bringing have changed their outlook on life as the years have passed by, particularly when they have been successful in a material way. The remarkable thing about Elbert Gary was that he was essentially the same in his luxurious New York office, when he was the directing head of the world's first billion dollar corporation, as he had been thirty-five years previously when he was first making a name for himself as a struggling young lawyer in the Middle West. As we look back upon the interesting panorama of the man's life, we realize what a boon it was to the stockholders of the United States Steel Corporation, to his associates in the Wall Street district, and to the people of the United States as a whole that, in spite of the laurels he achieved in a life of highly successful effort, Elbert Gary never in the slightest degree sacrificed his adherence to the principles of truth and honesty which he acquired in youth and maintained unsullied to the end.

Men are accustomed to boast of the improvement in business ethics which has occurred during the past twenty-five years, and it is a fact that today we do not lightly tolerate the kind of conduct which was condoned during the seventies, eighties, and nineties. We believe that the conscience of American business has been awakened, and that in spite of occasional scandals, the world of commerce and finance is cleaner today than it was a few short years ago. That such is the case is due primarily to a few men who have controlled the conduct of their associates and who have been strong enough to enthrone their ideals as an integral part of our national consciousness. Among such men Elbert Gary will always stand out as a leader. It is not too much to say that he was the father of a new business philosophy which we have been fortunate enough to inherit from him.

Morgan, however, did not promote Gary to be the head of the Federal Steel and subsequently to be chairman of the board of the United States Steel Corporation because of his moral qualities. That is not to say that Morgan did not recognize and appreciate them, but his choice was based chiefly upon his reliance on Gary's unusual combination of legal knowledge and business ability.

From the beginning of his administration, Judge Gary, as he always was called, proved a success as the chief executive of the Federal Steel Company, and in this his first position he displayed a vision of the future of the steel industry which was far more comprehensive than that exhibited by any of his contemporaries. In advance of the rest, he realized that the steel trade as a whole must be consolidated into one great unit if it was to be conducted on a really profitable basis. Of course this did not mean that every steel company was to be covered by a single corporate group, but it did mean that the core of the industry was to be represented by the biggest corporate development of modern times. This was made vitally necessary in Gary's judgment by the group situations which existed when Federal Steel was organized. On the one hand there were the Morgan companies and those put together by John W. Gates, and on the other the Carnegie Steel Corporation dominated and shrewdly conducted by the wily little Scotchman, who, in his economic position and peculiar ability, represented in his generation the element which Henry Ford typifies today. Carnegie understood this situation as well as Gary, and as has been mentioned before, used Charles M. Schwab as his ambassador. It was Gary's influence, however, which enabled Mr. Schwab to convince Pierpont Morgan of the advantages of a great consolidation, and it was Gary's genius which turned that consolidation, when once made, from a topheavy and inflated structure into a well-ordered and conservatively managed enterprise.

We may readily imagine the difficulties which confronted Judge Gary when he assumed the chairmanship of United States Steel. The company's total capital of bonds and stock amounted to a par value of over $1,300,000,000, a sum so huge that it staggered the imagination of mankind. Furthermore, the merged companies represented such a large segment of the steel trade that from the beginning they controlled approximately 65 per cent of the business. This alone constiuted an ever-present menace, for it meant that there was continual danger of dissolution at the suit of the United States Government acting under the authority of the Sherman Anti-Trust Law. There was really only one way out of trouble and that path was so direct and straightforward that it is doubtful if any experienced or hard-boiled eastern executive would ever have selected it. Yet it was the path that Gary chose and followed without interruption and in spite of much opposition, particularly in the early days of his leadership. It is only fair, however, to give J. P. Morgan part of the credit, because he was big enough in the first instance to comprehend dimly the necessity for business morality of a high order in a situation so complicated and so fraught with danger, and he was true enough to his own ideals and the interest of his investors to back Judge Gary with all the immense power at his command, even when Gary was bitterly opposed by Morgan's most intimate friends and loyal supporters.

We can perhaps best visualize the business ideals of both men if we reflect upon the interesting story connected with Judge Gary's induction into office as chief executive of the United States Steel Corporation. It is said that in 1900 when the Steel Corporation was first organized Judge Gary asked Mr. Morgan to be good enough to outline to him just what were to be his duties as chairman of the board and as chairman of the finance committee. Mr. Morgan replied as follows:

You are to take over all the executive responsibilities of the corporation except the production end; Charlie Schwab will attend to that. You are to keep the Corporation out of trouble. You are to make the Corporation the foremost example of American industry. You are to win for the Company the approval and respect of the public. You are to place its finances on so firm a basis that dividends may be assured regularly on both the preferred and common stock into the far-off future. That is all.

Most of us will readily agree that it was quite enough. Here is where Gary's early Methodist training came to his aid. Many more sophisticated men would have believed that Mr. Morgan was talking more or less for effect. Gary, however, took him seriously and started on a career which during the first ten years at least brought him into constant conflict with his own directorate and many other leaders in the world of steel. He knew that, in order to meet Carnegie's ruinous terms and to provide for all the other contingencies of the huge merger, the capital of the new corporation had been much inflated and its common stock represented little more than good will, and an optimistic mortgage on the future. Therefore, at the first good opportunity afforded by a rather welcome depression in business, Gary shut off dividends on steel common and commenced what was to resolve itself into a life-long practice, namely, to plow back earnings into the business and to accumulate considerable reserves. Also he began to enunciate certain business principles which shortly began to be known as "Gary policies," and with dogged determination he forced their acceptance upon what was frequently a reluctant board of directors.

It was Judge Gary who first insisted upon the acceptance of the theory that a clear line of demarcation existed between a good trust and a bad trust. He denied vehemently that any business consolidation should be condemned merely because of its size, and he emphasized the fact that a company, no matter how big, should be judged by its practices and by them alone. It is interesting to note in this connection that, when toward the end of the Taft administration the Steel Corporation was made the object of a dissolution suit by the Attorney General of the United States, it was able to assemble in its defense many of its leading competitors, who testified that under Gary's leadership the United States Steel Corporation was a blessing to the entire steel industry, that it stabilized prices, preserved fair competition, and made it easier for the independents to operate than if they had been playing lone hands. Such a tribute, it is believed, has never been paid to any other captain of industry by those who competed with him in the business world.

Judge Gary, however, had many other policies, and when the time seemed propitious he established one after another as the guiding principles of the steel business. He believed, for instance, in the widest publicity in connection with company operation, and he was one of the first men in the United States to insist upon a full disclosure to the stockholders of the most intimate details of company performance. On the question of dividend payments he was more conservative than he need have been. Undoubtedly most of the real opposition he experienced came from his insistence that the welfare of the business should be exhaustively protected before any part of the profits was handed over to the stockholders. This was indeed a revolutionary doctrine in the early days of the century, and one to which his Wall Street friends were thoroughly unaccustomed. His dividend policy was to place the regular dividend rate at a point which could reasonably be presumed to be earned in the worst probable year and to maintain it at that point in spite of the ups and downs which were bound to occur. He did not look on extra dividends with much favor, and for years he avoided a stock dividend, finally coming to it only under pressure. For a long time he retained a $5 per share dividend rate on Steel common. Gary's views of dividends may have been ultra conservative, but if so, he erred on the right side, the side of conservatism, the side of fidelity to those whom he represented.

Probably no corporation profited to a greater degree proportionately from the unusual conditions created by the World War than did the Steel Corporation, but even in such an unexampled situation, with money pouring in in a golden flood, the old executive departed reluctantly and slowly from the careful ideals and cautious policies based upon a lifetime of responsible leadership.

Another Gary policy which has been the subject of much discussion was his attitude toward labor. On this point there has been considerable conflict of views. It is undoubtedly true that organized labor hated Gary with peculiar venom because in the great steel strike of 1919 he steadfastly refused to meet the labor leaders or have any dealings with them whatever. In vain William Z. Foster, himself a brilliant man, and Samuel Gompers, probably the most powerful protagonist that labor ever knew, stormed and raged against the Judge and threatened him with dire retribution because of his reactionary behavior. To Gary, however, the issue was extremely simple. He maintained that he was willing to discuss labor conditions and wages with his own employees, but he positively declined to discuss his business with men like Foster and Gompers who did not work for him, never had worked for him, and, he maintained, if he kept his mind, never would work for him. In the tense situation during the great strike, Gompers in his capacity as president of the American Federation of Labor wrote to Gary trying to arrange for a workers' committee to meet him and discuss the conditions of the steel workers. Judge Gary never answered the letter. He simply stood pat and waited for the strike to break. It was really a tremendous effort on the part of labor, and it ran on from September 22, 1919, to January, 1920, when it collapsed. Judge Gary had won a great victory. He proceeded with his business as though nothing had happened, and not a single demand of the workers was conceded.

As usual there was an investigation by the United States Senate at which Mr. Gompers testified that Judge Gary was personally to blame for the strike and maintained that the workers had to quit to get any recognition from him. Judge Gary, on the other hand, declared with the utmost conviction that the steel workers employed by him would never have struck if they had not been made cats-paws and been utterly misguided by professional agitators who knew no more about the steel business than he did about piano playing. Now that more than ten years have elapsed since those troubled days, we probably can say that the judgment of the people upon well-considered second thought was in Gary's favor, and it has never been shown that in any way was he ever averse to the real interests of the men who worked for the Steel Corporation, nor did he ever refuse to listen patiently to their complaints and alleviate their difficulties to the best of his ability.

A more difficult problem in connection with Judge Gary's labor policies arose through his attitude toward the eight-hour day. Many investigators have shown the brutal conditions which existed for years in the steel industry when the twelve-hour day was in effect. Particularly obnoxious was the twenty-four-hour shift which then occurred every two weeks as a necessity in arranging the labor change in the working out of the twelve-hour schedule. It is not to be believed that Gary took pleasure in what he considered a necessity of labor in the industry, but to understand his opposition to an eight-hour day schedule we must visualize his own life experience. As a farmer's son he had been bred to work from sunrise to sunset. Throughout his long career as a lawyer and a business executive, he had been accustomed to work from fourteen hours a day upward whenever the necessity occurred for such intense application. Therefore he could hardly be expected to look with particular pity on laborers who bore little re-sponsibility, and were simply obliged to expend their physical effort over a rather prolonged period of time. He reasoned that if he worked as hard as he did, it would not hurt them to work equally hard in their way. This may seem severe to us moderns, but to one of Judge Gary's generation who had been raised in the strenuous school of which he was an emi-nent graduate, a different attitude of mind was wholly natural.

Another policy of Gary's, indeed almost the basis of his creed, was the maintenance of fair competitive conditions in the steel business. It was his adherence to this principle which endeared him to his competitors and made him particularly valuable to all his fellow citizens. He refused to tolerate the practices which were common when he first came to New York. Indeed, on one occasion he went directly to Mr. Morgan and in his straightforward way told the old chief that he believed he had better resign. He thought that his usefulness as chief executive of United States Steel was at an end. He could not and would not tolerate the deception and selfish policies which his fellow directors were constantly trying to force upon him. It is to Morgan's credit that he refused to entertain the idea of accepting Gary's resignation. He told him to go back to his office and continue to run the Steel Company, that he would support him to the limit, and if he did not like any of his associates all he had to do was to get rid of them, and he, Morgan, would back him up. It is probably a fact that in his latter years Morgan leaned heavily on Gary's unfaltering rectitude and frank insistence upon the elemental principles of business truth and honor. Morgan knew that Gary represented a fresh and unspoiled point of view in the thick atmosphere of Wall Street, and Morgan was big enough and clean enough in his own soul to appreciate the simple virtues of such a man.

It was quite in keeping with his character that Judge Gary should have been deeply attached to Theodore Roosevelt, and that he should have believed that Roosevelt was patriotically endeavoring to do his whole duty to the American people in spite of the fact that his "trust-busting" policy fell heavily upon Gary's friends and associates and constituted a real threat to the Steel Corporation itself. It took courage in those days for Judge Gary to support Roosevelt. It was a time when the men of Wall Street regarded the picturesque and colorful President of the United States with a thoroughly jaundiced

vision. They hated him because he threatened the most delicate portion of their anatomies—that is to say, the nerve which
runs from the pocket-book direct to the heart. Mr. Morgan's
dislike of Roosevelt was known to all, and Morgan was Gary's
best friend and most essential supporter. In spite of all that,
Gary maintained a loyal and devoted friendship with Theodore Roosevelt until Roosevelt died. On one occasion the directors of the Steel Corporation tried to pass a resolution the
purport of which was to direct Judge Gary not to call upon
the President. Naturally, Gary was greatly incensed at such
a piece of impertinence; in the end wiser counsels prevailed
and the resolution was withdrawn. The fact that it was offered,
however, shows how intense the feeling was at that time.

Ida M. Tarbell, the author of an interesting life of Judge
Gary, tells us that in 1907 Gary wrote to Roosevelt as follows:
"I do not hesitate to say that your influence as President of
this great Republic has been of great benefit to me personally
and I feel equally certain that it is beginning to have a good
effect upon others who have been reluctant to see their faults."
This was indeed a fine tribute from a man who, under ordinary circumstances and in the case of a less noble nature,
might have been supposed to be a severe critic of the President, if not an actual opponent. It was also thoroughly indica-
tive of Gary's fine social philosophy, devotion to moral standards, and broad mental viewpoint.

It is probable, however, that the most severe test of Judge
Gary's career arose in connection with the suit instituted to
dissolve the United States Steel Corporation in 1912. It is not
unfair to say that it now appears that the suit in question was
essentially political in character. United States Steel had been
in the public eye for a generation or more, and it had been
investigated on many occasions by officials of the Federal Government. A comparatively short time before the institution of
the suit, Judge Gary had asked Attorney-General Wickersham

if anything had been discovered in connection with his company which Wickersham considered illegal or which in his judgment ought to be in any way corrected, and the Attorney-General had told him that although his corporation was huge in size he knew of no reason for interference by the Federal Government.

Then suddenly, like a bolt out of the blue, came the famous suit against Steel filed near the end of the Taft administration when the Republican Party was already in great disfavor with the electorate, and for the apparent purpose of accumulating political capital. Mr. Gary took this legal action very hard. He believed it was unfair and wholly political. He considered it to be a direct attack upon him personally as well as the corporation he represented, and a most unjust arraignment of his established policies which he believed to be essentially fair and which he had devoted the best years of his life to establishing in the interest of a practical exhibition of a purer business philosophy than the American people had ever known before.

The history of this suit is peculiar and interesting. The Government charged that the corporation was a combination in restraint of trade and asked for its dissolution. The litigation continued for more than nine years. The Government's petition was denied by the United States District Court in 1915. An appeal was taken to the Supreme Court, and the Great War intervening before the case was decided, it dragged along until March 1, 1920, when the Supreme Court of the United States, in a long and carefully considered opinion, decided in favor of the Steel Corporation. The Supreme Court held that it was unfair and improper to condemn the Steel Corporation simply because of its size, and it found that the Gary policies, as exemplified in the business practice of the company, were so fair and just that no legal or practical reason existed for dissolving it, and that on the contrary it was in the interest of the people of the United States to allow it to continue its operations, for it really exerted a beneficial effect upon the entire steel industry and made it easier for the independent companies to carry on their business because of its fair attitude toward the trade as a whole. As a sort of a corollary, the Supreme Court gently admonished Judge Gary against his social gatherings where admittedly steel prices were a subject of discussion; the famous Gary dinners were held to be in the nature of a restraint of trade, and were ordered discontinued. This, however, was a mere trifle when the main allegations of the Government's bill are taken into consideration.

The Government's suit was in a sense the high-water mark of Gary's career, and the victory of his corporation was more important to him as a man than from any point of view of material gain. It justified his entire life and was indeed a glorious crown which enabled him to complete his career with an inner glow of pride and gratitude which no money could buy.

It is interesting to consider further the kind of man Gary was, because in answering this question we are explaining how it could happen that a huge aggregation of inflated capital could be turned into a conservatively financed and well-managed corporation in less than a quarter of a century. We will approach Gary once more, and this time wholly upon his personal side. The Judge was in truth endowed with the simplicity of the truly great. He was a family man. He was twice married and was always happy in his home circle. He had two daughters to whom he was devotedly attached. Furthermore, he had infinite capacity for friendship. He did not have a great sense of humor, for from the beginning life had been a serious matter to him in every respect. He had, however, some interesting personal characteristics. Though not a handsome man, he was trim and always extremely well groomed. He appreciated good clothes and sometimes liked to get a bit of color into his attire of which he was never quite certain that Mrs. Gary would thoroughly approve.

ELBERT H. GARY

He lived a full life and in his day he met all the prominent financiers, business men and lawyers of his generation. He was fond of the newspaper men, and when not too busy enjoyed talking things over with a group of the youngsters of the press. They repaid his kindly notice by a singular degree of genuine devotion to him and to his interests. They were always his friends, and it is a well-known fact that even a great man is fortunate if the gentlemen of the press are his sincere admirers. They have tremendous power to make or mar the reputation of any character in public life, no matter how outstanding or powerful he may be.

As the Judge grew older, he mellowed and he was never averse to stating his views on a great variety of subjects, although, of course, his first interest was in the world of steel. Thus on one occasion he discussed the new code of business ethics which he believed obtained in the modern world and to which he had contributed so greatly by his own personal efforts, stating that in his opinion morality was now as important as legality and paid as well in dollars and cents. In an article which he wrote for the *Century Magazine* toward the end of his life he said:

The United States Steel Corporation has been characterized as a "corporation without a soul." Whether or not the characterization is true might depend upon one's definition of the word "soul." A definition acceptable for this purpose is that a soul is a controlling influence, possessed by individuals or corporations, which recognizes as of equal importance with its own the rights, interests and welfare of others—no greater, no less. Under this definition the United States Steel Corporation has striven to secure in all who are interested in its conduct the conviction that it is possessed of a soul. To say that it has sometimes failed in this effort is but to assert that its managers are human.

The *New York Times*, in an interesting and sympathetic summary of the Judge's career published immediately after

his death, which occurred on August 15, 1927, gave the following interesting quotations which represent his ripe philosophy
during his last days on earth:

Judge Gary's last interview with newspaper men collectively, following the April 25 stockholders' meeting of the United States Steel
Corporation, suggested that he had a premonition of death. On that
occasion he said:

"I would not blame the members of the corporation if they
should decide to say, 'It is time for that old gentleman to lay himself on the shelf.' My age is such that I must expect such a thing to
happen.

"The question of health is something we cannot control. I might
be justified in saying, standing on my feet here, that I have at
least justified the conclusion that I am still alive. Whether my
health will continue as it is now I cannot tell. I ought to be, and
I am, thankful to a merciful Providence who has spared me up to
this time. I have had my share and more than my share. The support I have received from my associates in the Steel Corporation
has been so fair, so firm, unyielding and unfaltering that I ought
to be grateful and I am grateful."

And again when he granted an interview on October 8, 1926, his
birthday, Judge Gary disclosed that his thoughts were on his declining years. When some one mentioned the prospect of meeting
him again on his eighty-first anniversary, he said: "One can never
tell what the next year will bring."

In his last birthday interview the Judge dwelt largely upon his
boyhood days, and with tears in his eyes described the influence of
his father and mother.

"I would like to tell you a family secret," he said. "It concerns my
abstinence from tobacco. When I was a young man in college I
learned to smoke like the rest of the boys, and for a year and a half
I smoked considerably. One time when I returned home after a
considerable absence I kissed my mother and she said, 'I don't like
to kiss you today.' I asked her why, and she said, 'I don't like the
smell of your breath; you have been smoking.' After that I quit
smoking and I have never taken it up since.

"You may think it was a simple thing, but it was a big thing. The influence of my father and mother has been with me since I was very young. Parents as a rule do not realize how much harm they are doing with their own children by their own bad habits and practice. That is advice to old people."

Judge Gary told with open pride of the resolution which had been adopted by the directors of the United States Steel Corporation, praising his "great ability, loyalty to the ⌐orporation, respect for the opinion of others, his kindness and tact." Visibly moved by the testimonial, he told of his career, and how he came "by chance" to be engaged in the steel business.

"I came to New York to discuss, consider and decide legal questions," he said. "My experience as a lawyer had brought me into contact with business, so that I had considerable practical knowledge of it. After having finished most of my legal work I was drafted into the practical department of this business, and it has been a most pleasant experience."

Of the opportunities of the present Judge Gary had this to say:

"Any young man of intelligence, real ambition, must realize that of all the countries in the world, the United States offers the best opportunities for young men.

"If any young men think that business places are overcrowded, positions are scarce and that young men do not have the same chance they used to have, they should have rung in their ears the statement that there is plenty of room, if they will only get a little higher, and there is nobody preventing them from getting a little higher place. We are, all of us, slightly lazy."

In reviewing Judge Gary's life, one of the things which impresses one most is the ability he displayed when he had attained middle age to completely alter his vocation and to succeed in the field of business, after a training which had been entirely professional. All his early life had been devoted to the law. He was admitted to the Illinois bar in 1867, and as a young man he made a name for himself as a practicing lawyer in the town of Wheaton, Illinois. Inevitably he became interested in politics and his townsmen honored him with three terms as president of Wheaton, and on its incorporation as a city he was elected its first mayor. Later he served two terms as county judge of Dupage County, Illinois, and then, having progressed to a point where he was too big for his environment, he moved to Chicago and for twenty-five years practiced law actively in that city. In a short space of time he became a leading member of the Chicago bar, and this was evidenced by his service as president of the Chicago Bar Association from 1893 to 1894.

It was not until 1899 when he was fifty-three years old that he turned his attention to the operating end of the steel industry. From then on he embarked on an entirely new career, and his amazing success as a business executive, after a long career as a lawyer, is a marvel of personal achievement and unique in the annals of American business. It is, of course, true that he was never a practical steel operator like Charles M. Schwab and James W. Farrell, but he occupied a higher niche in the organization than that of a great productive agent. It has often been said that he was a statesman in the world of business, and it is true that his vision and sense of fair dealing proved to be the two greatest assets of the United States Steel Corporation. He will be long remembered for his splendid mind, his ability to absorb many details in a brief space of time and reach a correct decision, and for his successful selection of brilliant men to work with him. He will be much longer remembered, however, for the innate rectitude with which he enunciated and defended a series of ethical standards that came to be known as the "Gary policies"—standards which did more than any other single factor to revolutionize the principles of American business conduct, and in this way he made an unequalled contribution to the welfare of the nation.

Thus we have come at last to the end of a wonderful life, and we may close the book of Judge Gary's days with genuine reverence and affection. More than any other one man of his generation he was successful not merely by precept but by example in establishing in American business life a nobler set of ideals by which the conduct of men in their trade associations should be controlled and governed. As a great man he belonged to a notable generation. There were many others who were as great as if not greater than he; Morgan and Harriman, for instance, undoubtedly surpassed him in sheer ability and mental power. But he had a greatness peculiar to himself which no one of his contemporaries could possibly equal. His conquest was of the spirit, not of the mind. He was a pure soul in an age of corruption and unrestrained and unfair business competition. He was not only an honest man according to the strict rules of the game; he was that extremely rare human triumph—a man of genuine and unaffected goodness. His life was an inspiration; his memory is a national treasure.

BIBLIOGRAPHY

CHAPTER I

COLONIAL FINANCE

BEARD, CHARLES A. American Government and Politics, 1920.
AND MARY B. The Rise of American Civilization, 1930.
BOGART, E. L. Economic History of the U. S., 1929.
BRUCE, P. A. The Economic History of Virginia in the 17th Century, 1896.
BULLOCK, C. J. Essays on the Monetary History of U. S., 1900.
The Finances of the U. S. from 1775 to 1789, with Especial Reference to the Budget, 1897.
DAVIS, A. M. The Connecticut Land Bank of the 18th Century, *Quarterly Journal of Economics*, v. 13, 1900.
Currency and Banking in Massachusetts Bay Colony, *Publications of American Economic Association*, ser. 3, v. 1, 1901.
The Fund at Boston in New England, *Proceedings American Antiquarian Society*, 1903.
DAVIS, JOSEPH S. The Earlier History of American Corporations, 2 v., 1917.
DEWEY, DAVIS R. Financial History of the U. S., 10th edition, 1928.
DOUGLAS, C. H. Financial History of Massachusetts, 1629–1776, *Columbia Univ. Publications in Economics*, v. 1, no. 4, 1892.
HEPBURN, A. B. A History of Currency in the U. S., 1908.
LOTKA, A. J. The Size of American Families in the 18th Century, *Journal of the American Statistical Ass'n.*, 1927.
MACFARLANE, C. W. Pennsylvania Paper Currency, *Annals of the American Academy of Political and Social Science*, vol. 8, 1896.
MACLEOD, W. CHRISTIE. "The Business Corporation Takes a Hand

in Empire Building," chapter 2 of his The American Indian Frontier, 1928.

Big Business and the American Indian, *American Journal of Sociology*, 1928.

McCLELLAN, W. S. Smuggling—and the West Indian Trade, 1912.

PARKER, R. W. Taxes and Money in New Jersey before the Revolution, *New Jersey Historical Soc. Proceedings*, ser. 2, v. 6, 1883.

PHILLIPS, HENRY. Historical Sketches of the Paper Currency of the American Colonies, 1865.

RIPLEY, W. Z. The Financial History of Virginia, *Columbia Univ. Studies in History and Economics*, v. 4, 1904.

SWAN, C. H. The Spanish Silver Dollar in Massachusetts: An Illustration of Gresham's Law, *Sound Currency Magazine*, v. 6, 1901.

TAUSSIG, C. W. Rum, Romance and Rebellion, 1928.

VAN DOREN, MARK. Samuel Sewall's Diary, 1927.

WATSON, D. K. History of American Coinage.

WEEDON, W. B. Economic and Social History of New England, 2 v., 1890.

Indian Money in New England, *Johns Hopkins Univ. Studies in Politics and Economics*, v. 2, 1884.

WHITE, H. Money and Banking (Chap. 1), 5th edition, 1911.

WILDMAN, M. S. Money Inflation in the U. S. (Part 1), 1905.

Notes: (1) Attention may be called particularly to the instructive monographs by A. M. Davis, J. S. Davis and Douglas on early New England finances. (2) MacLeod analyzes the influence of the 17th century business corporations on early American settlement.

Chapter II

REVOLUTIONARY FINANCES

ANDREWS, C. M. The American Revolution: An Historic Interpretation, *American Historical Review,* 1926.
BACON, N. T. America's International Indebtedness, *Yale Review,* 1900.
BARRETT, W. The Old Merchants of New York City, 4 v., 1864–66.
BARTON, W. Memoirs on the Life of David Rittenhouse, 1813.
BOLLES, ALBERT S. Financial History of the U. S., 1774–1789, 4th edition, 1896.
BULLOCK, C. J. Finances of the U. S., 1775–1789, 1900.
DEWEY, DAVIS R. Financial History of the U. S., 10th edition, 1928.
EDELMAN, E. Thomas Hancock: Colonial Merchant, *Journal of Economics and Business History,* v. 1, 1929.
LODGE, HENRY CABOT. The Story of the Revolution, 1919.
MOORE, F. Diary of the Revolution, from Newspapers, 2 v., 1860.
ROOSEVELT, THEODORE. *Gouvenor Morris,* 1899.
SCHLESINGER, A. M. New Viewpoints in American History, 1922.
SPOFFORD, A. R. Lotteries in American History, *Annual Report of the American Historical Association,* 1892.
SUMNER, W. J. Financiers and Finances of the American Revolution.
VAN TYNE, C. H. England and the U. S., Rivals in the American Revolution, 1927.
YOUNG, R. C. The Financial Position of the U. S., 1929.

Notes: (1) The studies by R. C. Young and N. T. Bacon survey among other things the earlier history of American International financial relations. (2) In addition to the above see the references to Chapters III and IV.

CHAPTER III

LIFE AND TIMES OF ROBERT MORRIS

DEWEY, DAVIS R. Financial History of the U. S., 10th edition, 1928.
LEWIS, L. A History of the Bank of North America, 1882.
MICHENER, J. H. The Bank of North America, 1906.
OBERHOLTZER, E. P. Life of Robert Morris, 1903.
RUSSELL, C. E. Haym Salomon and the Revolution, 1930.
SCHLESINGER, A. M. The Colonial Merchants and the American Revolution, 1918.
SUMNER, W. J. Financiers and Finances of the American Revolution, 1891.

Note: See also the references to Chapters II, IV and VII.

CHAPTER IV

ALEXANDER HAMILTON—RECONSTRUCTION AFTER THE REVOLUTION

ATHERTON, GERTRUDE. The Conqueror, 1916.
BACON, CHARLES W. The American Plan of Government, 1918.
BAKER, W. S. Washington [George] after the Revolution, 1898.
BEARD, CHARLES A. American Government and Politics, 1920.
An Economic Interpretation of the Constitution of U. S., 1913.
Economic Basis of Politics, 1922.
Economic Origins of Jeffersonian Democracy, 1915.
BOWERS, C. G. Jefferson and Hamilton, 1925.
BUTLER, NICHOLAS MURRAY. Building the American Nation, 1923.
CULBERTSON, W. S. Alexander Hamilton: An Essay, 1911.
DEWEY, DAVIS R. Financial History of the U. S., 10th edition, 1928.
DORNETT, HENRY W. A History of the Bank of New York, 1784–1884, 1884.

DUNBAR, C. F. Some Precedents Followed by Alexander Hamilton, *Quarterly Journal of Economics*, v. 3, 1888.

DUPUY, H. A History of Some Loans Made to the U. S. During the Revolution, *Penna. Mag. of Hist. and Biography*, v. 31, 1907.

FLICK, A. C. Loyalists in New York during the American Revolution, *Columbia Univ. Studies in History and Economics*, v. 14, 1901.

HAMILTON's Report on Manufacture, *American State Papers*, Fin. I, 123–146.

   First Report on Public Credit, *Amer. State Papers,* Fin. I, 15–37.

   Second Report on Public Credit, *Amer. State Papers,* Fin. I, 64–67.

HERGESHEIMER, J. Balisand, 1924.

HUNT, G., AND SCOTT, J. B. (editors). The Debates in the Federal Convention of 1787 Reported by James Madison, 1920.

KNOX, J. J. A History of Banking in the U. S., 1900.

LODGE, HENRY CABOT. Life of Alexander Hamilton (Amer. Statesmen Series), 1882.

MACLAY, WILLIAM. The Journal of William Maclay, 1927.

MORSE, J. T. Life of Hamilton.

MULDOON, S. J. Alexander Hamilton's Pioneer Son, 1797–1850, 1930.

SUMNER, W. J. Hamilton, 1890.

WARREN, C. The Making of the Constitution, 1929.

WARSHOW, R. I. Alexander Hamilton, First American Business Man, 1931.

Notes: (1) The novel by Gertrude Atherton is based on the life of Hamilton. (2) The very splendid novel by Joseph Hergesheimer is a picture of life in tidewater Virginia during the period of reconstruction after the Revolution. (3) See also the references under Chapter IX.

CHAPTER V

ALBERT GALLATIN—AND THE METHODS EMPLOYED
TO FINANCE THE WAR OF 1812

ADAMS, H. C. Taxation in the U. S., 1789–1816, *Johns Hopkins
Univ. Studies,* v. 2, 1884.
BOLLES, ALBERT S. Financial History of the U. S., 1789–1860, 1883.
DEWEY, DAVIS R. Financial History of the U. S., 10th edition, 1928.
GALLATIN'S Consideration of the Currency Bank Systems (Works).
Views of the Public Debt, Receipts and Expenditures of the
U. S. (Works).
HOLLANDER, J. H. War Borrowing: A Study of Treasury Certifi-
cates in the U. S., 1919.
STEVENS, J. A. Life of Albert Gallatin, 1888.

CHAPTER VI

STEPHEN GIRARD

AREY, H. W. Biography of Stephen Girard, 1856.
Article published in the *Girard Letter* by Girard Trust Co. (Phila.).
BECK, JAMES M. Stephen Girard, Merchant and Mariner, 1897.
DUPONT, B. S. E. I. duPont de Nemours and Company: A His-
tory, 1802–1902, 1920.
ELIASON, A. O. The Rise of Commercial Banking in the U. S.,
1901.
GIRARD, STEPHEN. Will of Stephen Girard (Girard College).
HERGESHEIMER, J. Java Head, 1919.
HERRICK, CHEESEMAN A. Stephen Girard, the Founder, 1923.
KENT, FRANK. The Story of Alexander Brown and Sons, 1925.
LEACH, JOSIAH GRANVILLE. The History of the Girard National
Bank of Phila., 1834–1902, 1902.

MacMasters, John Bach. The Life and Times of Stephen Girard, 1918.

Minnegerode, Meade. Certain Rich Men, 1927.

Morrison, S. E. Maritime History of Massachusetts, 1783–1860, 1922.

Peabody, R. C. The Derbys of Salem, Massachusetts, 1908.

Putnam, G. F. Salem Vessels and Their Voyages, 1930.

Simpson, S. Biography of Stephen Girard, 1832.

Note: The volumes by Morrison, Peabody, and Putnam deal with various New England merchants of Girard's period. The novel by Hergesheimer is based on the Salem sea trade with China.

CHAPTER VII

LAND SPECULATION

Adams, H. B. Washington's Interest in Western Lands, *Johns Hopkins Univ. Studies in History and Economics*, v. 13, no. 1, 1885.

Alvord, C. W. Mississippi Valley in British Politics, 2 v., 1917.

Baker, W. S. Washington after the Revolution, 1898.

Churchill, Winston. The Crossing, 1904.

Dewey, Davis R. Financial History of the U. S., 10th edition, 1928.

Donaldson, T. G. The Public Domain; Its History and Statistics, 1863-1884.

Hart, A. B. Disposition of Our Public Lands, *Quarterly Journal of Economics*, v. 1, 1887.

Hibbard, B. H. History of the Public Land Politics, 1924.

Hurlburt, A. B. Methods and Operations of the Scioto Group of Speculations, *Mississippi Valley Historical Review*, v. 2, 1915.

McGrane, R. M. Panic of 1837, 1924.

McLendon, S. G. History of the Public Domain of Georgia, 1931.

MacLeod, W. Christie. "Jacob and Esau: On Why the Europeans

Bought Indian Land," chap. 15 of his The American Indian Frontier, 1928.

STEVENSON, G. M.   Political History of the Public Lands from 1840 to 1862.

SUTO, S.   History of the Land Question, *Johns Hopkins Univ. Studies*, v. 4, 1886.

WELLINGTON, R. G.   Political and Sectional Influence of the Public Lands, 1828–42, 1914 (Bibliography, pp. 119–125).

Note: The volume by McLendon deals with the notorious Yazoo companies.

CHAPTER VIII

JOHN JACOB ASTOR AND THE FUR TRADE

BANCROFT, H.   The History of the Northwest, 1890.

CHITTENDEN, H. M.   American Fur Trade of the Far West.
History of the Early Western Fur Trade, 3 v., 1902.

COMAN, K.   Economic Beginnings of the Far West, 2 v., 1921.

DAVIDSON, G. C.   The Northwest Company, 1918.
History of the Northwest Continent.

GREENBIE, S.   How China Set Us Exploring Our Northwest, *Asia Mag.*, 1925.

HOWDEN-SMITH, A. D.   Life of John Jacob Astor.

IRVING, WASHINGTON.   Astoria, 1851.

LAUT, A.   The Conquest of the Great Northwest, 1908.

MACLEOD, W. CHRISTIE.   "The Indian Trade," chap. 12 of his The American Indian Frontier, 1928.

MINNEGERODE, MEADE.   Certain Rich Men, 1927.

MYERS, G.   Great American Fortunes, 3 v., 1910.

NUTE, G. L.   The Papers of the American Fur Company, *Amer. Historical Review*, 1927.

PARTON, J.   Life of John Jacob Astor, 1865.

Porter, K. W. John Jacob Astor, Business Man, 2 v., 1931.

Reed, C. B. Masters of the Wilderness, 1914.

Schaeffer, J. History of the Pacific Northwest, chaps. 7 and 8, 1910.

Skinner, C. L. Adventurers of Oregon, 1921.

Smith, A. D. John Jacob Astor, 1929.

Stevenson, W. E. The Northwest Fur Trade, 1763–1800, *Univ. of Illinois Studies in the Social Sciences*, v. 14, no. 3, 1927.

Note: The history of Astor's businesses by Porter, recently published, is an exhaustive piece of research which will probably be the last word on this subject.

Chapter IX

MADISON, HAMILTON AND THE FIRST NATIONAL BANK

Bolles, Albert S. Financial History of the U. S., 1769–1860, chap. 7, 1883.

Butler, Nicholas Murray. Building the American Nation, 1923.

Dewey, Davis R. Financial History of the U. S., 10th edition, 1928.

Deyber, V. B. A History of Banking in the U. S.

George, W. M. Short History of Money and Banking in the U. S.

Hamilton, Alexander. Report in re First United States Bank Communicated to the House of Representatives, Dec. 14, 1790, *American State Papers*.

Heldermann, L. C. National and State Banks: A Study of Their Origins, 1928.

Holdsworth, J. T. The First Bank of the U. S., *National Monetary Commission Report, 61st Congress, 2nd Session, Senate Document 571*, 1910.

Note: See also the references to Chapter IV.

CHAPTER X

ANDREW JACKSON, NICHOLAS BIDDLE—GREAT CONTEST OVER SECOND NATIONAL BANK

BENSON, ALLAN L. Daniel Webster, 1929.

BOLLES, ALBERT S. Financial History of the U. S., 1789–1860, (chap. 7.), 1883.

BOWERS, C. G. The Party Battles of the Jackson Period, 1922.

BUTLER, NICHOLAS MURRAY. Building the American Nation, 1923.

CATTERALL, R. C. H. The Second Bank of the U. S., 1902.

DEWEY, DAVIS R. Financial History of the U. S., 10th edition, 1928.

DEWEY, DAVIS R. State Banking Before the Civil War, 1910.

DODD, WILLIAM E. Expansion and Conflict, 1920.

GIRARD LETTER, published by Girard Trust Company of Philadelphia, Sept., 1931.

JOHNSON, GERALD W. Andrew Jackson: An Epic in Homespun, 1927.

LONG, R. S. Andrew Jackson and the National Bank, *English Historical Review*, v. 12.

McGRANE, R. M. Correspondence of Nicholas Biddle.

PHILLIPS, J. B. Methods of Keeping the Public Money, *Pub's. Michigan Pol. Sci. Ass'n.*, 1900.

POLLACK, Q. Peggy Eaton, Democracy's Mistress, 1930.

ROOSEVELT, THEODORE. Life of Thomas Hart Benton (Amer. Statesmen Series).

SUMNER, W. G. Andrew Jackson (Amer. Statesmen Series), 1882.

CHAPTER XI

MARTIN VAN BUREN AND THE PANIC OF 1837

BOGART, E. L.　Economic History of American Agriculture, 1923.

BOURNE, A. G.　History of the Surplus Revenue of 1837.

BURTON, THEODORE E.　Financial Crises and Periods of Industrial and Commercial Depression, 1907.

COLLMAN, C. A.　Our Mysterious Panics, 1830 to 1930, 1931.

DEWEY, DAVIS R.　Financial History of the U. S., 10th edition, 1928.

FAULKNER, H. E.　American Economic History, 2nd edition, 1931.

HIRST, F. W.　The Six Panics, and Other Essays, 1913.

HURLBURT, A. B.　The Great American Canals, 2 v., 1904.

HYNDMAN, H. M.　Commercial Crises of the 19th Century, 2nd edition, 1902.

LAUCK, W. J.　Causes of the Panic of 1893, 1907.

LYNCH, DENIS T.　An Epoch and a Man, Martin Van Buren and His Times, 1929.

McGRANE, R. M.　The Panic of 1837, 1924.

MOFFRAN, R. H.　A History of Financial Speculation, 1929.

PHILLIPS, U. B.　History of Transportation in the Eastern Cotton Belts, 1918.

SCOTT, W. A.　The Repudiation of the State Debts, 1893.

SHEPERD, EDWARD M.　Martin Van Buren (Amer. Statesmen Series).

Note: Hyndman discusses in particular the European phases of the panics.

CHAPTER XII

SALMON P. CHASE AND JAY COOKE; FINANCING THE CIVIL WAR

BOGART, E. L.　Economic History of the U. S., 4th edition, 1929.

BOLLES, ALBERT S.　Financial History of the United States, 1861–1885, 1886.

BIBLIOGRAPHY   541

BRADBEEN, W. W. Confederate and Southern State Currency, 1915.

DAVIS, A. M. Origin of the National Banking System, *U. S. National Monetary Commission Report*, Washington, D. C., 1910.

DEWEY, DAVIS R. Financial History of the U. S., 10th edition, 1928.

HART, A. B. Life of Salmon P. Chase, 1889.

MINNEGERODE, MEADE. Certain Rich Men, 1927.

MITCHELL, W. The History of the Greenbacks, 1903.

OBERHOLTZER, E. P. Jay Cooke, Financier of the Civil War, 1907.

RIDDLE, ALBERT G. Recollections of War-times, 1860–65, 1895.

SCHWAB, J. C. The Confederate States, 1910.

SHUCKERS, J. W. Life of Salmon P. Chase, 1874.

CHAPTER XIII

JOHN SHERMAN AND THE RESUMPTION OF
SPECIE PAYMENT

BARRETT, D. C. The Greenbacks and the Resumption of Specie Payment, v. 36, *Harvard Economic Studies,* 1931.

BEALE, H. K. The Critical Years: A Study of Andrew Johnson and Reconstruction, 1931.

BOGART, E. L. Economic History of the U. S., 1929.

BOLLES, ALBERT S. Financial History of the United States, 1861–1885, 1886.

BOUTWELL, G. S. Reminiscences, 1902.

BOWERS, C. G. The Tragic Era: The Revolution after Lincoln, 1929.

BURTON, THEODORE E. Life of John Sherman (Amer. Statesmen Series), 1906.

CARROTHERS, N. The History of Fractional Currency in the U. S., 1930.

CLEVELAND, F. A., AND POWELL, F. W. Railroad Finance, 1912.

DEWEY, DAVIS R. Financial History of the U. S., 10th edition, 1928.

HICKS, FREDERICK C. High Finance in the Sixties, 1929.

KERR, W. S. John Sherman; His Life and Public Services, 2 v., 1908.

LYNCH, DENIS T. "Boss" Tweed, 1927.

McCULLOUGH, H. Men and Measures.

MILTON, G. F. The Age of Hate: Andrew Johnson and the Radicals, 1930.

NOYES, ALEXANDER D. Forty Years of American Finance, 1865–1907, 1907.

OBERHOLTZER, E. P. Jay Cooke, Financier of the Civil War.

PAXSON, FREDERICK L. The New Nation, 1924.

SHERMAN, JOHN. Recollections of Forty Years in the House, Senate and Cabinet, 1895.

CHAPTER XIV

THE TARIFF AS AN ISSUE IN THE U. S.

BURTON, THEODORE E. John Sherman (Amer. Statesmen Series), 1906.

DEWEY, DAVIS R. Financial History of the U. S., 10th edition, 1928.

ELLIOT, O. L. The Tariff Controversy from 1789 to 1833, *Leland Stanford Univ. Studies in History and Economics.*

KERR, W. S. John Sherman, 1908.

NOYES, ALEXANDER D. Forty Years of American Finance, 1909.

ROOSEVELT, THEODORE. Thomas H. Benton (Amer. Statesmen Series), 1887.

SHERMAN, JOHN. Recollections of Forty Years in the House, Senate and Cabinet, 1895.

TAUSSIG, F. W. The Tariff History of the U. S., 1914.

CHAPTER XV

CORNELIUS VANDERBILT, MASTER OF TRANSPORTATION

ADAM, C. F., AND ADAM, H. Chapters of the Erie, 1871.
CARTER, C. F. When Railroads Were New, 1910.
CLEVELAND AND POWELL. Railroad Finance, 1910.
DEWEY, DAVIS R. Financial History of the U. S., 10th edition, 1928.
FULLER, ROBERT H. Jubilee Jim, Life of Col. James Fisk, Jr., 1929.
HEPBURN, A. B. Artificial Waterways and Commercial Development—with a History of the Erie Canal, 1909.
HICKS, FREDERICK C. High Finance in the Sixties, 1929.
HOWDEN-SMITH, A. D. Commodore Vanderbilt.
MERRICK, G. B. Jos. Reynolds and the "Diamond Jo Line" Steamers, 1862–1911, *Proceedings of the Miss. Valley Historical Ass'n.,* v. 8, 1914–15.
MINNEGERODE, MEADE. Certain Rich Men, 1927.
MOODY, JOHN. Masters of Capital, 1926.
NOYES, ALEXANDER D. Forty Years of American Finance, 1909.
SHIPPEE, L. B. Steamboating on the Upper Mississippi after the Civil War, *Miss. Valley Historical Review,* v. 6, 1919–20.
STEVENS, —. The Beginnings of the New York Central R. R.
TWAIN, MARK. Life on the Mississippi, 1883.
WARSHOW, R. I. Jay Gould, The Story of a Fortune, 1920
    The Story of Wall Street, 1930.

Note: Merrick and Shippee afford studies which describe early steamboating which may be compared to that of the early Hudson River. Mark Twain's introduction to his novel is interesting in the same connection.

CHAPTER XVI

JAY GOULD AND THE AGE OF INNOCENCE

CORNWALLIS, K. The Gold Room and the New York Stock Exchange, 1879.

FULLER, ROBERT H. Jubilee Jim, Life of Col. James Fisk, Jr., 1929.

GOULD, JAY. History of Delaware County and Border Wars of N. Y., Containing a Sketch of the Early Settlements in the County and the History of the Late Anti-rent Difficulties in Delaware with Other Historical and Miscellaneous Matter Never Before Published, 1856.

HICKS, F. C. High Finance in the Sixties, 1929.

LYNCH, DENIS T. "Boss" Tweed, 1927.

MEDBERRY, J. K. Men and Mysteries of Wall Street, 1870.

SPARKS, B. Hetty Green: A Woman Who Loved Money, 1928.

WARSHOW, R. I. The Story of Wall Street, 1929.

   Jay Gould, The Story of a Fortune, 1928.

WHARTON, EDITH. The Age of Innocence, 1920.

WHITE, BOUCK. The Book of Daniel Drew, 1910.

CHAPTER XVII

GEORGE WESTINGHOUSE, ENGINEER, INVENTOR
AND BUSINESS LEADER

CRANE, F. George Westinghouse, 1925.

DEWEY, A. S. Corporate Promotions and Organizations.

LEUPP, FRANCIS E. George Westinghouse, His Life and Achievements, 1918.

NOYES, ALEXANDER D. Forty Years of American Finance, 1909.

PROUT, HENRY L. Life of George Westinghouse, 1922.

WARREN, A. George Westinghouse, 1914.

CHAPTER XVIII

GROVER CLEVELAND AND THE SILVER PROBLEM

DEWEY, DAVIS R. Financial History of the U. S., 10th edition, 1928.
   National Problems, 1885–1897, 1907.
HEPBURN, A. B. History of Currency in the U. S., 1908.
HICKS, J. D. The Populist Revolt: A History of the Farmer's
   Alliance and the People's Party, 1931.
LAUGHLIN, J. L. History of Bimetalism in the U. S., 3rd edition,
   1896.
LYNCH, DENIS T. Grover Cleveland, a Man Four-Square, 1932.
MACELROY, ROBERT. Grover Cleveland, the Man and the States-
   man, 1923.
NOYES, ALEXANDER D. Forty Years of American Finance, 1909.
SHERMAN, JOHN. Recollections of Forty Years in the House, Senate
   and Cabinet, 1895.

CHAPTER XIX

THE RISE OF THE PACKING INDUSTRY

CLEMEN, R. The American Livestock and Meat Industry, 1923.
GOODSBY, THOMAS W. Life of Gustavus F. Swift.
SINCLAIR, UPTON. The Jungle, 1906.
SWIFT AND COMPANY. Yearbooks and Other Publications.
WOOD, W. The Meat Industry, 1928.

Note: Sinclair's famous novel is included for its valid picture of
packing of this period and for its influence in creating a public
demand for changed conditions.

CHAPTER XX

ANDREW CARNEGIE—KINGDOM OF STEEL

ALDERSON, BERNARD. Andrew Carnegie, The Man and His Work, 1909.

BRIDGE, J. H. Inside Story of the Carnegie Steel Company.

CARNEGIE, ANDREW. The Gospel of Wealth and Other Timely Essays, 1901.
   The Empire of Business, 1902.
   Triumphant Democracy, 1896.
   Autobiography, 1920.

CASSON, H. A. The Romance of Steel: The Story of a Thousand Millionaires, 1907.

CLEVELAND, F. A. Mr. Carnegie as Economist and Social Reformer, *Annals, American Academy of Political and Social Science,* v. 17, 1901.

DEPEW, CHAUNCEY. One Hundred Years of American Commerce, 1895.

DREISER, THEODORE. The Financier, 1912.

HARVEY, G. Henry Clay Frick, 1928.

HAZARD, L. L. "The Gilded Age of Industrial Pioneering," chap. 6 of her The Frontier in American Literature, 1927.

MOODY, JOHN. Masters of Capital, 1926.

MYRES, G. History of the Great American Fortunes, 1911.

NOYES, ALEXANDER D. Forty Years of American Finance, 1909.

WINKLER, J. K. Incredible Carnegie, 1931.

Note: Carnegie's own writings are amazingly illuminative of his personality and, as shown in Hazard, of his era.

CHAPTER XXI

JAMES J. HILL, BUILDER OF THE NORTHWEST

BENSON, RAMSEY. Hill Country, the Story of James J. Hill and the Awakening of the West, 1928.
HILL, JAMES J. Highways of Progress, 1910.
HUSBAND, J. "James J. Hill," chap. 4 of his Americans by Adoption, 1920.
LAUT, A. C. The Romance of the Rails, 1929.
NOYES, ALEXANDER D. Forty Years of American Finance, 1909.
PYLE, J. J. Life of James J. Hill, 1917.
SKELTON, O. D. The Railroad Builders (Canadian), 1910.
STARR, J. One Hundred Years of Railroading, 1931.

CHAPTER XXII

CAREER OF EDWARD H. HARRIMAN AND ITS EFFECT ON AMERICAN RAILWAY FINANCE

ADAMS, C. F. The Granger Movement, *North American Review,* v. 120, 1875.
COUNTY, ALBERT JOHN. The Penna. R. R. Company, 1906.
DAGGETT, S. History of the Southern Pacific, 1922.
DAVIS, JOHN P. The Union Pacific Railway, *Annals of the American Academy of Political and Social Science,* v. 8, 1896, following his book: The Union Pacific Railway: A Study in Railway Politics, History, and Economics, 1894.
DODGE, G. M. How We Built the Union Pacific Railway, 1910.
HAFER, L. R. The Overland Mail, 1849–69, Precision of the Railroad, 1927.
KENNAN, GEORGE. Life of Edw. H. Harriman, 1922.
KERR, J. L. Missouri Pacific Railway, 1928.
Report of Interstate Commerce Commission, v. 12, p. 278, etc., "On

the Importance of Consolidation and Combinations of Carriers."

SCHOLTER, H. W. Growth of the Penna. R. R. Company, 1927.

SEITZ, W. D. The Penna. R. R., 1875.

TROUTMAN, N. History of the Union Pacific.

TRUESDALE, W. H. Development of Railway Systems in the U. S., *Trust Companies Mag.*, v. 1, 1904.

CHAPTER XXIII

J. PIERPONT MORGAN

ALDERSON, BERNARD. Andrew Carnegie: The Man and His Work, 1909.

ANONYMOUS. A New Home for an Old House, Drexel and Co., 1927.

COREY, L. The House of Morgan, 1930.

DEWEY, DAVIS R. Financial History of the U. S., 10th edition, 1928.

HICKS, J. D. High Finance in the Sixties, 1928.

HOVEY, C. The Life and Story of John Pierpont Morgan, 1911.

KENNAN, GEORGE. Life of Edw. H. Harriman, 1922.

MACELROY, ROBERT. Life of Grover Cleveland.

MOODY, JOHN. The Masters of Capital, 1926.

NOYES, ALEXANDER D. Forty Years of American Finance, 1865, 1907, 1909.

OBERHOLTZER, E. P. Life of Jay Cooke.

PYLE, J. J. Life of James J. Hill.

RIPLEY, W. Z. "United States Steel Corporation: Capitalization and Finance, 1901," in his Trusts, Pools and Corporations, 1905.

SHERMAN, JOHN. Recollections of Forty Years in the House, Senate and Cabinet, 1895.

TARBELL, IDA M. History of the Standard Oil Company, 1904.

WARSHOW, R. I. The Story of Wall Street, 1929.

     Jay Gould, The Story of a Fortune, 1929.

WHITE, B. Book of Daniel Drew, 1910.

WINKLER, J. K. Morgan, the Magnificent, 1929.

Note: Corey's fine study is probably the outstanding writing on the subject. It is a great deal more than a mere biography.

CHAPTER XXIV

ELBERT H. GARY—THE PHILOSOPHY OF MODERN BUSINESS

ALDERSON, BERNARD. Andrew Carnegie: The Man and His Work, 1909.

BERGLUND, A. The U. S. Steel Corporation: A Study of the Growth and Influence of Combination, *Columbia University Studies in Economics,* 1907.

GULICK, C. A. The Labor Policy of the U. S. Steel Corporation, 1924.

MOODY, JOHN. The Masters of Capital, 1926.

TARBELL, IDA M. The Life of Elbert H. Gary, the Story of Steel, 1926.

INDEX

Great Northern R.R., 433, 459, 490; takes over Northern Pacific, 438-440

Great Northern Ry. System, 436

Greenback circulation reduced, 281-282

Greenback heresy, 376, 486

Greenback Party, 275, 279, 280

"Grundy, Mr.," 329

Guaranty Trust Co., 396, 499, 500

Hallgarten and Co., 396

Hamilton, Alexander, 24, 41, 46-82, 134, 208; characteristics of, 46-47; army activities, 48-49; admitted to New York bar, 50; attitude on democracy, 52-53, 56; advocacy of constitution, 56; "Letters of Junius," 56; early reports of, 59-61; plans for paying debts, 60-64; on payment of domestic debts, 65; on need of national bank, 71-73; attacks Jefferson, 78; attitude towards France, 80; breaks with Adams, 81, 86; opposes Burr, 81; death, 82; impression on people, 87; reports of expenditures demanded, 92-93, 105; on national bank, 156-168; idea of tariff, 289; report on manufacturing, 291

Hamilton, James A., 199

Hancock, General, on tariff, 287-288

Hand, Phebe, 303, 306

Harding, W. G., 302

Harriman, Edward H., 324, 338, 443-470, 475, 479, 492, 495, 507-508, 529; resemblance to Hill, 437; designs on Northern Pacific, 439-440; early life, 443; buys seat on Stock Exchange, 444; as an athlete and philanthropist, 445; turns from bonds to rails, 447; opposes Morgan, 449-450; runs Illinois Central, 451-452; buys Union Pacific stock, 453-454; personal influence on employees, 456; and the Central Pacific, 457; need of Chicago, Burlington and Quincy, 458-460; surprise attack on Northern Pacific, 460-464; with Northern Securities Corp., 464-465; and Roosevelt quarrel, 465-466; Chicago and Alton inquiry, 467-468; death, 469; purposes of building, 470; contest over dissolving of the Northern

Securities Corp., 498-499; plans world domination, 499-500

Harriman, Edward H., estate, 471, 472, 473

Harriman, Oliver, 444

Harrison, Benjamin, 379

Hathaway and Swift, 402-403

Hayes, D. C., 444

Hayes, Rutherford B., 266, 282; makes Sherman Secretary of Treasury, 283; vetoes silver act, 378

Hayes-Tilden controversy, 282-283

Helm, Peter, 126

Henry, Patrick, 134

Hero fund, 423

Hill, Isaac, 199

Hill, James J. 428-442, 447, 458-460, 475, 479, 495; early life, 428-429; with the St. Paul and Pacific, 431; meets Smith, 432; resemblance to Harriman, 437; idea regarding stockholders, 437; connection with Morgan, 439-440; art collector, 441; becomes suspicious of market of Northern Pacific stock, 461-463; first meeting with Morgan, 490

Hillsboro, Lord, 133

"History of Delaware County, New York," 334

Hocking Valley R.R., 490

Holland, loans to colonies, 32, 35

Homestead laws, 140

Homestead Steel Works, 412

Homestead strike, 421-422

Hudson Bay Co., 146

Hudson River Ry., 323

Hughes, Charles Evans, 350

Huntingdon, Collis P., 455, 456, 457

Illinois Central R.R., 439, 446-447, 448, 457, 465, 499; Harriman's interest in, 450-452

Illinois General R.R., 499

Illinois Steel Co., 502, 512

Import duties, used by Morris, 28

Imports, types of, 8

Income tax, increase in during Civil War, 263

Inflation in 1837, 218, 225